Greater Cincinnati
Bicentennial History Series

Board of Editors

Zane L. Miller
Gene D. Lewis

RACE AND THE CITY

RACE

AND THE

CITY

Work, Community, and Protest in
Cincinnati, 1820–1970

EDITED BY

Henry Louis Taylor, Jr.

University of Illinois Press

Urbana and Chicago

Publication of this book was supported by a grant from the Greater Cincinnati Bicentennial Commission.

This book is printed on acid-free paper.

Library of Congress Cataloging-in-Publication Data

Race and the city : work, community, and protest in Cincinnati,
   1820–1970 / edited by Henry Louis Taylor, Jr.
      p.   cm. — (Greater Cincinnati bicentennial history series)
   Includes bibliographical references and index.
   ISBN 0-252-01986-5 (cl)
      1. Afro-Americans—Ohio—Cincinnati—History. 2. Afro-Americans—
   Ohio—Cincinnati—Social conditions. 3. Afro-Americans—Ohio—
   Cincinnati—Economic conditions. 4. Cincinnati (Ohio)—Social
   conditions. 5. Cincinnati (Ohio)—Economic conditions. 6. Cincinnati
   (Ohio)—Race relations. I. Taylor, Henry Louis. II. Series.
F499 . C59N426 1993
977 . 1'7800496073—dc20   92-37088
                                                                    CIP

To Henry Louis Taylor, Sr.

Contents

This book derives from the celebration of Cincinnati's bicentennial in 1988. As part of that celebration, the Cincinnati Historical Society, under the auspices and with the financial support of the Cincinnati Bicentennial Commission, sponsored a three-day conference on the history of African Americans in Cincinnati. Henry L. Taylor, Jr., organized this conference, to which he invited senior and younger scholars, who presented and discussed formal papers. From these Taylor selected for publication those which, in his view, most deftly integrated black and urban history, and to them he added one previously published essay. The collection follows a scheme of periodization based on urban development, and the essays especially highlight the themes of work, housing, community, and the struggle for advancement. Though the historical literature on black urban history is growing, this is the only volume that attempts an examination of the black urban experience in one city from the early nineteenth century through the first half of the twentieth century.

This is the third volume in the Greater Cincinnati Bicentennial History Series, which focuses on a broad range of topics relating to the Cincinnati region. Additional volumes will be published for the next several years. The series is a joint venture of the Cincinnati Historical Society and the Department of History and the Center for Neighborhood and Community Studies at the University of Cincinnati. We are indebted to the Cincinnati Bicentennial Commission for assistance in defraying the cost of publishing this volume.

Gene D. Lewis
Zane L. Miller

Preface

Cincinnati holds a distinctive place in the history of race relations and African Americans in the United States. It is part of the borderland, a border city in a border state, and sits astride the boundary between the North and South.[1] This marginality was most pronounced during the antebellum era, when Cincinnati was a real dividing line between slavery and freedom, and the population was composed of large numbers of southerners—including a black population consisting primarily of former slaves—and aggressive abolitionists.[2]

In its early days Cincinnati was a very racist city. After denying blacks the right to vote at its first constitutional convention in 1802, Ohio enacted in 1804 and 1807 a series of Black Laws to discourage black immigration and settlement in the state. These laws required blacks to register and post five hundred dollars' bond, excluded them from jury service and from testifying in cases involving whites, barred them from participating in the militia, and denied them the benefits of the Poor Law and of institutions for the physically and mentally infirm. Although they paid taxes to support local schools, blacks were excluded from public schools and no provisions were made for their education until 1829. Prejudice and discriminatory behavior kept many blacks from learning new skills and practicing the ones they already possessed. Although slavery was made illegal by the Northwest Ordinance, slaveholders visited Cincinnati so frequently and lived there so comfortably that no one even challenged their right to bring their peculiar property into the state. These attitudes and practices were reinforced by the many conservative white southerners settling in Cincinnati.[3]

At the same time, northerners and liberal-minded southerners moved to the city as well. As a result, antebellum Cincinnati became a hotbed of abolitionism, a major station on the Underground Railroad, and a battleground to determine if slaveholders would, in fact, be allowed to bring their slaves into the state.[4] Yet Cincinnati was not simply a northern city looking South. The city had a dual personality, a schizophrenic northern and southern personality occupying the same urban body. Across time Cincinnati would feel this duality— a northern city, a southern city; two cultures, two unreconciled strivings; two warring ideals in a single city. And throughout Cincinnati's history these warring souls produced constant tension while simultaneously providing Cincinnati with a unique culture and way of life. This duality, this dialectic, this contradiction, is central to understanding the history of both Cincinnati and its African American population.[5]

Borderland culture, where North meets South, then, creates in part the setting and backdrop to the African American experience in Cincinnati. In this city blacks lived on the edge, the margin, as they never could in Philadelphia, Buffalo, Detroit, Chicago, or even Cleveland. At the same time, because black Cincinnatians lived in the northern borderland, they lived on the edge, the margin, as they never could in Louisville, Baltimore, Washington, D.C., or even St. Louis.[6]

Although Cincinnati was a city with a northern/southern personality, Ohio still was not Mississippi, Alabama, Georgia, Louisiana, or South Carolina, and Cincinnati was not Richmond, New Orleans, or Charleston. Both before and after the Civil War the political rights of blacks in the South (and, in a certain sense, those of their white allies) were severely circumscribed. This did not happen in Cincinnati. After the Civil War blacks faced the future with great optimism. The legal foundation of racism was dismantled. The Black Laws, including the state's separate school law, were all repealed by 1887.[7] By contrast, during the same period, Jim Crow and white supremacy were written into the southern law of the land. Law became the foundation upon which racism was based in the South.[8]

Nevertheless, the postbellum dreams of African Americans were deferred. Although discriminatory laws were lacking, public opinion, prejudices, and social custom still hindered blacks' quest for equality and successful integration into white-dominated society.[9] The hiring and promotional practices of white employers and the racist attitudes of white workers combined to keep blacks at the bottom of the occupational ladder. As the old walking city crumbled, the evolving land use system, based on housing cost and type and buttressed by white hostility to the idea of having black neighbors, led to ghetto-slum formation.

Still, prejudice and discrimination notwithstanding, the color-caste system did not rest on a legal foundation, and naked terror was not systematically employed to keep blacks in their "place." In Cincinnati blacks could speak out and meet openly; they could petition and protest.[10] After securing the right to vote in 1870, they never experienced the horror and tragedy of disenfranchisement.[11] Yet, by living on Dixie's border, African Americans were not allowed to forget the proscriptions hampering southern blacks. Life on the edge constantly reminded them of their marginal position in white-dominated society.[12] This, combined with their relative freedom, caused black Cincinnatians to develop a tradition of aggressiveness and political activism that differed significantly from that of African Americans living just across the Ohio River in the southern borderland and in the deep South.[13] So a history of the black experience in Cincinnati is particularly important because it sheds light on black urban history in the borderland, that northern place situated betwixt and between the North and South.

The history of African Americans in Cincinnati is also tied to the development of the city, the city-building process, and the theoretical constructs, definitions, and policy formulations of those urban leaders who shaped the physical environment and determined, in part, where blacks lived within that environment. This book spans a period of about 140 years. During this time Cincinnati underwent dramatic changes as it passed through several distinct epochs—the commercial, industrializing, industrial, and postindustrial eras.[14]

Over this broad span of time the city's population grew from less than 100,000 to over 500,000; its territorial boundaries expanded from six square miles to more than seventy square miles; its internal organization changed from a pattern of overlapping land uses to one of segregated land uses; its method of electing representatives changed from a ward-based system to a complex 9X limited voting system; and its economy shifted from commerce to industry, then to service and high technology.[15]

In each stage of its development Cincinnati was characterized by a specific type of economic base, transportation system, structure ("the spatial organization of key functional areas and essential services facilities in response to certain fundamental living needs and activities of human society"), and form ("the visually perceptive features of the city which this structure produces, both the two-dimensional and three-dimensional forms created by surfaces, spaces, structures, and circulatory systems in a defined natural setting"),[16] which shaped the everyday life and culture of its people. As Cincinnati moved through time, changes in its economy and transportation system had a profound impact on its structure and form, as well as a profound effect on the behavior and life chances of its people.[17]

The events of the late nineteenth and early twentieth centuries are suggestive. During this period Cincinnati made the transition from a commercial to a modern industrial city.[18] Not only did the physical boundaries of the city expand to include many surrounding towns and villages, but its internal organization, structure, and form shifted fundamentally. These physical changes shattered the narrow perimeters of the "old walking city" and scattered people and industry across the urban hinterland.[19]

The changes taking place in Cincinnati affected the everyday life and culture of African Americans. At each of these stages in Cincinnati's development, African Americans faced a different set of problems, opportunities, and challenges as the city moved from the commercial to the industrializing to the industrial and into the postindustrial age. So the realities and possibilities facing blacks were constantly changing. For example, the types of jobs and opportunities available to blacks in 1850 were very different from those available in both 1890 and 1950. The location of the black community changed from epoch to epoch as well. In the commercial city most blacks lived in the East End; by the turn of the century they were concentrated in the West End; and by 1960 the black population center had shifted to the hilltop neighborhood of Avondale.[20]

Even racism changed over time. In the antebellum era blacks faced Black Laws, race riots, and open hostility from whites.[21] After the Civil War the laws were repealed and legally sanctioned racism stopped. But popular culture, social custom, and public opinion promoted segregation and fueled prejudice and discrimination. The discriminatory hiring and promotional practices of white employers, the prejudicial behavior of white workers, and restrictive covenants, zoning laws, building codes, and subdivision regulations replaced the Black Laws as the primary vehicles of black repression.[22]

After World War II and the high tide of the civil rights movement, most manifestations of socially sanctioned racism disappeared and institutional racism gained dominance. For example, between 1950 and 1970 residential segregation dropped in Cincinnati, and places of public accommodation opened to people regardless of skin color.[23] Employers stopped the practice of openly rejecting job applicants solely on the basis of race.[24] But a second black ghetto-slum appeared. The "job ceiling" still kept African Americans tied to the bottom of the economic ladder. And although the black population increased dramatically after 1950, Cincinnati's limited voting system kept black political representation at a minimum.[25] Finally, the anger and frustration of blacks exploded with the riot of 1967.[26]

As the city changed over time, a host of social groups, including workers, women, physicians, politicians, builders, architects, real estate dealers, developers, industrialists, and businessmen, struggled for the triumph of their vision of a new Cincinnati and to secure for themselves a prominent place in the new social order.[27] In the ensuing search for order, middle-class whites and blacks imposed their notion of order onto the rest of society.[28] It was their definitions of good government, of city "beautiful" and city "practical," of good housing and residential development, and of the place of various groups in the social order that guided the city-building process and that defined the context within which the African American experience evolved.[29]

The reform movement elevated Cincinnati to national prominence as a model of efficient government and a pioneer in the city planning and housing reform movements.[30] Most significant, the reformers' notions about city building provided the broad framework within which Cincinnati evolved throughout the twentieth century.[31] The emergence of Cincinnati as an exemplary efficient city and as a leader in city planning and housing reform provides yet another reason why the study of black Cincinnati is so important. Simply put, how did African Americans fare in this well-run city with a model approach to planning and housing reform? Did "good" government and innovative approaches to residential development make life better for black Cincinnatians?

Thus the essays in this book locate the black experience within the context of the city-building process. They illuminate that experience at specific moments in Cincinnati's history, as well as across time. Conceptually, then, the focus is on city building and how the changing urban environment and the decisions, definitions, and policy formulations of urban leaders affected the life chances of African Americans and their fight for equality and social justice. In this sense, the collection grapples with both the external and internal forces that shaped the black experience as Cincinnati moved through successive stages of economic, social, and political development.

So at one level the analytic focus is on the role played by city building and urban leaders in creating the urban environments in which the black experience unfolded. At another, it is on the response of African Americans to the city-building process and to the changing conditions produced by the city as it moved through time. Here the concern is with how African Americans organized their residential environment and built communities and how they fought against racism. By looking at black Cincinnati from an urban history perspective and by focusing on the themes of work, housing, community, and the struggle for advancement, hopefully this volume will offer insight into the critical linkages that bind together the past and present—and create perspective for the future.

Notes

1. The term "borderland" refers to those states that stand on the line separating the North and South. In this sense there are both northern and southern borderland states and cities. For instance, Missouri, Kentucky, Virginia, Maryland, and Delaware are southern border states, while Pennsylvania, Ohio, Indiana, Illinois, and New Jersey are northern border states. The cities lying on both sides of the borderline separating the North and South are referred to as borderland cities. Using this definition, Cincinnati and Cairo, Illinois, would be borderland cities but not Cleveland and Chicago. Other borderline cities would include Pittsburgh, Steubenville, Wheeling, Evansville, Louisville, Paducah, Baltimore, Washington, D.C., and St. Louis. Although there have been several important books written on borderland cities, only in George C. Wright's *Life behind a Veil: Blacks in Louisville, Kentucky, 1865–1930* (Baton Rouge: Louisiana State University Press, 1985) do we find an effort to conceptualize the borderland as a unique region with a unique urban experience. For examples of studies of borderland cities that do not employ a borderland conceptual framework, see Peter Gottlieb, *Making Their Own Way: Southern Blacks' Migration to Pittsburgh, 1916–30* (Urbana: University of Illinois Press, 1987); James Borchert, *Alley Life in Washington: Family, Community, Religion, and Folklife in the City, 1850–1970* (Urbana: University of Illinois Press, 1980). Although it is not an urban history, John H. Fenton's *Politics in the Border States: A Study of the Patterns of Political Organization, and Political Change, Common to Border States—Maryland, West Virginia, Kentucky and Missouri* (New Orleans: The Hauser Press, 1957) is helpful in developing an understanding of borderland culture. Ira Berlin's "Comments on the Historical Backdrop: Black Cincinnati, Journey across Time" (Black Cincinnati: Journey across Time: A Bicentennial Symposium, Cincinnati, 26 December 1988) triggered my thinking on borderland culture.

2. Cincinnati was located on the banks of the Ohio, just across the river from Covington and Newport, Kentucky. In 1850 17 percent of Cincinnati's native population came from the South. Charles Cist, *Cincinnati in 1851* (Cincinnati: W. H. Moore, 1851), 46; John D. Barnhart, "Sources of Southern Migration into the Old Northwest," *Mississippi Valley Historical Review* 22 (June 1935): 59–62; Barnhart, "The Southern Influence in the Formation of Ohio," *Journal of Southern History* 3 (Feb. 1937): 28–42; Richard N. Campen, *Ohio: Architectural Portrait* (Chagrin Falls, Ohio: West Summit Press, 1973); 14–23; Cole Patrick Dawson, "Yankees in the Queen City: The Social and Intellectual Contributions of New Englanders in Cincinnati, 1820–1850" (Ph.D. diss., Miami University, 1977); William E. Barringer, "The Politics of Abolition: Salmon P. Chase in Cincinnati," *Cincinnati Historical Society Bulletin* 29, no. 2 (1971): 79–99.

3. Henry Louis Taylor, Jr., "The Northwest Ordinance and the Place of Ohio in African American History," *The Old Northwest: A Journal of Regional Life and Letters* 14 (Summer 1988): 131–44; Charles Hickock, *The Negro in Ohio, 1802–1870* (1896; repr., New York: Negro University Press, 1976); David A. Gerber, *Black Ohio and the Color Line, 1860–1915* (Urbana: University of Illinois Press, 1976), 3–7.

4. Larry Gara, *The Liberty Line: The Legend of the Underground Railroad* (Lexington: University of Kentucky Press, 1961); Charles L. Blockson, *The Underground Railroad: First-Person Narratives of Escapes to Freedom in the North* (New York: Prentice Hall, 1987).

5. The idea of conceptualizing the contradictions in Cincinnati's history in this specific manner came from W. E. B. DuBois, "The Souls of Black Folk," *Writings,* ed. Nathan Huggins (New York: The Library of America, 1986), 364–65.

6. Antebellum Buffalo, New York, offers an interesting contrast to Cincinnati. Buffalo lies on the northeastern edge of the Great Lakes, just across the river from Canada. Frederick Douglass once called Canada the only place in North America that was truly north of slavery. Some blacks, like William Wells Brown, settled in Buffalo because they felt threatened by the slave catchers. Buffalo stood on the edge of a truly free territory, and if a runaway were threatened, he or she could easily slip across the border to safety. No such haven existed for Cincinnati blacks. Fear was a constant companion of fugitives living in this Queen City. See T. J. Davis, "Black Buffalo: A Historical Backdrop," in *African Americans and the Rise of Buffalo's Post-Industrial City, 1940 to Present,* ed. Henry Louis Taylor, Jr. (Buffalo, New York: Buffalo Urban League, 1991).

7. Following the Civil War and Reconstruction, northern states had no laws requiring segregation in places of public accommodation and in public institutions. In fact, in a number of northern states segregation was actually against the law. For a detailed discussion of this issue in Ohio, see Gerber, *Black Ohio,* 44–59.

8. C. Vann Woodward, *The Strange Career of Jim Crow* (New York: Oxford University Press, 1974); Joel Williamson, *A Rage for Order: Black-*

White Relations in the American South since Emancipation (New York: Oxford University Press, 1986); Howard N. Rabinowitz, *Race Relations in the Urban South, 1865–90* (Urbana: University of Illinois Press, 1980).

9. Frank U. Quillin, *The Color Line in Ohio: A History of Race Relations in a Typical Northern State* (1913; repr., New York: Negro University Press, 1969).

10. For example, in the 1880s Cincinnati blacks formed the Civil Rights League to fight for the right to use public accommodations. Gerber, *Black Ohio*, 58.

11. Ibid., 44–59.

12. Unlike Cleveland and Columbus, blacks in Cincinnati continued to face hostility from whites as de facto segregation took root. Restaurants, including those of the highest quality, drew the color line, and blacks encountered insult and humiliation. For example, Cleveland's John Green, a state representative who had recently won the gratitude of labor by sponsoring a bill to establish an annual Ohio Labor Day, was asked to address a Labor Day gathering at Cincinnati in 1890. He was refused rooms at several hotels before finally finding accommodations. Ibid., 58–59.

13. For a look at the role of politics in the life of black Cincinnatians, see Ralph A. Straetz, *PR politics in Cincinnati: Thirty-two Years of City Government through Proportional Representation* (New York: New York University Press, 1958), 109–25; Gregory R. Coor, "Black Politics and Education in Cincinnati: 1870–1890" (Ph.D. diss., University of Cincinnati, 1984).

14. This book employs an urban history scheme of conceptualization that seeks to understand the city in dynamic terms. By locating the black experience within the context of the city's changing ecological structure and in the changing theoretical constraints, definitions, and policy formulations of urban leaders, this work hopes to link the experiences of African Americans to aspects of the particular environments in which they live. Moreover, by tracing the black experience over time, we hope to offer insight into how the changing city creates different problems and challenges for African Americans at various points in time. And we hope to gain insight into how blacks responded to their challenges. This approach is based on the work of Theodore Hershberg. See Hershberg, "The New Urban History: Toward an Interdisciplinary History of the City," in *Philadelphia: Work, Space, Family, and Group Experience in the Nineteenth Century*, ed. Hershberg (Oxford: Oxford University Press, 1981), 3–35; Theodore Hershberg, Alan N. Burnstein, Eugene P. Ericksen, Stephanie W. Greenberg, and William L. Yancey, "A Tale of Three Cities: Blacks, Immigrants, and Opportunity in Philadelphia, 1850–1880, 1930, 1970," in *Philadelphia*, 461–91. For a detailed look at the intellectual roots of the approach used in this book, see also W. E. B. DuBois, *The Philadelphia Negro: A Social Study* (1899; repr., New York: Shocken Books, 1967); St. Clair Drake and Horace R. Cayton, *Black Metropolis: A Study of Negro Life in a Northern City* (New York: Harcourt

and Brace, 1945); Amos H. Hawley, *Human Ecology: A Theory of Community Structure* (New York: Ronald Press, 1950); Eric E. Lampard, "American Historians and the Study of Urbanization," *American Historical Review* 67 (Oct. 1961): 49–61; Roy Lubove, "The Urbanization Process: An Approach to Historical Research," *American Institute of Planners* 33 (Jan. 1967): 33–39; Sam Bass Warner, Jr., "If All the World Were Philadelphia: A Scaffolding for Urban History, 1774–1930," *American Historical Review* 74 (Oct. 1968): 26–43.

15. The 9X election system is designed to minimize either the risk of partisan, at-large elections in which one party sweeps all seats or the risk of excluding minorities from representation. In this system the number of nominees allowed each party is limited to less than the total number of council seats or the number of candidates a voter may check is restricted (or both). In the Cincinnati system three parties (Democrats, Republicans, Charter) make unofficial nominations. There is no primary, and the voters are allowed to mark as many as nine Xs on the ballot. There are nine councilmanic seats. See Howard D. Hamilton, *Electing the Cincinnati City Council: An Examination of Alternative Electoral-Representation Systems* (a report to the Stephen H. Wilder Foundation, June 1978), 6–7; Henry Louis Taylor, Jr., "The Use of Maps in the Study of the Black Ghetto-Formation Process: Cincinnati, 1802–1910," *Historical Methods* 17, no. 2 (1984): 44–58; Zane L. Miller, *Boss Cox's Cincinnati: Urban Politics in the Progressive Era* (New York: Oxford University Press, 1968).

16. Lubove, "The Urbanization Process," 33; Hershberg, "The New Urban History," 3–40.

17. Richard Rhonda, "Urban Transport and the Expansion of Cincinnati, 1858 to 1920," *Cincinnati Historical Society Bulletin* 35, no. 1 (1977): 43–70; Miller, *Boss Cox.*

18. This transition had a profound impact on the city and produced significant changes in the everyday life and culture of its residents. For example, see Steven J. Ross, *Workers on the Edge: Work, Leisure, and Politics in Industrializing Cincinnati, 1778–1890* (New York: Columbia University Press, 1985); Janet A. Miller, "Urban Education and the New City: Cincinnati's Elementary Schools, 1870 to 1914," *Ohio History* 88, no. 2 (1979): 152–72; Alan I. Marcus, "Professional Revolution and Reform in the Progressive Era: Physicians and the City Elections of 1897 and 1900," *Journal of Urban History* 5, no. 2 (1979): 183–208; Barbara L. Musselman, "The Shackles of Class and Gender: Cincinnati Working Women, 1890–1920," *Queen City Heritage* 41, no. 4 (1983): 35–40.

19. Zane L. Miller, "Boss Cox's Cincinnati: A Study in Urbanization and Politics, 1880–1914," *Journal of American History*, 54, no. 4 (1968): 823–38.

20. Henry Louis Taylor, Jr., "On Slavery's Fringe: City-Building and Black Community Development in Cincinnati, 1800–1850," *Ohio History* 95 (Winter/Spring): 5–33; Gerber, *Black Ohio*, 60–92; Taylor, "The Use of

Maps," 44–58; [George Schermer], "A Background Paper for the Greater Cincinnati Conference on Equal Opportunity in Housing," 18 Nov. 1964, 5, University of Cincinnati, Archives and Rare Books Department, Census Tract Data Bank.

21. Otto A. Lovett, "Black Laws of Ohio" (Master's thesis, Ohio State University, 1929); Leonard Harding, "The Cincinnati Riots of 1862," *Cincinnati Historical Society Bulletin* 25, no. 4 (1967): 229–39.

22. Gerber, *Black Ohio,* chapters 2–4.

23. For example, between 1940 and 1970 the segregation index for Cincinnati dropped significantly. In 1940 the index was 90.6, and by 1970 it had dropped to 83.1. During this same period the segregation index for Pittsburgh rose by 1.9 percentage points, and in Cleveland it dropped by only three points. See James N. Upton, "Theories on Urban Violence," *Journal of Social and Behavioral Sciences* 29, no. 3 (1983): 78–90.

24. Ohio Civil Rights Commission, *Second Annual Report* (Columbus: The Commission, 1960).

25. An important result of the change of Cincinnati's electoral system in 1957 from proportional representation to the 9X system was the infrequent election of black candidates. Hamilton, *Electing the Cincinnati City Council,* 42; Straetz, *PR Politics,* 109–25.

26. James N. Upton, "Urban Violence: A Case Study of Three Cities" (Ph.D. diss., Ohio State University, 1976).

27. Ross, *Workers on the Edge;* Miller, *Boss Cox;* Larry G. Osnes, "The Birth of a Party: The Cincinnati Populist Convention of 1891," *Great Plains Journal* 10, no. 1 (1970): 11–24; Lyle Koehler, "Women's Rights, Society, and the Schools: Feminist Activities in Cincinnati, Ohio, 1864–1880," *Queen City Heritage* 42, no. 4 (1984): 3–17; Brian Williams, "Petticoats in Politics: Cincinnati Women and the 1920 Election," *Cincinnati Historical Society Bulletin* 35, no. 1 (1977): 43–70; Marcus, "Professional Revolution."

28. Robert H. Wiebe, *The Search for Order: 1877–1920* (New York: Hill and Wang, 1967); John D. Buenker, John C. Burnham, and Robert Crunden, *Progressivism* (Cambridge: Schenkman, 1977).

29. This process suggests that urban development was determined by the interplay between objective and subjective growth factors. In other words, Cincinnati's growth and development were determined in part by a continuous process of people defining and solving problems. Miller, *Boss Cox;* Robert B. Fairbanks, *Making Better Citizens: Housing Reform and the Community Development Strategy in Cincinnati, 1890–1960* (Urbana: University of Illinois Press, 1988); Richard E. Foglesong, *Planning the Capitalist City: The Colonial Era to the 1920s* (Princeton, N.J.: Princeton University Press, 1986).

30. Hamilton, *Electing the Cincinnati City Council;* Straetz, *PR Politics;* Fairbanks, *Making Better Citizens,* 1–11.

31. This is not to suggest that people's ideas about the city were static. They were not. Notions about city building were constantly changing as

urban leaders confronted and solved problems. Particularly in the postindustrial age, that period between 1940 and the present, the way that Cincinnatians thought about the city shifted. Still the new ideas operated within the scaffold constructed by the urban reformers who "built" New Cincinnati. Fairbanks, *Making Better Citizens,* 146–78; Zane L. Miller, "History and the Politics of Community Change in Cincinnati," *The Public Historian* 5, no. 4 (1983): 17–35; Martha S. Reynolds, "The City, Suburbs, and the Establishment of the Clifton Town Meeting, 1961–1964," *Cincinnati Historical Society Bulletin* 38, no. 1 (1980): 6–32; Zane L. Miller and Geoffrey Giglierano, "Downtown Housing: Changing Plans and Perspectives," *Cincinnati Historical Society Bulletin* 40, no. 3: 167–90; Hamilton, *Electing the Cincinnati City Council.*

Acknowledgments

I wish to thank the many people who assisted in the preparation of this book. I gratefully acknowledge the assistance given to this project by the Greater Cincinnati Bicentennial Commission, the Cincinnati Historical Society, the Friends of Harriet Beecher Stowe House, Citizens' Committee on Youth, and the Black History Archives Committee of the Cincinnati Historical Society. These organizations played a critical role in marshaling the resources to fund the project and in putting together the team that organized the bicentennial symposium, "Black Cincinnati: Journey across Time."

I wish to express my gratitude to the members of the Bicentennial Symposium Planning Committee for organizing the symposium, which allowed us to share the findings of our study with Cincinnati residents and created a forum for us to receive criticisms, suggestions, and further encouragement: Frank Allison, Johnnie Mae Berry, J. Kenneth Blackwell, Herb Brown, Rev. Roy E. Eiland, Barbara H. Ford, Joseph B. Hall, Bertha L. Jones, Phyllis H. Layton, Roland C. McGoodwin, Zane L. Miller, Charles B. Nuckolls, Lorena O'Donnell, Harriet Marsh Page, Gale E. Peterson, Halloway C. Sells, Nia W. Terry, W. Monty Whitney, and Reggie Williams. These individuals made the symposium a success. Also I wish to thank Theodore M. Berry, Charles Cooper, Allen Howard, John Fleming, Dewey Fuller, Virginia Coffey, and Myrtis Powell for their participation in the symposium.

An important debt goes to the following institutions for providing financial support for this project: the Greater Cincinnati Bicentennial

Commission, the *Cincinnati Daily Enquirer*, Foxx and Company, Gannett Foundation, Ohio Humanities Council, Omni Netherland Plaza, Westin Hotel, and Wilson and Associates. A special thank you goes to the Greater Cincinnati Bicentennial Commission for providing a subvention to help defray publishing costs.

A number of colleagues commented on portions of this book. I owe them a debt of gratitude for their questions, comments, and suggestions. I wish to thank Ira Berlin, Henry Binford, Darlene Clark Hine, Clayborne Carson, Roger W. Lotchin, Judith Spraul-Schmidt, Roger Daniels, Robert Forbes, Lois E. Horton, Mark Ledbetter, Marie McGraw, Elsie Mosqueda, Gene Lewis, and a reviewer for the University of Illinois Press for their critical thoughts. A special thank you also goes to David L. Calkins, who made his Cincinnati newspaper card files available, and to Frances Forman of the Cincinnati Historical Society, who always thought of one more way to search for sources. A debt is owed to the staffs at the Cincinnati Historical Society and the University of Cincinnati Libraries, Department of Archives and Rare Books.

I would like to offer special thanks to research assistants at the Center for Applied Public Affairs Studies at the University at Buffalo. Radhika Suresh, Pawan Bajpai, Carlos Lugo, Spencer Reed, John Joseph, Therese Aboujaoude, David Rodriguez, Rafael Morales, and Rosa Camacho all played an important role in the preparation of the manuscript for this book. A special debt of gratitude goes to Lalit Goel and Chien-Hwa Wang for their role in "crunching numbers" for the project. The work of Lisa R. Monpere and Vicky Dula stands out. Both put much hard work into the preparation of this book. Their dedication and professionalism were inspiring.

I wish to thank Theodore Hershberg and Michael Frisch, whose ideas provided a scaffolding for my thinking on urban history. Of course, I owe a very special thank you to Zane L. Miller. His patience, encouragement, wisdom, and knowledge made this project possible. Charles B. Nuckolls was the driving force behind the project. He was the individual who made it all happen. His enthusiasm and optimism were contagious. More than any other individual, he made this unique partnership work.

I wish to thank my wife, Carol, and my children, Jean-Jacques, Keeanga, and Chad-Cinque. They endured my long absences and gave me encouragement along the way. Dr. Henry Louis Taylor, Sr., has been my hero and was the inspiration behind this project. He always supported and encouraged my scholarship. He was my role model and mentor. Thank you, Dad.

RACE AND THE CITY

1

HENRY LOUIS TAYLOR, JR.

Introduction: Race and the City, 1820–1970

The history of black Cincinnati from 1820 to 1970 is a narrative about the stages and determinants of black community development and about the internal and external forces that shaped the black experience over time. Both continuity and discontinuity characterize the history of black Cincinnati. Some things changed in dramatic ways, while other things remained essentially unchanged. Antebellum Cincinnati is the reference point in the chronicle. It is the backdrop against which changes that took place in the city and in the black experience are described, analyzed, interpreted, and explained.

The Antebellum Preindustrial Commercial City

Black Cincinnati formed in a booming river town with a social world characterized by Negrophobia, proscription, segregation, and the constant threat of violence. Denied citizenship and protection under the Constitution of the United States, blacks faced legal, political, and social restrictions in their quest for freedom.[1] Therefore, black Cincinnatians had to create their community in a city offering expanding economic opportunities yet tinged with the stench of racism.

Within this protean setting, African Americans sensed that they could survive Cincinnati only by fashioning their lives in an environment put together by independent organizations reflecting their concept of being a people, filled with pride, confidence, and self-determination.[2] White friends were important, but to secure real freedom blacks had to rely on their own resources, not benevolence. They had to build organizations, forge a group identity, and act in their own interest.[3] Operating within this philosophical context, African Americans built churches, schools, benevolent organizations, orphanages, homes for widows, and secret societies, including stations on the Underground Railroad.[4]

The leaders of these organizations and institutions were drawn from the ranks of the groups in the community with the most stability and the highest status. They were elites, dominated by skilled workers and business people, most of whom were barbers, carpenters, hucksters, teachers, painters, tanners, and whitewashers. These black leaders were usually democratically elected at citywide meetings. Thus the black masses, not white patrons, formed the social base of their power. Consequently, antebellum leaders did not become an isolated elite, out of touch with the black community (see chapter 3).

The black residential structure reinforced this pattern of leadership. African Americans lived in a series of residential clusters scattered throughout the city. These clusters formed without reference to class, family structure, nativity, or stage in the life cycle (see chapter 4). Therefore, those who spoke and acted on behalf of black Cincinnati lived among the masses. Proximity and social interaction reinforced the bonds of unity between leaders and their constituencies and help to explain the vitality of black organizational life.

The struggle against racism and the abolition of slavery stood at the center of the African American experience. Yet blacks did not simply react to whites. They formed their own culture, developed their own worldview, and fought constantly to control their own destiny. This is what young John Mercer Langston and other youths observed when they walked the streets of antebellum Cincinnati. They saw black men and women, against great odds, building a tightly knit community and establishing themselves as skilled workers, entrepreneurs, property owners, and leaders fighting for freedom (see chapter 2).

Still, African Americans lived on the edge in Cincinnati. Although the Queen City was a prosperous place, most blacks did not gain access to many of the jobs and opportunities there. A color-caste occupational system existed in Cincinnati.[5] Its segmented labor market not only featured different types of jobs for men, women, and children, but it was partitioned along racial lines.[6] Institutions, such as government, education, and trade unions, and white employers and workers (outside the unions) colluded to perpetuate the "colored" and white sections of the labor market. This resulted in the "floor" of white economic opportunity becoming a "ceiling" for black economic opportunity. Racism, not human capital deficits, created the obstacles encountered by African Americans in Cincinnati's labor market (see chapter 5).

Nevertheless, a handful of blacks achieved phenomenal economic success. Robert Harlan made a fortune buying and selling racehorses; Robert Gordon captured the imagination of a generation with his exploits in the coal business; Thomas Schooley had a successful pickling establishment; and Alfred V. Thompson ran a thriving tailoring business. Pressley Ball and Alexander Thomas were well-known photographers, and Samuel T. Wilcox succeeded as a grocer. Henry Boyd manufactured, and owned the patent for, a popular pre-Civil War, corded bed.[7]

Remarkable and inspirational, these great individual accomplishments, nevertheless, did not reflect the realities or the possibilities available to most blacks. The color-caste occupational system and openly hostile forms of racism, including violence and discrimination, kept the vast majority of African Americans securely locked in the lower chambers of the city's economic structure.

Race and class played a major role in determining where blacks lived in the city.[8] In the antebellum period, however, black Cincinnati was not a territorial community with specific boundaries, and no one perceived African American culture or behavior as connected to the particular "place" (as a physical/social environment) occupied by blacks.[9] When people used terms like "Little Africa" and "Bucktown," they were identifying where large clusters of African Americans and their institutions were located, not making statements about a relationship between the physical/social environment and black behavior (see chapter 4).[10]

This is not surprising. African Americans were spatially integrated into the entire city. Although white prejudice, discrimination, and hostility infiltrated every aspect of life in Cincinnati, racial residential segregation did not exist. Blacks were concentrated but did not live in homogeneous, racially segregated neighborhoods. They shared the living space with whites from various ethnic groups and social classes. The houses of the rich and the hovels of the poor stood within a stone's throw of each other. Many blacks and whites huddled together in wretched neighborhoods. And almost everywhere dwelling units coexisted with stores, offices, shops, warehouses, and factories. No one group could claim the living place as its own. In such a setting, the riveting of African American behavior to "place" could not occur (see chapter 4).[11]

Finally, it would be a mistake to conclude that the pervasiveness of racism meant that blacks were consumed with white machinations in this or any other period in Cincinnati's history. African Americans lived in a social universe apart from whites. The sights, sounds, smells, rhythms, melodies, and improvisations of black life existed independent of the white world and gave shape, form, texture, and vibrancy to black Cincinnati.[12] In the intimate atmosphere of home, church, and the backroom bar, blacks loved, told stories, joked, laughed, sang, danced, and enjoyed friendships without conscious thought of whites, racial hostility, and the ever-present threat of violence.[13]

Race, Class, and the Rise of the Industrial Metropolis

In the decades following the Civil War, African Americans flocked to Cincinnati, hoping to build a better life for themselves and their families. Before the war blacks viewed slavery, their lack of citizenship, and their inability to participate in the political process as the cornerstones of prejudice, discrimination, and segregation.[14] With slavery abolished and the legal fetters of racism broken, blacks expected Negrophobia, proscription, discrimination, and segregation to retreat.[15] They were mistaken. Obstacles to their full participation in American society remained in force. Black Cincinnatians' quest to transform their dreams into reality and the thwarting of those efforts are dominant themes in the postbellum experience.

Economic restructuring looms large in the growth and development of Cincinnati after the mid-nineteenth century. Industrialization was the driving force behind the change process. The value of Cincinnati's manufactured products, for example, increased from $54 million in 1851 to $262 million in 1910. The developing economy spurred population growth, including an influx of southern blacks. Between 1850 and 1940 the total population increased from 115,438 to 455,610, while blacks shifted from 3,172 to 37,222 and went from comprising 3 percent of the population to 18 percent. Meanwhile the city expanded its territorial boundaries from six to more than fifty-two square miles (see chapter 6).

The Queen City's transition from a compact settlement with an economy centering on the waterfront and on steamboat traffic to a sprawling industrial city with a diverse manufacturing base brought havoc into the lives of many workers. For example, as the pace of industrialization accelerated in the 1870s and 1880s, the workplace changed for individual workers. The small workshop was transformed into the modern factory, production was reorganized and rationalized, mechanization increased dramatically, a sharp division of labor emerged, and many jobs became highly specialized. Both the number of occupations requiring highly skilled workers and those requiring little or no skills proliferated (see chapter 5).

The change process eroded the old ways of life and marginalized large segments of the working class. Not only did numerous jobs and opportunities disappear, but many workers, especially craftsmen, lost status.[16] They became obsolete in a rapidly changing world. Yet the greatly expanded economy did produce new jobs and opportunities. In the newfangled industrial world, a different category of workers achieved status. For example, machinist, clerical, sales, professional, and white-collar positions gained in prestige. Moreover, the growth of industries in such areas as foundry and machine shops, liquors, clothing, slaughtering and packing, boots and shoes, printing and publishing, carriages and wagons, soap, and lumber products created a great demand for skilled workers and laborers (see chapter 5).[17]

Cincinnati did not keep pace with its competitors, but the city still thrived. Black workers, however, did not fare well. The Civil War abolished slavery but left the color-caste occupational system intact. Racism and Negrophobia continued to circumscribe the jobs and opportunities available to African Americans. Moreover, the progress that blacks did make resulted from occupational filtering, not a free labor market. As the expanding economy produced new jobs, whites moved up the occupational ladder. The jobs that they did not want filtered down. This occupational filtering became the primary vehicle for black advancement during the industrial age (see chapter 5).[18]

The experience of the Irish, a downtrodden group in antebellum Cincinnati, provides one measure of how whites benefited from industrialization. The Irish, who had held lowly positions on the waterfront in the commercial era, made significant gains during the industrial period. By 1890 significant proportions of Irish-born men and women had jobs as clerical and salesworkers, traders and dealers, blacksmiths, masons, policemen, and workers in the iron and steel, textile, cigar, and boot and shoemaking industries. None of these categories were important for black workers (see chapter 5).

In fact, blacks actually lost occupational ground during the period. For example, their monopoly on barbering disappeared. Black entrepreneurs attracted fewer and fewer white customers. With the dismantling of the colored school system, the elite corp of black teachers declined. And increasing numbers of black men and women were forced to take jobs as unskilled and semiskilled laborers and domestic servants. By 1920 86 percent of black Cincinnati worked as un-skilled laborers and domestic and personal servants. There were no black bankers, brokers, moneylenders, wholesale dealers, importers, exporters, city officials, or inspectors (see chapter 6).

The black middle-class was very small, and its income base fragile. For instance, blacks comprised only 2 percent of professionals and 2 percent of proprietors, managers, and officials. And most black professionals were ministers, musicians, and teachers of music, not doctors, dentists, lawyers, judges, mechanical engineers, editors, and reporters (see chapter 6). Blacks remained at the bottom of the oc-cupational ladder. Everything had changed, but everything had re-mained the same.[19]

Still the economic gains made by blacks were important. Prole-tarianization (the creation of a black industrial working class) and the growth of the black middle class strengthened the black com-munity.[20] This small group of entrepreneurs, professionals, social workers, teachers, industrial workers, Pullman porters, and federal employees formed the critical core of black leadership during the in-dustrial age. The college-educated black, in particular, became a ma-jor force in the community-building effort.[21] Even so, low wages and the limited range of opportunities stunted the development of black Cincinnati, distorted its class structure, and made both class and race determinants of the life chances of blacks.[22]

The place of class and race in fashioning the life chances of African Americans is most clearly reflected in their quest to find good housing and good neighborhood conditions. African Americans migrating to Cincinnati in the late nineteenth and early twentieth centuries en-tered a city whose physical environment was being structurally reor-ganized. Not only were separate zones being set up for commercial and industrial activity, but the residential environment was being re-shaped. In the old walking city the rich and poor had lived near each other. Big mansions and rickety shanties had coexisted. Mosaic best describes these neighborhoods, where a collage of people and houses shared space. The industrial city altered this pattern.[23] Neighbor-hoods became increasingly segregated on the basis of housing type and cost. Low incomes, coupled with this reorganization of the res-idential environment, limited the housing options of African Ameri-cans (see chapter 6).

Mass homeownership and residential land use regulation were the driving forces behind this change process. As the population grew and the transportation revolution made city expansion possible, people moved into neighborhoods that were emerging in the space between the basin and the city's boundary line. This space became the center of residential development in the years between 1880 and 1940.[24]

A residential building boom accompanied population growth in these emergent neighborhoods. The owner-occupied, single-family house became the dominant type of structure. Between 1900 and 1938 84 percent of the new residential buildings constructed in Cincinnati were single-family dwellings, most owner-occupied. The number of people who owned their homes increased dramatically, and ownership changed residents' attitudes toward the living place. They wanted to keep out people or establishments that might threaten their investment (see chapter 6).

As new communities emerged in the hilltop and valley region, neighborhoods in the basin deteriorated. The area became a volatile land use conversion zone as it turned into metro Cincinnati's economic center. Industrial, commercial, and government activity replaced residential development as the predominant form of land use. At the same time, housing costs in hilltop and valley neighborhoods kept many low-income workers from leaving the basin.[25]

But housing costs alone could not keep low-income workers out of the emerging middle-income residential areas. Cincinnati had land speculators, lenders, building materials companies, and an army of carpenters who catered to low-income workers. This made it possible for these workers to "invade" neighborhoods with expensive, owner-occupied houses. In the industrial city the regulation of residential land use, without laws, did not work.

In an unregulated residential environment workers could buy cheaply developed lots and build inexpensive, poorly constructed homes on them. Moreover, industrial and commercial enterprises could locate in thriving middle-income neighborhoods and, if they felt the need, build modest cottages for their workers. Housing leaders felt that these forms of residential land use threatened homeownership and the development of homogeneous neighborhoods.[26]

They believed that middle-income communities had to be protected from invasion by low-income workers and commercial and industrial establishments. "It would be a shortsighted policy to encourage the construction of small homes and to foster home ownership and at the same time fail to take every precaution to see to it that the residence districts are not properly protected," said the Better Housing League (BHL) in its 1921 annual report.[27] As a result, the BHL, and other reform groups, passed building codes, zoning laws, and subdivision regulations to keep out the unwanted. These regulations structured the framework within which residential development took place in Cincinnati.

Zoning laws proved to be the most powerful of these regulatory mechanisms.[28] Enacted in 1924, Cincinnati's comprehensive zoning law created three different types of residential areas. Class A reserved land exclusively for single-family homes, while Class B permitted both two- and four-family detached housing. Class C allowed for neighborhoods where any type of house could be built. The zoning law codified the city's emerging class-stratified residential environment and legally reinforced the economic walls partitioning the various residential districts (see chapter 6).

Large numbers of African Americans arrived in Cincinnati when residential land use regulation, the rise of homeownership, and market forces were producing neighborhoods stratified on the basis of housing cost and type. The emergence of this type of residential environment, in combination with the low incomes of blacks and racism, produced the ghetto.[29] The residential options of black Cincinnatians were severely limited by their low incomes. Much of the new owner-occupied and rental housing units were beyond their economic reach. The residential land-rent structure, then, forced the majority of African Americans to search for housing in the low-rent district, located in the West End of the basin. By 1930 more than thirty thousand blacks, comprising 67 percent of the African American population, lived here. The concentration of thousands of blacks in this part of the city caused a ghetto to form (see chapter 6).

The West End was not simply a ghetto. It was also a slum.[30] Housing here was the oldest and most dilapidated in the metropolis. When in 1913 members of the National Housing Association called housing in Cincinnati among the worst in the United States, they were referring to dwelling units found in the basin. The basin's metamorphosis into the region's economic center exacerbated the problem. Between 1900 and 1940 it became a land use conversion zone where hundreds of tenements were destroyed to make way for new development. Almost 50 percent of the buildings demolished in Cincinnati were found there, while one-third of the city's new factories, offices, and service shops had basin locations. The blending of omnipresent destruction and construction with a concentration of social problems caused the basin to become a very undesirable place to live. Not surprising, many blacks wanted to move from the ghetto to more stable residential locations. They wanted to find a good place to live and raise their families (see chapter 6).

A major goal of the housing reformers was to keep poor blacks confined to the basin. By restricting cheap housing to specified zones and by having visiting social workers and housekeepers encourage blacks not to move into white neighborhoods, reformers hoped to keep African Americans living in the ghetto-slum. Their activities were complemented by realtors and white homeowners who likewise wanted to confine blacks to segregated neighborhoods. Class melded with race to determine where in the metropolis African Americans lived. Thus a combination of the city's physical structure, public policy, economic forces, and racism gave birth to the ghetto-slum (see chapters 6 and 7).

It should be stressed that ghetto-slum formation was more complex than the mere separation of blacks and whites in physical space. It involved the segregation of blacks and whites in very different types of neighborhoods. Uneven development is the concept that best describes the emerging differentials between the living place occupied by blacks and whites.[31] Blacks increasingly lived in a residential environment characterized by dilapidated housing, congestion, crime, and a proliferation of social problems. Whites increasingly lived in a residential environment characterized by good housing, amenities, safety, and stable neighborhood conditions.[32]

The emergence of a ghetto-slum led to a shift in thinking about the relationship between place and behavior. Before the ghetto-slum, people did not believe that such a relationship existed. Now they argued that the ghetto-slum not only identified the place where African Americans lived in the city, it also defined their behavior.[33] The West End was a material reflection of the attitudes, values, beliefs, and traditions of black Cincinnatians, not simply the location of their community. This interweaving of place and culture made it appear that African Americans were responsible for the blight and social problems found in their neighborhoods. This is what the newspaper editor and black chronicler, Wendell P. Dabney, had in mind when he said,

> The whites claim that the property of a locality depreciates in value when Negroes become residents. That cause for such depreciation arises from the Negro's failure to keep his property up to the right standard, the neglect of its appearance, his tendency to make money by subletting his rooms to irresponsible people who lower the tone of, as well as become a nuisance to, the neighborhood. . . . Whenever one Negro comes, the others feel they have the right to follow, and that while the firstcomer may be all right, those who follow will be the opening wedge for a number of undesirables, with their business signs, for hair straightening, toilet preparations, and furnished rooms.[34]

In essence, the idea was that wherever African Americans go within the metropolis, they will reproduce the ghetto-slum. This linking of culture to place, and the fear that black people blight neighborhoods, fueled the residential segregation movement and exacerbated race relations.

Not all blacks lived in the ghetto-slum. Some escaped.[35] More than one-third were scattered across the city. In predominantly white residential settings these blacks built small residential clusters similar to those that existed in the antebellum period. A number of low-income blacks even moved into the suburban region, where they built crudely constructed "shacks," located on poorly developed lots with unpaved roads.[36]

To the housing reformers these communities of homeowners were "bad spots" that threatened suburban residential development. But to the people who resided there the shacks were home sweet home. So, then, in the city residential land use regulation placed home-ownership beyond the economic reach of many blacks and limited their housing options, while in the suburb the lack of such regulation brought homeownership and stable communities within the grasp of the poor, albeit on cheaply developed land with wobbly houses.[37]

The reformers' emphasis on promoting homeownership and regu-lating residential land use did not mean that they eschewed the hous-ing problem of low-income workers. On the contrary, attacking the low-income housing problem was an important part of their residen-tial development strategy. The reformers believed that dilapidated housing, congestion, and slums produced anomie and bad citizens. Such conditions, they posited, threatened Cincinnati's economic, so-cial, and political well-being. Based on this perspective, they formed a strategy centering on the goal of building both houses and commu-nities that produced good citizens imbued with the middle-class val-ues of hard work and participatory democracy. But in spite of the reformers' lofty goals, their housing program failed; it did not create good housing and neighborhoods for low-income workers (see chap-ter 7).

The reasons are complex. Racism, the business creed, and the re-formers' economic goal of transforming the basin into the economic center of the metropolis conflicted with and canceled out their social goal of building good housing and neighborhoods for low-income workers. During the teens and twenties their strategy consisted of using building codes and constructing model tenements to pro-vide housing for low-income workers. But code enforcement led to the demolition of hundreds of tenements without the simultane-ous construction of new dwelling units to house displaced residents.

Since blacks were overrepresented in the worst housing units and since most blacks could not afford either the new owner- or rental-occupied houses, the restrictive legislation movement increased crowding and exacerbated the black housing problem.[38]

In response to the inability of blacks to purchase new housing, the reformers developed a "filter-down" housing strategy. White workers were encouraged to move out of the West End so that their old housing could provide lodging for blacks. For instance, when black leaders and members of the Cincinnati Community Chest asked the Better Housing League to develop a plan for addressing the worsening black housing problem, they were told that the friends of African Americans should be encouraged to invest their money in the building of new houses for whites. "This," the BHL indicated, "while not relieving colored families directly would tend to relieve them indirectly by drawing white families out of the district now occupied for the most part by colored people."[39] The big problem with this scheme is that most housing was ready for demolition by the time it filtered down to low-income blacks. Moreover, the reformers, by encouraging white flight, reinforced the emerging pattern of racial residential segregation in the West End (see chapter 7).

In the 1930s and 1940s the effort to provide good housing and neighborhoods for low-income workers shifted from the private to the public housing front. The Great Depression led to a federally supported public housing program designed to replace crowded, insanitary slum housing with good housing and neighborhoods for the poor. By clearing slums and rehousing the poor in low-rent housing units, reformers hoped to create vibrant neighborhoods where people mired in poverty were redeemed. But again, racism and the business creed thwarted their efforts (see chapter 7).

Housing officials divided the city's low-income population into two groups, the deserving and undeserving poor. The undeserving poor, according to the housing reformers, lived in those sections of the slum where housing was the most dilapidated and where social problems were most heavily concentrated. These places, they posited, not only identified where the undeserving poor resided but reflected their behavior as well. Nothing could be done for the individuals in this group. They were best left to the social workers, the police, and the courts. In contrast, the deserving poor, reformers believed, were either newcomers to the city or workers temporarily down on their luck. They could be helped (see chapter 7).

Consistent with their philosophy of homogeneous neighborhoods, reformers felt that the deserving and undeserving poor should be separated in geographic space, lest the latter adversely affect the former.

Within this context the reformers sought to rehabilitate the deserving poor by bringing them into a public housing environment, where strong communities were to be established. Since the majority of the white poor were members of the deserving poor and the majority of the black poor were not, it only made sense, the housing leaders probably reasoned, to build most of the new public housing units in the white section of the West End and in white-dominated areas of the metropolis. In this regard, housing authorities attempted to use public housing as a means of solving the housing problem of low-income whites.[40]

Black admission to public housing was further curbed by high minimum-income requirements and rentals. Public housing's goal was to furnish the poor with a supply of low-rent housing, but the cost of land acquisition, demolition, and construction pushed the cost of living in these units beyond the economic reach of most blacks (see chapter 7). In the end, public housing, like tenement regulation and model homes, failed to provide African Americans with good housing and neighborhood conditions. Consequently the ghetto-slum persisted.

One response to the formation of the ghetto-slum, the housing problem, the growth of socioeconomic problems among blacks, and persistent racism was the emergence of a black social welfare movement (see chapter 8). Within this context the black sociologist and social worker assumed great importance. They became frontline workers grappling with the complex social and economic problems confronting African Americans on a day-to-day basis. They played a central role in helping blacks survive the city.

The sociologist and the social worker represented a new type of black leader. Coming out of the Progressive era's social justice movement, these leaders sought to apply the new methods of the social sciences to the analysis and resolution of social and economic problems facing African Americans. The Progressive era social reformers believed that the problems facing blacks were not caused by their innate racial inferiority, but by racism, lack of training, and society's failure to provide them with adequate education, health services, housing, and stable neighborhoods. All these causes, they believed, were susceptible to improvement through organized social reform. Therefore, they placed great emphasis on the use of careful study or investigation as the foundation upon which to build the reform movement.[41]

The idea of cultural pluralism guided the activities of both black and white social reformers. This viewpoint conceptualized the United

States as having one culture that was composed of a series of equal, or potentially equal, racial and ethnic groups, each with its own subcultures. In many ways the notion of cultural pluralism seemed to be an ideological reflection of the new urban form, with its segregated patterns of land use and its residential environment partitioned on the basis of homogeneous neighborhoods. It seemed both to explain and justify the separation of racial and ethnic groups, along with the various social classes, in physical space (see chapter 8).

The black sociologist James Hathaway Robinson and the Negro Civic Welfare Committee were the driving forces behind the black social welfare movement in Cincinnati during the 1920s, 1930s, and 1940s. For Robinson and his contemporaries, improved race relations and the alleviation of social and economic problems among blacks did not mean racial integration but rather the development of black institutions and the ability of African Americans to influence the larger, pluralistic community. Robinson saw no contradiction in the building of a strong African American community and the participation of blacks, as a group, in the larger Cincinnati community. To him the internal development and strengthening of the black community did not mean segregation (separation) and social isolation. Based on this viewpoint, Robinson developed a two-pronged approach to organizing the black community—strengthening it internally and also making it an equal participant in the larger metropolitan community (see chapter 8).[42]

Robinson, the quintessential social reformer, initiated the city's black social welfare movement with a detailed survey of the black community that described the social and economic problems facing black Cincinnati and the nature of social work among blacks. Robinson then used this information, along with the founding of the Negro Civic Welfare Committee, which he headed, to guide the social welfare movement in Cincinnati for three decades.

The Negro Civic Welfare Committee represented a new type of organization in black Cincinnati. What made it novel was its centralizing and coordinating role. Under Robinson's leadership it guided the work of all social agencies operating in the African American community. Robinson even sought to bring the social welfare activities of the churches and other black institutions under its umbrella. This centralization of work, he believed, was one key to addressing the myriad problems faced by the race. Focusing on the everyday problems facing African Americans, however, did not blind him to the broader issues of racism and race relations. He believed that educating whites on the history and plight of blacks was central to improving race relations and creating a climate of opinion that would facilitate the struggle of African Americans.

The Postindustrial City: Urban Change and Protest

The Second World War ushered in a third period in the development of Cincinnati and the black community. In this period black population growth, slum clearance, superhighway construction, and the rise of the metropolis led to the formation of a second ghetto in the once-exclusive hilltop region of Cincinnati. The war triggered a second wave of blacks who left the South for the North in the Great Migration. Between 1940 and 1970 Cincinnati's black population more than doubled as it jumped from 55,593 to 125,070, and blacks as a proportion of the total population grew from 12 to 28 percent. As blacks moved into the city an even greater number of whites moved out. In the postwar era the suburban region became the center of neighborhood development and population growth in metro Cincinnati.

Slum clearance in the basin and superhighway construction marched in tandem with the demographic changes. Both projects required the clearance of large sections of the West End. In the 1940s and 1950s the demolition of housing units displaced so many people that it scattered the population, especially African Americans. The destruction of hundreds of housing units at a time of significant population increase created a housing shortage. By 1943 vacancies in the basin were almost nonexistent. The West End black population had no choice but to deconcentrate. With existing black neighborhoods bulging at their seams, old patterns of residential segregation began to break down as blacks began to move into hilltop and valley neighborhoods.

The black housing crunch and the white exodus to the suburbs led to an easing of racial restrictions on real estate mortgages and a new willingness among realtors to sell and rent houses and apartments to blacks in previously all-white neighborhoods. In many ways, the black "invasion" of white hilltop and valley neighborhoods was a new variation of the old "trickle-down" housing theory. As whites vacated their used central city housing for new suburban housing and neighborhoods, blacks moved in.

Still the process of neighborhood change generated racial tensions. Some realtors and property owners tried to keep their neighborhoods all white, and when blacks did move into these communities, they faced hostility. Another source of tension came from the "blockbusting" activities of realtors. Blockbusters used a variety of tactics to pressure whites in a target area to sell their homes. The resulting panic contributed both to neighborhood change and racial tension.

Although the dispersed black population moved into different neighborhoods in the city and suburbs, their primary destination was the Walnut Hills–Avondale section of the city. Before 1940 this area had been a haven for middle-income blacks. After the war it became the center of black population growth and the place where a second ghetto formed. Ironically, during the 1950s as the second ghetto formed, housing reformers ended their support for residential segregation and suggested that the creation of integrated neighborhoods might help to relieve housing congestion in the basin. Blacks and poor whites did not cause slums, they argued, poverty and racial segregation did. Allowing higher-income blacks to move into white neighborhoods would make dwelling units available for those with lower incomes. This way, as the income and educational level of blacks improved, they could move out of the ghetto-slum. This approach would enable African Americans to climb the same housing and neighborhood ladder as whites.[43]

The fight for open housing and integrated neighborhoods became a new tactic for combating the consequences of living in a ghetto-slum. Nevertheless, income still played the principal role in determining where most blacks lived. African Americans moved into those neighborhoods where they could afford the housing. And with a relaxation of building codes and zoning regulations in those neighborhoods undergoing change, housing conditions worsened.[44] Consequently, the neighborhoods experiencing the highest degree of integration were those neighborhoods adjacent to neighborhoods undergoing rapid changeover from white to black occupancy. Thus as Cincinnati's new ghetto emerged in the Walnut Hills–Avondale area, the neighborhoods located on the ghetto's outer perimeter became the most integrated in the city.[45]

The influx of blacks into northern cities during the forties increased racial tensions and created an atmosphere where the threat of violence was omnipresent. Then Detroit exploded on June 20, 1943. When peace was restored, twenty-five African Americans and nine whites were found to have been killed. Property valued at several hundred thousand dollars had been destroyed. In response to the riot, many cities across the country, including Cincinnati, made efforts to prevent interracial violence. On October 7, 1943, an interracial delegation led by the executive directors of the National Association for the Advancement of Colored People (NAACP) and the Community

Chest's Division of Negro Welfare, Harold Snell and Arnold Walker, met with Mayor James G. Stewart to discuss establishing a politically independent organization to fight for the protection of minorities. Both the mayor and city council supported the idea, and on November 17 the council passed a resolution authorizing the creation of a committee on race relations, known as the Mayor's Friendly Relations Committee (MFRC) (see chapter 10).

The concept of cultural pluralism determined the structure and function of the MFRC. By promoting tolerance for cultural diversity, the MFRC sought to minimize tensions between groups and to keep violence from breaking out in Cincinnati. Although this goal forced it to address the issues of prejudice and discrimination, the MFRC's definition of pluralism caused it to formulate an action program based on the concept of neutrality. The MFRC would not champion the cause of any single group; thus, shortly after its formation it stated that it was not a black advocacy group. Yet as an official arm of city government charged with the responsibility of reducing intergroup tension, preventing racial violence, and promoting harmony among all citizens, the MFRC helped to create an environment that aided the black protest movement. The MFRC's role in this was not accidental; the MFRC formed at a time when blacks were beginning to step up their struggle to desegregate public places and to end racial discrimination in hiring. And African Americans worked to involve the MFRC, at some level, in their own struggle (see chapter 10).

Blacks had their own interpretation of cultural pluralism. They believed, as did whites, that American society consisted of varied racial and ethnic groups, each with its own culture. Theoretically these groups existed on a horizontal plane, with no one group superior to the others, but blacks felt that racism bred inequities that kept them from competing with whites. This meant that the cultural pluralism ideal could be realized only through struggle. Indeed, based on the activities of James Hathaway Robinson and other black leaders, cultural pluralism became a variant of black nationalist ideology. To them the philosophy meant building and developing black Cincinnati while fighting against the forces that kept blacks economically, politically, and socially unequal.[46]

The MFRC did not actively participate in the black protest movement, and it carefully avoided taking any stand that might be interpreted as supporting blacks and refused to engage in any activity that might increase racial tensions. Even so, the MFRC spent most its time grappling with issues that divided blacks and whites. Whenever racial tensions heated up, the MFRC tried to put out the fire. For example, in 1944 and 1945 when blacks began to challenge racial discrimination in employment and in public places, the MFRC served as an "honest broker" to reconcile differences and to minimize the possibility of violence. In 1946 when racial violence threatened to explode following the alleged rape of a white woman by four black men, the MFRC labored to defuse the racial time bomb. They launched an educational campaign and worked with ministers, civic leaders, and others to create an atmosphere of calm and reason. To change "anti-Negro" attitudes among the police, the MFRC established a race relations detail within the police department and promoted the idea of providing policemen with training in minority problems. When blacks sought housing in all-white neighborhoods and racial tensions boiled, the MFRC made efforts to cool down the situation (see chapter 10).

The MFRC's success in combating prejudicial thinking and discriminatory practices is debatable, but its effectiveness in helping to bring about conditions that facilitated the black protest movement is not. Indeed, its crusade to assuage racial tensions and promote cultural diversity might explain why the civil rights movement did not generate as much violence in the North as it did in the South.[47] Finally, the MFRC's role in the protest movement demonstrates the complex way in which blacks approached their struggle. African Americans did not simply join the MFRC and adopt its program, they brought their own agenda there and sought to impose it on the MFRC. And to a degree they were successful.

This suggests that African Americans recognized the need for different types of organizations and for different approaches to their struggle. Although tensions existed among organizations aiding the black cause, and although many had varying ideologies and agendas, their activities were nevertheless complementary. Some marched, demonstrated, picketed, and harangued; some strategized, petitioned, and litigated; and still others worked quietly behind the scenes, educating, negotiating, and pleading the case for change. But regardless of the approach, their collective action pushed forward the struggle for civil rights.

One black organization that believed in working behind the scenes during these turbulent years was the Cincinnati Urban League (CUL) (see chapter 11). Shortly after its founding in 1948, the CUL launched a struggle against hiring discrimination, which was a bastion of the color-caste occupational system. A secondary goal of the league was to stop the practice of companies refusing to promote blacks when they did hire them. In most businesses and industries African Americans were confined to entry-level jobs when they were hired.

Blacks were excluded from many jobs in the city. For example, in 1948 half of the companies in Cincinnati, each of which employed more than 1,500 workers, did not hire blacks. Those that did, employed them only in menial jobs. For example, only fifty of the telephone company's three thousand workers were African Americans, and they all had low-wage jobs. Most companies had policies that stressed job promotion on the basis of race, not merit. So when blacks did get jobs in large companies, they remained locked in entry-level positions (see chapter 11).

Dismantling the color-caste occupational system became the league's top priority. To spearhead its jobs program the CUL established an Industrial Relations Program, headed by Francis L. Dowdell, a graduate of the Atlanta University School of Social Science. The program used quiet diplomacy, featuring behind-the-scene negotiations and a willingness to compromise, to attack the color-caste occupational system. Dowdell and CUL leaders met with select heads of business and industry and urged them to hire blacks and to upgrade workers on the basis of merit, not race. Concurrently, the league recruited qualified workers, prepared them for the desegregation experience, and tried to find them jobs. The league believed that once a company broke the color line, it would hire other blacks. Those breaking the color line, then, represented a wedge of opportunity for the workers who would follow. Breaking the job color barrier was the goal, and quiet diplomacy the means (see chapter 11).

Between 1948 and 1953 the league perfected its behind-the-scenes approach to black protest. It would start by establishing a close working relationship with the heads of a given company. Then the CUL used quiet persuasion to convince the owners to hire or promote blacks. The league experienced some success with this method. Five years after starting the program, it had placed 523 workers in jobs that had previously been closed to blacks. This process was slow, but the CUL believed that agitation and confrontation would not open doors marked "For Whites Only." Gradualism was the only viable option. The league remained wedded to behind-the-scenes activities.

As activity on the civil rights front stepped up, the CUL extended its behind-the-scenes approach to other arenas. The lengthy fight to desegregate Coney Island, Cincinnati's major amusement park, is a model of how the CUL operated during the stormy fifties. The struggle to desegregate Coney Island lasted nine years and involved a broad coalition including the NAACP, the Cincinnati Committee on Human Rights (an affiliate of the Congress of Racial Equality), the black church, the Jewish Community Relations Committee, and the Civil Liberties Union.

In 1952 when the conflict broke out, the league, based on a recommendation to Coney Island officials from the MFRC, became involved in the struggle. Throughout the prolonged fight the league worked behind the scenes, educating, persuading, negotiating, and constantly speaking about the struggle's negative consequences. As the league talked, other organizations engaged in more aggressive activities. The NAACP went to court, harangued, and joined with other groups that repeatedly sought entry to the park, even though they were repeatedly denied admission. Direct action was used in the fight to desegregate the Coney Island swimming pool and dance hall. Finally, on May 27, 1961, the long battle ended. A decision was made to desegregate all facilities at Coney Island, beginning on May 30 (see chapter 11).

The league played an important role in this struggle. Its success, however, depended on two factors. First, the league relied on the cooperation of white power brokers. The CUL always asked; it never demanded. And the CUL retreated whenever it encountered stiff resistance. So whenever it could not convince power brokers that it was in their best interest to end discrimination, progress stalled. Second, the militancy of groups that did not participate in quiet diplomacy created conditions favorable to behind-the-scenes activity. The aggressiveness of "troublemakers" pressured power brokers into negotiating with groups like the CUL. Their demonstrating, picketing, petitioning, and haranguing made the power brokers want to discuss the issue with "responsible" leaders. This suggests that victories on the civil rights front were usually caused by the complementary activities, conscious or unconscious, of a number of different organizations. Thus, only by viewing organizations within the context of other groups can their role in the protest movement be fully understood and appreciated.

Conclusion

On June 13, 1967, black Cincinnati exploded. Riots took place in the communities of Avondale, Walnut Hills, Evanston, Corryville, Mt. Auburn, Clifton, Millville, and the West End.[48] The anger and deep frustration that led to the "fires, acts of hoodlumism, looting, and anarchy" are best captured in Langston Hughes's poem "Harlem": "What happens to a dream deferred? Does it dry up like a raisin in the sun? . . . or does it explode?"[49] Inquiries into the causes of the riot pinpointed unemployment, bad housing, poor neighborhood conditions, and the lack of political representation.[50]

More than 140 years had passed since blacks first settled in Cincinnati. During that period the battle for civil rights, political representation, decent housing and neighborhood conditions, and jobs and opportunities had been constant themes. As the city moved through the commercial and industrial eras and into the postindustrial age, the nature of the problems facing blacks changed, and so too did the organizations fighting for advancement.

Race and class defined the position of blacks in Cincinnati's plural but unequal society. Prejudicial thinking, discrimination, segregation, and location on the economic margin determined the life chances of African Americans at every stage in Cincinnati's development. Through the years African Americans fought to control their own destiny and to change their location in Cincinnati's social, economic, and political order. Blacks marched, demonstrated, picketed, harangued, and worked behind the scenes to educate, plead their case, and negotiate. They formed organizations that protested and agitated and grappled with the complex day-to-day problems of the race. They also formed social clubs, fraternities, sororities, and secret societies that reinforced cultural bonds and enabled them to enjoy a life apart from whites. Over time racism changed, the doors of opportunity, once closed, opened, and blacks, once highly concentrated, were scattered across the city. Many moved from the river bottoms to the hilltops and valleys, while others settled in the suburban hinterland. The ranks of the middle-class and higher-paid workers swelled, the idea of segregation gave way to integration, and open, hostile forms of racism retreated.

Yet on several hot summer nights in 1967, as hundreds of national guardsmen and city policemen armed with rifles, pistols, and machine guns roamed through black sections of Cincinnati, as armored tanks roared up and down the streets, and as angry young blacks burned, looted, and marauded, it seemed remarkable how much things had changed yet remained the same.[51] Most blacks remained confined to the bottom of the job market; unemployment became a big problem; African Americans lived in dilapidated houses and run-down neighborhoods; and family stability tottered.

In retrospect, the riot was both an epilogue and prologue of the black experience in Cincinnati. It summarized decades of having dreams deferred, of living in a world where things seemed immutable, fixed in time and space; and it introduced the dawning of a new era when unemployment and underemployment, declining participation in the labor force, poverty, the rise of an underclass, and catastrophic social problems would replace civil rights as the dominant issues on the black agenda for advancement.[52]

Notes

1. Gary B. Nash, *Forging Freedom: The Formation of Philadelphia's Black Community, 1720–1840* (Cambridge, Mass.: Harvard University Press, 1988), 246–79; Leon Litwack, *North of Slavery: The Negro in the Free States, 1790–1860* (Chicago: University of Chicago Press, 1961); Stephen Middleton, "The Growth of the Law of Freedom in Ohio, 1837–1845" (unpublished manuscript, University of Buffalo Center for Applied Public Affairs Studies, Cincinnati Files, Center Archives).

2. Richard W. Pih, "Negro Self-Improvement Efforts in Ante-Bellum Cincinnati, 1836–1850," *Ohio History* 78 (1969): 179–87; Richard Wade, "The Negro in Cincinnati," *Journal of Negro History* 39 (Jan. 1954): 43–55.

3. The concept of black people "acting in their own interest" is the central theme in Earl Lewis, *In Their Own Interest: Race, Class, and Power in Twentieth-Century Norfolk, Virginia* (Berkeley: University of California Press, 1991).

4. Pih, "Negro Self-Improvement"; Wade, "The Negro in Cincinnati."

5. My notion of the color-caste occupational system is based on a theory of labor market segmentation. In general terms the theory argues that political and economic forces within American capitalism have given rise to segmented labor markets and perpetuated them and that it is incorrect to view the sources of segmented markets as exogenous to the economic system. Michael Reich, David M. Gordon, and Richard C. Edwards, "A Theory of Labor Market Segmentation," *Papers and Proceedings,* American Economic Association (May 1973): 359–65; S. Bowles, "Understanding Unequal Economic Opportunity," *American Economic Review Proceedings,* May 1973; Robert T. Averitt, *The Dual Economy: The Dynamics of American Industry Structure* (New York: W. W. Norton, 1968).

6. Lyle Koehler, "Women's Rights, Society and the Schools: Feminist Activities in Cincinnati, Ohio, 1864–1880," *Queen City Heritage* 42 (Winter 1984): 3–17; Barbara L. Musselman, "The Shackles of Class and Gender: Cincinnati Working Women, 1890–1920," *Queen City Heritage* 41 (Winter 1983): 35–40.

7. Carter G. Woodson, "The Negro in Cincinnati Prior to the Civil War," *Journal of Negro History* 1 (Jan. 1916): 1–22; Wendell P. Dabney, *Cincinnati's Colored Citizens: Historical, Sociological, and Biographical* (Cincinnati: Dabney, 1926).

8. The melding of race and class as key determinants of black life in Cin-

cinnati is a central theme in this book. Many scholars have counterposed the two in their discussions of the black experience. Rather than viewing race and class as separate analytic frameworks, I merge them into a single framework. Blacks were oppressed as a racial group. Regardless of their educational level or class position in terms of social economic status, African Americans faced life chances that were shaped by prejudicial thinking and discrimination. At the same time, blacks were overwhelmingly members of the working class, and their class position in society determined their life chances. Where blacks lived, the type of dwelling units they occupied, the social problems they encountered were all functions of their class position. Even race relations were deeply influenced by class. As the most exploited segment of the labor force and as victims of a dual wage and labor market system, blacks needed to develop unity with white workers. There was only one labor force and one labor market. Consequently, the ability of blacks to fight for higher wages, improved working conditions, and shorter hours was riveted to the plight of the white working class. Without working unity with this group, African Americans would be unable to make persistent economic gain. At the same time, the preferential treatment that white workers received in the work force, combined with their own racism, made them see black workers as competitors. Regardless, however, of the conflicts between black and white workers, the stubborn fact remains: class was a major determinant of the life chances of African Americans. For a discussion of this issue, see Clarence E. Walker, *Deromanticizing Black History: Critical Essays and Reappraisals* (Knoxville: University of Tennessee Press, 1991), chapters 2, 4, and 5.

9. For a detailed discussion of the concept of place and its relationship to culture, see Henry D. Shapiro, "The Place of Culture and the Problem of Identity," in Allen Bateau, ed., *Appalachia and America: Autonomy and Regional Dependence* (Lexington: University Press of Kentucky, 1983), 111–41; Zane L. Miller, "Race-ism and the City: The Young DuBois and the Role of Place in Social Theory, 1893–1901," *American Studies* 30 (Fall 1989): 89–102. Miller uses the notion of place to describe the city as the primary spatial unit. In this sense, Miller analyzes DuBois's view on how blacks fared in the city (as a particular type of physical/social environment). In my approach I examine linkages between the behavior of blacks and a particular place within the city. I am concerned about determining when neighborhoods come to be viewed as a "place" that exerts influence on human behavior.

10. See also Kathleen Neils Conzen, "Immigrants, Immigrant Neighborhoods, and Ethnic Identity: Historical Issues," *Journal of American History* 66 (Dec. 1979): 603–15; Sam Bass Warner, Jr., and Colin B. Burke, "Cultural Change and the Ghetto," *Journal of Contemporary History* 4 (1969): 173–87.

11. See also Henry Louis Taylor, Jr., "On Slavery's Fringe: City Building and Black Community Development in Cincinnati, 1800–1850," *Ohio History* 95 (Winter-Spring 1986): 5–33.

12. See Lewis, *In Their Own Interest*, 3.

13. This is not to suggest that African Americans lived in a bifurcated society where the problems they confronted on a daily basis evaporated when they entered their homes or bars and joined with friends and family. Life was more complex than this. In small and large ways, living in a racist, class-stratified society influenced private times. Yet blacks did escape from the pressures and stresses of living and working around whites. There were moments when they had no conscious thoughts of their oppressor or their oppression. The point is that either/or conceptual frameworks obfuscate social reality, and I am not employing one in this interpretation. The concept employed here is dominance. What type of attitude or feeling dominated a particular social or work setting? This is the central question. For a discussion of the problem of interpretation in African American history, see Walker, *Deromanticizing Black History*, xi–xxvi. Walker is particularly critical of John Blassingame's classic study, *The Slave Community: Plantation Life in the Antebellum South* (New York: Oxford University Press, 1972). He argues that Blassingame romanticizes slave life by splitting the plantation into two environments, one controlled by the master and the other by the slave. Blassingame, he argues, overemphasizes the extent to which the slave actually controlled the quarters and the extent to which slaves were free of white influences.

14. Litwack, *North of Slavery*, especially chapters 3–5; John H. Bracey, Jr., August Meier, and Elliott Rudwick, *Blacks in the Abolitionist Movement* (Belmont, Calif.: Wadsworth Publishing Co., 1971).

15. David A. Gerber, *Black Ohio and the Color Line, 1860–1915* (Urbana: University of Illinois Press, 1977).

16. Steven J. Ross, *Workers on the Edge: Work, Leisure, and Politics in Industrializing Cincinnati, 1788–1890* (New York: Columbia University Press, 1985); idem, "The Politicization of the Working Class: Production, Ideology, Culture and Politics in Late Nineteenth-Century Cincinnati," *Social History* 11 (May 1986): 171–95; Philip S. Foner, "Peter H. Clark: Pioneer Black Socialist," *The Journal of Ethnic Studies* 5 (1977): 17–35.

17. See also Charles R. Hebble and Frank P. Goodwin, *The Citizens Book* (Cincinnati: Chamber of Commerce, 1916), 174–83.

18. Also, for a detailed look at jobs, class, and race, see Diane Meisenhelter, "Black Workers in Cincinnati during the Opening Decades of the Twentieth Century" (unpublished paper, University of Buffalo, Center for Applied Public Affairs Studies, Cincinnati Files, Center Archives); and Edna Bonacich, "Advanced Capitalism and Black-White Race Relations in the United States: A Split Labor Market Interpretation," *American Sociological Review* 41 (Feb. 1976): 34–51.

19. Lewis, *In Their Own Interest*.

20. Joe William Trotter, Jr., *Black Milwaukee: The Making of an Industrial Proletariat* (Urbana: University of Illinois Press, 1985).

21. It is important to note that the social and class composition of black leadership changed with the rise of the industrial metropolis. In the earlier

period entrepreneurs, skilled workers, and teachers dominated black leadership. In the industrial age middle-class professionals, especially college-educated blacks, dominated leadership. While the earlier groups remained important, they became secondary to the middle-class professionals. I might add that I am talking about major organizations that led the black community as a whole and that most often interacted with whites.

22. Wendell P. Dabney, in a section of his chronicle of black Cincinnati, offers biographical sketches of important city leaders. These sketches are invaluable for gaining insight into the early twentieth-century black leadership. Dabney, *Colored Citizens*, 197–436.

23. These shifts in the residential environment were connected to the evolution of a new housing market that was dominated by single-family dwelling units and the rigid application of residential land use regulation. The emergence of this new housing market melded with other aspects of structural change in the social and economic geography of the city to separate the population according to race and class and, in some places, ethnicity. For a discussion of the relationship of housing markets to the social geography of the city, see Richard Harris, "Self-Building and the Social Geography of Toronto, 1901–1933: A Challenge for Urban Theory," *Transactions of the Institute of British Geography* 15 (1990): 387–402.

24. Between 1920 and 1930, the period when homeownership exploded in Cincinnati, virtually all of the census tracts beyond the basin experienced growth. This growth took place during a period when the city's total population grew by 12 percent. This shows not only that Cincinnati retained its population during the decade but that the number of people living in the city grew. At the same time, the black population was restricted to select areas of the city, primarily in the basin and Avondale–Walnut Hills. It was not until the 1930s that the shift toward the suburban region became noticeable. Even so, the dynamic center of population growth was still within the city proper. Not surprising, the building of new single-family homes also took place in these tracts where the population grew. James A. Quinn, Earl Eubank, and Lois E. Elliott, *Population Changes—Cincinnati, Ohio, and Adjacent Areas, 1900–1940*, Research Monograph No. 47 (Columbus: Bureau of Business Research, Ohio State University Press, 1947); idem, *Cincinnati Building Permits: Trends and Distribution, 1908–1938* (Columbus: Bureau of Business Research, Ohio State University, Special Bulletin, 1947); Robert G. Barrows, "Beyond the Tenement: Patterns of American Urban Housing, 1870–1930," *Journal of Urban History* 9 (Aug. 1983): 395–420; Calvin Skinner, "Some Aspects of Population Characteristics and Trends in Greater Cincinnati," Report No. 89 (Cincinnati Bureau of Government Research, Dec. 1945); William S. Groom, "Population Shifts in Cincinnati and Hamilton County: A Study of Changes by Race, Sex, and Age Groups, U.S. Census 1930 to U.S. Census 1940" (Public Health Federation, Health Division of the Community Chest, Oct. 1942).

25. National Industrial Conference Board, *The Cost of Living among Wage-Earners: Cincinnati, Ohio*, Special Report No. 13 (July 1920, pam-

phlet); Department of Sociology, University of Cincinnati, "Summary of Cincinnati Data," Dec. 1938, Archives and Rare Books Department, University Libraries, University of Cincinnati, file S.28.10.17. This summary compares select variables between the basin and the rest of the city. In 1930, for example, the median rental in the basin was $22.80, while in the rest of the city it was $57.74.

26. Henry Louis Taylor, Jr., "The Building of a Black Industrial Suburb: The Lincoln Heights Story" (Ph.D. diss., State University of New York at Buffalo, 1979).

27. Better Housing League, *Housing Progress in Cincinnati: Second Report,* July 1921, 29 (cited in chapter 6).

28. To get a sense of the extent to which zoning had became a force in shaping the residential environment during the 1920s, see Norman L. Knauss, *Zoned Municipalities in the United States* (Washington, D.C.: Department of Commerce, May 1931).

29. Ghetto formation suggests that a dual housing market existed in Cincinnati. There was one market for whites and another for blacks. Of course, there are always exceptions to the rule. But the exceptions were just that, exceptions.

30. It cannot be overly emphasized that blacks did not just live in a ghetto, they lived in a slum. Many blacks wanted to escape the ghetto, not because it was a community of African Americans, but because it was a slum. And slums have negative characteristics that stable working- and middle-class neighborhoods do not possess. David A. Snow and Peter J. Leahy were among the first scholars to link the ghetto-slum to the process of neighborhood change, while Thomas Philpott was the first scholar to make a distinction between the ghetto and slum. Snow and Leahy, "The Making of a Black Slum-Ghetto: A Case Study of Neighborhood Transition," *The Journal of Applied Behavioral Science* 16 (1980): 459–81; Philpott, *The Slum and the Ghetto: Neighborhood Deterioration and Middle-Class Reform, Chicago, 1880–1930* (New York: Oxford University Press, 1978).

31. For a discussion of the concept of uneven development, see Henry Louis Taylor, Jr., "Toward a Historiography of Black Urban History: An Essay Review of Lester Lamon's *Black Tennessean: 1900 to 1930*" (Knoxville: University of Tennessee Press, 1978); idem, *Afro-Americans in New York Life and History* 4, no. 2 (July 1980): 71–80; Joe T. Darden, Richard Child Hill, June Thomas, and Richard Thomas, *Detroit: Race and Uneven Development* (Philadelphia: Temple University Press, 1987).

32. A snapshot of the extreme differences in the residential environment of blacks and whites can be seen in the "Summary of Cincinnati Data," December 1938, University of Cincinnati Department of Sociology.

33. This view is found in many of the reports and newspaper articles that deal with slums and slum clearance. A good example of this new way of thinking about place and culture is found in the BHL pamphlet promoting homeownership. BHL, *The Home is the Heart of the World* (May 1929, Cincinnati Historical Society, BHL Papers). This linking of culture to place be-

came a critical concept in the Chicago school of sociology's perspective on urban life. Ernest W. Burgess, ed., *The Urban Community* (Chicago: University of Chicago Press, 1926).

34. Dabney, *Colored Citizens,* 144. This same kind of thinking undergirded the struggle to outlaw cheap housing in the suburbs. See the flyer urging support of Senate bill 232, designed to "give county commissioners the right to prevent the spread of county slums." The Sponsoring Committee, "Stop the Spread of County Slums," March 1941, box 12, folder 44, Cincinnati Historical Society.

35. The historiography of black urban history has ignored this critical fact. Ghetto formation is the dominant theme. The result is that we know very little about residential development and community life outside the ghetto in this critical 1880–1940 period. Here I am referring to residential development not only in the central city but also in the suburban region, where a surprising number of blacks lived. We know even less about the southern black urban experience, especially the impact that urbanization had on rural blacks living in the rural zone of the metropolis. In my forthcoming book, *A Good Place to Live: Black Suburbanization and the Rise of Metropolitan Cincinnati, 1900 to 1940,* I place the black residential experience within a metropolitan context while stressing that black suburbanization was part of the urbanization process that transformed rural areas surrounding central cities during the industrial age.

36. Rhoza A. Walker, "Housing as an Educational Problem for Negroes in Cincinnati" (Master's thesis, University of Cincinnati, 1940); Susan Redman-Rengstorf, "To Better the Conditions: The Annexation Attempts of West College Hill," *Queen City Heritage* 43 (1985): 3–16; James E. Cebula, "Kennedy Heights: A Fragmented Hilltop Suburb," *Cincinnati Historical Society Bulletin* 2 (1976): 78–101.

37. For a complete discussion of these forms of suburban developments, see Richard Harris, "American Suburbs: A Sketch of a New Interpretation," *Journal of Urban History* 15 (Nov. 1988): 98–103; idem, "Working-Class Home Ownership in the American Metropolis," *Journal of Urban History* 17 (Nov. 1990): 46–69; idem, "Self-Building in the Urban Housing Market," *Economic Geography* 67 (Jan. 1991): 1–21; idem, "The Impact of Building Controls on Residential Development in Toronto, 1900–40," *Planning Perspectives* 6 (1991): 269–96; Andrew Wiese, "Driving a Thin Wedge of Suburban Opportunity: Black Suburbanization in the Northern Metropolis, 1940–1980" (Paper presented at the Fourth National Conference on American Planning History, 7–10 Nov. 1991, Richmond, Virginia); Henry Louis Taylor, Jr., "Black Suburbanization in the Twentieth Century: Myths and Realities" (paper presented at the Advanced Placement Conference, "Seeking the Good Life: Changing Perception of the American Middle Class," Strong Museum, Rochester, New York, 29–30 Jan. 1992).

38. Edith Elmer Wood complains that restrictive legislation, while outlawing bad housing, does not lead to the construction of new housing for the low wage earner. Thus the use of restrictive legislation to solve the housing

problem of poor workers leads to a zero-sum gain. Wood, *The Housing of the Unskilled Wage Earner: America's Next Problem* (New York: Mac-Millan, 1991), 57.

39. BHL, *Minutes*, Special Committee on Negro Housing Problem, 4 Feb. 1924, BHL Papers, box 1, folder 4, Archives and Rare Book Department, University of Cincinnati (cited in chapter 6).

40. This practice also took place in other cities. In Buffalo, New York, for example, public housing units were built in white residential areas. Early white public housing residents said that these units were superior to dwellings in their neighborhood. And residents succeeded in Buffalo's Commodore Perry Projects to raise the rent caps so that more neighborhood residents would be eligible to live there.

41. Arvarh E. Strickland, *History of the Chicago Urban League* (Urbana: University of Illinois Press, 1966), 1–24.

42. August Meier discusses the place of cultural pluralism in the thinking of African Americans in his classic study, *Negro Thought in America, 1800–1915: Racial Ideologies in the Age of Booker T. Washington* (Ann Arbor: University of Michigan Press, 1968), 51, 54–55, 167, 195, 204, 247, 256, 262, 266, 268–69. See also Harold Cruse, *Plural But Equal: A Critical Study of Blacks and Minorities in America's Plural Society* (New York: William Morrow, 1987); David A. Gerber, *The Making of An American Pluralism, Buffalo, New York, 1825–60* (Urbana: University of Illinois Press, 1989), especially the introduction.

43. Paul F. Cressey, "Population Succession in Chicago, 1898–1930," *American Journal of Sociology* 4 (July 1938): 59–60.

44. It is interesting to note that as zoning laws and building codes were being relaxed in those neighborhoods undergoing racial transition, they were being strengthened in the suburban region where the dreaded shack towns were located.

45. U.S. Bureau of the Census, *Census Tracts: Cincinnati, Ohio and Kentucky: Standard Metropolitan Statistical Area: U.S. Census of Population and Housing: 1960* (Washington, D.C.: U.S. Department of Commerce, 1961). A more detailed look at the census tracts into which blacks were migrating can be obtained by looking at the city block data. Idem, *City Blocks: Cincinnati, Ohio: U.S. Census of Housing: 1960* (Washington, D.C.: U.S. Department of Commerce, 1961); John G. Vaughan, "Housing for Negroes in Cincinnati," BHL report, May 1962, 7–10, BHL Papers, Archives and Rare Books Department, University of Cincinnati.

46. Meier refers to this as ethnic dualism, which reflected the thinking of one trend of nationalism in the African American community. Meier, *Negro Thought*, 51, 54–55, 167, 195, 204, 247, 256, 262, 266, 268–69; Cruse, *Plural But Equal*. Both chapters 7 and 9 of this volume deal with the cultural pluralism theme.

47. For a good survey of the civil rights movement, see Sean Dennis Cashman, *African Americans and the Quest for Civil Rights, 1900–1990* (New York: New York University Press, 1991).

48. The riot took place between June 12–18. One person was killed and sixty-three persons were injured. There were 404 arrests. The estimated property damage was $2.6 million. The riot was focused in the Avondale section of the city, but violent acts also took place in other neighborhoods. *Cincinnati Enquirer,* 14 June 1967, np., from *Cincinnati Enquirer Newspaper Clip Files,* Cincinnati Historical Society; idem, June 14, 1967, np.

49. Amiri Baraka, "A Critical Reevaluation: A Raisin in the Sun's Enduring Passion," in *A Raisin in the Sun and the Sign in Sidney Brusrein's Window,* ed. Robert Nemiroff (New York: New American Library, 1987), 9–20. This article discusses the meaning of Hughes's poem in relation to Lorraine Hansbury's play "A Raisin in the Sun."

50. *Cincinnati Post Times-Star,* 13 June 1976, *Race Riot Newspaper Clip File,* Cincinnati Historical Society; *Cincinnati Daily Enquirer,* 20, 22 June 1967; BHL, "Staff Report: Housing Aspects of the June Riots," 28 July 1967, Papers on Cincinnati Riots, box 11, folder 9, Cincinnati Historical Society; Grant G. Cannon, Robert Beck, and Charles M. Judd, "Why Did It Happen?," BHL, 29 Aug. 1967, Papers on Cincinnati Riots, box 11, folder 9. Cincinnati Historical Society; James N. Upton, "The Politics of Urban Violence: Critiques and Proposals," *Journal of Black Studies 5,* no. 15 (Mar. 1985): 243–58, Center Archives; Donald West, "Urban Renewal, Residential Transformation, and the 1967 Cincinnati Riots" (Unpublished paper, Center Archives).

51. This way of thinking about the changes that took place over time in the black experience is central to Earl Lewis's important study of Norfolk, Virginia. Lewis, *In Their Own Interest,* 199–208.

52. Henry Louis Taylor, Jr., *African Americans and the Rise of Buffalo's Post-Industrial City, 1940 to Present* (Buffalo, New York: Urban League, 1991); William Julius Wilson, *The Truly Disadvantaged: The Inner City, the Underclass, and Public Policy* (Chicago: The University of Chicago Press, 1987).

2

WILLIAM CHEEK AND AIMEE LEE CHEEK

John Mercer Langston and the Cincinnati Riot of 1841

A multifaceted leader whose career in black protest, politics, education, and the law spanned half a century, John Mercer Langston (Dec. 14, 1829–Nov. 15, 1897) was in the vanguard of the nineteenth-century African American struggle. Educated at Oberlin College (A.B., 1849, seminary, 1853), Langston managed to gain admittance to the previously all-white Ohio bar in 1854. The next year his election as clerk of Brownhelm, a township not far from Oberlin, made him the first African American elected to public office in the United States. During his subsequent fifteen-year residence in Oberlin, he solidified his reputation as an able public executive and adroit defense attorney. Throughout the 1850s Langston played a major role in both the strong black civil rights movement in Ohio and radical antislavery politics. In 1863, once the North finally agreed to accept black soldiers, he threw himself into black recruitment, directing recruiting efforts in the Midwest for the pioneering 54th and 55th Massachusetts regiments. He then became the head of recruiting for the first black regiment in Ohio. The national black convention in Syracuse in October 1864 recognized Langston's contributions by naming him president of its newly formed National Equal Rights League.

After the Civil War Langston took a leading role in Reconstruction as an inspector for the Freedmen's Bureau and an organizer for the Republican party in the South. He was the first law dean of

Howard University and a member of the Washington, D.C., Board of Health. After serving as the U.S. minister to Haiti for eight years, he became the president of the Virginia Normal and Collegiate Institute, the state college for African Americans at Petersburg. Finally, in 1888 he waged a hotly fought race for Congress in Virginia's fourth district. After a protracted contest of the election results he was declared the victor—so late in his term, however, that he served only a few months in 1891. He was the first and, for at least a century afterward, the only African American elected to Congress from Virginia.

Langston's career seems the more remarkable in light of his early years. Though relatively privileged, his childhood was marked by emotional trauma and social dislocation. Born free on a Virginia plantation, he was the son of Ralph Quarles, a wealthy slaveholder, and Lucy Jane Langston, a part-Native American, part-black emancipated slave. The deaths in 1834 of both parents left four-year-old John Mercer and his older brothers, Gideon Q. and Charles H. Langston, financially well provided for but unprotected by Virginia law and prompted Gideon and Charles to move to Ohio. (Gideon's career is sketched below. Charles became a major figure in northern black political agitation in prewar Ohio and postwar Kansas and is best known as a hero of the Oberlin-Wellington fugitive slave rescue case.) Little John Mercer lived as part of the family of William Gooch, white friends of his father, on a farm near Chillicothe. Treated like a son and called Johnnie Gooch, the light-skinned boy attended the whites-only public school. In 1839 young Langston suffered, in effect, a second orphaning when a court decree abruptly parted him from the Gooches, who were moving to the slave state Missouri. He returned to the farm to board with its new white owners. In late 1840 his brother Gideon arranged for him to move to Cincinnati. Still struggling with his sense of being abandoned by the only family he knew and being labeled as racially distinct from the Gooches, without experience in being black, John Langston, just turning eleven, embarked on life in the black community of the most race-conscious city in the state.

———————

Placed in an amphitheater of hills giving onto the Ohio River, where boats and barges teemed against the backdrop of the slave shores of Kentucky, the Queen City of the West—Porkopolis to the unromantic—provided a spectacle of Jacksonian aspirations. Animated, striving, growing in four decades from a frontier settlement to the sixth largest city in the nation in 1840, it was a town of red and white houses on clean well-paved streets with tiled walkways, attractive shops, and neat and elegant private residences, and a town of swampy bottoms, rickety tenements, and mean, malodorous alleys; protean and joltingly democratic, where yesterday's raisin cake vendor was today's state congressman; progressive and reform-minded, boasting a system of public schools in which even the poorest Irish child might receive a free education but no black child could; violence prone, with "gentlemen of property and standing" not loathe to form a mob against abolitionists and blacks; above all, exuberantly committed to exemplifying the potential of free men working in a free society and shamelessly dedicated to placating its good customers of the South. With the city's economy revolving around commerce and trade—hogs, cattle, whiskey, flour, lumber, and a variety of manufactured products—leading businessmen took pains to nourish the commercial match with southern cotton that had been struck early on. Even in the midst of the nationwide depression set off by the panic of 1837 and despite losses to business, the city grew at record rates, its population swelled by immigrants from the hard-hit eastern urban centers. Mechanics and builders were busy. Carriages bearing generously petticoated ladies rattled over the cobblestones; rich southern planters in tall beaver hats pushed through the throngs of horny-handed Ohio and Kentucky farmers; burly German butchers festooned stalls in the famous market with garlands of sausages; newly arrived Irish families stood in bewilderment on the docks; rough rivermen, black and white, sought out satisfaction in brothels and bars. Steamboats anchored while others lined up for berths, travelers above deck, cargo and slave coffle below. On the waterfront muscular black roustabouts hoisted bales of cotton, tierces of tobacco and salt pork, barrels of flour, sugar, coffee, molasses, fish, and whiskey. Black porters hustled for baggage to carry to the elegant hotels where Kentuckians liked to pass the summer months; black draymen clattered from wharf to warehouse; black stewards looked to the buying of fresh produce; well-dressed black waiters pocketed their tips.[1] The alert farmboy who simply walked the broad streets of Cincinnati acquired an education.

Yet beneath the bustle, for a boy who was black, harder lessons lay. Although blacks struggled against crippling restrictions throughout Ohio, discrimination was nowhere more entrenched than in Cincinnati. All black Ohioans had to contend with the state's infamous Black Laws. The Ohio constitution of 1802 denied blacks the franchise. Subsequently, the Black Laws, a series of discriminatory laws and court decisions, were adopted to discourage black immigration through such requirements as registration and the posting of surety;

to exclude blacks from jury service and from testifying in legal cases involving white persons; to bar them from the militia; to deny them the benefits of the Poor Law and of institutions for the physically or mentally infirm; and, despite equal taxation of black-owned property, to exclude black children from the public school system.[2] In Cincinnati, moreover, blacks met with all-but-universal segregation, proscription, and recurring violence or threats of violence. News that a slave had disappeared from a ship, or that white southerners were in town to search for their missing bond servant, usually set off a hue and cry in which city authorities joined to look for signs of stolen property in the homes and shops of black residents and white abolitionists. In 1829 and in 1836 large-scale riots directed against blacks engulfed the city. The first riot resulted in the exodus of a large number of black residents; the second proved costly to white abolitionists as well as to blacks, when rioters destroyed the presses of the *Philanthropist*, an antislavery newspaper then edited by James G. Birney.[3]

In this volatile setting John Mercer Langston first experienced the life of a black community. As luck would have it, when he arrived in Cincinnati in late 1840, it was just at the moment when a white backlash, triggered by the rising socioeconomic status of the city's blacks in combination with other factors, was about to erupt into yet another of Cincinnati's periodic manifestations of mob violence. Nonetheless, it was here that the impressionable boy first was exposed to enterprising black men and women who had established themselves as skilled workers and property owners, to vigorous black institutions, and to black community leaders. The evidence supports the mature Langston's own judgment: "If there has ever existed in any colored community of the United States, anything like an aristocratic class of such persons, it was found in Cincinnati. . . . In fact the entire negro community of the city gave striking evidences, in every way at this time, of its intelligence, industry, thrift and progress; and in matters of education and moral and religious culture, furnished an example worthy of the imitation of their whole people."[4] During his two years in Cincinnati, John Langston, barely eleven when he arrived, began to learn about the black kinship and culture that would sharpen his perceptions and help to give purpose and direction to his life.

Blacks were so drawn by the ever-expanding economic opportunities to be found in the Queen City—some blacks called Cincinnati "the emporium of the West"—that the black population there became the largest in the state, growing from an estimated 690 in 1826 to an official 2,240 by 1840 (5.1 percent of the city's 44,000 people).

The city's black residents tended to be young and of southern origin; indeed, self-bought, manumitted, and freeborn southerners fueled much of the dynamism and egalitarian idealism observed in the youthful black Cincinnati society of 1840, in which 80 percent of the population was less than thirty-six years of age.[5] The 1840 residential and occupational directory for the city listed 313 "Colored" persons, who probably constituted the most successful group, 74 percent of whom had come from the slaveholding District of Columbia or slave states, principally Virginia and Kentucky. Augustus Wattles, a dedicated white abolitionist who as a young man immersed himself in black community life, in 1834 calculated that 1,129 blacks in Cincinnati had known slavery. Of these ex-slaves, 476 had purchased themselves at a total cost of $215,522, or an average of about $450 per person, while many were currently involved in purchasing family members or friends. When a concerned Wattles visited a family to learn the reason for its children's irregular school attendance, he found the youngsters in the care of the eldest child, a ten-year-old, who explained, "I'm staying at home to help buy father." An 1845 canvass by Wattles's brother John revealed 369 self-emancipated slaves, about one-fifth of the adult population, who had paid $166,050 for their freedom. Such men and women, the black editor Rev. Charles B. Ray of New York was disposed to declare after a protracted stay in 1839, had the "proper materials in their character to become industrious, economical, and reputable citizens."[6]

Combining skills learned in slavery[7] with the ingenuity suggested by their playful saying "If you can't find it, make it,"[8] and benefiting from the assistance of committed white sympathizers, black Cincinnatians registered economic gains in the late thirties. As migrants flowed into the city, the demand for essential services increased: workers were necessary to hew and dig and haul, whitewash the walls, scrub the clothes and floors, mend and polish the shoes, cook the food, and saw the wood. Although always indifferent in reporting the women who performed many of these tasks, the city directory in 1840 listed 146 blacks so engaged, almost double the figure of four years earlier. Because Irish immigrants, who would compose 12 percent of the population by 1850, had just begun to arrive, blacks had as yet few competitors for such work.[9] In the wake of the 1837 panic, blacks also took advantage of the depression-induced lower cost of living and the institution of a near-barter economy. Moreover, river and canal commerce continued to thrive, providing major employment opportunities. By 1840 nearly one-fourth of the black work force had jobs either on the several hundred steamboats that operated from Cincinnati's wharves or in other services and trades connected with the river. "Besides their ordinary wages, which are good," Ray observed, black rivermen availed themselves of plentiful "opportunities for trading at great profit" in "the lower country."[10]

Among the 287 blacks listed as employed in the 1840 directory, 92 (an increase of 250 percent in four years) can be classified as semi-skilled, that is, workers at jobs demanding some talent and under-standing of the marketplace such as whitewasher, drayman, steward, cook, huckster, butler, trader, gardener, fruit dealer, and barkeeper. The traditional classification of such workers as unskilled is cast in doubt by the fact that thirty-eight of the eighty-eight blacks worth $1,000 or more according to the 1850 census fall in this category. Furthermore, although laborers are always characterized as un-skilled, six black Cincinnatians who held this title somehow managed to accumulate $1,000 or more by 1850. Indeed, three of the black community's most respected men were listed in unskilled occupa-tions: the intellectual stevedore John I. Gaines ($3,000); the huckster Richard Phillips ($13,000); and the huckster Joseph J. Fowler ($18,000).[11] Traditional classifications of work are patently inade-quate to measure either the worth or worthfulness of mid-nineteenth-century black Cincinnatians.

In 1840, 90 blacks were recorded in 21 skilled occupations: 46 bar-bers, 10 carpenters, 6 shoemakers, 4 coopers, 3 bricklayers, 3 plas-terers, 1 schoolteacher, 1 livery stable owner, and single assorted other artisans. "Colored mechanics were . . . getting as much skilled labor as they can do," an observer remarked. Like the port cities of St. Louis and Boston, but in substantially more occupations, Cincin-nati was beginning to employ black men in a variety of jobs that re-quired a certain amount of expertness and responsibility.[12] From 1836 to 1840 the number of blacks in the higher occupational tier increased from 83 to 182.[13]

The city's rise in population particularly benefited black barbers. It was no accident that a black parade in Columbus in the mid-1850s featured a giant razor and a plow, for throughout Ohio, barbering, a trade relegated exclusively to blacks, along with farming, offered the most economic security to black men. An exemplar of the economic potential of barbering in Cincinnati was William W. Watson, an able community leader and young John Langstons's future protector. Pur-chased from slavery by a family member only eight years before, by 1840 Watson owned two brick houses and lots in town and another 560 acres in the Mercer County black farming settlement, as well as

his own barbershop (expanded to include a bathhouse) advanta-
geously situated in the heart of the business district of Cincinnati. By
1850, when the number of black barbers had risen to 134 from the
46 of a decade earlier, Watson ranked as one of the community's
outstanding financial successes, with declared property holdings of
$5,500.[14] His actual worth may have been greater: the white aboli-
tionist James Freeman Clarke put it at some $30,000, while the black
abolitionist Frederick Douglass put the barber on the same rung as
Henry Boyd, the carpenter and bedstead manufacturer who was
widely advertised as the richest black man in Cincinnati. Besides the
possibility of abolitionist exaggeration, the discrepancy in the reports
of the wealth of such prospering and publicly protesting blacks as
Watson may have arisen from several related factors: a copy of the
census was deposited in the courthouse; blacks were excluded from
public facilities maintained by property taxes; and black success
might invite white retaliation. For example, Boyd's renowned furniture factory was burned again and again until finally, in 1859, he was
no longer able to obtain fire insurance, and he closed his business.[15]

Despite the special strains of purchasing family members from
slavery and of coping with white harassment, by 1840 an impressive
number of black Cincinnatians, persuaded that to possess a home-
stead was to be "independent and wealthy,"[16] had become property
owners. Noting that their property "consists in that which is permanent and valuable, in household lots, and country land, two thousand
or more acres of which they own in one plot," Rev. Charles B. Ray in
1839 assessed their holdings as proportionately higher than those in
other black communities in the North. Moreover, "they are still ac-
cumulating faster than our people elsewhere."[17] The white abolitionist Amzi D. Barber reported in 1840 that nine-tenths of the black-
owned houses and lots in the city had been purchased within the last
four years. Besides individual holdings, a joint stock enterprise titled
the Iron Chest Company, whose vice president was Gideon Langston,
had been organized in September 1838. From the weekly dollar investments of its members, the company had erected three large brick
buildings that it rented to whites. Including the $19,000 valuation on
three black churches, the total property worth of Cincinnati blacks in
1840 was estimated at $228,600.[18]

Blacks lived in some ten clusters located around the city's outer perimeter and in the center of town. Although many of them lived close
together for purposes of self-defense, society, and access to their own
community institutions, the residential segregation practiced in Cincinnati during the prewar era—given the constant stream of low-

income immigrants—was more economic than racial. The bulk of the unskilled, black and white, tended to concentrate in the most densely settled areas. Some 950 blacks and 8,000 whites lived in the east central section, where both "Germany" (or "Over-the-Rhine"), so called for its large number of Germans, and "Bucktown," so called for its large number of blacks, were situated.[19] Within this section, housing conditions varied considerably, from the relative comfort of Germany, where the black schoolteacher and whitewasher Owen T. B. Nickens and other respected black leaders lived, to the misery of Bucktown (referred to as the "Bottoms" by the compassionate and probably by the residents themselves). In this wretched basin of tenements and shanties drained by an odiferous stream that carried the bloody runoff from pork processing houses, blacks and whites "herded together," as a white journalist put it. As many as six family members found shelter in an eight-by-twelve-foot room. Under such circumstances, poverty, disease, violence, and criminality were good neighbors.[20]

In the mid-1830s abolitionist commitment, in combination with a large, growing, and youthful black population and improving economic conditions, helped to invigorate black institutional life in Cincinnati. Building on a foundation of black community-directed efforts extending back at least a decade,[21] a group of young white abolitionists—the famous "Rebels" of Lane Seminary led by the Connecticut Yankees Theodore Dwight Weld and Augustus Wattles—rendered valuable assistance.[22] In 1834, working closely with black leaders[23]—including the Baptist minister David Nickens,[24] the African Methodist Episcopal (A.M.E.) minister William Paul Quinn,[25] the painter William M. Johnson,[26] and the schoolteacher Owen Nickens[27]—the Rebels instituted an extensive program of instruction and uplift in an effort, as Weld put it, to create a "spectacle of free black cultivation." Three young white female teachers brought in from the East, called the "Sisters," worked zealously on the project.[28] Besides a lyceum and a library, day and night schools were established for both sexes and all ages, with instruction on topics ranging from the ABCs, sewing, and housekeeping to mathematics, abolitionism, and salvation.[29]

Morally and materially, the abolitionists contributed to the upsurge in black property holdings that occurred during the late thirties. "Before you commenced schools," a black Cincinnatian confided in 1840, "I did not feel any interest in laying up property. I did not feel that I had a home here. If I earned property, I knew not but my house would be pulled down over my head by a mob. All I cared for was to have enough to eat and wear." Outside the city black Cincinnatians' large landholdings in Mercer County resulted from Augustus Wattles's investment of their funds in the all-black farming community he instigated; at home, whites, on occasion following an example set in Mercer County, may have recorded property in their names while making out second titles to the actual black owners.[30]

The schooling and moral reform efforts of the reformers bore fruit. By 1839 the Colored Education Society, founded in 1836, was overseeing three private schools for black children in the city, two of them entirely supported by the black community and one by the white Ladies' Anti-Slavery Society of Cincinnati, while black financial contributions had risen from $150 in 1835 to $900. This performance, in combination with petitioning by blacks and white abolitionists, led to the city council's unprecedented allocation of black tax money to support a short-lived school in 1839–40 for the "children of the colored people."[31] Under a constitution drafted by the schoolteacher Owen Nickens, the Moral Reform Society—which was organized shortly after the founding of its educational counterpart and had many of the same officers—pledged its members of both sexes to uphold the "true principles of morality and integrity" and to work for the "suppression of intemperance, licentiousness, gambling, sabbath-breaking, blasphemy, and all other vices." At the end of the decade one-quarter of the adult black population of the free-swinging port city belonged to temperance societies, with the result that black whiskey peddlers had to operate surreptitiously, and drunken blacks seldom appeared on the streets.[22]

Respectable black life in Cincinnati had long centered on the black community's churches, particularly the abolitionist Bethel A.M.E. and Union Baptist. Bethel's origins dated back to 1824, when several black Methodists, rebelling against the requirement that blacks come last to the communion table at the city's predominantly white church, withdrew from it and, inspired by the itinerant missionary Moses Freeman, formed an A.M.E. congregation. Both Freeman and the convert Owen Nickens, who was appointed a "local" preacher, later recalled meetings in a cellar dubbed "Jericho," while other gatherings occurred in homes, a blacksmith shop, and a house for processing lime. In 1834 the congregation purchased a lot on Sixth Street east of Broadway, where, using the combined labors of the fellowship, it erected a church designed by one of the members.[33]

One of the oldest black Baptist churches in the West and probably the largest, the Union congregation separated from the white Baptists in 1831, although it continued an uneasy coalition with them.[34] In

1839 the black Baptists moved from the small brick church they had
constructed to an imposing structure on Baker Street formerly occupied by their white counterparts. Within five years, by using proceeds
from fairs conducted by women of the church, converting donated
goods into cash, and relying on contributions from members (the
barber Watson in particular), the church had paid all but $2,000 of
the property's $9,000 purchase price; by 1848 it had cleared the en-
tire debt.[35] During the 1840s, when young John Langston attended,
the ministers were two ex-Virginians—Charles Satchell, also a self-
employed dyer,[36] and the Oberlin-educated fugitive slave, William P.
Newman.[37] Both, Langston recalled, "were possessed of large ability,
piety, and eloquence." Under their leadership, coupled with Watson's
faithful service, the Union Baptist functioned as a missionary church
to the black destitute and a "mother church to nearly all the colored
churches of its order in the great valley and in Canada."[38] Fervent
in condemning slavery and in opposing the church's pro-slavery
apologists (as was the Zion Baptist, founded in 1843 by the pioneer
minister-missionary Wallace Shelton),[39] the Union Baptist congregation infused its other major interests—the Sabbath school and the
"secular education of youth"—with Christian abolitionist principles.[40]

Worship in these churches combined emotional release with reform values. Newman in later years endorsed as accurate a white
woman's account of her visit to a black church that must have resembled the Union Baptist: "No surly pew occupant placed a forbidding
hand on the pew door. Seats, hymn-books, crickets, and fans were
at my disposal. The hymn was found for me. Everybody sang. It
was infectious. I was among people to whom Sunday was neither a
bugbear nor a bore. And such hearty singing!—sometimes too fast,
sometimes too slow, but to my ear music, because it was soul, not
cold science. . . . I went home happy, for I had not fed on husks."
Similarly, on a Sunday afternoon in late 1850 the Swedish traveler
Fredrika Bremer called at the Bethel A.M.E. Church, which John
Langston also attended during his sojourn in Cincinnati. The house
was filled. The celebrants sang their own hymns, which Bremer found
crowded with "naiveté, imagery, life." The singing "ascended and
poured forth like a melodious torrent, heads, feet and elbows moved
all in unison amid evident enchantment and delight." A "very black"
young minister, in "flowing eloquence," alluded to the recently enacted fugitive slave law and entreated the congregation to pray for the
runaway and for a nation that would pass such oppressive legislation.
And in 1849 a British minister and his wife came away from a tea

invitation at the neat and clean dwelling of the Zion Baptist minister Wallace Shelton, assured that blacks "were deeply and justly disaffected towards the American people and the American laws."[41]

Arguably, the extensive religious conversions that occurred during the late 1830s, stimulated by pious blacks as well as evangelizing white radicals, helped to move black Cincinnatians toward self-help and protest. In 1840 Amzi D. Barber, an Oberlin theological student and former teacher of black children in Cincinnati, reported about five hundred conversions over the past four years, bringing the total membership in the Union Baptist, Bethel A.M.E., and M.E. churches to some eight hundred. Religion for some was "excitement merely."[42] But there was more. Historians argue convincingly that evangelical Christianity (the Oberlin brand in particular, with its emphasis on moral excellence) stirred many whites to acts of benevolence (the most potent manifestation being the abolitionist crusade). That same force mixed with African-American religion brought from the South, with its stress on emotional and sensory fulfillment—the two faiths having in common a respect for freedom, education, and individual responsibility and dignity—was seemingly no less effective in energizing a black self-help movement in the city and around the state. If the revolution in race relations was to occur, if "the cause of truth and justice, . . . one God will sanction," as the devout Gideon Langston put it, was to prevail, it had to begin, Cincinnati's black leadership generally agreed, in the churches. The poet Madison Bell, who worshiped in the Bethel congregation during this period, later reflected, "These Negro churches have done more to educate the heart and mind for freedom's blessings held in store than every other means combined."[43]

By the time John Langston came to the city, twenty-two men, including his brother Gideon, had emerged as leaders in church and society as well as in educational, moral, and abolitionist enterprises. Nearly three-fourths of the group were native Virginians. All were employed—six as barbers, four as carpenters, three as hucksters, two as whitewashers, and one each as schoolteacher, painter, plasterer, tanner, dyer, steward, and livery stable operator.[44] Newspaper readers and keen observers, these leaders profited from occupations that positioned them to receive and transmit political intelligence.[45] This was particularly true of the barbers, who included Andrew J. Gordon, one of the state's premier black orators; the literate W. H. Yancy, coeditor of the *Colored Citizen,* one of two black newspapers published briefly in the city during the 1840s; John Liverpool, a pioneer leader in Cincinnati and corresponding secretary in Ohio for the early national black convention movement; John Hatfield and William O'Hara, key conductors for the Underground Railroad;[46] and William W. Watson.

Certain traits distinguished them, individually and as a group. Augustus Wattles, who enjoyed more intimate terms with the black community than any other white man in Cincinnati, singled out the leaders' honesty, uprightness, and industry. A sophisticated black observer, the Baptist minister Newman was struck by the pride and strength the leaders seemed to derive from their community's advancing "number, intelligence, and wealth." The well-traveled editor Ray believed that—to a greater extent than in any other black community he had visited—"important principles" prevailed among the leaders, primarily union and "confidence in each other's integrity." Taking in leadership and community, Ray pronounced black Cincinnatians "the best population of our people I have ever seen or heard of."[47] Moreover, these black men of property and standing embodied a sense of racial obligation, the essence of which several articulated in 1837: " 'Ethiopia shall soon stretch forth her hand to God,' is the declaration of infinite goodness and wisdom. It must take place, and will doubtless be effected by human agency; and who so proper as educated colored people to be the heralds of the gospel, and teachers of science and civilization to their benighted brethren in all lands."[48] Speaking in 1845, Salmon P. Chase of Cincinnati, a future state senator, governor of Ohio, and chief justice of the U.S. Supreme Court, who had already made a name for himself with his legal defense of fugitive slaves and in antislavery politics, summed up the achievements of the black community. Contrasting the situation in his boyhood, twenty years before, when "the colored inhabitants [were] hardly in a better condition than slaves," to their current "visibly improved condition," Chase declared, "Debarred from the public schools, you have established schools of your own; thrust by prejudice into the obscure corners of the edifices in which white men offer prayer, you have erected churches of your own. . . . Excluded from the witness box, you have sought that security which the law denies, in a favorable public opinion propitiated by your good conduct."[49] On the self-help foundation of the thirties, the leadership went on to build a broad array of political and protest activities in the two decades before the war, working aggressively in cooperation with other black communities in the state to further the objectives of full freedom and equality.

Although Gideon Langston and other leaders of the Cincinnati black community eased the way, eleven-year-old John, fresh from the Chillicothe farm and still harboring wistful memories of the

Gooches, doubtless was more confused than impressed by his introduction to the black social and political culture of the city. Any hopes he had of living with his brother Gideon were dashed. After coming to Ohio, Gideon had entered Oberlin Institute's preparatory department in 1835, where he and his brother Charles were Oberlin's first black students. Gideon then established himself in business in Cincinnati, opening a barbershop and, shortly thereafter, the only black-owned livery stable in the city. But he had remained a bachelor and, as such, was unprepared to care for the boy.[50]

Instead, Gideon found John a boarding space with John Woodson, a fellow community leader whose home was situated on Sixth Street, east of Broadway and north of the canal, in the section the boy knew as Germany. Like Gideon, Woodson, a master carpenter, was an officer and stockholder in the Iron Chest Company. "Steady, industrious, and cherishing proper ideas of what is necessary for [black] elevation," as the *Philanthropist* editor Gamaliel Bailey said of him and two other black builders, Woodson, a former Virginian, was compiling a solid record of involvement in local and state organizations for education, moral elevation, and self-help. As superintendent of the Sabbath school of the Bethel A.M.E. Church, Woodson, whom Langston characterized as "fairly educated" and efficient, entered John into its membership. It is likely that John also joined the children's temperance group, which had existed for more than five years and was of special interest to Woodson as an officer of the Moral Reform Society.[51]

On weekdays John went to the basement of the black Baptist church on Baker Street, some distance away, to the school taught by the Reverends Mr. Denham and Goodwin. Langston later remembered these white teachers, who had been at the work for several years, as even-tempered, enthusiastic men of considerable learning, able to win the respect and confidence of their pupils. Charging three dollars per quarter in advance and affording the rare opportunity of a full-year term, the school enjoyed a healthy enrollment, drawing not only local children but also those who, like John, had been sent from other more deprived areas for the educational advantages of the city. An average of sixty-five boys and girls attended. According to Langston's recollection, the pupils displayed a high order of morality and scholarship; Cincinnati schoolchildren had been praised for eagerness since the opening of the first Lane Rebel project school in 1834, when children had "begged to be taken in."[52]

Nevertheless, on initial acquaintance, Johnnie's new school, like his new surroundings as a whole, must have seemed strange and constricted. Although his schooling had been neglected of late, it was

soon apparent that he was one of the better scholars. As for his classmates in general, years of enforced ignorance and poverty had left
deep imprints on their young minds. Some of them may have been
among those students at Hiram Gilmore High School in 1848 who
struck the visiting black abolitionist Martin Delany as having learned
"comparatively nothing, except perhaps a little business education
and some music for show purposes," but no science and no English
composition—"They don't capitalize i." The effects of limited opportunity were also apparent at John's Sabbath school, where white
abolitionists, while praising the "neat dress, good order, and appear-
ance of intelligence" of the pupils, noted with regret that this was the
solitary instruction some received.[53] For John, moreover, the Bethel
church's demonstrative services may well have seemed strange after
the proper Presbyterians of Chillicothe. And what was he to make
of men and women of the black upper class, like Woodson and his
associates, whose constant striving to maintain home and institutions contrasted sharply with the easy circumstances of the white
families he had known? Even while the boy responded to the culture—learning new phrases such as "you creature, you!," "a squash
of fat," and "studies about it";[54] stopping off at a confectioner's shop
for a sugarplum or a stick of candy from the big barrel; playing at
marbles or splashing in the canal on hot summer days; sniffing the
strong odors of frying pork or fatback in narrow alleys; listening to
the music of the black boatmen, one man singing the stanzas, others
coming in on the chorus[55]—he had few clues to the puzzle of his
own place in it. The grammatical questions of "I" were simple for
Johnnie Langston, the psychological more than ordinarily complex
and painful.

The city's turbulent racial and anti-abolitionist climate that spring
and summer of 1841 could only heighten the boy's anxieties. A number of factors—a controversial court decision regarding a fugitive
slave, the activities of blacks and some white abolitionists to help
slaves escape set against the often-violent attempts to reclaim them,
the building white resentment of rising black prosperity and confidence, and the general economic unrest—all contributed to the rise of
the impending conflict.

In late May the Cincinnati attorney Salmon Chase appeared in the
Hamilton County court to represent Mary Towns, a Kentucky slave
who had lived in Cincinnati as a free woman for ten years before being charged as a fugitive by her master. Judge Nathaniel C. Read,
conforming to arguments earlier advanced by Chase in two highly
publicized cases, granted Towns her freedom. Since the slaveowner's

affidavit did not explicitly charge her with having escaped from Kentucky into Ohio, Chase argued, she could not be considered a fugitive slave. In freeing Towns, Judge Read declared that in Ohio "liberty is the rule, involuntary servitude the exception." The decision alarmed conservative business leaders who feared it might alienate trading partners in the South. In response, playing on fears of damage to the southern trade, the influential *Cincinnati Daily Enquirer* renewed its periodic alert about the malign influences of abolitionism. Condemning the practice of assisting fugitive slaves as particularly disruptive of relations with the South, the *Enquirer* began a summer campaign of demanding action against those responsible.[56]

New to the city and young as he was, John nonetheless doubtless already knew something of the operations of the Underground Railroad, in which his brother Gideon, his landlord, John Woodson, and such notables as William W. Watson were involved. Helping slaves off the steamboats or from over the river and concealing them once they were in the city, blacks, assisted by white sympathizers, over the years had made Cincinnati a major portal from slavery to freedom. While members of the Bethel church regularly helped runaways, the Iron Chest Company also included among its enterprises the care and protection of fugitives. "Such matters are almost uniformly managed by the colored people," the abolitionist James G. Birney confided to Lewis Tappan in 1837, an assertion echoed by Levi Coffin, who was called the superintendent of the Underground Railway, when he took up residence in the city a decade later. Although the work was necessarily clandestine—one black man referred to "under-railway" agents as being "initiated into the mysteries of Syble"—and dangerous, it engendered the kind of personal satisfaction expressed by the trusted agent John Hatfield: "I never felt better pleased with anything I ever did in my life, than in getting a slave woman clear, when her master was taking her from Virginia."[57]

If John's imagination could enter into not only the adventure but also the morality of violating the law to aid a fellow human being to freedom, the boy was all the more alarmed by the recurrent mob action against those who succored fugitives. "When . . . their hiding places were discovered it mattered little what the color of the protector was," Langston remembered. "Popular feeling was quickly aroused and in not a few cases manifested itself in violence against those concerned in such [a] transaction." Thus the entire black community had reason for concern in early August 1841 when a letter purportedly from a fugitive to his still-enslaved wife came to light. Naming two black residents of Cincinnati, William O'Hara, a barber, and "George" Casey (probably William Casey, a riverman), from whom help could be expected, the escapee advised his wife to tell her trusted friends "that if they can once get to Cincinnati, they can get liberty; and that the colored men in the boats will whisper in their ears where to find abolitionists." Enraged by this evidence of a "nefarious conspiracy," the *Enquirer* declared the city overrun by free blacks, "laboring, when they do labor, in competition with white citizens, and when they do not, subsisting by plunder." It called on township trustees to enforce the seldom-observed state law of 1807 requiring blacks to post five hundred dollars bond within twenty days of their arrival in Ohio. If they did not post bond and could not, the *Enquirer* demanded that they leave the city.[58]

In the company of landlord or brother, Johnnie Langston surely attended the ceremonies held on August 1, 1841—despite the growing hostility—to commemorate the abolition of slavery in the British West Indies. Since 1838, when black Cincinnatians had held a watchnight service to mark the official termination of the apprenticeship system in the British possessions, celebration of the First of August had become an annual event, as it was in a growing number of black northern communities. With many of the city's black leaders taking part, William M. Johnson presided over the 1841 observance, an elaborate family-oriented affair that opened at Bethel A.M.E., continued at Baker Street Baptist, and concluded with "an elegant temperance dinner" prepared by a black caterer and served outdoors. Young Joseph Henry Perkins—who on a like occasion in 1849 would proudly describe black contributions and excoriate "the fiery famished brood of Anglo Saxons, that continue to suck at the vitals of Afric's bleeding, but unoffending children"—acted as orator of the day. Woodson's foreman, J. L. Tinsley, led the toast to "the day we celebrate—Honored for an event which must ultimately result in the abolition of slavery throughout the world," and A. M. Sumner declared that the West Indies' independence "admonished all oppressors in every nation that the day is at hand when the hand of Almighty God will sunder the chains of the oppressed in every land."[59] As much as the forthright rhetoric, the success of the well-organized celebration evinced the considerable socioeconomic progress and political awareness that the Cincinnati black community had attained.

Nonetheless, these very factors were stimulating rancor among whites. On a psychological level, the Englishman Edward Abdy's observation, made during a visit to Cincinnati in 1834, was still apt: whites spoke of self-improving blacks "with a degree of bitterness that dictated a disposition to be more angry with their virtues than with their vices." Whether or not blacks actually "assume[d] the air of fellows in authority" or "took the inside of the pavement upon all occasions," as critics charged, more than one Cincinnatian was angered simply by respectable and responsible black behavior. "White men . . . are naturally indignant," a white workingman explained, "when they see a set of idle blacks dressed up like ladies and gentlemen, strutting about our streets and flinging the 'rights of petition' and 'discussion' in our faces."[60]

The economy and the weather exacerbated the festering discontent. In early August drought and heat dropped the Ohio River to an unprecedented low watermark, throwing many white, as well as black, laborers out of work. Meanwhile, overall economic conditions remained unstable, with new bank closings imminent. As the *Enquirer* continued to charge blacks and abolitionists with the major responsibility for business difficulties and job losses, the *Philanthropist* indulged in provocative statements of its own. In the defiant spirit of the First of August proceedings, the *Philanthropist* rebuked those southern editors who were threatening that the South would sever business relations with Ohioans if alleged fugitive slaves were not returned to their owners. "Madmen! a pretty thing for you to be talking of non-intercourse, while nothing but respect for the power of the free states protects you from the desolating vengeance of the united black race of the Western Hemisphere."[61]

Little was needed to trigger a riot. As August turned to September, violent incidents began. Not far from the Woodson home where Johnnie lived a youthful white gang pelted several well-dressed black men with gravel. As other blacks joined in, a fight ensued that wounded several persons on both sides; rumor had it that a white youth was "so badly cut, that his bowels fell out." Sometime after midnight the following day an armed white party burst into a black hotel, the Dumas House on McAllister Street, demanding a black man's surrender to them, only to be repulsed. Yet another scuffle between whites and blacks, reportedly with some injuries to the former, broke out in the Lower Market soon after.[62]

By Friday, September 3, even a black child could recognize that a full-scale white attack seemed inevitable. As numbers of Kentuckians swelled the crowds and city officials made no move to intervene, Johnnie Langston heard "high and open threats, conveyed in vulgar base expressions which indicated the possibility and probability of an early attack." It was Langston's recollection, which subsequent events seemed to confirm, that black elders, stiffening for the onslaught, armed themselves with guns, planned their defense, and—in an all-but-unique action in the history of prewar race riots—chose a leader to direct it. The man was Major J. Wilkerson. A twenty-eight-year-old self-purchased mulatto who acted as an A.M.E. missionary to establish churches and schools in the West, Wilkerson offered this family history in his memoirs: "A Virginian by birth, born not far from Little York, a town of no little renown, and as to his blood, he is of the Bengal of Africa, Anglo-Saxon of Europe, Powhatton of America; but strictly the grandson of Col. Wilkerson, who fought with one of the bravest of the brave, namely General Gates, at the battle of Saratoga, N.Y." Langston recalled that the Cincinnati black community had full confidence in the man.[63]

By 8:00 P.M. that night a white mob, having assembled openly in Fifth Street Market, moved toward the black homes and businesses clustered around Sixth and Broadway, the section where Johnnie Langston boarded. In the "outrageous, barbarous and deadly attack upon the entire class of the colored people" that followed, as Langston put it, the mob assaulted blacks "wherever found upon the streets, and with such weapons and violence as to cause death in many cases, no respect being had to the character, position, or innocence of those attacked." Behind windows and doors and on rooftops of houses at Sixth and Broadway and along the alley leading from New to Sixth, armed blacks waited. The rioters, after razing a black confectioner's shop and shouting down the mayor, who had attempted to remonstrate with them, advanced into New Street, brandishing bludgeons and demanding of white residents where the blacks lived.[64] Suddenly the black defenders, doubtless under orders from Major Wilkerson, launched their counterattack, opening fire from the alley with rifles and muskets and wounding several whites. "The crowd gave back towards Broadway," a white witness reported. "The negroes rallied, and came into the street firing their guns, and throwing missiles at the crowd as it was retreating, . . . and pursued the crowd to Broadway." To cover the black charge, shots were fired into the retreating mob from a frame house in Broadway occupied by the black steamboat steward Asbury Young.[65] Reportedly yelling out "a wild shout of triumph and defiance," some fifty armed black men succeeded in pushing the mob "full one hundred yards from their houses." Despite a heavy rain shower and further firing from the black defenders, by 1 A.M. the attackers had collected themselves sufficiently to drag an iron six-pounder from the river to the corner of Sixth and Broadway, stuff the cannon with boiler punchings, and discharge it at least three times down Sixth. Far into the night the fighting continued, until a military contingent summoned by the mayor moved in to keep the mob at bay.[66]

Although the black defense had succeeded, the struggle was not over. An early morning meeting of white citizens at the courthouse, presided over by the mayor, resulted in a hasty agreement on a number of issues: the enforcement of the Black Laws, including the requirement for bonding, the return of all fugitive slaves, the repudiation of the doctrines and activities of abolitionists, and, most immediately, complete disarmament of blacks and the arrest of black lawbreakers. With the riot area under martial law for blacks but under mob law for whites (none of whom were arrested), "swarms of improvised police officers" spread across the city in search of blacks, dragging off servants or waiters or barbers, combing black residences for men and arms, collecting what the *Enquirer* described as enough weapons to supply "an Algerine pirate vessel." In a futile gesture toward conciliation, some blacks met to promise compliance with the laws and thank city officials for their efforts to protect them. Herded into the square at Sixth and Broadway and penned in by a guard of soldiers, blacks were not permitted to leave even when they gave bond; late in the day some three hundred black men, whether sound or maimed, were marched off to jail while whites struck and kicked and jeered at them.[67]

Early that morning John Langston was in Woodson's home when a black neighbor dashed in to warn him of the impending arrests of blacks. Although allegedly the jailing was for their self-protection, Langston later wrote that in actuality "the colored men were imprisoned because it had been thoroughly shown by their conduct that they had become so determined to protect themselves against whatever odds, that great and serious damage might be expected were they again assaulted."[68] After watching Woodson and his assistant Tinsley hide themselves in the chimneys of the house, the boy took off through the backyard and garden, jumped over the fence into the alley, and headed down Main Street to the canal bridge. He was determined to warn Gideon, whose barbershop was near Fourth and Main, more than a mile away. At the middle of the bridge John heard police officers behind him ordering him to stop. Terrified, he raced onward until nearly to his goal, stumbled into a drugstore, and fainted. The white druggists, friends of his brother, carried him to Gideon's rooms, where he was revived and told his story. Well aware of the city order and already in hiding, fearful that Johnnie might have been followed, Gideon settled in behind barred doors and win-

dows to listen and wait, his exhausted brother at his side. Gideon's
five employees hid with them. Finally, in the concealing dusk the boy
ventured out with the helpful white merchants to a confectionary
to buy food for the hungry men, who had eaten nothing for some fifteen hours.

Listening in the darkness, Johnnie heard the "howls, and yells, and
screams, and oaths, and vulgarities" of the rioters as they dragged
the press of the *Philanthropist* down Main Street and threw it into
the river.[69] They destroyed the bakery of the naturalized Englishman Cornelius Burnett, who often succored fugitives, and attacked
an abolitionist book depository. Raiding parties searched out blacks'
homes, where "windows were broken, doors smashed, children
frightened, and poor women insulted." Late in the night they descended on Sixth and Main, battered the Bethel church, and again attacked the houses, where only women and children remained. The
Daily Cincinnati Chronicle reported "scenes of greater real atrocity,
though with less personal injury" than on the evening before; the
Daily Cincinnati Gazette acknowledged that the city had been "in a
complete anarchy, controlled mostly by a lawless and violent mob."
Although Governor Thomas Corwin issued a proclamation calling
for cessation of the violence, neither military companies, police, nor
the large numbers of deputized citizens offered effective resistance to
the rioters. At length, after a few arrests were finally made, the mob
dispersed from sheer exhaustion.[70]

On Sunday John came out of hiding to a dazzlingly sunshiny day.
The "solemn, awful tread and tramp" of the mounted constabulary
intruded on an almost-religious silence. Like Ishmael, the boy was
struck by the cruel dissonance of natural serenity and human violence: "It would have been a day fit for the calm and peaceful worship
of our Heavenly Father in a civilized and Christian community. As it
was, however, the horrid sight of the vast company of such policemen, . . . with the recollection of the sad, dire events of the preceding nights and days, drove every feeling of love and veneration out of
the hearts of those who had thus been outraged and terrified."[71]

It had been the most destructive and violent rioting in the city's
history; indeed, it may well have been the most severe urban outbreak
against blacks in pre-Civil War America. Although Langston remembered a high death toll among white attackers and black defenders,
no accurate count of the dead and wounded or of the amount of
property damage was attempted.[72] In accordance with the rioters' demand that the state law of 1807 be enforced, however, a city official
did disclose the posting of bonds by more than one hundred blacks

and mulattoes; Kentucky slaveholders, invited to inspect the black prisoners before their release, claimed one as a fugitive slave.[73] Not appeased, a group of anti-abolitionists formed a new society to forward their aims. On the other hand, the *Philanthropist* continued publication, picking up a few new subscribers and renewed support from the old. Langston believed that the riot had also served to embolden such antislavery adherents as Salmon P. Chase and Samuel Lewis, who subsequently joined with Gamaliel Bailey in giving force to the fledgling Liberty party.[74]

The effect on the black community was profound. An abolitionist's census of black Cincinnatians in 1845 showed that despite a population increase of about six hundred since 1840, their private property holdings had dropped by nearly fifty thousand dollars during the five-year period—an indication, however imperfect, of the extent of the property loss and the difficulty of economic rebuilding in a time of increased financial retrenchment. In the months immediately following the riot, another white observer of black Cincinnatians noted "a manifest depression of their energy and zeal in behalf of the schools and even of their private interests"; blacks themselves began seriously considering emigration to Canada. By the fall of 1842 a black Oberlin student reported that nine of the city's most respectable black families, in addition to several young men, already had left for Canada, explaining that "times are very dull, money very scarce, nothing doing, & prejudice very great." At the same time, black community leaders took pains to contradict a rumor that a number of blacks desired or intended to move to Liberia. Within two months of the riot, before a large crowd assembled at the abolitionist Sixth Presbyterian Church, such leaders as George Cary, William O'Hara, John Liverpool, Charles Satchell, A. M. Sumner, and William W. Watson repudiated the American Colonization Society and its Liberian project.[75] Over the long term the riot of 1841—as repeated references to it at public gatherings demonstrated—exercised a strong hold on the black consciousness. At the 1843 National Convention of Colored Citizens in Buffalo, New York, Sumner, speaking also for fellow delegates Watson and Andrew J. Gordon, voiced opposition to the adoption of Rev. Henry Highland Garnet's militant *Address to the Slaves*. Sumner argued that the call for a slave insurrection could endanger not only those free blacks living in the South but also those who lived in the border areas of free states. "We of Cincinnati," he declared, "[are] ready to meet anything that may come upon us unprovoked, but we [are] not ready injudiciously to provoke difficulty." Despite the legacy of fear left by the riot, because of the black defense

there was also a legacy of pride, which the black abolitionist William
C. Nell, visiting the city with Langston fifteen years later, observed.
From the perspective of his own years in the black movement, Langston later wrote that the riot and the restrictive measures failed to
"hush the voices of the eloquent colored men themselves who
through such experience, were learning what their rights were and
how to advocate and defend them."[76]

For young John Langston the riot may well have served as an emotional watershed. The desperation that pushed the boy over Woodson's fence to seek out and warn the one person he could claim as his
family in that dangerous city was a telling measure of his lonely in-
security in this new life. The pulse-pounding moment on the canal
bridge when he was identified as a black, his race to his brother, and
his venture into the night to procure food for Gideon and his workers
may all have made him feel intensely a participant in the black experience. Repelled and frightened by the depravity of the white attackers, thrilled by the courage of the black defenders, he could have
felt the sense of unity engendered in members of groups by sudden
adversity; later he may have experienced the survivor's sense of his
own, as well as the community's, uniqueness and value and of kinship
to one's fellows. The knowledge that white abolitionists, too, were
suffering could take him toward an appreciation of the possibilities of
black-white union for the cause. Moreover, it is possible that the very
savagery of the riot served to vent the violent and inexpressible anger,
fear, and grief that had seized him when he was torn from the
Gooches, moving him toward a sense of closure and to an acceptance
of his black identity.

Toward the beginning of John's second year in Cincinnati, he
looked up from his school desk at the sound of a familiar voice and
saw Col. William Gooch. Together on a bench, Johnnie and Gooch
passed an emotional afternoon reviewing their separate existences—
the boy asking eagerly after Matilda and Virginia Gooch, the women
he had considered his mother and sister; the colonel, who was back
in Ohio to make final settlement of his property in Chillicothe, assuring him of their affectionate concern. John promised that when he
reached his majority he would rejoin the Gooch family in Missouri.
Gooch's departure left the boy deeply affected but not despairing;
in school and out, he had duties to attend to and associations to
explore.[77]

Shortly after the riot John changed his address from the eastern
to the south central part of the city, a move that brought him closer
to school and to Gideon, and into the household of the redoubt-
able William W. Watson. Watson's classic story of bondage and free-

dom, already well known among abolitionists, contained more than enough drama to thrill his young boarder. In 1832 in Lexington, Kentucky, Watson, then twenty-four and a "sable son" of Virginia, was put up for sale. Standing on an auction table, Watson pointed to his weeping wife and little daughter and pled successfully with potential buyers to abstain from bidding; instead, he was purchased by his brother-in-law for $650. The latter, a Cincinnati barber, had raised the purchase price by persuading two white merchants to endorse his note, on which he had then borrowed at exorbitant interest. Working in his brother-in-law's shop and also as a waiter, not only did Watson pay off the note within the year, he subsequently purchased four other family members for a total exceeding $3,000 while embarking on his own barbering business and making substantial investments in real estate. In her published justification for *Uncle Tom's Cabin*, Harriet Beecher Stowe, a resident of Cincinnati during the time she was gathering material for the book, named Watson, along with five other former slaves she had met there, as men who exemplified the capability of the race, "conquering for themselves comparative wealth and social position" by their "self-denial, energy, patience, and honesty."[78]

John Langston, who found Watson's brick house with its well-furnished and pleasant rooms and parlors attractive, rightly perceived the social position of Watson and his wife, Ruthellen, as "conspicuous and influential." Besides the large number of family members and boarders—a total of seventeen persons was recorded in the home by the 1840 federal census—frequent visitors kept the household lively. Frederick Douglass, noting in 1850 that Watson, his "esteemed friend," was the first black Cincinnatian to offer him hospitality, advised, "He who would know whether colored people know how to live in a state of freedom might soon receive the desired information by making Mr. W. W. Watson a visit."[79] Because the children of Cincinnati's enterprising black families, "the very best and most highly educated and cultured young persons," as Langston put it, congregated in the Watsons' parlor, John made new friendships and deepened others initiated during his first tentative months in the city. The most notable was with Peter H. Clark, the son of the successful barber Michael Clark. A precocious youngster exactly John's own age, Peter Clark—so forward in his studies that he would be employed as a teaching assistant after only two years of study at Gilmore High School, where he "finished" his education—was destined to become an eminent educator and political leader. Riveted in young manhood by common reform concerns, Langston and Clark began a relationship that lasted until Langston's death, when Clark referred brokenly to the loss of the "only friend who remains to me from my boyhood days."[80]

Like others in the industrious Watson household, where the 1840 census recorded nine males employed, John, while continuing his schooling, began to work at his landlord's barbershop and bathhouse. On Saturdays from early morning to midnight he blacked boots, ran errands, and carried towels for whatever tips came his way. Rendered inconspicuous by age and role, John could closely observe the black barbers and their patrons, the majority of whom were white, although—since Watson and his companions in black reform repeatedly reproved those Cincinnati barbers who operated racially segregated shops—black customers may well have been accommodated. The propensity of men to talk over the small beer of the week in such a setting acquainted the boy with current issues and ideas. At the same time, he could appreciate the personal qualities of the black barber—diplomacy, a liking of good talk and companionship, and a need to be abreast of events both abroad and in his own provincial sphere—that often made him an able politician and community leader, not only in Cincinnati but elsewhere. Watson and his staff "pleased and won" their customers, John concluded, by skill, efficiency, decorum, and honesty. As for the patrons, one at least provided John an object lesson in thrift and temperance: the well-heeled dandy, who often tossed fifty cents and sometimes a dollar to the boy for polishing his boots, "commenced drinking and gaming, and I have lived to see him willing to black my boots for ten cents had I asked him." Under the masks of lather, moreover, men sometimes revealed their passions and prejudices. Peter Clark, Langston's friend, who as a young man worked in his father's barbershop, once related that a white man whom he was shaving had asked to be introduced to colored women. When Clark refused, the customer sneeringly referred to his shop's serving "niggers," whereupon Clark hurled the shaving cup to the floor, avowing never to shave a white man again unless to "cut his throat." If Watson and his workers also resented being at the beck and call of offensive white men, the bootblack might note the mechanisms of self-defense under the disguise of accommodation—unimpeachable politeness, but perhaps an accidental nick of an offensive customer's chin, a topcoat brushing so assiduous it scraped the shoulders beneath, a flattering appraisal of an unappealing cut of hair or beard. Past midnight, when black masks descended, in the sweepings of the day the young bootblack would count out his earnings before his encouraging elders, who offered counsel on pleasing customers, hard work, and frugality. Delighted to have mounting savings as well as pocket money, John began to envision himself a "successful and thrifty man."[81]

Business, however, he observed, was to be balanced with larger obligations. Watson, a staunch Baptist who agreed with white abolitionists that the Sabbath should be reserved for worship, refused to open his shop from the Saturday closing until 5 A.M. Monday. Any financial loss he suffered was set against a psychological gain that could hardly have escaped John's notice—the transformation from Saturday night's barber, as liable to be called "boy" as John himself, to Sunday morning's "Rev. Watson" and "Mr. Watson" in a society whose religious and secular joys and sorrows existed outside of white reckoning. John again enjoyed the reflected glory of his landlord's prestigious position in the church for, like Woodson at the Bethel A.M.E., Watson served as superintendent of the Sabbath school for the Union Baptist on Baker Street, of which he was also a trustee. This man of "vigorous mental parts, with limited education," as Langston described him—whose command of religious discourse was such that black political gatherings frequently called upon him to offer prayer—taught the most advanced Bible class, in which he enrolled Johnnie. In this church where good oratory and, as a white visitor remarked, "hymns beautifully and exquisitely sung" were staples, the boy added to his store of knowledge of the rhythms and variety of black oral expression and to his appreciation of the black American's religious music—music that depicted an enlarged universe, roaming between past history, present circumstance, and future promise, bestowing a sense of peace and inner freedom, calling up thoughtful reflection. Most important, John experienced in the Union Baptist Church, as in the Bethel A.M.E., the power of black self-determination. The black church, a mature John Langston later maintained in describing the founding of the African Methodist Episcopal church, not only represented "the organized Christian protest of the colored American against unjust, inhuman, and cruel complexional discriminations," but also offered him the "opportunity to be himself, to think his own thought, express his own conviction, make his own utterance, test his own powers, cultivate self-reliance, and thus, in the exercise of the faculties of his soul, trust and achieve."[82]

During his second year at Denham and Goodwin's school, John progressed rapidly to the point where he and one other boy, probably Peter H. Clark, composed the highest class. Despite the traditional nature of the curriculum—ancient history, advanced arithmetic and grammar, and elementary science—the preoccupations of students and teachers meant that John was acquiring the rudiments of an antislavery education as well. In a typical assignment for the day— to write an essay on Alfred, King of the Saxons—a sixteen-year-old black pupil in a similar Cincinnati school responded: "at one time [Alfred] did not know his a, b, c, but before his death he commanded . . . nations. . . . I think if the colored people study like King Alfred they will soon do away with the evil of slavery. I cant see how the Americans can call this a land of freedom where so much slavery is." Just as the white Ohio schoolboy William Dean Howells, wearing a paper hat and flourishing a wooden sword, dreamed of the martial glory of English and American heroes,[83] John and his classmates also fastened for inspiration on these classic figures, but they emulated modern black liberationists as well.

In particular, with the terrifying events of the riot impressed upon his memory, John was excited by the story of the slave mutineers of the ship *Amistad* and their leader, the valiant Cinque (or, as Langston and other contemporaries spelled it, Chinque). In the summer of 1839 Cinque, said to be an African prince, led an uprising of his fifty-two fellow captives aboard the Spanish schooner *Amistad*. Though the Africans gained control of the ship, they were overtaken by a U.S. government brig off the coast of Long Island and arrested, but not before Cinque had dived overboard, swimming "like an otter, first upon his back, then upon his breast," evading his captors for nearly an hour. With the ex-president John Quincy Adams representing the Africans, their case was eventually decided in their favor by the U.S. Supreme Court. The abolitionists extracted full publicity value from it, using such devices as the sale of Cinque's picture for a dollar. Like blacks in other communities, Cincinnati's blacks not only tacked Cinque's likeness to their walls and told their children his story, they contributed to his defense fund. After the Africans had finally won their freedom, Gideon Langston, speaking for the black community, was able to thank Adams personally for his "able defense . . . by which means a number of our fellow men were raised from a level with the brute creation, and placed in the scale of human existence." So meaningful was the memory of this story to John Mercer Langston, he went on to name his first daughter Chinque.[84]

In 1843 Haiti was also much in the news because of the attempt of several congressmen—Adams's "untiring efforts" won Gideon Langston's praise—to extend official recognition to the black Caribbean republic. This issue also caught John's interest. Excited by the Haitian revolution and its heroes, whom black Cincinnatians frequently toasted at First of August celebrations, the boy familiarized himself with Haitian history. Langston would later name his first son Dessalines after one of the heroes of the Haitian revolution.

The antislavery crusade provided ready topics for John's early rhetorical efforts. Like the youthful white orators in the common schools—whose "vehement action" led Harriet Martineau to wonder in mock dismay which of them would "speak in Congress hereafter"—John and his classmates frequently participated in plays, special exercises, and public exhibitions, the boys decked out in starched collars, the girls in "kid slippers, neat pantalettes and tastefully-plaited and ribboned hair." With his extended family and adult friends present to hear and applaud, John, honored to be chosen for special parts, soon discovered how much he liked reciting and speaking.[86]

Having tasted the exhilaration of performing, the boy, accompanying his brother or Watson to public forums addressed by white abolitionists or black community leaders, witnessed the power of oratory to express ethical values and laudable goals as well as to inspire protest and resistance. None ranked higher in the boy's pantheon of heroes during these months than four talented young black orators: Joseph Henry Perkins, whom Peter H. Clark would call the "great orator of the Ohio valley";[87] John I. Gaines, then barely in his twenties but already active in state and local black reform; Andrew J. Gordon; and Gideon Langston. In 1850 Frederick Douglass singled out both Perkins and Gaines for their "great powers over the minds and feelings of our people."[88] A barber noted for his dignity, Gordon was the speaker at a notable ceremony in 1845 (after John had left the city) to honor Salmon Chase.[89] Presenting the attorney with an engraved silver pitcher in recognition of his contribution toward establishing a slave's right to freedom if brought voluntarily by his owner into the state, Gordon praised not only Chase's service to the enslaved but also his sensitivity to "the deprivation of rights endured, and the wrongs inflicted upon the free colored people." In return the normally restrained Chase made his most radical utterance to date, a firm declaration of support for the black's rights to civil and political equality, including suffrage.[90]

Although all of these "fearless and able defenders of the rights of their people" inspired John, his brother Gideon, who "manifested large ability and learning with commanding and surprising qualities of oratory," excited his warmest admiration. Probably John was present on the brisk March 1843 evening when the "gifted and eloquent" Gideon, as Gaines characterized him, severely denounced colonization as having "no other tendency than to sacrifice the free colored population for the purpose of rendering the system of slavery more secure." Abolition of slavery, Gideon declared, was the only means to achieve the "entire liberation" of the black. A leader in the black reform movement at the state level as well as in Cincinnati, Gideon was chosen in November 1843 to head the black delegation that welcomed John Quincy Adams to the city—privately because blacks were barred from participating in the official welcoming ceremony. In his remarks, Gideon—whom Adams described in his diary as a "young mulatto, son of wealthy Virginia planter, but bearing the name of negress mother"—expressed gratitude for the congressman's fight against slavery. "Although we have no honors of state to confer," Gideon said, "yet we offer you a far higher reward in the approbation of a grateful people. Injuries we write upon sand, but favors on marble, not to be erased; and these acts of yours are as indelibly written on the tablets of our hearts, and can never be obliterated." The occasion provided John Langston with a proud family memory, the more poignant since Gideon had fallen victim to tuberculosis, apparently contracted after his exposure to severe winter weather because of his livery stable work. He was soon forced to drop from public life and died at the age of forty-six.[91]

When the thirteen-year-old John left Cincinnati to return to Chillicothe in the spring of 1843, invitations from Woodson and Watson to stay with them whenever he might return helped soften his real regret at leave-taking. Of Watson, at least, John had early news, for the Baptist deacon offered "an impressive appeal to the throne of Grace" at the black state convention in Columbus in August, attended by both John's brother Charles and his half-brother William Langston, delegates from Chillicothe. Indeed, in the fraternity of talent and need that developed between black Ohioans, such meetings were inevitable. Growing into manhood, John Mercer Langston would maintain his ties with these men and their families, who had become, in a real sense, his own. In his maturity, he would express his gratitude to the outspoken leaders of the black community, "all of whom, it was the privilege and advantage of the boy John to hear and to know, their eloquent efforts serving him in large measure as inspiration and purpose."[92] His experience in Cincinnati had left him little ground to doubt that black people, afforded half a chance, could earn their way and justify their claim to full citizenship rights in American society— and defend themselves by force of arms when appropriate to their struggle. The determination, sacrifice, and achievement exhibited daily by the reform-minded men and women with whom he had associated undergirded his future resolve to win them at least that half a chance.

Notes

This chapter, with minor changes, is excerpted from William Cheek and Aimee Lee Cheek, *John Mercer Langston and the Fight for Black Freedom, 1829–65* (Urbana: University of Illinois Press, 1989).

1. Charles Dickens, *American Notes and Pictures from Italy* (London: MacMillan and Co., 1908), 162; George Wilson Pierson, *Tocqueville and Beaumont in America* (New York: Oxford University Press, 1938), 554–65; Harriet Martineau, *Retrospect of Western Travel,* vol. 2 (New York, 1838; repr., New York: Haskell House, 1969), 37–52; Ohio Writers Project, *Cincinnati: A Guide to the Queen City and Its Neighbors* (Cincinnati, 1943), 58–59, 35–36; Leonard L. Richards, *"Gentlemen of Property and Standing": Anti-Abolition Mobs in Jacksonian America* (New York: Oxford University Press, 1970), 136–50; Robert McColley, *Slavery and Jeffersonian Virginia* (Urbana: University of Illinois Press, 1964), 176; David Carl Shilling, "The Relation of Southern Ohio to the South during the Decade Preceding the Civil War," *Quarterly Publication of the Historical and Philosophical Society of Ohio* 8 (Jan. 1913): 6–15; *Colored American,* 17 Oct. 1840; Carter G. Woodson, "The Negroes of Cincinnati Prior to the Civil War," *Journal of Negro History* 1 (Jan. 1916): 1–22.

2. Helen M. Thurston, "The 1802 Ohio Constitutional Convention and the Status of the Negro," *Ohio History* 81 (Winter 1972): 21–37; Betty Culpepper, "The Negro and the Black Laws of Ohio, 1803–1860" (Master's thesis, Kent State University, 1965), 16–17; Leonard E. Erickson, "The Color Line in Ohio Public Schools, 1829–1890" (Ph.D. diss., Ohio State University, 1959).

3. Richard C. Wade, *The Urban Frontier* (Chicago: University of Chicago Press, 1964), 223–29; John Mercer Langston, "Action of the Federal Government," manuscript of a speech, John Mercer Langston Papers, Fisk University Library; Amzi D. Barber, *Report of the Colored People of Ohio* (Cincinnati, 1840); *Rights of All,* 7 Aug. 1829; *Cincinnati Sentinel,* 20 Aug. 1829, quoted in *Rights of All,* 7 Sept. 1829; Marilyn Bailey, "From Cincinnati, Ohio to Wilberforce, Canada: A Note on Antebellum Colonization," *Journal of Negro History* 68 (Oct. 1973): 427–40; Richards, *"Gentlemen of Property and Standing,"* 92–100; Ohio Anti-Slavery Convention, *Report on the Condition of the People of Color in the State of Ohio . . . Putnam . . . Apr. 1835* (n.p., 1835), 2; *Philanthropist,* 27 Feb. 1838, 11 Nov. 1840, 19 May 1841, 24 Mar. 1841.

4. John Mercer Langston, *From the Virginia Plantation to the National Capitol; or, The First and Only Negro Representative in Congress from the Old Dominion* (Hartford, 1894; repr., New York: Johnson Reprint, 1968), 61–62.

5. The Board of Managers of the Colored Education Society to Editor, *Emancipator,* 22 Apr. 1837; C. B. Ray to Dear (Philip) Bell, 13 Sept. 1839, *Colored American,* 12 Oct. 1839; Ray to Bell, 16 Sept. 1839, *Colored American,* 5 Oct. 1839; U.S. Bureau of the Census, Population Census of 1840, Hamilton County, City of Cincinnati, reel 398, National Archives.

6. David Henry Shaffer, *The Cincinnati, Covington, Newport and Fulton Directory for 1840* (Cincinnati, 1840), 467–77; *Report on the Condition of the People of Color . . . 1835*, 8–9, 12, 6; Augustus Wattles to Mr. Editor, 6 Mar. 1834, *Utica Western Recorder*, n.d., reprinted in *Emancipator*, 22 Apr. 1834; John O. Wattles, "Colored People in Cincinnati," Cincinnati *High School Messenger and Reformer*, n.d., quoted in *Philanthropist*, 30 Apr. 1845; *Colored American*, 5 Oct. 1839.

7. On the African-American work patterns and culture that developed in slavery and around it, see Ira Berlin, *Slaves without Masters: The Free Negro in the Antebellum South* (New York: Pantheon Books, 1974); John Blassingame, *The Slave Community: Plantation Life in the Antebellum South* (New York: Oxford University Press, 1979); Dena J. Epstein, *Sinful Tunes and Spirituals* (Urbana: University of Illinois Press, 1977); Eugene D. Genovese, *Roll, Jordan, Roll: The World the Slaves Made* (New York: Pantheon Books, 1974); Herbert Gutman, *The Black Family in Slavery and Freedom, 1750–1925* (New York: Pantheon Books, 1976); Lawrence W. Levine, *Black Culture and Black Consciousness* (New York: Oxford University Press, 1979); Gerald W. Mullin, *Flight and Rebellion: Slave Resistance in Eighteenth-Century Virginia* (New York: Oxford University Press, 1972); Leslie Howard Owens, *This Species of Property* (New York: Oxford University Press, 1976); Albert J. Raboteau, *Slave Religion* (New York: Oxford University Press, 1978); Thomas L. Webber, *Deep Like the Rivers* (New York: Norton, 1978); Peter Wood, *Black Majority: Negroes in Colonial South Carolina* (New York: Knopf, 1974).

8. Frances Trollope, *Domestic Manners of the Americans*, ed. Donald Smalley (New York: Knopf, 1949), 427.

9. Edward Deering Mansfield, *Personal Memories, Social, Political, and Literary, with Sketches of Many Noted People, 1803–1843* (Cincinnati, 1879; repr., New York: Arno Press, 1970), 305–7; Ohio Writers Project, *A Guide to the Queen City*, 58–59; Shaffer, *Cincinnati Directory, 1840*, 467–77; J. H. Woodruff, *Cincinnati Directory, 1836–1837* (Cincinnati, 1836); *Daily Cincinnati Gazette*, 4 Dec. 1839.

10. Shaffer, *Cincinnati Directory, 1840*, 483; Mansfield, *Personal Memories*, 307. The population census of 1840 for Cincinnati lists 229 boatmen out of 1,005 blacks recorded as employed. In 1840 thirty-three steamboats were built in Cincinnati. Charles Cist, *Cincinnati in 1841: Its Early Annals and Future Prospects* (Cincinnati, 1841), 252–55; *Colored American*, 12 Oct. 1839.

11. Shaffer, *Cincinnati Directory 1840*, 467–77; Francis J. Mastrogiovanni, "Cincinnati's Black Community, 1840–1850" (Master's thesis, University of Cincinnati, 1967), 97–100. John Isom Gaines (Nov. 6, 1821–Nov. 17, 1859) was born in Cincinnati, the eldest son of Isom and Elizabeth (Betty) Gaines (Betty had been the slave and mistress of Major William Clark, the noted explorer of the Pacific Northwest with Merriwether Lewis). Forced into active life at an early age by his father's death, Gaines began to work as a stevedore before setting up a very successful riverfront

store to sell foodstuffs and other provisions to steamboats. He steadily improved upon a meager formal education by self-study and a sustained participation in black conventions and other protest activities, beginning with the first Ohio state black convention in 1837 when he was only sixteen. Although proud of his dark skin color and African ancestry, he steadfastly opposed both colonization and black nationalist emigration movements.

A powerful orator and fluent writer, Gaines worked indefatigably to secure a common school education for black children in Cincinnati. When the city council in 1849 refused to appropriate funds for black schools under a newly enacted state law, Gaines helped to instigate a successful suit against the city. In 1856, with Peter H. Clark, his half-nephew (see note 80), he successfully lobbied the state assembly to restore to Cincinnati blacks the right to elect trustees for black schools (a right bestowed by the 1849 law but rescinded in 1853). Gaines then served as clerk of the black school board for several years.

In his eulogy of Gaines, Langston recalled that his colleague in black reform, although disabled by disease for several years, insisted on being carried to a school board meeting a few days before he died to defend a measure he deemed significant. When a black secondary school was finally established in 1866, with Clark as its first principal, the school was called Gaines High School.

See John M. Langston, "Eulogy ... of John I. Gaines," Xenia, 3 Jan. 1860, *Liberator,* 27 Apr. 1860; William Wells Brown, *The Rising Son,* 450–52; Samuel Matthews, "John Isom Gaines: The Architect of Black Public Education," *Queen City Heritage* 45 (Spring 1987): 41–48; John B. Shotwell, *A History of the Schools of Cincinnati* (Cincinnati, 1902), 455–56, 457–59; *Eighth Annual Report of the Board of Trustees for the Colored Public Schools of Cincinnati* (Cincinnati, 1857), 12–23; *National Anti-Slavery Standard,* 16 Feb. 1856; *History of Schools for the Colored Population from the Special Report of the Commissioner of Education on the Improvement of Public Schools in the District of Columbia, 1871,* 2 vols. (rept., New York: Arno Press, 1969), vol. 2, 371–72. For examples of his speeches, see *Oration Delivered on the First of August 1849* (Cincinnati, 1849); "Response to Speech by Martin Delany," *North Star,* 2 June 1848; "A Plea for Colored Americans," *Anti-Slavery Bugle,* 21 May 1853.

12. Shaffer, *Cincinnati Directory, 1840,* 467–77; *Philanthropist,* 21 July 1840. Blacks were engaged in 46 different occupations in 1840, and in 66 by 1850. In St. Louis in 1850 blacks worked in 33 different categories of employment; in Boston, 44. Shaffer, *Cincinnati Directory, 1840,* 467–77; Patricia Mae Riley, "The Negro in Cincinnati, 1835–1850" (Master's thesis, University of Cincinnati, 1971), 59, 66.

13. Woodruff, *Cincinnati Directory, 1836–1837;* Shaffer, *Cincinnati Directory, 1840,* 467–77.

14. *Frederick Douglass' Paper,* 11 Aug. 1854; *Philanthropist,* 14 July 1840; Shaffer, *Cincinnati Directory, 1840,* 476; Harriet Beecher Stowe,

Uncle Tom's Cabin (Boston, 1852; repr., Columbus: Charles E. Merrill, 1969), 320; Mastrogiovanni, "Cincinnati's Black Community, 1840–1850," 40.

15. *The Free People of Color,* ed. William Loren Katz (New York, 1969), 251; *Anti-Slavery Bugle,* 10 Aug. 1850; George Washington Williams, *A History of the Negro Race in America,* 2 vols. (New York: G. P. Putnam's Sons, 1883), vol. 2, 138–40.

16. "Report of Committee Upon Agriculture," *Minutes of the National Convention of Colored Citizens . . . Buffalo . . . Aug. 1843* (New York, 1843), 31, reprinted in *Minutes of the Proceedings of the National Negro Conventions, 1830–1864,* ed. Howard Holman Bell (New York, 1969).

17. *Colored American,* 5 Oct. 1839. Amzi D. Barber, who taught school in black Cincinnati in the mid-thirties, reported in the spring of 1837 that more than twenty blacks in Cincinnati had purchased land in Mercer County. Barber, "Of the Present Condition of the Colored People in Cincinnati, Apr. 1837," *Report of the Second Anniversary of the Ohio Anti-Slavery Society . . . Mt. Pleasant . . . Apr. 1837* (Cincinnati, 1837), 62. See also *Philanthropist,* 30 Apr. 1845, and *North Star,* 9 June 1848, for reports of "many" black Cincinnatians owning farms and tracts of land in the country.

18. Barber, *Report of the Colored People of Ohio,* 12–13.

19. Useful in drawing these conclusions were three masters' theses: Riley, "The Negro in Cincinnati, 1835–1850," 92–95, 101–4 (maps, 86–91); Mastrogiovanni, "Cincinnati's Black Community, 1840–1850," 14–19, 28–38; Leonard Harding, "The Negro in Cincinnati, 1860–1870: A Demographic Study of a Transitional Decade" (Master's thesis, University of Cincinnati, 1967), 20–28. See also Ray to Dear Bell, 3 Oct. 1839, *Colored American,* 2 Nov. 1839. On black residential clusters in Cincinnati in 1850, see Henry Louis Taylor, Jr., "On Slavery's Fringe: City Building and Black Community Development in Cincinnati, 1800–1850," *Ohio History* 95 (Winter-Spring 1986): 5–33.

20. Shaffer, *Cincinnati Directory, 1840,* 474; Population Census of 1840, Cincinnati; Trollope, *Domestic Manners,* 52; *Daily Cincinnati Gazette,* n.d., quoted in *Philanthropist,* 24 Mar. 1840.

21. *Proceedings of the Semi-Centenary Celebration of the African Methodist Episcopal Church of Cincinnati Held in Allen Temple, Feb. 8th, 9th, and 10th, 1874,* ed. Arnett (Cincinnati, 1874), 13–20, 62; Shotwell, *A History of the Schools of Cincinnati,* 447.

22. *Letters of Theodore Dwight Weld, Angelina Grimke Weld and Sarah Grimke, 1822–1844,* Gilbert H. Barnes and Dwight L. Dumond, eds. 2 vols. (New York: D. Appleton-Century, 1934), vol. 1, 132–35, 211–21, 250–54; Augustus Wattles to Henry Howe, n.d., in Henry Howe, *Historical Collections of Ohio* (Cincinnati, 1847), 356.

23. *Weld-Grimke Letters,* vol. 1, 192, 218, 179; Augustus Wattles to Susan Lowe, 28 Apr. 1835, Augustus Wattles Papers, Kansas State Historical Society; Shotwell, *A History of the Schools of Cincinnati,* 447.

24. David Nickens, a likely candidate for the honor of being the first ordained black Baptist minister in Ohio, served as pastor of the African Baptist

church organized in Chillicothe in the early 1820s. In a militant speech delivered in Chillicothe on July 5, 1832, Nickens called for black self-help and solidarity, asserting that once freed of white oppression, "we could stand forth with the enlightened men of the earth." By the mid-thirties he was in Cincinnati as pastor of the Union Baptist Church, a post he retained until his death in 1838 at the age of forty-four. William J. Simmons, *Men of Mark: Eminent, Progressive and Rising* (Cleveland, 1887; repr., Chicago: Johnson Publishing, 1970), 375–76; *Weld-Grimke Letters,* vol. 1, 192; Wendell P. Dabney, *Cincinnati's Colored Citizens: Historical, Sociological, and Biographical* (Cincinnati, 1926; repr., New York: Johnson Reprint, 1970), 371–72; Wattles, *Memorial . . . 1838,* 18–19. Quote from David Nickens, "Address to the People of Color in Chillicothe," 20 July 1832, *Liberator,* 11 Aug. 1832.

25. Quinn's ministry soon took him elsewhere. Daniel A. Payne, *History of the African Methodist Episcopal Church* (Nashville, 1891), 131, 137, 146, 170.

26. The Virginian William M. Johnson and his wife were in the 10-to-24 age category in the 1840 census; a female child and an elderly man resided in the household. An agent for the *Colored American* and the *Liberator* in Cincinnati, Johnson was prominent in local protest meetings and presided at the 1841 First of August ceremonies. He was the president of the 1843 black state convention in Columbus. Population Census of 1840, Cincinnati; *Colored American,* 2 Sept. 1837; *Philanthropist,* 20 Feb. 1838, 5 Mar. 1839, 18 Aug. 1841, 2 Oct. 1843.

27. After joining the A.M.E. church in December of 1824 in Cincinnati, the native Virginian Owen Nickens was appointed a local preacher. In March 1834, independent of the Lane Rebels, he started the "first successful colored school" in the city; three months later he was in New York, representing the state at the national black convention. The 1840 census puts Nickens in the 36-to-55 age category, head of a family of four. In 1844, with the ex-Tennessean A. M. Sumner, whose own experience as a schoolteacher added up to a "score of years," he edited Cincinnati's initial black newspaper, the *Disfranchised American.* When public education finally came to black Cincinnati in 1852, Nickens was awarded one of the three black teaching positions available. As late as 1874 Nickens was still teaching, but in a rural Ohio community. Owen T. B. Nickens to Rev. B. W. Arnett, 4 Feb. 1874, printed in *Proceedings of the Semi-Centenary,* ed. Arnett, 31; Payne, *History of the A.M.E. Church,* 61–63; Shotwell, *A History of the Schools of Cincinnati,* 447; *Minutes of the Fourth Annual Convention, for the Improvement of the Free People of Colour in the United States . . . New York, 1834* (New York, 1834), 9, reprinted in *Proceedings of the National Negro Conventions,* ed. Bell; Population Census of 1840, Cincinnati; *Palladium of Liberty,* 1 May 1844; *Philanthropist,* 24 Apr. 1844; *Eighth Annual Report . . . Colored Public Schools, Cincinnati, June 30, 1857* (Cincinnati, 1857), 13.

28. Theodore Weld to Louis Tappan, 18 Mar. 1834, *Weld-Grimke Letters,* vol. 1, 135; on the "Sisters," Emeline Bishop, Phoebe Matthews, and Susan Lowe, see *Weld-Grimke Letters,* vol. 1, 211–21, 250–54.

29. Edward Abdy, *Journal of a Residence and Tour in the United States of North America from April 1833 to October 1834*, 3 vols. (London, 1834), vol. 2, 400–404; *Report on the Condition of the People of Color, 1835*; A. Wattles to Editor, 3 July 1834, *Emancipator*, 26 Aug. 1834.

30. *Colored American*, 17 Oct. 1840; *Free Labor Advocate*, n.d., quoted in *Anti-Slavery Bugle*, 6 Nov. 1846; *Report on the Second Anniversary of the Ohio Anti-Slavery Society*, 62; Emma Wattles Morse, "Sketch of the Life and Work of Augustus Wattles," Wattles Papers.

31. *Philanthropist*, 9 Dec. 1836, 21 July 1840; Barber, *Report of the Colored People of Ohio*, 13; Cincinnati Board of Education, *Annual Report*, 30 June 1840. From April 1830, a year after the start of the public school system, until at least the end of 1843, blacks regularly petitioned the city council for a share of the public school funds. Shotwell, *A History of the Schools of Cincinnati*, 447; Abdy, *Journal*, vol. 2, 393–94, 400–401; *Philanthropist*, 24 Dec. 1842; *Cincinnati Herald*, 22 Dec. 1843.

32. *Report of the Second Anniversary of the Ohio Anti-Slavery Society*, 59–64; Barber, *Report of the Colored People of Ohio*, 13; *Philanthropist*, 26 Mar. 1839. John Wattles's census listed 509 members in 1845. *Philanthropist*, 30 Apr. 1845.

33. *Proceedings of the Semi-Centenary*, ed. Arnett, 13–21; Daniel Alexander Payne, *Recollections of Seventy Years* (Nashville, 1888), 104; Nickens to Arnett, 4 Feb. 1874, *Proceedings of the Semi-Centenary*, 31.

34. Oberlin *Evangelist*, 28 Aug. 1844; William J. Simmons, *Men of Mark: Eminent, Progressive, and Rising* (Cleveland, 1887; repr., Chicago: Johnson Publishing, 1971), 375–77; Wendell P. Dabney, *Cincinnati's Colored Citizens: Historical, Sociological, and Biographical* (Cincinnati, 1926; repr., New York: Johnson Reprint, 1970), 370–71.

35. Simmons, *Men of Mark*, 377; Barber, *Report of the Colored People of Ohio*, 12–13; *The Free People of Color*, ed. Katz, 253; *Cincinnati Daily Enquirer*, 2 June 1841; *Philanthropist*, 14 July 1841; *Daily Cincinnati Gazette*, 23 July 1844; Oberlin *Evangelist*, 28 Aug. 1844; *North Star*, 9 June 1848. The oldest church in black Cincinnati was the Union Chapel M.E. Church on Seventh Street, organized in 1815. *Proceedings of the Semi-Centenary*, ed. Arnett, 59. A city directory for 1846 lists five black churches: African Union Baptist, Zion Baptist, Bethel African Methodist, Episcopal Methodist, and New Wesleyan African. Charles Cist, *The Cincinnati Miscellany* . . . (Cincinnati, 1846), 81.

36. The first pastor of the Union Baptist Church was David Nickens. Charles Satchell, his successor, held the position from late 1838 to 1845. The 1840 census lists Satchell and his wife in the 24-to-36 age category and indicates that two children and an elderly woman were also in the house. Satchell was elected president of the Moral Reform Society of the Colored of Ohio in 1838. He attended the 1844 black state convention in Columbus. Simmons, *Men of Mark*, 371, 375–76; Shaffer, *Cincinnati Directory, 1840*, 475; Population Census of 1840, Cincinnati; *Philanthropist*, 20 Feb. 1838; *Palladium of Liberty*, 25 Sept. 1844.

37. William P. Newman, a fugitive slave from Virginia, studied for five years at Oberlin until 1843, the end of his sophomore year in college. A mercurial personality and fiery orator, he traveled extensively in Canada, helping to establish black schools as an agent of the Ladies' Education Society of Ohio and raising funds both for the society and the Union Baptist Church of Cincinnati. He served as Union Baptist's pastor from late 1848 until passage of the Fugitive Slave Law in September 1850. Pledging to "kill any so-called man who attempts to enslave me or mine," Newman immediately took his family (he and his wife and six children by 1864) to Chatham in modern-day Ontario—the first stop on an odyssey that included Haiti and Jamaica. In late 1864 he again became pastor of the Union Baptist. He died of cholera in Cincinnati in August 1866. His congregation erected a monument to him in its new cemetery and paid $1,000 for a homestead in Appleton, Wisconsin, for his family. *Philanthropist*, 2 July 1839, 14 Oct. 1843, 28 Aug. 1844, 24 Apr. 1844; Oberlin *Evangelist*, 17 Aug. 1842, 16 Aug. 1843, 20 Dec. 1843, 3 Jan. 1844, 28 Aug. 1844, 3 Jan. 1849; *Aliened American*, 9 Apr. 1853; *Palladium of Liberty*, 27 Dec. 1843; Dabney, *Colored Citizens*, 371; *Voice of the Fugitive*, 15 Jan. 1851; Robin Winks, *The Blacks in Canada* (New Haven, Conn.: Yale University Press, 1971), 164–65, 196, 199–201, 203, 231, 395; W. P. Newman to Editor, *American Baptist*, n.d., quoted in *Anti-Slavery Bugle*, 16 Mar. 1861; William P. Newman to Salmon P. Chase, 30 Nov. 1863, Chase Papers, Library of Congress; *Proceedings of the National Convention of Colored Men . . . Syracuse . . . Oct. 1864* (Boston, 1864). Quote from William P. Newman to Frederick Douglass, 1 Oct. 1850, *North Star*, 24 Oct. 1850.

38. Langston, *Virginia Plantation*, 62; Oberlin *Evangelist*, 28 Aug. 1844; Dabney, *Colored Citizens*, 371.

39. In the 1820s and 1830s Wallace Shelton organized Baptist churches in various parts of Ohio. An ex-slave, he was the chaplain of the first Ohio black state convention in 1837. The same year he was one of the nearly two hundred black Cincinnatians who petitioned the state legislature to abolish the Black Laws. In the late thirties and early forties Shelton occupied pulpits in Dayton and Columbus. In early 1843 he and thirty-nine other members of the Baker Street Baptist Church in Cincinnati decided to form the Zion Baptist Church, of which he was the minister for thirty years. An Underground Railroad agent, Shelton was active in local and state protest causes throughout the forties and fifties. In 1873 he became the acting pastor of the newly organized Mt. Zion Baptist Church. Lewis G. Jordan, *Negro Baptist History* (Nashville, 1930), 61; *Frederick Douglass' Paper*, 11 Aug. 1854, 18 Aug. 1854, 1 Sept. 1854; *Philanthropist*, 8 Sept. 1837, 20 Feb. 1838, 13 Aug. 1839, 31 May 1843, 12 July 1843, 10 June 1846, 11 Nov. 1846; Columbus, Ohio, Chapter of the Frontiers of America, ed., *Negroes' Contribution in Franklin County, 1803–1953* (Columbus, 1954), 7; *Proceedings of the Semi-Centenary*, ed. Arnett, 62; Wilbur Henry Siebert, *The Mysteries of Ohio's Underground Railroads* (Columbus, 1951), 31; *State Convention of the Colored Citizens of Ohio . . . Columbus . . . Jan. 1849* (Oberlin, 1849); *Cleve-*

land Leader, 25 Oct. 1858. A picture of the "Father of the Zion Baptist Church" is in Dabney, *Colored Citizens*, 94.

40. Simmons, *Men of Mark*, 376.

41. *Provincial Freeman*, 19 Jan. 1856, 8 Dec. 1855; Fredrika Bremer, *The Homes of the New World*, 2 vols. (New York: Harper and Brothers, 1853), vol. 2, 157–59; Ebenezer Davies, *American Scenes and Christian Slavery* (London: J. Snow, 1849), 156, 152–53.

42. *Weld-Grimke Letters*, vol. 1, 179, 192, 218; Barber, *Report of the Colored People of Ohio*, 13; Augustus Wattles, *Memorial of the Ohio Anti-Slavery Society to the General Assembly of the State of Ohio* (Cincinnati, 1838), 17; *State Convention of the Colored Citizens of Ohio, 1849;* Payne, *History of the A.M.E. Church*, 193–94.

43. *Philanthropist*, 22 Nov. 1843; J. Madison Bell, "Poem—Now and Then," in *Proceedings of the Semi-Centenary*, ed. Arnett, 91.

44. The twenty-two leaders were Thomas Bascoe, Va., plasterer; Henry Boyd, Ky., carpenter and bedstead manufacturer; George Cary, Va., huckster; Thomas Crissup, Va., carpenter; Joshua B. Delany, Ohio, steward; Thomas Dorum, Ky., whitewasher; Joseph Fowler, Va., huckster; A. J. Gordon, Va., barber; John Hatfield, Pa., barber; Dennis Hill, Md., tanner; William M. Johnson, Va., painter; Gideon Quarles Langston, Va., barber and owner of a livery stable; John Liverpool, Va., barber; Owen T. B. Nickens, Va., white-washer; William O'Hara, Va., barber; Richard Phillips, Md., huckster; Charles Satchell, Va., dyer; A. M. Sumner, Tenn., schoolteacher; John Tinsley, Va., carpenter; William W. Watson, Va., barber; John Woodson, Va., carpenter; and W. H. Yancy, Va., barber. A partial list of sources for the twenty-two leaders includes the newspapers, directories, censuses, antislavery convention reports, published church records, and masters' theses cited throughout these chapter notes. Also beginning to be active in the early forties in black protest were two very young men, John I. Gaines (see note 11), a stevedore, and Joseph Henry Perkins (see note 87), who worked in navigation. By the late forties, Langston's contemporary Peter H. Clark was active (see note 80). All three were to become major local and state leaders. Rev. Wallace Shelton became an important leader in the city when he finally settled there permanently in the early forties (see note 39).

45. John Wattles found that an adult black population of 1,903, of whom 343 could read and write, accounted for a total of seven hundred newspaper subscriptions. See *Philanthropist*, 30 Apr. 1845; list of subscribers in *Philanthropist*, 30 June 1841, 17 Nov. 1841; George Cary to editor, 18 Aug. 1837, *Colored American*, 2 Sept. 1837; Ray to Bell, 16 Sept. 1839, *Colored American*, 5 Oct. 1839.

46. On Gordon, see note 89. The two black newspapers were the *Disfranchised American* (1844), edited by O. T. B. Nickens and A. M. Sumner, and the *Colored Citizen* (1845–46), edited by W. H. Yancy and Rev. Thomas Woodson. On Liverpool's association with the national convention movement, see *Minutes and Proceedings of the First Annual Convention of the People of Color . . . June 1831* (Philadelphia, 1831), 9; *Minutes and Pro-*

ceedings of the Second Annual Convention . . . June 1832 (Philadelphia, 1832), 15, both reprinted in *Proceedings of the National Negro Conventions*, ed. Bell. For the Underground Railroad activities of O'Hara, see *Philanthropist*, 23 Oct. 1840, and *Cincinnati Daily Enquirer*, 9 Aug. 1841; for Hatfield, see Laura Haviland, *A Woman's Life-Work* (Chicago, 1889; repr., New York: Arno Press, 1969), 166, and Wilbur Henry Siebert, *The Underground Railroad from Slavery to Freedom* (New York: MacMillan, 1898), 422.

47. *Emancipator,* 22 Apr. 1834; *Provincial Freeman,* 3 Nov. 1855; *Colored American,* 12 Oct. 1839.

48. Statement of the Board of Managers of the Colored Education Society, *Emancipator,* 13 Apr. 1837.

49. *The Address and Reply on the Presentation of a Testimonial to S. P. Chase, by the Colored People of Cincinnati* (Cincinnati, 1845), 19, 33–34.

50. Henry Cowles, "Oberlin College Catalogue and Records of Colored Students, 1835–62," Manuscript, Henry Cowles Papers, Oberlin College Library; *Daily Cleveland Gazette,* 24 Dec. 1892; Charles Cist, *Cincinnati Directory for the Year 1842* (Cincinnati, 1842), 395.

51. Langston, *Virginia Plantation,* 60–61; *Philanthropist,* 20 Feb. 1838, 14, 21 July 1840, 4 Nov. 1840, 21 Dec. 1842; *The Free People of Color,* ed. Katz, 252; Dabney, *Colored Citizens,* 357, 106–7. The 1840 census lists Woodson and his wife in the 24–to–36 age category. Population Census of 1840, Cincinnati; *Report of the Second Anniversary of the Ohio Anti-Slavery Society,* 64.

52. Langston, *Virginia Plantation,* 60; Barber, *Report of the Colored People of Ohio,* 13; Shotwell, *A History of the Schools of Cincinnati,* 452–53; Abdy, *Journal,* vol. 2, 401.

53. *Philanthropist,* 26 Nov. 1839, 14 July 1840; *Report of the Second Anniversary of the Ohio Anti-Slavery Society,* 59, 65; *North Star,* 9 June 1848. On Hiram Gilmore's high school, see the sketch written by Peter H. Clark and L. D. Easton in Shotwell, *A History of the Schools of Cincinnati,* iii, 453–54.

54. Trollope, *Domestic Manners,* 427–28; *Weld-Grimke Letters,* vol. 1, 216. "Studying" meant prayerful reflection.

55. *Emancipator,* 21 Dec. 1843; Epstein, *Sinful Tunes and Spirituals,* 165–66.

56. Frederick J. Blue, *Salmon P. Chase: A Life in Politics* (Kent, Ohio: Kent State University Press, 1987), 31–34, 36; J. W. Schuckers, *The Life and Public Services of Salmon Portland Chase* (New York, 1874; repr. Miami: Mnemosyne Publishing, 1969), 41–44; *Philanthropist,* 30 June 1841, 18 Aug. 1841; *Cincinnati Daily Enquirer,* 26 June 1841.

57. *The Free People of Color,* ed. Katz, 253; *Anti-Slavery Bugle,* 24 Aug. 1850; *Philanthropist,* 4 Nov. 1840; *Proceedings of the Semi-Centenary,* ed. Arnett, 19; Siebert, *The Mysteries of Ohio's Underground Railroads,* 31; Abdy, *Journal,* vol. 3, 23; Dwight L. Dumond, *Letters of James Gillespie Birney,* 2 vols. (New York, 1938), vol. 1, 376; Levi Coffin, *Reminiscences of*

Levi Coffin (Cincinnati, 1892; repr., New York: Arno Press, 1968), 297; "Cincinnatus" to Frederick Douglass, 3 July 1848, *North Star*, 11 Aug. 1848; interview with John Hatfield in Benjamin Drew, *The Refugee: A North-Side View of Slavery* (Boston, 1856; repr., Reading, Mass.: Addison Wesley, 1969), 256.

58. Langston, *Virginia Plantation*, 62; *Philanthropist*, 30 June 1841; *Cincinnati Daily Enquirer*, 9, 10 Aug. 1841. Although George Cary, the president of the Iron Chest Company (of which O'Hara was treasurer), did aid fugitives, William Casey, whose occupation and residence in Post Office Alley abetted his Underground Railroad work, was even better known in this capacity. *Philanthropist*, 4 Nov. 1840; Shaffer, *Cincinnati Directory, 1840,* 468; Haviland, *A Woman's Life-Work,* 112, 129, 135, 161, 166; Coffin, *Reminiscences,* 308, 330–32, 339, 347–48; *Cincinnati Herald*, n.d., quoted in *Anti-Slavery Bugle*, 7 July 1848.

59. *Philanthropist*, 18 Aug. 1841; *Colored American*, 25 Aug. 1838; J. H. Perkins, *Oration, Delivered on the First of August 1849 Before the Colored Citizens of Cincinnati* (Cincinnati, 1849), 25.

60. Abdy, *Journal*, vol. 1, 117; *Cincinnati Daily Enquirer*, 9, 10, 25 Sept. 1841; "A Workey" to Editor, *Cincinnati Daily Enquirer*, 10 Sept. 1841.

61. *Cincinnati Daily Enquirer*, 10 Aug. 1841; *Emancipator*, 23 Sept. 1841; *Philanthropist*, 4 Aug. 1841.

62. All of the city's newspapers covered the riot. See reprints in the *Philanthropist*, 8 Sept. 1841, and summaries of precipitating events in the *Daily Cincinnati Gazette*, 6 Sept. 1841; *Daily Cincinnati Chronicle*, 4 Sept. 1841; *Cincinnati Daily Enquirer*, 3, 4, 9 Sept. 1841; see also Richards, *"Gentlemen of Property and Standing,"* 124–29; and Woodson, "The Negroes of Cincinnati," 12–16.

63. Langston, *Virginia Plantation*, 63–64. An elder of the A.M.E. church, Wilkerson acted as the principal fundraiser for the church's Union Seminary, a manual labor school set up some twelve miles west of Columbus in 1845. During the Civil War Wilkerson reportedly became a Quaker. Major James Wilkerson, *Wilkerson's History of His Travels and Labors in the United States, as Missionary, in Particular that of the Union Seminary* (Columbus, 1861), 25, 4, 33–34, and passim; Payne, *History of the A.M.E. Church,* 161, 185–86; A. G. B. to Editor, *Anglo-African*, 28 Feb. 1863.

64. Langston, *Virginia Plantation*, 63; *Daily Cincinnati Gazette*, 6 Sept. 1841; *Daily Cincinnati Chronicle*, 4 Sept. 1841; *Cincinnati Republican*, 6 Sept. 1841, quoted in *Philanthropist*, 8 Sept. 1841; *Cincinnati Daily Enquirer*, 9 Sept. 1841.

65. James Hall et al. to Editor, *Cincinnati Daily Enquirer*, 18 Sept. 1841. Young, a steamboat steward and later a cook, by 1850 was one of the wealthiest blacks in the city, with property valued at $3,900. The ex-Virginian also served as a trustee of the Colored Orphan Asylum. Shaffer, *Cincinnati Directory, 1840,* 477; Riley, "The Negro in Cincinnati, 1835–1850," 74; *Cleveland True-Democrat*, 22 Feb. 1848.

66. *Liberator*, 17, 24 Sept. 1841; *Cincinnati Daily Enquirer*, 9 Sept. 1841; *Philanthropist*, 8 Sept. 1841.

67. *Daily Cincinnati Gazette*, 6 Sept. 1841; Langston, *Virginia Plantation*, 64; *Daily Cincinnati Chronicle*, 6 Sept. 1841, quoted in *Philanthropist*, 8 Sept. 1841; *Philanthropist*, 8 Sept. 1841; *Cincinnati Daily Enquirer*, 9 Sept. 1841.

68. Langston, *Virginia Plantation*, 64–65; see similar argument in *Philanthropist*, 8 Sept. 1841.

69. Langston, *Virginia Plantation*, 65–66.

70. *Daily Cincinnati Chronicle*, 6 Sept. 1841, quoted in *Philanthropist*, 8 Sept. 1841; *Philanthropist*, 8, 22 Sept. 1841; *Daily Cincinnati Gazette*, 6 Sept. 1841.

71. Langston, *Virginia Plantation*, 67.

72. Leonard P. Curry, *The Free Black in Urban America, 1800–1850* (Chicago: University of Chicago Press, 1981), 107; Langston, *Virginia Plantation*, 64. Casualty reports varied: 30 whites seriously wounded, *Daily Cincinnati Gazette*, 6 Sept. 1841; 15 to 20 injured, primarily whites, 4 dead (2 white, 2 black), *Niles' National Register*, 11 Sept. 1841; J. Nicholson, a white man from Newport, Ky., dead, 2 unnamed black men dead or dying, *Cincinnati Daily Enquirer*, 6 Sept. 1841.

73. *Cincinnati Daily Enquirer*, 8, 10 Sept. 1841; *Daily Cincinnati Gazette*, 7 Sept. 1841; *Philanthropist*, 22 Sept. 1841.

74. *Cincinnati Daily Enquirer*, 10, 11, 14, 18, 21, 25 Sept. 1841, 24 Jan. 1842; Richards, *"Gentlemen of Property and Standing,"* 129; Joel Goldfarb, "The Life of Gamaliel Bailey, Prior to the Founding of the *National Era* . . . " (Ph.D. diss., University of California at Los Angeles, 1958), chapter 16, cited in Richards, *"Gentlemen of Property and Standing,"* 128; Langston, *Virginia Plantation*, 66.

75. *Philanthropist*, 30 Apr. 1845; "Annual Report of the Ladies Education Society," *Philanthropist*, 29 June 1842; "A Colored Man" to Editor, *Philanthropist*, 28 Dec. 1842; William E. Walker to Hamilton Hill, 7 Oct. 1842, Oberlin College Library; *Daily Cincinnati Chronicle*, n.d., quoted in *Philanthropist*, 10 Nov. 1841.

76. *Minutes of the National Convention of Colored Citizens . . . Buffalo, N.Y . . . Aug. 1843* (New York, 1843), 18, reprinted in *Proceedings of the National Negro Conventions*, ed. Bell; William C. Nell to Editor, *Liberator*, 21 Nov. 1856; Langston, *Virginia Plantation*, 66–67.

77. Langston, *Virginia Plantation*, 69–71; Deed Record 40, Ross County Courthouse, Chillicothe, Ohio; *San Francisco Post*, 5 Apr. 1877, in John Mercer Langston Scrapbooks, 4 vols., vol. 1, Moorland-Spingarn Research Center, Howard University.

78. Langston, *Virginia Plantation*, 61; *Colored American*, 17 Oct. 1840; *Philanthropist*, 14 July 1840; *Anti-Slavery Bugle*, 10 Aug. 1850; Stowe, *Uncle Tom's Cabin*, 319–21.

79. Langston, *Virginia Plantation*, 61; Population Census of 1840, Cincinnati; Frederick Douglass, "Character and Condition of Colored of Cincinnati," *North Star*, n.d., quoted in *Anti-Slavery Bugle*, 10 Aug. 1950.

80. Langston, *Virginia Plantation*, 61; Peter Clark to Caroline Langston, 11 Dec. 1897, Caroline W. Langston Papers, Fisk University Library; "Rem-

iniscences—Professor Peter H. Clark" (at John Mercer Langston Memorial Meeting, St. Louis, 6 Feb. 1898), news clipping, n.d., John Mercer Langston Papers, Fisk University Library. There is no biography of Peter Clark. The best account of his life is David A. Gerber, "Peter Humphries Clark: The Dialogue of Hope and Despair," in *Black Leaders of the Nineteenth Century,* ed. Leon Litwack and August Meier (Urbana: University of Illinois Press, 1988), 173–90. Gerber errs in describing Clark as the stepson of John Isom Gaines; in actuality Clark's grandmother Elizabeth was Gaines's mother (see note 11). See also Herbert Gutman, "Peter H. Clark: Pioneer Negro Socialist, 1877," in *Journal of Negro Education* 34 (Fall 1965); Philip S. Foner, "Peter H. Clark, Pioneer Negro Socialist," *Journal of Ethnic Studies* 5 (1977); Lawrence Grossman, "In His Veins Coursed No Bootlicking Blood: The Career of Peter H. Clark," *Ohio History* 83 (1977); Dovie King Clark, "Peter Humphries Clark," *Negro History Bulletin* 5 (May 1942): 176; Simmons, *Men of Mark,* 244–49.

81. Langston, *Virginia Plantation,* 72; *Report of the Proceedings of the Colored National Convention . . . Cleveland . . . Sept. 1848* (Rochester, 1848), 17, reprinted in *Proceedings of the National Negro Conventions,* ed. Bell; Cleveland *Leader,* 2 Aug. 1866; Simmons, *Men of Mark,* 244–45.

82. Langston, *Virginia Plantation,* 72, 61; *Report of the Second Anniversary of the Ohio Anti-Slavery Society,* 65; Barber, *Report of the Colored People of Ohio,* 13; Bremer, *Homes of the New World,* vol. 2, 157; John Mercer Langston, *Freedom and Citizenship* (Washington, D.C., 1883; repr., Miami, Mnemosyne Reprint, 1969), 135–36.

83. Langston, *Virginia Plantation,* 60; Ohio Anti-Slavery Convention, *Report on the Condition of the People of Color of Ohio,* 5; W. D. Howells, *A Boy's Town* (New York: Harper and Brothers Press, 1890), 124–25.

84. Langston, *Virginia Plantation,* 66, 181; Howard Jones, *Mutiny on the Amistad* (New York: Oxford University Press, 1987); Brown, *The Rising Son,* 325–28; Joseph Sturge, *A Visit to the United States in 1841* (London, 1842; repr., New York, A. M. Kelley Reprint, 1969), 50, appendix E, xxxi–li; *Weld-Grimke Letters,* vol. 2, 811; *Philanthropist,* 18 Nov. 1840, 9 Dec. 1840, 22 Nov. 1843. One of the *Amistad* captives, Mar-gru [Sarah Kinson] attended Oberlin while Langston was a student there.

85. *Philanthropist,* 22 Nov. 1843; Langston, *Virginia Plantation,* 355, 157.

86. Martineau, *Retrospect of Western Travel,* vol. 2, 52–53; *Philanthropist,* 9 Dec. 1836, 26 Jan. 1844; Langston, *Virginia Plantation,* 60.

87. Of the major Cincinnati black leaders of the period, least is known of Perkins. The 1840 census lists him and his wife in the 10–to–24 age category. A student at Gilmore High School in the mid-forties, he attended the 1844 state convention and delivered the 1849 First of August oration in Cincinnati. Shotwell, *A History of the Schools of Cincinnati,* 454–55; Population Census of 1840, Cincinnati; *Palladium of Liberty,* 25 Sept. 1844; Perkins, *Oration.*

88. *Anti-Slavery Bugle,* 24 Aug. 1850.

89. Andrew J. Gordon, a native Virginian listed, along with his wife, in the 10–to–24 age column in the 1840 census, took a leading role in black affairs on a local, state, and national level for more than two decades. In 1843, having served as secretary of a meeting in New York to determine whether to have a national convention, he served as a delegate from Cincinnati to the convention, which was held in Buffalo, New York, in August. President of the 1853 Ohio state convention at Columbus, Gordon was a barber in Cleveland during the fifties, where he served as a member of the "Committee of 9," the city's black Underground Railroad directors. In 1859 he advised the members of a black meeting in Cincinnati against adopting a strong resolution in favor of John Brown, reminding them of the damage done to the community by the 1841 riot. In June 1860 he was elected a trustee of the Colored Public Schools for the Western District of Cincinnati. Shaffer, *Cincinnati Directory, 1840,* 471; Population Census of 1840, Cincinnati; *National Convention, 1843,* 3, reprinted in *Proceedings of the National Negro Conventions,* ed. Bell; *Frederick Douglass' Paper,* 6 July 1854; *Official Proceedings of the Ohio State Convention of Colored Freemen . . . Columbus . . . Jan. 1853* (Cleveland, 1853); *Cincinnati Daily Enquirer,* 16 Nov. 1859; *Daily Cincinnati Gazette,* 26 June 1860.

90. *Address and Reply on the Presentation of a Testimonial to S. P. Chase,* 17 and passim. On Chase's serious commitment to black America, see Blue, *Salmon P. Chase.*

91. Langston, *Virginia Plantation,* 67; Gaines's comment, *Eighth Annual Report . . . Colored Public Schools, Cincinnati,* 12; John Quincy Adams, *Memoirs of John Quincy Adams* (Philadelphia, 1886), 428–29; *Philanthropist,* 15 Mar. 1843, 22 Nov. 1843, 14 Oct. 1846; John Mercer Langston, "The Langstons," *Daily Cleveland Gazette,* 24 Dec. 1892.

92. *Philanthropist,* 2 Oct. 1843; Langston, *Virginia Plantation,* 73, 67.

3

JAMES OLIVER HORTON AND STACY FLAHERTY

Black Leadership in
Antebellum Cincinnati

Standing before the Ohio state gathering of black representatives in the Bethel Church of Columbus in early January 1849, Cincinnati delegate Rev. Wallace Shelton, addressed the two major issues of the convention. On the question of slavery, Rev. Shelton stood firmly on the ground of abolition, urging that blacks be willing to work with those whites who advocated freedom but dismiss those who refused to condemn slaveholding and those who "would fellowship with slaveholders or their abettors."[1] On the question of colonization, the other burning issue of the convention, Rev. Shelton was just as candid. "We are free born Americans, but are robbed of our rights by our American-born brethren." Not limited to a concern for the rights of free blacks alone, he desired to maintain and increase the pressure of the antislavery movement. Rev. Shelton counseled rejection of the American Colonization Society's plan to transplant free blacks to West Africa. "Stay where you are," he urged, "and never leave this land as long as one chain is to be heard clanking, or the cry of millions is to be heard floating on every breeze."[2]

For the free blacks of Cincinnati in the years before the Civil War, these were the great national issues. And with minor exceptions, these were the popular positions. In this regard, Shelton and his fellow Cincinnati representatives, Charles M. Wilson, John T. Ward, and James McGowan, reflected the views of the city's black community. They were chosen in the fall of 1848 at a citywide meeting of Cincinnati blacks called to consider local and national concerns of the race. During the next two decades black Cincinnatians gathered on numerous occasions to discuss mutual problems and to plan concerted action. In the process they selected from their number those deemed specially suited for leadership. This chapter is a study of those chosen to lead.

It focuses on leaders drawn from the local Cincinnati community, even though African Americans in antebellum Cincinnati were not unaware of, or unaffected by, the great national black leaders of the period. Frederick Douglass, Sojourner Truth, William Wells Brown, Martin R. Delany, and other nationally and internationally known black Americans visited the city and commanded the respect and loyalty of black Cincinnati, but theirs was a more periodic and a more distant influence. Those who provided day-to-day direction lived in the local community.

The relative importance of national and local black leaders is a well-discussed issue. Many nineteenth-century blacks believed that "the only leaders among the colored people [were] those whom they personally [knew] and [who] live[d] and associate[d] among them." A century later historian Nell Irvin Painter argued that we are likely to misunderstand local concerns if we focus on the influence of national black leaders. She and others have argued persuasively that although national black leaders influenced local black communities, they often depended on white patronage for the basis of their power and were not necessarily in touch with grass-roots black sentiment.[3]

The local leaders of Cincinnati's black community had many distinguishing characteristics. They were in several ways advantaged members of the community. Yet they were not an isolated elite. Most lived among and interacted with black Cincinnatians regularly, sharing their concerns.

These assertions are based on our analysis of data on eighty-two Cincinnati blacks whose names were drawn from primary documents produced between 1830 and 1860. These included lists of officers elected at community gatherings of black Cincinnatians, lists of community representatives selected to attend local, state, and national conventions, lists of organizational leaders, and lists of those elected to serve on the school committee of the separate African American school system created during the 1840s.

We distinguish between local black achievers and leaders. Those eligible for our leadership list (see Table 3.1) must have headed a group or have been selected for an organizational office or position.

Table 3.1. Cincinnati African American Leaders Identified by
This Study

Alexander, William	Harrison, William Henry
Anderson, Alfred J.	Hatch, Richard
Austin, Alphea	Hawkins, Julius
Ball, James P. (J. Presley Ball)	Hill, Dennis
Ball, R. G. (Robert)	Hunster, Jerusha (Mrs. William)
Ball, Thomas	Jackson, Jane J.
Ball, V. (Victoria; Mrs. James Ball)	Jackson, John
Beeckley, William	Johnson, George
Bentley, Milton	Johnson, James
Bowman, Jeremiah	Jones, Marshall P. H.
Boyd, Henry	Keith, Ismael
Brodie, G. W.	Lewis, Hensley
Brown, James	Liverpool, John
Buckner, Rev. William A.	Mann, William (W. H. Mann)
Carrel, Samuel	McGowan, James (Jesse)
Casey, William	Moore, Jackson
Clark, Peter H.	Moore, Joseph H.
Cole, Coleman	Nelson, William
Coleman, Elizabeth	Nickens, Vurn T. B. (Owen)
Collins, Jesse	Param, W.
Conrad, Richard	Parham, Hartwell
Cooper, E. (Emma)	Perkins, Joseph Henry
Cooper, Eveline	Peterson, George
Corbin, Joseph C.	Phillips, Richard
Darnes, William	Robinson, W.
Early, Joseph H.	Roots, George W.
Ellison, William	Satchell, Charles
Ernest, Sarah	Speer, Henry (H. P. Spears)
Ferguson, P. B.	Thomas, Alexander
Ferguson, William	Thompson, Alfred V.
Fluellan, L. C. (Lovewell)	Tilley, Virginia
Fowler, Joseph J.	Toliver, Philip
Gaines, John I.	Troy, Isaac M.
Gibson, Daniel	Ward, John T.
Gibson, Mary	Watson, William W.
Goff, William D.	West, William P.
Goode, Thomas	Wilcox, Samuel I.
Gordon, Andrew J.	Williams, Amelia
Gordon, Robert	Wilson, Charles M.
Gray, Daniel	Wilson, Isaac
Harris, Catherine	

It was not enough to have been successful in business or to have accumulated great wealth. Jesse Beeckley, for example, was a wealthy roofer from Virginia with real estate worth more than $10,000 in 1850, but he was not included in our list of Cincinnati leaders. Although he achieved great local prominence, became a man of influence, and associated with several community leaders, so far as we could determine, Beeckley did not lead any community organization, nor was he elected to any representative office. It might be argued that achievers are leaders in terms of the example they set, especially in view of the importance placed on black role models, but we elected a more narrow and, we believe, a more defensible definition.[4]

We traced the names of black leaders on our list through the federal censuses for 1850 and 1860, Cincinnati probate records (including wills and personal property inventories), city directories, local and national newspapers, a list of officials elected to the city's African American school board, the records of Ohio state colored conventions, and the records of the national colored conventions. The extensive records compiled by the Black Abolitionist Papers project were also used to track the activities of Cincinnati black leaders.[5]

There are disadvantages inherent in this methodology. Because our leadership list was assembled from public documents and from formal organizational records, it is heavily biased in favor of men. Black women were less likely to be elected to organizational office or be community delegates to state or national conventions. In fact, black men disagreed over whether women should be allowed to attend these gatherings other than in limited, often domestic, roles. In a few instances black women successfully protested their exclusion, but they remained underrepresented among the community-wide elected representatives. Several women's organizations were active in the city throughout the antebellum period. The Colored Ladies' Anti-Slavery Sewing Circle of Cincinnati, the Daughters of Temperance, and countless bazaars and fairs organized and administered by black women raised funds for community services and protest action. African American women played a vital role in the financial support of Cincinnati's many male-dominated political and social organizations. Unfortunately, records of these activities are not abundant, and even when they are available they tend not to give the names of elected officers. It is also noteworthy that leadership roles among women were generally different from those among men. Decision making in female organizations was often by the consensus of the membership, with less emphasis placed on individual leaders. Names of women were gathered where possible, but it is certain that black female leadership was more extensive and of greater consequence than the data here suggest.[6]

Another disadvantage of our selection process is that it favors the leaders of established, and thus more middle-class—oriented, organizations over the leaders of less formally organized actions of the poor. Yet since this study is concerned with the extent to which formally selected community leadership associated with the masses of poor that constituted black Cincinnati during this period, it does reveal information about leadership at all levels of the society.

To judge the connections between these leaders and the city's black community we drew several comparisons. We compared leaders and non-leaders in terms of regional birthplace, shade of color, marriage patterns, literacy rate, residential patterns, and occupational patterns. Our findings not only shed light on the differences and similarities between black leaders and non-leaders but also suggested structural patterns within the black community that marked Cincinnati's distinctive position as a border city.

Our analysis is mindful of the specific social, economic, and political setting within which the Cincinnati black community took shape. As blacks traveled from one community to another in the United States they found many familiar lifestyles and institutional forms, but no single model explains the variety of black community structures except in the most general sense. Although they shared common concerns and problems with blacks elsewhere, Cincinnati's African Americans shaped their community to fit their local circumstances.

The city was geographically northern, but it looked southward economically and politically. It was a border city within which the traditions of North and South met, shaping lifestyles and race relations. The Northwest Ordinance of 1797 made slavery illegal within the Ohio territory, and when Ohio joined the Union in 1803, it did so as a free state. Yet Cincinnati, the fifth largest city in the nation by 1850 and the most important city west of the Alleghenies, was situated on the southern boundary of the state, just across the Ohio River from slaveholding Kentucky. Thus it had substantial and regular contact with the South. The Cumberland Road traversed Ohio and brought settlers from the slave states of Virginia, Maryland, and Delaware. The Ohio River, which connected to the Mississippi, regularly carried not only southern settlers but traders and planters from the deep South on their way to do business in the city. Southern businessmen, attracted by the city's reputation as "Porkopolis," came to Cincinnati to buy meats and other foodstuffs for the South's plantations.

Economically and socially Cincinnati was tied to the southern port cities along the Mississippi River.

By 1829 Cincinnati's river commerce, which began modestly in 1805, had a value of over seven million dollars. Much of this money came from trade with the South. Throughout the antebellum years Cincinnati remained a major commercial and financial center for southern planters. The patronage of visiting planters became an important part of the city's restaurant and hotel business. Although some visitors to Cincinnati during these years were unimpressed with the unstructured growth of this "this ditch between the hills," by 1840 the steamboat had turned this once-small muddy riverfront town into the "Queen City of the West."[7]

The strong southern influence in the city greatly affected white attitudes toward the free black community. White Cincinnatians, many of whom had migrated from the South to escape the presence of blacks, slave or free, were troubled by the growing African American presence, and they launched local and statewide efforts to curb the growth of the black population. In 1804 and again in 1807 the Ohio legislature passed Black Laws that, among other things, restricted African American settlement in the state. These laws required black migrants to register with local authorities within twenty days of their arrival in Ohio and to post a five-hundred-dollar bond guaranteeing their good conduct and self-support.[8]

Despite restrictions and periodic violence against the African American community, the black population of Cincinnati grew to 1,100 in 1830 (of 24,831 total population), to over 3,200 (of 112,198) by mid-century, and to over 3,750 (of 161,044) by 1860. The city never faced a realistic threat of overwhelming numbers of African Americans, however, because the white population, especially Irish and German immigrants, grew even more rapidly. The percentage of blacks in the city population actually dropped from almost 4.5 percent in 1830 to just over 2 percent on the eve of the Civil War.[9]

Still Cincinnati's black community was among the most important in the antebellum North. It was on the front lines of the Underground Railroad and the antislavery movement. The city was the receiving ground for untold numbers of runaway slaves from south of the Ohio River. Individual blacks provided food, clothing, shelter, and a variety of other services, from financial support and jobs to direct action in defense of fugitives in need. Community leaders often coordinated and facilitated these activities, sometimes calling upon the assistance of white reformers with whom they had influence.

Table 3.2. Regional Origins of Cincinnati Blacks

	1850			1860		
	South (%)	North (%)	Other (%)	South (%)	North (%)	Other (%)
All blacks	72	26	2	72	26	2
Black leaders	74	26	0	55	43	2
When Ohio-born Blacks Were Removed from the Count						
All blacks	84	13	3	88	10	2
Black leaders	95	5	—	89	8	3

Source: Compiled from the manuscript schedules of the U.S. population censuses, 1850 and 1860, for Cincinnati.

They also filled crucial roles in civil rights actions and in efforts at community self-help. Peter H. Clark, for example, led the fight for black education. Although public education was mandated in Cincinnati through state law as early as 1825, no public schools were made available for African Americans. A series of provisions throughout the 1830s alternated between allowing property taxes collected from blacks to go toward the support of black education and disallowing such a provision.

Finally, in 1849 blacks were assured by the state that a portion of their taxes would be applied toward the support of their schools. Further, they were given control over their own schools, and males were permitted to elect an independent school board. Clark was elected as the head of the board, and under his leadership, the community at last received enough public funds to construct a school building in 1858.[10]

Within a hostile and restrictive atmosphere Cincinnati blacks carved out a community that both reflected and contrasted with the city's wider society. Like its whites, Cincinnati's African Americans were largely southern born, a fact that added to the city's distinctly southern flavor. At mid-century over 70 percent of the city's officially recorded adult black population was southern born (see Table 3.2). Almost two-thirds of them were born in the states of neighboring Virginia and Kentucky, but a number of them (almost one-fifth) came from the deep South, reflecting the significance of Mississippi–Ohio River travel routes. These figures do not include the hundreds of fugitive slaves in the city and, therefore, underestimate the true proportion of southern-born blacks.[11]

The southern character of the city and of its black community helped to determine the demographics of the local black leadership. At mid-century more than three-quarters of those who spoke and acted for the community or who led it into action were southern born, just two percentage points more than for Cincinnati blacks generally.

By 1860 the percentage of leaders born in the South had dropped to 55 percent, but this decline was not as dramatic as it appeared. It did not indicate a rise in the number of blacks entering Ohio from other northern states and taking over leadership roles. Instead, it reflected the numbers of Ohio-born blacks growing to maturity and becoming leaders, often following in the footsteps of their southern-born parents. Like others in the community, most non-Ohio-born leaders hailed from southern border states. And, like other southern-born blacks, they were deeply concerned about the welfare of friends and family left behind in slavery.

Elizabeth Coleman and Sarah Ernest were examples of southern-born women who led groups in Cincinnati dedicated to assisting fugitive slaves. They led the Anti-Slavery Sewing Society, which produced clothing for runaways. Generally fugitives arrived in Cincinnati with inadequate winter clothing, so the society's efforts were especially important to fugitives bound for Canada. James Brown was a leader in the Canadian emigration movement, and he was also a southerner from Kentucky. He made several trips into his home state from Cincinnati to aid slaves in escaping to Ohio. On one occasion he was captured in Louisville, but he was able to escape, after which he settled in Canada.[12]

Other southerners, active in the Underground Railroad, also gained influence among Cincinnati blacks. P. B. Ferguson, a cabinetmaker from Virginia, represented Cincinnati at the 1858 Ohio state convention of free blacks, while William D. Goff, a barber from Tennessee, was elected secretary to that body. The Kentuckian Dennis Hill was president of the Cincinnati Union Society of Colored Persons during the 1830s and remained active throughout the 1840s in various leadership roles within that and several other local organizations.[13]

In 1850 the proportion of leaders born in northern states approximated the proportion of northern-born black Cincinnatians. Almost all of these northern-born leaders, however, were natives of Ohio. Only four leaders were not—three from Pennsylvania and one from Indiana. The most prominent non-Ohio-born leader was William Darnes of Pennsylvania, who was vice president of the 1852 state freedmen convention and chairman of a Cincinnati black antislavery group during the 1830s that heartily endorsed the militancy of

Table 3.3. Age Distribution, in Years

	1850	1860
All Cincinnati Black Adults		
Mean age	33.4	34.2
Median age	29.6	30.0
Cincinnati Black Leaders		
Mean age	35.7	36.8
Median age	33.5	35.5

Source: Compiled from the manuscript schedules of the U.S. population censuses, 1850 and 1860, for Cincinnati.

William Lloyd Garrison. By 1860 Darnes and his fellow northern-born leaders had been joined by two New Yorkers, but the number of northerners among the leadership remained small, reflecting the small number of northern-born African Americans in the city. Thus on the eve of the Civil War Cincinnati's black leaders were more likely to hail from the local region than other African Americans in the city, but most continued to reflect the southern flavor of the general population.[14]

The leaders were generally more mature than their fellow black Cincinnatians (see Table 3.3). Their mean age was 35.7 years in 1850, about three years older than that of all black adults in the city. Their median age (33.5 years) was also higher than that of all black adults, indicating the higher proportion of leaders over 40 years of age. Almost two-fifths (38 percent) of the leaders were 40 years or older as compared to one-fifth of other black adults. By 1860 the mean age of all black adults in the city had advanced, but the leadership remained older than other Cincinnati blacks. The proportion of black leaders over 40 rose to 49 percent, moving further ahead of the general African American population, in which the same proportion stood at less than 25 percent. The increased percentage of black leaders over the age of 40 and the general rise in the mean age reflected the fact that those who led in the 1840s continued to lead in the 1850s even as they grew older. This age difference between leaders and non-leaders suggests that maturity was a consideration in the selection of community leadership.

Ohio-born leaders were an exception to this rule. With an average age of just over 25 years in 1850 and under 30 by 1860, they were quite a bit younger than other leaders, younger even than the general African American population of the city. Black Ohioans were also overrepresented among the city's black leaders. This seems to indicate the importance of residential persistence. Ohio-born William Henry Harrison was active in the local abolition movement and was also elected trustee to the "colored school board committee." Serving with Harrison on the school board was Joseph C. Corbin, also an Ohio native. Only in his mid-twenties by 1860, Corbin was one of the youngest on the board. Another young Ohio-born leader was Eveline Cooper, who served on the black state convention and was an officer of the Ohio Female Anti-Slavery Society. The relative youth of Ohio-born leaders notwithstanding, by the mid-nineteenth century those chosen to lead were mature adults, typically older than community people generally.

African American leaders, reflecting their maturity, were generally married people with families. John Liverpool, while in his early forties, led the campaign against African colonization. Like most blacks in Cincinnati, he opposed the aim of the American Colonization Society to encourage free African Americans to migrate to West Africa. Frances, his wife, John Jr., his son, Eliza Ann Elizabeth, his daughter-in-law, and Thomas, his grandson, were all active in the cause of anti-slavery and civil rights. Liverpool remained active through the early 1850s and was selected to represent Hamilton County at the state convention of colored freemen in 1852. By that time he was in his fifties, one of Cincinnati's older black leaders.[15]

It was common for several members of a single family to be involved in reform activities. Four of the twelve women in our leadership group had male relatives who were also identified as leaders, and all of them had relatives who were active in one way or another. Jane J. Jackson and Mary Gibson headed up a committee that put on a fair in 1858 for the benefit of the Ohio Anti-Slavery Society. They were also delegates to the Ohio black convention during the late 1850s, as were both their husbands. Jane Jackson's husband, John, served on the central committee for the convention. Victoria Ball also served on various committees of the convention, while her husband, James, was an elected official of several local abolitionist meetings. This pattern was not limited to Cincinnati but was significant elsewhere in the state as well. A large number of the women who attended Ohio black conventions between 1849 and 1858 were related to men in attendance.[16]

Although some men would have had "the ladies" present only in supportive roles, providing music and food for the gatherings, black women made clear their intention to assert themselves as full members of these conventions. In one of the earliest statewide meetings the women in attendance served notice that they did not intend to take an inferior role. "Whereas we the ladies have been invited to attend the Convention, and have been deprived of a voice, which we the ladies deem wrong and shameful. Therefore, Resolved, That we will attend no more after tonight, unless the privilege is granted."[17]

A resolution encouraging women's participation was immediately brought to the floor. Two men, W. Hurst Burnham, of Muskingham County, and G. J. Reynolds, from Erie County, were opposed, but the sense of the gathering was favorable and the resolution passed, "inviting the ladies to share in the doings of the Convention." Among those who favored the resolution from the outset were J. L. Watson, chair of the session, and T. J. Merritt, a member of the business committee who brought the women's resolution to the floor initially. Both men's wives were present at the convention and supported the resolution. There is no record of any representative from Cincinnati voting or speaking against the women's participation in the convention. This incident reflected the reality of black society in Cincinnati, which saw significant roles in the family and community economy assumed by black women translated into important political influence.[18]

The African American leaders of Cincinnati were a literate group. Almost all were able to read and write. This was due, in large part, to the availability of private, and later public, education to the black community. Literacy was one of the most important areas of difference between black leaders and non-leaders in the city, although the significance of this difference should not be exaggerated. The general literacy rate among Cincinnati blacks was between 60 and 70 percent during the 1840s and 1850s. That is a relatively high literacy rate for a predominantly southern-born black community, reflecting the general commitment to education among Cincinnati's black people. This commitment was demonstrated in the struggle for increased public support for black instruction. It resulted in the establishment of a separate black-controlled administrative board for African American schools. Education was an important consideration when leaders were being chosen in black Cincinnati. Yet the relatively high literacy rate for the entire community lessened the possibility that this leadership would become an isolated intellectual elite adrift in a sea of illiteracy.[19]

The most important evidence of an elite leadership was revealed by our analysis of the significance of color among Cincinnati African Americans. There is strong evidence that color stratification was an important source of division within the community. Such division was not unique to black Cincinnati. The literature is replete with evidence that light-skinned African Americans often held favored positions within the general society and sometimes formed a special elite within the black community. Thus we were particularly interested in comparisons based on shade of color. The U.S. censuses of 1850 and 1860 designated African Americans as either black or mulatto. This designation depended largely on the judgment of the census taker and was likely to reflect color rather than ancestry.[20]

Most of Cincinnati's free blacks, especially those born in the South, were of racially mixed ancestry and likely to be light in complexion. The fact that masters were most willing to free their mulatto offspring partly explains the large percentage of mulattoes in the free southern black population. Also, because masters were sometimes willing to allow their slave kin to learn trades, many mulatto slaves had skills that they could use to generate funds to purchase their own freedom. Thus mulattoes were freed in disproportionate numbers and were able to leave the South, many migrating to antebellum Cincinnati and "lightening" the city's black community.[21]

By 1850 mulattoes accounted for 54% of adult African Americans in Cincinnati. Although this figure dropped to just over 47% by 1860, this high proportion of light-skinned blacks was far in excess of the regional average for the North (31%) or even the upper South (35%). Cincinnati's percentage of mulattoes in its free black population was higher than that for the midwestern region comprised of Ohio, Indiana, Illinois, Michigan, and Wisconsin. Only in the lower South was the percentage higher (76%).[22]

A partial explanation for the high number of mulattoes in Cincinnati was the tendency of free blacks from the neighboring slaves states of Kentucky and Virginia to move into southern Ohio. The Virginia Assembly ruled in 1806 that any slave set free after May of that year must be transported out of the state or face re-enslavement. After the Nat Turner slave uprising of 1831 Virginia passed additional measures that made life almost intolerable for free blacks. Thus during the 1830s and continuing through the 1840s Ohio received a sizable migration of free blacks, many of them the racially mixed offspring of slaveholders and their slaves. John Mercer Langston and his brothers, Gideon and Charles, were among those free blacks who came to Ohio during the 1830s. They were supported in part by a legacy from their father, Ralph Quarles, a white Virginia planter. John stayed for a brief time in Cincinnati before going on to northern Ohio and eventually to Oberlin Collegiate Institute, where he made a name for himself educationally and in local politics. At Oberlin Langston found several other mulattoes whose education, like his own, was funded to varying degrees by well-to-do white fathers.[23]

Such financing of the education of mixed-race blacks from the South in northern schools was not unusual. Cincinnati's Hiram Gilmore High School, established in 1844, offered the only advanced education available to blacks in the region. Growing from an initial student body of twenty, enrollment reached almost two hundred by 1847. Among those who attended were a number of mulattoes sent there by southern white slaveholding families. Although scholarship aid was available for students unable to finance their education, some of these mulattoes were supported by a white parent. P. B. S. Pinchback of New Orleans, who became a powerful political force in Louisiana during Reconstruction, was educated at the school for a time before the death of his father and benefactor, a white planter, forced him to cut his schooling short.[24]

In this city with so many mulattoes it is not surprising that the African American leadership was disproportionately light. By 1850 at least seven out of every ten leaders were of racially mixed ancestry, and although by 1860 the figure had dropped slightly to 65 percent, there was no mistaking the distinctive shade of the city's black leadership. The high percentage of mulattoes in Cincinnati reflected the general southern character of the city and illustrated the general southern structure of the black community. In southern cities like Charleston and New Orleans, where mulattoes formed well over half of the African American population, they often separated themselves into an elite mulatto society. Partly influenced by Caribbean and Latin American traditions related to color distinction, whites sometimes encouraged this phenomenon by according lighter-skinned African Americans privileges not extended to darker blacks.[25]

In antebellum Charleston, for example, several prominent mulatto families amassed great wealth and lived in relative comfort. They associated with others of their shade in sociopolitical organizations like the Brown Fellowship Society, which limited its membership by wealth and lightness of skin color. William Ellison and his family were economically secure within the mulatto community of nineteenth-century Charleston. The Ellisons held slaves, were successful in business, and could count on the patronage of some of the wealthiest and most powerful whites in the city. They had extremely limited contact with the black masses and almost never interacted socially with the darker, poorer members of their race. The Ellisons and others like them consciously isolated themselves from other black people as one strategy for ensuring continued tolerance and paternalistic support from elite whites. This pattern of mulatto self-separation to maintain important white support was distinctly southern, found most explicitly in the port cities of the old South. As one historian explained South Carolina, "The Palmetto state . . . refused to relegate free mulattoes to the status of blacks, slave or free."[26]

The voluminous literature on the special role of quadroons and octoroons and the elite social and political clubs in nineteenth-century New Orleans that catered to them complements the Charleston illustration. New Orleans' mulattoes, while not treated on a par with whites, were a privileged class. As in Charleston, they formed a social and economic elite with special ties to the white aristocracy. Local ordinances restricting the association of free mulattoes and dark-skinned slaves gave official sanction to color distinctions. Unofficially, New Orleans society winked at regularly held quadroon balls at which sexual liaisons between mulatto women and white men were commonplace.[27]

Some mulattoes in both cities held slaves, and one report showed that in 1830, 735 New Orleans free African Americans, almost all of them mulatto, held a total of more than 2,300 slaves. Outside of the city lived some of the wealthiest mulattoes in the country, including the Metoyer family, which owned over one thousand acres and 300 slaves. These mulattoes thought of themselves as very different from other African Americans and acted "as a distinct racial ethnic group." At the opening of the Civil War mulatto planters in and around New Orleans formed the Native Guard to protect the elite against slave uprisings. They subsequently offered their military services to the Confederacy, and in the spring of 1861 the governor authorized the formation of an African American military unit to guard New Orleans against Union attack.[28]

The position and status of mulattoes in Cincinnati confirmed this regional pattern of mulatto privilege. Although antebellum Ohio law restricted the franchise to white males, twice in the 1840s state courts upheld the right of mulattoes to vote, claiming that they were not "Negroes." In 1859 the state legislature, then dominated by Democrats, passed a measure forbidding anyone from voting who had a "distinct and visible admixture of African blood." The Ohio Supreme Court, however, further recognized a distinction between mulattoes and other African Americans, ruling that this law could not stop males with more than 50 percent white ancestry from voting.[29]

Although there is little evidence that Cincinnati mulattoes voted in significant numbers before the Civil War, these legal distinctions may be an important indication of the general advantages they had in dealing with whites. This fact would have made lighter blacks valuable as African American spokesmen to white society and might help to account for their disproportionate representation among the black leadership. It also might have given rise to a color elite such as that found in cities farther South. However, there was an important difference between the role of mulattoes in New Orleans, Charleston, and other port cities of the deep South and that in Cincinnati. In the deep South prominent light-skinned blacks were sometimes singled out as targets of racial hostility by those intolerant of African American success. Often mulattoes found the protection of paternalistic influential whites their only shield from capricious racial attack. In order to attract and reassure these white patrons southern mulattoes found it advantageous to distance themselves from darker blacks. By contrast, mulattoes in Cincinnati were less likely to be detached from, and more likely to be politically allied with, the masses of blacks in community-wide activism.

The complexity of this issue is increased in light of the marriage trends among the city's African Americans. Marriage patterns of the local leaders indicate a consciousness of color among that group comparable to that found in Charleston, New Orleans, and other deep South cities. The rate of intracolor marriage—that is, mulattoes marrying mulattoes and blacks marrying other blacks—was strikingly high. Almost every male mulatto (93% in 1850, dropping slightly to 89% by 1860) who married chose a mulatto spouse. The rate was comparable for mulatto women, although slightly lower (84% in 1850 and 80% in 1860). Darker black men and women who married were almost as likely to marry someone of their approximate hue (76% in 1850 and 74% in 1860).[30]

Among the African American leadership the importance of color in the selection of a mate was comparably high. In 1850 all married mulatto leaders had mulatto spouses, and in 1860 every mulatto leader was married to a mulatto except for one, George Johnson, a barber from New York, whose wife was a white Englishwoman. In 1850 darker black leaders appear to have had greater access to lighter spouses than other darker blacks in the community. In that year 50 percent of them were married to mates lighter than themselves, an indication, perhaps, of the status accorded community leaders.

These marriage patterns grouped blacks and mulattoes into separate households, clustering them in the wards of the city by shade of color (see Table 3.4). At mid-century mulattoes were overrepresented in two of the city's most heavily African American wards (wards 6 and 9) and underrepresented in two others (wards 1 and 4).[31]

By 1860 a population shift and the redrawing of ward lines increased the clustering of African Americans by color (see Table 3.5).

Table 3.4. Residential Patterns by Ward in 1850

Ward	For Blacks		For Mulattoes	
	No.	%	No.	%
1	181	14.0	253	12.9
2	81	6.3	121	6.2
3	31	2.4	73	3.7
4	331	25.7	242	12.4
5	44	3.4	123	6.3
6	131	10.2	277	14.2
7	93	7.2	82	4.2
8	31	2.4	67	3.4
9	247	19.2	574	29.3
10	71	5.5	86	4.4
11	48	3.7	59	3.0

Largest Ward Concentrations of All
African Americans *(% Mulatto)*

1	434	(58)
4	573	(42)
6	409	(68)
9	821	(70)

Source: Compiled from the manuscript schedules of the U.S. population censuses, 1850 and 1860, for Cincinnati.

Mulattoes, who accounted for slightly more than half of the city's blacks, were underrepresented in two wards, slightly overrepresented in two others, and substantially overrepresented in another.[32]

Mulattoes were not isolated from darker blacks, however. This clustering by shade of color, apparently within wards, did not occur within neighborhoods. Henry Louis Taylor, Jr., in his study of residential patterns in antebellum Cincinnati, plotted the black community street by street. He concluded that there was no substantial clustering by color within neighborhoods (see chapter 4). While mulattoes tended to cluster in a few wards of the city, within these wards blacks were not separated by shade of color.[33]

The residential distribution of African American leaders reflected this pattern. Although leaders lived disproportionately in wards 1 and 9, substantial numbers of them resided in every ward in which there were black people. As we shall see shortly, the occupations held by these leaders should have made it economically possible for them to live in the more desirable residential areas. Nevertheless, in 1850

Table 3.5. Residential Patterns by Ward in 1860

Ward	For Blacks		For Mulattoes	
	No.	%	No.	%
1	188	11.0	126	6.4
2	94	5.5	65	3.3
3	74	4.3	8	0.4
4	563	33.0	241	12.2
5	41	2.4	98	5.0
6	116	6.8	175	8.8
7	52	3.1	69	3.5
8	20	1.2	60	3.0
9	15	0.9	21	1.1
10	6	0.4	60	3.0
11	5	0.3	15	0.8
12	31	1.8	1	0.1
13	356	20.9	618	31.2
14	38	2.2	219	11.1
15	26	1.5	91	4.6
16	10	0.6	23	1.2
17	5	0.3	—	—
22	3	0.2	—	—
25	61	3.6	88	4.4

Largest Ward Concentrations of All
African Americans   *(% Mulatto)*

1	314	(40.1)
4	804	(30.0)
6	291	(60.1)
9	36	(58.3)

Source: Compiled from the manuscript schedules of the U.S. population censuses, 1850 and 1860, for Cincinnati.

almost two of every five leaders lived in the East End factory district of ward 9, an area known as Bucktown, one of the city's poorest sections. Although the percentage of leaders living in Bucktown dropped by 1860 to under one-quarter, this area remained the section of greatest leader residence. Other leaders were scattered through the other heavily African American wards. This residential intermingling of leader and non-leader households encouraged and facilitated regular contact between the community leadership and its constituency. It also reflected the racial discrimination that limited the areas of the city open to blacks and enforced their residential clustering. Even if leaders had wanted to spatially separate themselves from other blacks, it would have been impossible.[34]

The residential integration of leaders with other blacks occurred despite their occupational dissimilarity. The great majority of the blacks in Cincinnati (85 percent in 1850 and 1860) worked in unskilled or very low skilled jobs. This was true partly because most blacks had few skills but also because there was strong opposition to blacks employing any skills they did possess. White employers who were willing to hire blacks in skilled jobs often faced extreme censure from those white workers who saw themselves in direct competition with African American labor. Trade associations, dominated by German and, to a lesser extent, Irish immigrants, not only forbade black membership but also pressured white businesses not to take on black workers in any but "appropriate"—that is, low-level and unskilled—employment. In 1830 one leader of a local trade group was tried by his organization for the "crime" of assisting a young black man in learning a trade.[35]

A few African American craftsmen found work within the black community, but general poverty among blacks ensured that such work was limited. Sometimes white abolitionists hired black skilled workers. One local newspaper called upon all friends of the colored people to "encourage their industry" as a part of the "great duty of abolitionists." Yet "few abolitionists ever call[ed] upon them [black artisans]" to do other than menial work. One black Cincinnatian complained, "We have among us carpenters, plasterers, masons, etc., whose skill as workmen is confessed—and yet they find no encouragement—not even among [white] friends."[36]

Mulattoes fared better in this restrictive environment than darker blacks. A strengthening economy, especially after 1840, and a large pool of skilled mulatto workers, combined with southern traditions adhered to by the large numbers of southern-born whites and blacks in the city, was enough to temper some of the objections to employment opportunities for lighter African Americans. In 1850 18% of mulattoes versus 10% of darker blacks found work above the lowest skill levels. In 1860 the percentages were 20% for mulattoes and 10% for darker blacks. Thus the occupational structure of the city's black community favored its lighter members and in so doing resembled the southern urban pattern, which reserved many skilled positions for mulattoes. Yet the advantage of light skin must not be exaggerated because the vast majority of mulattoes (80%) remained in the ranks of the unskilled.[37]

Leaders were, however, more likely to hold jobs above the un-skilled level than any other single group of African Americans. Lead-ership status was a better predictor of relatively high occupational level than shade of color. African American leaders held higher-level jobs (47% in 1850 and 43% in 1860), roughly twice the rate for mulattoes in the community. The percentage for mulatto leaders was even higher, over 50% in 1850 and just slightly less in 1860.

Barbering and hairdressing accounted for a significant proportion of mulatto skills and was the most popular profession among leaders. Immigrant workers were generally tolerant of blacks holding these service jobs. Those jobs, like storekeeper and small business owner, that were not directed primarily toward serving whites tended to deal with customers from the black community. Thus Cincinnati, with its sizable black community, offered not only middle-level jobs in the general economy but also employment opportunities for blacks serv-ing their own community. It was hardly surprising, then, that from among these predominantly southern-born blacks, already advan-taged mulattoes stepped forward to run these local businesses. From this occupationally advantaged group came a disproportionate num-ber of the community's leaders, who were more economically stable than most of their followers.

In several ways, then, Cincinnati's African American leaders were distinct from most of the city's blacks. They were disproportionately lighter in skin color and more secure occupationally. They were also more highly literate and just a bit older than the average black Cincinnatian. These observations point to the presence of a local leadership that stood at a social and economic level above other Cin-cinnati blacks.

Yet these leaders were very much like others in the black commu-nity in other important ways. They were generally southern-born and shared a general social, economic, and political environment that was restrictive for all black people. When the Black Laws were applied, they were applied to all identified as "colored people." When white mobs invaded the black community in 1829, 1836, and again in 1841, they attacked blacks indiscriminately and destroyed the prop-erty of those fortunate enough to own any, regardless of their status in the community. Cincinnati African Americans of all social and economic levels shared a common vulnerability, and leaders emerged as advocates of programs and projects that held community-wide ap-peal. Education for black children and adults, care for widows and orphans, the fight against the restrictive laws under which all blacks suffered, and the antislavery crusade were the causes of black leaders and of their constituents.

Nor was there a major attempt by any single group within the community to take exclusive control over the leadership. Given the advantages held by mulattoes within the city, one of two situations might have existed within black Cincinnati. Mulattoes might have formed a separate community and run their own affairs independently of the city's darker African Americans, as happened in several southern port cities. They might also have used their relatively privileged status to freeze darker blacks out of leadership positions. Neither happened in Cincinnati. Darker blacks were not excluded from leadership positions. They increased their proportion among leaders (30 percent in 1850 and 35 percent in 1860) at roughly the same rate as their presence grew in the city.

Nor were darker blacks relegated to unimportant positions of leadership. When black Cincinnatians were represented outside their local community, they selected delegates of many hues. John I. Gaines, John Liverpool, William Casey, and other mulattoes served with darker blacks like Joseph J. Fowler, a huckster originally from Kentucky, John Jackson, a cooper from Virginia, Isaac Wilson, a laborer from North Carolina, and William W. Watson, a barber born in Virginia. All were part of the delegation elected from Hamilton County to the Convention of the Colored Freedmen of Ohio in 1852. Jackson represented his community several times during the 1850s, serving on a variety of committees, including the convention's central committee in 1852. Watson served on the finance committee for the convention.[38]

When black Cincinnatians addressed more local problems, darker blacks also participated as leaders along with mulattoes, and during community celebrations darker blacks were not given inferior roles. Daniel Gray, darker than most of his brethren, was selected as the grand marshal for the annual "Fifth of July" parade in 1834. He was aided by two assistant marshals, the mulattoes William and Josiah Smith. Fifteen years later, when an observer reported on the annual "colored procession" in honor of the abolition of slavery in the British West Indies, he noted, "Among them we noticed every shade of color, from the darky so black that charcoal would almost make a white mark, to those of straight hair and nearly white."[39]

Darker skin did not exclude African Americans from community leadership, and leaders were alert to any situation that might exacerbate the sensitive issue of color. In 1844 John I. Gaines, a mulatto member of the central committee of the Convention of the Colored Freedmen of Ohio, warned white authorities in the city that black people would not tolerate the establishment of a separate school for mulattoes. "This I anticipate would be fraught with evil consequences," he argued. "It would not only divide the colored children, but create prejudices too intolerable to be borne." Instead Gaines demanded that public education be provided for all black children regardless of color.[40]

African American leaders in Cincinnati, and many other blacks in the community who could not be identified as leaders, often expressed this view of racial solidarity, and, more important, they worked both through formally organized groups and informally to aid those in need. Robert Gordon, a black coal dealer born in Virginia, devoted much of his life to establishing a Colored Orphan Asylum and then bequeathed twenty-five thousand dollars to start the Home for Colored Widows. William Casey, a prominent leader throughout most of the antebellum years, adopted Emily, a young girl who worked as a washerwoman. He gave her his last name, and for many years Emily lived with the Casey family. After William died in the mid-1850s Emily inherited a portion of his estate and continued to live with his widow, Maria Casey.[41]

There was also significant association between the community leaders and those less well known and less well placed in the community. John Liverpool, a prominent Virginia-born mulatto barber, was willing to post bond of surety for debts on the modest estate of Thomas Bascoe, a black boatman from Virginia. This was a great service, no doubt, to the widow Mildred Bascoe, who, even with this aid, was forced to take in washing to make ends meet within a few years of her husband's death. Bascoe was not Liverpool's only associate who worked at a less prestigious job; Liverpool's son-in-law worked, for a time, as a boatman.[42]

Other examples of such associations can be found in the probate records of black Cincinnatians, which reveal many associational networks that cut across class and color lines within the African American community. Perhaps the community was too small and its problems too broad and too critical to allow hard and fast distinctions. Not that there were no groupings of choice—marriage patterns clearly show that color preference was exercised. But these preferences did not detach a light, wealthy elite from black society, nor did they predict community leadership. Other factors were also important. Samuel Carrel, an active member of the "Life Guards," which protected fugitive slaves seeking shelter in the city, was selected to represent the community before city authorities because "being a Pennsylvania man . . . he could speak up 'pert' before white folks." The report went on to say, "Most of the others were from Kentucky and were afraid of white men."[43]

Thus the intangible, often unpredictable factors of personality and personal experience were also important considerations in the selection of community leaders. Surely the most educated and the most financially secure held advantages in this regard, but leadership was not closed to others.

Local black leaders did comprise a distinct and comparatively privileged group. They pushed for middle-class goals. Education, civil rights, and economic opportunity were high on their list. But these were also the goals of most black Cincinnatians. These leaders were forced to deal with white authority, but they did not hold their leadership positions at the pleasure of that authority. Unlike the mulatto elite of the southern port cities, Cincinnati leaders, whatever their shade of color, were responsible directly to the black community and held their positions because they were elected at community mass meetings. They were selected by, and therefore could be rejected by, the community.

Not only were the African American leaders of Cincinnati and most of their followers committed to self-help and civil rights for free blacks, they also spoke and acted against slavery individually and in organized groups, and they raised funds to support the abolition movement. They were not willing to abandon their friends and families bound in slavery any more than they were willing to ignore the injustices they suffered in their daily lives as "free people of color."

This study strongly suggests that local leaders in antebellum Cincinnati were people with advantages. As a group they were comparatively mature, literate, and well employed. They were not, however, isolated from their constituents. This was so partly because the relatively small size of the black community made isolation difficult and because racial restrictions were imposed upon all African Americans regardless of position. The situation in Cincinnati, with the major proportion of its black and white citizenry southern-born and its comparatively privileged mulatto population, exhibited many of the same characteristics as the situation in southern cities. Yet in many ways it also illustrated a northern pattern that allowed for public black protest and social and political activism. In the slaveholding South free blacks were restricted from holding open mass gatherings, and mulattoes were likely to remain socially and politically separated from the masses of darker blacks, at least publicly. In Cincinnati, although mulattoes married among themselves and held a disproportionate share of skilled employment and wealth, they did not constitute a separate color caste. Instead, they led black protest against slavery and racial restrictions. Cincinnati was a city in the middle, a border city in the truest sense. Its black leadership reflected that position. It constituted something of an elite but achieved its status by engaging in public protest instead of drawing inward and isolating itself from the rest of the black community. The nature of Cincinnati's local black leadership was determined not only by the special talents of individuals but also by the structural patterns of the city straddling North and South.

Notes

The names of the leaders identified in this study were taken from membership lists, special reports, minutes of meetings, articles, and other accounts, which appeared in the following published sources:

Records of Ohio state colored conventions
Records of the national colored conventions
Black Abolitionist Papers (microfilm edition in 17 rolls)
The Liberator (Boston)
Cincinnati Daily Enquirer
Cincinnati Daily Commercial
Daily Cincinnati Gazette
Colored American (New York)
The Rights of All (New York)

1. Philip Foner and George Walker, eds., *Proceedings of the Black State Conventions, 1840–1865* (Philadelphia: Temple University Press, 1979), 224.
2. Ibid., 226.
3. Nell Irvin Painter, *Exodusters: Black Migration to Kansas after Reconstruction* (New York: Knopf, 1976), 28.
4. Nathan Irvin Huggins made a similar distinction between achievers and leaders in his discussion of twentieth-century black leadership. Huggins, "Afro-Americans," in *Ethnic Leadership in America,* ed. John Higham (Baltimore: Johns Hopkins University Press, 1978), 91–118. See Records of Probate for Richard Phillips (1858), Hamilton County, Ohio (copies of this and other probate records cited herein are on file at the Afro-American Communities Project, Smithsonian Institution).
5. The Black Abolitionist Papers are available on microfilm through the Microfilm Corp. of America.
6. For an extensive discussion of the importance of black women in antebellum black society see James Oliver Horton, "Freedom's Yoke: Gender Conventions among Antebellum Free Blacks," *Feminist Studies* 12 (Spring 1986): 51–76.
7. For the negative quote about Cincinnati see "Our Colored Population" in the *Cincinnati Commercial,* 31 Mar. 1867, 1–2; Richard C. Wade, *The Urban Frontier* (Chicago: Howard University Press, 1959), 53–59.

8. Leonard P. Curry, *The Free Black in Urban America, 1800–1850: The Shadow of the Dream* (Chicago: University of Chicago Press, 1981), 104.

9. Unless otherwise noted, all population figures are from the Afro-American Communities Project data file of the U.S. Censuses for 1850 and 1860. The total population of Cincinnati was almost 26,000 in 1830, over 115,000 in 1850, and over 160,000 by 1860.

10. Carter G. Woodson, "The Negroes of Cincinnati Prior to the Civil War," *Journal of Negro History* (Jan. 1916): 1–22.

11. Woodson, "The Negroes of Cincinnati"; Richard C. Wade, "The Negro in Cincinnati, 1800–1830," *Journal of Negro History* 39 (Jan. 1954); David A. Gerber, *Black Ohio and the Color Line, 1860–1915* (Urbana: University of Illinois Press, 1976).

12. *Cincinnati Commercial*, 19 Jan. 1850, and Wendell P. Dabney, *Cincinnati's Colored Citizens* (Cincinnati, 1926), 60; Benjamin Drew, *A Northern View of Slavery* (Boston: Negroes University Press, 1856).

13. Foner and Walker, eds., *Black State Conventions; Liberty Hall and Cincinnati Gazette*, 11 Aug. 1836; *Daily Cincinnati Gazette*, 4 July 1834.

14. Foner and Walker, eds., *Black State Conventions*. The single northern-born leader in 1850 may be less significant, given the small number of leaders relative to the black population of the city. The chances of such a regional representation among the leadership occurring by accident are high, and the importance of this phenomenon should not be overstated.

15. "Proceedings of the Convention, of the Colored Freedmen of Ohio, Held in Cincinnati, January 14–19, 1852" in Foner and Walker, eds., *Black State Conventions*, vol. 1, 274–96.

16. Foner and Walker, eds., *Black State Conventions*. For examples of this kind of family participation elsewhere, see James Oliver Horton, "Generations of Protest: Black Families and Social Reform in Antebellum Boston," *New England Quarterly* (June 1976): 142–56.

17. Foner and Walker, eds., *Black State Conventions*, 227.

18. Ibid. For a discussion of gender roles in antebellum black society, see Horton, "Freedom's Yoke."

19. For an examination of black education in Cincinnati, see Thomas P. Kessen, "Segregation in Cincinnati Public Education: The Nineteenth-Century Black Experience" (Ph.D. diss., University of Cincinnati, 1973).

20. For information on color stratification among Cincinnati's blacks, see James Oliver Horton, "Shades of Color: The Mulatto in Three Antebellum Northern Communities," *Afro-Americans in New York Life and History* 7, no. 2 (July 1984): 37–60.

21. Free blacks in the South were more likely to be mulattoes than to be darker African Americans. By 1850, for example, mulattoes constituted 65 percent of Virginia's free black population but only 22 percent of the state's slaves. The farther south one moved, the greater the possibility that free African Americans would be lighter in skin color than slaves. By 1860 mulattoes in the deep South accounted for only 8.5 percent of the slave population but more than three-quarters of the free blacks. See U.S. Bureau of

the Census, *Negro Population of the United States, 1790–1915* (Washington, D.C., 1918), 221. Also see Ira Berlin, *Slaves without Masters: The Free Negro in the Antebellum South* (New York: Pantheon Books, 1974) (see p. 178 for 1860 figures on the percentage of mulattoes in the free black population in the South).

22. The figures for the percentage of mulattoes among African Americans in antebellum Cincinnati are given for adults (eighteen years of age and over) because such figures make for a more meaningful comparison with the percentage of mulattoes among black leaders, all of whom were adults.

23. William Cheek and Aimee Lee Cheek, *John Mercer Langston and the Fight for Black Freedom, 1829–65* (Urbana: University of Illinois Press, 1989).

24. L. D. Easton, "The Colored Schools of Cincinnati," in *History of the Schools of Cincinnati and Other Educational Institutions, Public and Private,* ed. Isaac M. Martin (Cincinnati, 1900).

25. See John G. Mencke, *Mulattoes and Race Mixture: American Attitudes and Images, 1865–1918* (New York: Umi Research Press, 1976); Carl N. Degler, *Neither Black Nor White* (New York: MacMillan, 1971); and Joel Williamson, *New People* (New York: Free Press, 1980).

26. The quotation is from Williamson, *New People,* 17–18. For an important look at free African Americans in antebellum Charleston, see Michael P. Johnson and James L. Roark, *No Chariot Let Down* (Chapel Hill: University of North Carolina Press, 1984); and see also idem., *Black Masters* (New York: Norton Press, 1984).

27. John W. Blassingame, *Black New Orleans, 1860–1880* (Chicago: University of Chicago Press, 1973).

28. The quote is from Williamson, *New People,* 21. See also David O. Whitten, *Andrew Durnford: Black Sugar Planter in Antebellum Louisiana* (Natchitoches: Northwestern State University of Louisiana Press, 1981).

29. Paul Finkelman, "Prelude to the Fourteenth Amendment: Black Legal Rights in the Antebellum North," *Rutgers Law Journal* 17: 407, 425.

30. Horton, "Shades of Color."

31. In 1850 the four wards with the largest African American population were wards 1 (434), 4 (573), 6 (409), and 9 (821). The proportion of mulattoes and darker blacks in these wards illustrated color clustering. Mulattoes, 59% of the total African American population, were overrepresented in wards 6 (68%) and 9 (70%) and underrepresented in ward 4 (42%). They were slightly underrepresented in ward 1 (58%).

32. In 1860 the boundaries of the largest black wards in the city were redrawn and expanded. These wards were 1 (314), 4 (804), 6 (291), 13 (974), and 14 (253). Mulattoes, who accounted for over 53% of the city's blacks in 1860, were underrepresented in wards 1 (40%) and 4 (30%). They were slightly overrepresented in wards 6 (59%) and 13 (63%) and substantially overrepresented in ward 14 (85%).

33. The best work on residential clustering in Cincinnati is Henry Louis

Taylor, Jr., "The Use of Maps in the Study of the Black Ghetto-Formation Process: Cincinnati, 1802–1910," *Historical Methods* 17, no. 2 (1984): 44–58. The index of dissimilarity, an indicator of residential separation measured at the ward level, was 34.8 when computed for darker blacks' and mulattoes' residence in Cincinnati for 1860. It shows that there was as much residential separation between darker blacks and mulattoes in the "Queen City" at the ward level as there was between blacks and whites in Brooklyn (35.5) or San Francisco (34.6). Taylor is rightly critical of the index of dissimilarity for exaggerating the degree of racial segregation of nineteenth-century cities; it is used here only as a striking point of comparison between ward-level residential separation of the races in San Francisco and Brooklyn and that of mulattoes and blacks in Cincinnati.

34. In 1850 the wards in which most leaders lived were 1 (20%) and 9 (39%). The redrawing of ward lines by 1860 created an apparent, but not an actual, shift in leader residence. In that year one-third of the leaders lived in ward 13, and less than 15% lived in ward 6.

35. Ohio Anti-Slavery Society, *Proceedings of the Ohio Anti-Slavery Convention Held at Putnam on the Twenty-second, Twenty-third, and Twenty-fourth of April 1835* (n.p., n.d.), 19.

36. *Philanthropist*, 10 Nov. 1841, 21, 28 Dec. 1842.

37. Curry, *The Free Black in Urban America;* Berlin, *Slaves without Masters.*

38. The above information is compiled from the U.S. censuses of 1850 and 1860 and from Foner and Walker, eds., *Black State Conventions.*

39. *Cincinnati Daily Gazette,* 4 Aug. 1834, 3 Aug. 1849.

40. *Morning Herald,* 20 Jan. 1844. See also Richard W. Pih, "Negro Improvement Efforts in Antebellum Cincinnati, 1836–1850," *Ohio History* (Summer 1969): 179–87.

41. Records of Probate for Robert Gordon (1883) and Emily Casey (1862).

42. Records of Probate of Thomas Bascoe (1855) and John Liverpool (1863).

43. The *Cincinnati Commercial,* 31 Mar. 1867. Here one is reminded that Martin Luther King, Jr., was selected to lead the 1956 Montgomery Bus Boycott, in part because blacks felt that with his northern education and erudite speaking style, he could effectively address white authority.

4

Henry Louis Taylor, Jr., and Vicky Dula

The Black Residential Experience and Community Formation in Antebellum Cincinnati

In the antebellum period, northern blacks built tightly knit, well-organized communities that helped them successfully confront the challenge of urban living.[1] "Community" is one of those shadowy terms that demand careful definition. In 1955 George A. Hillery, Jr., found no fewer than ninety-four meanings given to the concept.[2] Yet, despite the variations, most definitions of community imply something both geographical and sociopsychological and stress the following themes: proximity and propinquity, territoriality, social interaction, consciousness of kind, socialization, and shared values and institutions.[3]

A number of scholars have emphasized the geographical dimension in their definition. Thomas Bender suggests that the most common definitions used today focus on community as an aggregate of people who share a common interest in a particular locality. Territorial-based social organizations and social activity thus define a community.[4] Roland L. Warren stresses the interplay between the territorial and sociopsychological dimensions of community, with special emphasis on the place of institutions in community formation.

> The community concept, in addition to factors of space and population, includes the notion of shared institutions and values. Putting this another way, geographic area and people do not in themselves constitute a com-

munity. One must also look for institutions commonly held by the local population. As we have seen, the area of shared institutional services, far from being secondary, is actually one of the most important ways of delineating communities. But more than this, the shared institutional services are thought to constitute a shared way of life, a level of participation on which people come together in significant relationships for provision of certain necessary living functions.[5]

The historian James Borchert and the sociologist Gerald D. Suttles define community as a form of activity that occurs within a common geographical area that permits and, we might add, encourages social interaction. Borchert adds to this, in his study of alley life in Washington, D.C., that the existence and form of community can be glimpsed through the alley (or neighborhood) as a commons and community center and also by the level of residential persistence and satisfaction.[6]

Other scholars have argued that community can exist beyond the boundaries of a common territorial base. Bender indicates that community can also be defined as a network of social relations marked by mutuality and emotional bonds.[7] This network, says Kai T. Erikson, is the essence of community, and it may or may not be coterminous with a specific, contiguous territory.[8] Martin Buber writes, "A real community need not consist of people who are perpetually together; but it must consist of people who, precisely because they are comrades, have mutual access to one another and are ready for one another."[9] Stressing the significance of sociopsychological aspects of community, Robert A. Nisbet says that community "draws its psychological strength from levels of motivation deeper than those of mere volition or interest. . . . Community is a fusion of feeling and thought, of tradition and commitment, of membership and volition."[10] To these scholars the existence of social networks makes it possible for people to form communal ties, or community, even when they live in different locations. Social structures allow groups to transcend spatial structures in community formation.[11]

The ability of African Americans to form a community in antebellum Cincinnati raises important questions about the relationship between the residential experience and community building in the pre-ghetto era.[12] African Americans faced major obstacles in the community formation process. They were scattered throughout a white-dominated residential environment. Although concentrated in the eastern portion of the city, they were still dispersed across Cincinnati's face. Dispersal and the lack of territorial domination erected barriers to community formation.

Moreover, although racially homogeneous, black Cincinnatians were divided in significant ways. Regional differences created variations in the experiences African Americans brought with them to the city. Slavery differed from region to region and from state to state. And these differences, as Ira Berlin has suggested, could be quite significant.[13] African Americans gained their freedom in various ways—some were manumitted, others escaped, and still others were born free. Occupational differences created not only class divisions but also diversity in the content of work. In the antebellum commercial city, Stephanie W. Greenberg has shown, occupation played a significant role in shaping the residential pattern. Different jobs were often located in different parts of the city, and this usually affected where people lived.[14] Differences in family and household type and in the age structure further fragmented black Cincinnati. Then there were divisions along the color line. James Oliver Horton, Theodore Hershberg, and others have shown that color represented a source of tension inside the black community. These internal divisions represented another major obstacle to community formation among African Americans.[15]

How, then, did African Americans overcome the barriers of dispersal and internal division to build a tightly knit, well-organized community? How were they able to form a community without the territorial base characteristic of the twentieth-century black ghetto? The answers to these questions will deepen our understanding of the northern black residential experience in the pre-ghetto era.[16]

The central thesis, or hypothesis, is that the internal organization and structure of the black residential environment tied the African American population together despite diversity and tensions within the group. Moreover, although African Americans were dispersed, the unity generated within the residential environment made possible the creation of a shared institutional life. Most significant, black institutions were concentrated in one section of the city; while African Americans lived in every section of Cincinnati, their institutions were clustered in one locale. The concentration of important institutions formed a "commons" where a high degree of social interaction took place among the dispersed population. This interaction strengthened communal bonds and tied the group together.

The Black Residential Pattern in 1850

Built on slavery's fringe, Cincinnati was a northern city deeply influenced by southern notions of race and race relations. Still its lo-

Table 4.1. Distribution of Blacks and Whites by Ward, 1850

Ward	Black	White	Total	% Black
1	434	6,411	6,845	6.34
2	187	8,026	8,213	2.28
3	101	7,567	7,668	1.32
4	563	10,394	10,957	5.13
5	161	5,122	5,283	3.04
6	401	9,229	9,630	4.16
7	178	9,167	9,345	1.90
8	96	14,328	14,424	0.66
9	816	9,889	10,705	7.62
10	145	12,887	13,032	1.09
11–12	90	19,246	19,336	0.46
Total	3,172	112,266	115,438	2.74

Source: Charles Cist, *Cincinnati in 1851* (Cincinnati: W. H. Moore, 1851), 44.

cation across the river from Kentucky and its proximity to Virginia combined with a booming economy to make the Queen City a favored site for blacks fleeing the slave states. So despite the existence of Black Laws, high levels of racial hatred, and periodic outbreaks of racial violence, the number of blacks migrating to Cincinnati steadily increased. By 1850, 3,172 African Americans lived in the city, making it home to the largest black community in Ohio and one of the largest in the North.[17]

In 1850 Cincinnati was an extremely compact city in which business, industry, transportation, and residential space were jammed into six square miles. Only New York City was more congested. The limited spatial margin precluded the dominance of any part of the city by a single racial or ethnic group.[18] Not surprising, no black ghetto existed in Cincinnati at mid-century. African Americans were dispersed across the face of the city (Table 4.1).

The ward-level distribution pattern suggests that African Americans did not live in a residential world separate and apart from whites. Yet the pattern does not tell the complete story. Ward boundaries are political divisions that ignore residential boundaries, where social relations, which lay the foundation for community formation, are established.[19] At the ward level we cannot determine to what extent blacks and whites actually shared the living place, nor can we determine how African Americans organized and structured their residential environment within this white-dominated milieu.

Table 4.2. Residential Areas in Cincinnati's Commercial City, 1850

Section	Ward	Blacks	White	% Black
East End Factory District	9, 1, 3	1,351	23,867	5.3
Central Waterfront	4, 6	964	19,623	5.0
Central Core	2, 5, 7	526	22,315	2.3
West End	8	96	14,328	0.7
Over-the-Rhine	10, 11–12	235	32,133	0.7

Source: Charles Cist, Cincinnati in 1851, 44.

To understand the complex social interactions that take place among people of different races, ethnic groups, and classes and to see how African Americans were spatially incorporated into the city, it is necessary to reconstruct the 1850 residential environment so that the subward distribution, and interaction, of the population can be studied. To achieve this objective a spatial methodology was developed that allowed us to divide Cincinnati into several residential areas and then to study the subward distribution of the African American population.[20]

Initially a three-tiered approach was used to identify Cincinnati's major residential areas.[21] First, we identified those wards where blacks were most heavily concentrated.[22] Second, we analyzed the geographic distribution of economic activity within the city. Finally, we identified conspicuous landmarks, such as major streets or the Erie Canal, that might create natural boundaries for residential areas.[23] Using this approach, the city's twelve wards were organized into five residential areas: East End Factory District, Central Waterfront, Central Core, West End, and Over-the-Rhine (Table 4.2 and Map 4.1).[24]

An examination of the residential area's distribution pattern showed that 73 percent (N = 2,315) of the African American population lived in the East End Factory and Central Waterfront districts. Blacks were concentrated there, even though they lived in every section of the city. Yet they did not spatially dominate any one residential area. A ghetto did not exist. Even in the two districts where most blacks lived, they constituted only a tiny fraction of the area's population (Table 4.2). African Americans shared the living space with whites in the pre-ghetto era.

This poses two intriguing questions. What type of residential structure did African Americans build within this white-dominated environment? Were they randomly distributed among the white population, or did they cluster together? To answer these questions, we

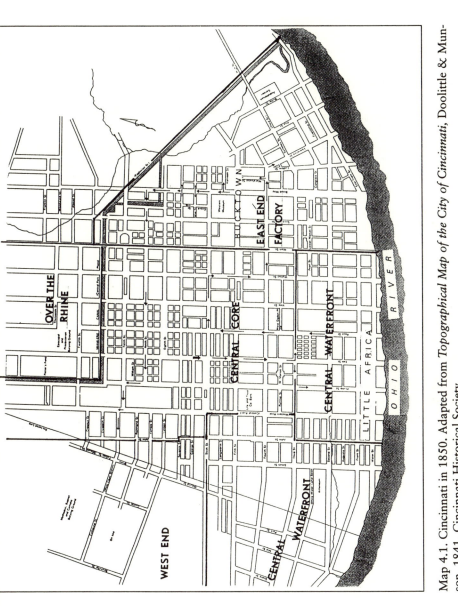

Map 4.1. Cincinnati in 1850. Adapted from *Topographical Map of the City of Cincinnati*, Doolittle & Munson, 1841, Cincinnati Historical Society.

developed a two-step procedure to give us a street-level view of the spatial organization of African Americans and their geographic relation to whites. This methodology was based on the 1850 U.S. manuscript census and the city directory.[25] The data showed that even at the street level, blacks had white neighbors. On virtually every block and street where African Americans resided, whites could also be found living there in large numbers. African Americans lived in a multiracial residential environment where they shared the living place with white ethnic groups and with whites from every social class.

Yet blacks were not randomly distributed throughout the residential environment. Instead they formed small residential clusters that were sandwiched in among the larger white population. A residential cluster is defined as two or more families that live in the same dwelling unit with another African American family, next door to an African American, or a few doors away from other African American households. Two or more families living in the same household would not constitute a cluster, however. In the pre-ghetto era, we argue, the residential cluster was the basic unit of spatial organization among African Americans. It was equivalent to a twentieth-century neighborhood characterized by intimate, face-to-face relations.

David M. Katzman, in *Before the Ghetto,* first pointed out that in the pre-ghetto era urban blacks were not just concentrated in specific areas of the city but actually lived in small residential clusters that were scattered throughout a white-dominated residential environment. A similar observation was made by James Borchert.[26] While Katzman and Borchert identified the black residential cluster, they did not analyze its internal organization and structure. A detailed examination of these clusters will show how African Americans organized and structured their residential environment and will provide insight into the interactive social process that facilitated the formation of communal bonds among this diverse population.

The Black Residential Cluster

The spatial analysis showed that the majority of Cincinnati's African American population lived in 106 residential clusters. Not all African Americans, however, lived in these clusters (Table 4.3). Twenty-three percent (N = 702) of Africans Americans were either randomly distributed throughout the residential environment (18 percent) or lived in white households (5 percent). Yet for safety, mutual aid, and the desire simply to live with friends, relatives, or other members of the race, African Americans clustered together.

Table 4.3. Distribution of Black Residential Clusters by Ward, 1850

Ward	Clusters		Pop. of NC	B/WH
	No.	Pop.		
1	17	393	38	20
2	9	122	65	41
3	1	42	48	11
4	14	372	167	8
5	8	117	25	5
6	17	225	47	12
7	8	101	50	18
8	3	60	36	7
9	16	755	20	4
10	8	106	28	18
11–12	5	70	20	4
Totals	106	2,363	543	159

NC = non-clustered blacks; B/WH = blacks in white households
Source: U.S. Bureau of the Census, Manuscript Census, 1850.

An examination of the cluster pattern shows that even the clustering of African Americans did not lead to their residential separation from whites. The clusters were always bracketed by groups of whites. And in many instances, one or two white families resided within the cluster boundaries (Table 4.4). The particular class or group of whites sharing residential space with blacks depended on the specific residential area in which blacks lived. For example, in the East End Factory and Central Waterfront districts blacks were most likely to live next door to Irish and German workers. In the Central Core they lived near middle-class native whites and Germans, while in the West End and Over-the-Rhine blacks had German neighbors.[27]

The Internal Organization and Structure of the Residential Cluster

The residential cluster was the basic unit of spatial organization among African Americans in the pre-ghetto era. To study it in detail we selected a random sample of twenty clusters and analyzed them in terms of nativity, occupation, family-household type, age structure, and shade of color.[28]

The sample clusters contained 109 households with a population of 538.[29] This population lived in eighty dwelling units with an average

Table 4.4. A Residential Cluster in Cincinnati, Ward 2, 1850

Dwellings	Family	Household Head	Race	Occupation
761	996	Martha Alcorn	white	unknown
762	997	Robert Armstrong	black	waiter
	998	Samuel Brown	mulatto	barber
	999	Nelson O'Neil	mulatto	steward
763	1,000	William Casey	mulatto	cook
764	1,001	Samuel Jasson	white	watchmaker
	1,002	Max Hanover	white	peddler
	1,003	Donald Davison (?)	white	clerk

Note: The numbers listed under dwellings and family refer to the order of visitation. Multiple family units are shown whenever more than one family is listed for a dwelling. When the name of the person listed in the census is unclear, a question mark is used to denote that the name of the household head is uncertain. Ward Two is located in the central core of the city, where large numbers of middle-income whites resided.
Source: U.S. Manuscript Census for Cincinnati (microfilm), Ward 2, 163.

of 6.7 persons per house. The average cluster contained 5 households and 27 people. Still, there was considerable variation in the size of clusters. Some were very large. Five clusters, for instance, contained at least 8 households and 40 residents. The largest cluster contained 17 households and 87 people and was located in the Central Waterfront district. This suggests that in those sections of Cincinnati where large numbers of African Americans lived, clusters could grow to mammoth proportions. The smallest cluster contained only 2 households and 10 people and was located in the East End Factory district. Not surprising, 12 of the 20 clusters were located in the East End Factory and Central Waterfront districts. As you will recall, 70 percent of black Cincinnati lived in these two districts. The remaining 8 clusters were found in the Central Core and Over-the-Rhine districts. No sample clusters were located in the West End.[30]

The Cluster Population

In the cluster population women outnumbered men, just as they did in the general population. There were 231 males (43 percent) and 307 (57 percent) females in the sample.[31] These were young men and women in the prime of their lives. Their average age was 24 years.[32] There was a large number of children, 10 years old and under, in the sample population. Twenty-five percent (N = 132) of the sample population fell into this age category. There were only 42 people (9 percent) in the 46-and-over age category. The cluster population had

Table 4.5. Major Places of Birth for Sample Population

Birthplace	Number	Percent
Washington, D.C.	8	1
Georgia	21	4
Kentucky	55	10
Louisiana	13	2
Maryland	14	3
Mississippi	21	4
North Carolina	11	2
Ohio	167	31
Pennsylvania	25	5
South Carolina	8	1
Tennessee	15	3
Virginia	154	29
Other states	19	4
Unknown	7	1
Total	538	100

Source: U.S. Bureau of the Census, Manuscript Census, 1850.

a very diverse family-household structure, with eleven different types of structures represented.[33] Seventy percent of the family-households were headed by males, with the remaining 30 percent headed by females. The nuclear family (N = 129) and the extended family (175)—containing a father, mother, children, and relatives and/or boarders—were the most common forms of family-household structures. Fifty-seven percent of the sample population lived in these two types of structures. Most important, 86 percent of the sample lived in some type of family-based household structure. On the other hand, 73 individuals (14 percent) lived in households with unmarried people.[34]

Women headed five different types of households. Fourteen of the thirty-one households headed by females were composed of unmarried people. Sixty-four people (or 12 percent of the sample population) lived in this type of family-household structure. Nine households (containing a total of fifty-two people) consisted of mother, children, and relatives and/or boarders. Seventy-four percent of the female-headed households fell into these two categories. Significantly, there were only six households (containing twenty people) that consisted of a mother and only her child.[35]

The sample population was regionally diverse, with twenty-two states, Canada, and Cuba represented (Table 4.5). Sixty-five people (12%) came from the deep South, 262 (49%) came from the upper

Table 4.6. Occupational Categories for Sample Population

Occupation	No.	%
Barbers	32	26
Boatmen	33	27
Carpenters	4	3
Cooks	9	7
Grocers	3	2
Laborers	14	11
Servants	4	3
Traders	2	2
Waiters	5	4
Whitewashers	7	6
Miscellaneous	10	8
Total	123	100

Source: U.S. Bureau of the Census, Manuscript Census, 1850.

South, and 202 (38%) from the North, with one person coming from Cuba and one from Canada. The nativity of 7 individuals was unknown. Although diverse, about 76 percent (N = 376) of black Cincinnati came from just three states: Ohio (167), Virginia (154), and Kentucky (55).[36]

Occupational data were available on 123 males (the 1850 census did not provide data on the occupations of women). Sixty-five of the males in the sample were ten years old or younger. When these individuals were eliminated, we had data on about 73 percent of the male population. The data showed that blacks were tied to the bottom of the economic ladder, with most laboring as roustabouts on the river or as barbers, laborers, cooks, servants, waiters, carpenters, and whitewashers (Table 4.6).[37] Although data are not available on female occupations, it is reasonable to believe that most women worked as domestics, servants, cooks, and washerwomen.[38] Even though blacks were concentrated at the bottom of the economic ladder, they were nevertheless an occupationally diverse group.

In antebellum Cincinnati African Americans were divided along color lines. In the sample population there were 332 mulattoes (63%) and 193 blacks (36%).[39] This is not surprising. Fifty-six percent of the free blacks in Ohio and 60 percent in Cincinnati were mulattoes.[40] The color of 13 African Americans (2%) could not be determined. To what extent did these differences among African Americans affect the organization and structure of the black residential clusters? Did clusters differ in terms of nativity, occupation, family-household type, age structures, and shade of color? Or were they formed with little or no regard for these variables?

Nativity

People from different states and regions came together to form the various residential clusters. In eighteen of the twenty clusters the residents came from at least four states. With reference to nativity, it appears as if the clusters were formed in a random fashion. For instance, in cluster 3, which contained four households and twenty people, the residents came from five different states: Ohio, Kentucky, Virginia, Pennsylvania, and New York. Cluster 1 was smaller, with only three households and twelve people, yet the residents came from eight different locations: Cuba, Louisiana, Mississippi, Missouri, North Carolina, Ohio, South Carolina, and Virginia. Diversity was the characteristic feature among all clusters, both large and small. Nativity was not a factor in cluster formation.

Occupational Structure

In only one case did occupation appear to have played a major role in cluster formation.[41] Cluster 7 contained 12 households and 74 people. Data on occupation were available on 35 cluster residents, revealing that barbers (N = 24 or 67 percent) dominated this cluster.[42] Cluster 7 is located in the East End Factory district,[43] an occupationally diverse residential area. Yet the only barbers living in the area resided in cluster 7. Even so, the cluster was occupationally diverse, including five steamboat workers, two laborers, and four servants. Cluster 10 was the largest and, occupationally, the most diverse cluster in the sample.[44] It was located in the Central Waterfront district[45] and contained 12 households and 87 residents. This cluster contained most of the occupational categories found in the sample population. In all other cases, either the data were inconclusive, or else a clear pattern of occupational diversity existed.

The data show that the residential clusters were quite diverse and that occupation did not play a significant role in their formation. There is, however, one caveat. The number of cases analyzed is small, so generalizations must be made with extreme care. For example, in an earlier study of the black residential structure in Cincinnati, Henry Louis Taylor, Jr., found that occupation did play a role in determining where in the city people lived. At the same time, Taylor emphasized that blacks were an occupationally diverse group, and this diversity was reflected in every section of the city.[46]

Family-Household Type

Family-household structure did not form a basis for cluster formation.[47] A variety of different types of family-household structures
existed in each of the clusters. These differences reflected divisions
within the black community. There were married and single people,
married people with children, and single parents. There were older
residents and those in the prime of life. And women outnumbered
men. These divisions, however, were not reflected in the spatial organization of the residential environment.[48]

Surprisingly, although women headed 30 percent of the households in the sample population, there was not a single cluster composed exclusively of female heads of households. In every instance,
the households headed by women were spatially mixed with those
headed by men. And households consisting of single persons were
not spatially separated from those consisting of families and married couples.[49]

Age Structure

Black Cincinnati was composed of a diverse population consisting
of people at various stages in the life cycle. To determine if the African American community was stratified on the basis of stage in the
life cycle, each residential cluster was analyzed in terms of its age
structure. To do this the age structure was divided into five age categories: 10 years and under, 11 to 19 years, 20 to 35 years, 36 to 45
years, and 45 years and over.

Every cluster had children 10 years and younger, and 90 percent of
the clusters had residents in the 11-to-19 age group. All clusters had
residents in the critical 20-to-35 age category. People in the 36-to-45
year category were found in 95 percent of the clusters. And 70 percent of the clusters had residents in the 46-and-over age group. Here
it should be remembered that only forty-two people in the sample fell
into this age group. The data are clear. Age was not a factor in the
formation of black residential clusters. People from across the age
spectrum lived together.[50]

Shade of Color

The shade of color question lies at the center of our quest to understand community formation among African Americans in the pre-
ghetto era. Scholars agree that color represented an important source
of tension among African Americans during the antebellum period.[51]
At a time when class divisions were weak among African Americans,
color was an explosive issue that had the potential to create deep di-

vision within the race. Preferential treatment was the source of this tension. Within the context of the slave era, mulattoes were given preferential treatment over darker-skinned blacks. This was most strikingly reflected in the large number of mulattoes found in the free African American population. Some mulattoes felt culturally superior to blacks and sought to separate themselves from darker-skinned members of the race. In some southern cities this trend led to the formation of "Brown" societies.[52]

At the same time, social scientists have argued that inner tensions and conflicts do not necessarily erect insurmountable barriers to community formation. René Konig says that the presence of community "does not exclude the existence of powerful inner tensions, definite power groupings, and even a lack of inner homogeneity, which can, under certain circumstances, break into open conflict."[53] Likewise, James E. Blackwell suggests that shared life experiences can create communal bonds even when great differences exist within a group.[54]

Still the question lingers. Did shade of color create an obstacle to community formation among African Americans in Cincinnati? One way to answer this question is to determine if African Americans residentially separated themselves along color lines. Did mulattoes segregate themselves from blacks in the residential environment? Did shade of color play a significant role in shaping the African American residential environment?

The concept social interaction must be used in conjunction with segregation to understand fully the residential experience of blacks and mulattoes in Cincinnati and to determine if shade of color erected a barrier to community formation. There is evidence to suggest that the type and degree of social interaction, or face-to-face contact, that occurs among people will determine if friendships develop and groups are formed. While not all contacts will lead to friendships and the formation of groups, contacts do form the framework within which such social relations are established.[55] Stressing this point, Leon Festinger, Stanley Schachter, and Kurt Back in a study of housing at the Massachusetts Institute of Technology said,

> In the ordinary process of going in and out of a home, of working around it, one will occasionally meet others. It is reasonable to suppose that by means of this process one is more likely to meet someone who lives close by than someone who lives farther away. Our hypothesis, then, would state that, other things being equal, the greater the physical proximity between two people, the greater the probability that, within a given unit of time, a contact between them will occur. . . . Whether or not such a further development occurs depends upon a host of factors which might be loosely subsumed under such terms as "liking" and "congeniality."[56]

Table 4.7. Distribution of the Sample Population by Color

Color	No.	Cumulative No.	%	Cumulative %
Missing data	13	13	2.4	2.4
Black	193	206	35.9	38.3
Mulatto	332	538	61.7	100.0

Source: U.S. Bureau of the Census, Manuscript Census, 1850.

The point is that the frequency and intensity of social contacts create the foundation upon which friendships and group solidarity are built. It is within this context that the role played by color in the residential location decision of blacks and mulattoes assumes great importance. To gain insight into the place of color in the organization and structure of the African American residential environment, we examined the distribution of blacks and mulattoes at the ward, cluster, and household and dwelling unit levels. Also, we operated on the assumption that the distribution pattern would be affected by the fact that mulattoes outnumbered blacks in the sample population (Table 4.7). We wanted to answer two questions. First, were blacks and mulattoes segregated in the African American residential environment? If so, did the level of segregation erect significant barriers to social interaction? In other words, did physical distance, or dispersal, reduce the possibility of frequent contacts between blacks and mulattoes within the residential environment?

The Ward-Level Pattern

Although imperfect, the distribution pattern at the ward level appears to mirror the proportion of blacks and mulattoes in the African American population (Table 4.8). For example, mulattoes comprised 63 percent of African Americans in the sample population.[57] In the nine wards represented in our sample, mulattoes were slightly overrepresented in three wards and slightly underrepresented in three. Yet the maldistribution does not appear to be significant. We find no evidence of a strong tendency toward self-segregation among blacks and mulattoes at the ward level.

The Cluster-Level Pattern

At the cluster level there is evidence of a tendency toward the segregation of blacks and mulattoes. In 11 of the 20 clusters, mulattoes

Table 4.8. Distribution of Sample Population by Color and Ward

Ward	Black	%[a]	Mulatto	%[b]	Total	% Mulatto in Ward
1	27	13.9	51	15.4	78	65.3
2	25	12.9	59	17.8	86	68.6
4	59	30.6	79	23.7	142	55.6
5	10	5.2	30	9.0	40	75.0
6	7	3.6	18	5.4	26	69.2
7	17	8.8	12	3.6	32	37.5
9	11	5.7	34	10.2	46	73.9
10	27	13.9	25	7.5	53	47.2
11–12	10	5.2	24	7.2	34	70.5
Total	193	100.0	332	100.0	525	63.2

Note: The color of thirteen African Americans could not be determined.
[a]Percent of total black population.
[b]Percent of total mulatto population.
Source: U.S. Bureau of the Census, Manuscript Census, 1850.

comprised 70 percent or more of the cluster population (Table 4.9). And in 5 of those clusters, they comprised 80 percent or more of the population. We computed Chi-Square to determine the strength of the relationship between color and cluster formation. The computations showed that a significant association existed between color and cluster formation. The data have to be interpreted with great caution, however, because of the small size of the sample clusters.[58] While the relative strength of this association between cluster formation and shade of color might be questionable, the data do show that segregation played a role in cluster formation.

Yet the data do not tell the complete story. The black residential cluster represented a small circumscribed environment. It consisted of a constellation of houses and a small group of people huddled together in an environment dominated by whites, many of whom were hostile toward African Americans, regardless of shade of color. From this perspective, it is significant that blacks were represented in every cluster within the sample. Moreover, there were nine clusters that contained large numbers of both blacks and mulattoes. And 57 percent of the sample population (297) lived in such clusters. So, while a tendency toward segregation did exist in cluster formation, caution must be exercised in interpreting the social meaning of this "segregation." There were many blacks and mulattoes living in close proximity to each other. In the small world of the residential cluster,

Table 4.9. Distribution of the Sample Population by Color
and Cluster

Cluster	Black	Mulatto	Total	% Mulatto
1	8	4	12	33
2	4	6	10	60
3	5	15	20	75
4	10	30	40	75
5	4	10	14	71
6	11	35	46	76
7	27	47	74	64
8	6	6	12	50
9	2	10	12	80
10	40	43	83	52
11	1	12	13	92
12	9	13	22	59
13	21	29	50	58
14	3	19	22	86
15	11	6	17	35
16	5	15	20	75
17	7	18	25	72
18	8	4	12	86
19	2	12	14	86
20	9	8	17	47
Total	193	332	525	63

Note: The color of thirteen African Americans could not be determined.
Source: U.S. Bureau of the Census, Manuscript Census, 1850.

mulattoes and blacks probably came into frequent contact with one
another. They may have been separated, but they were not socially
isolated from each other.

Household and Dwelling Units

An examination of the color composition of households and
dwelling units shows a clear pattern of segregation by color in the
formation of households by African Americans (Table 4.10). The
sample population lived in 109 households. Sixty-nine percent of
these households—containing 331 people, or 63 percent of the African American population—were segregated on the basis of color.
This suggests that mulattoes may have consciously separated themselves from blacks when they formed households.

Table 4.10. Distribution of Sample Population by Color
Composition of the Household

Household	No.	%	Population	% Type
Black	29	27	101	19
Mulatto	46	42	230	44
Mixed	34	31	194	37
Total	109	100	525	100

Note: The color of thirteen African Americans could not be determined.
Source: U.S. Bureau of the Census, Manuscript Census, 1850.

Yet when we look at the distribution of these households by dwelling unit, this notion of mulattoes isolating themselves from blacks must be greatly tempered (Tables 4.11 and 4.12).

The 109 households contained in the sample population were distributed among eighty dwelling units or houses. Thirty-three, or 41 percent, of these dwelling units provided lodging for both blacks and mulattoes. Put another way, 48 percent of the African American pop-

Table 4.11. Population of Mixed Dwelling Units by Color

Cluster	No. Mixed Dwelling Units	Black	Mulatto	Total
1	1	8	4	12
3	1	5	1	6
4	1	6	14	20
5	1	4	1	5
6	2	22	4	26
7	2	9	7	16
8	1	6	6	12
10	10	34	31	65
11	1	1	6	7
12	1	9	5	14
13	5	21	10	31
14	1	1	8	9
16	2	5	3	8
17	1	1	3	4
18	1	1	5	6
19	1	2	5	7
20	1	6	2	8
Total	33	141	115	256

Source: U.S. Bureau of the Census, Manuscript Census, 1850.

Table 4.12. Distribution of the Sample Population by Dwelling
Unit, Cluster, and Dwelling Unit Type

Clusters	No. Dwelling Units	Population	No. Mixed Dwelling Units
1	1	12	1
2	2	10	0
3	3	20	1
4	4	40	1
5	2	14	1
6	5	48	2
7	12	74	2
8	1	13	1
9	3	13	0
10	15	87	10
11	2	13	1
12	4	23	1
13	6	40	5
14	2	22	1
15	2	17	0
16	3	20	2
17	4	26	1
18	3	12	1
19	2	14	1
20	4	20	1
Total	80	538	33

Source: U.S. Bureau of the Census, Manuscript Census, 1850.

ulation (N = 256) lived in houses that contained both blacks and
mulattoes. Most significant, a striking 73 percent (N = 141) of blacks
lived in dwelling units with mulattoes. Although most blacks and
mulattoes lived in separate households, they nevertheless shared the
same dwelling unit.

Under these circumstances, it is reasonable to believe, especially
given the high levels of racial hostility in antebellum Cincinnati, that
meaningful social contacts took place between blacks and mulattoes
who shared the same dwelling unit. In the hallways or on the front
porches of these houses, blacks and mulattoes probably met and talked
with each other. And it would not be surprising if the resulting face-
to-face contact did not give rise to friendships or neighboring, which
probably reinforced communal bonds and facilitated the community
formation process. Here it should be remembered that 31 percent of

the households contained both blacks and mulattoes. In Cincinnati shade of color did not erect a barrier to community formation.

In summary, the data suggest that there was a trend toward segregation in the organization of the African American residential environment. In a number of residential clusters mulattoes were overrepresented, and the majority of African American households were formed along color lines. At the same time, it is clear that this trend toward self-segregation was overshadowed by the fact that blacks and mulattoes lived within close proximity and that the great majority of blacks lived in dwelling units with mulattoes. Moreover, every cluster in the sample contained both blacks and mulattoes; 73 percent of blacks lived in dwelling units with mulattoes, and 31 percent of the households contained both blacks and mulattoes. So, then, the social relations between the two groups were characterized by intimate, face-to-face contact, which increased the probability of friendships forming, of neighboring occurring, and of communal bonds being strengthened.

The Formation of Community and High Visibility

As previously mentioned, although scattered across the city, most blacks were concentrated in the East End Factory district and along the Central Waterfront district, where they formed two big cluster-concentrations. A cluster concentration is a series of residential clusters that are located in a particular geographical area. Contemporaries referred to these two locales as "Bucktown" and "Little Africa," respectively.[59] Why? After all, African Americans did not spatially dominate the two locations. We argue that the location of institutions determines the importance of a geographic area to a social group, especially when that group is residentially dispersed. Further, when combined with large numbers of group members living in the area, the concentration of institutions makes a region highly visible to other people as well as to members of the group.[60] This suggests that "Bucktown" and "Little Africa" were highly visible not simply because large numbers of blacks lived there but also because of the concentration of African American institutions there. And it was this concentration of institutions in the locale that caused it to become a "central place" or meeting ground for African Americans, who lived in various parts of Cincinnati.[61] In essence, this clustering of institutions created a "commons" for black Cincinnati during the pre-ghetto era. The commons served as a focal point of social interaction for blacks.

To test this hypothesis we identified and found the approximate location of eighteen black institutions: four schools, eleven churches,
one orphanage, one hotel, and a stop on the Underground Railroad.
These institutions were then located on an 1855 map of Cincinnati
(Map 4.2).[62] The mapping project showed that ten of the institutions
were located in the East End Factory district, four in the Central
Waterfront, and four outside the cluster-concentrations. These black
institutions were not randomly distributed within the two main residential areas but were concentrated. For example, nine of ten institutions found in the East End Factory district were located in ward 9,
primarily in the area between Fifth and Seventh streets, near Sixth
and Broadway. A similar pattern of clustering took place among the
institutions located in the fourth ward section of the Waterfront area.
The concentration of institutions gave these two areas high visibility
and explains why contemporaries referred to them as "Bucktown"
and "Little Africa."

Finally, both the concentration and variety of institutions located
in the East End Factory district suggest that it was the cultural center
of black Cincinnati and the hub around which the rest of the community operated. In other words, "Bucktown" probably served as
the central place for black Cincinnati and represented the location
that first came to mind when Cincinnatians, both black and white,
thought of the African American community. This highly visible
section of the black residential component represented the social glue
that held African Americans together, especially those who lived outside the cluster-concentrations. These institutions served as gathering
places, nodal points where social interaction took place. For example,
the Dumas Hotel, located on McAllister Street in "Bucktown" (the
East End Factory district), was a place where free and slave blacks
met to exchange information.

Conclusion

Howard P. Chudacoff, in a study of ethnic neighborhoods in
Omaha, Nebraska, between 1880 and 1920, indicated that the pattern of residential dispersion tended to minimize the importance of
the residential component in the urban experience of immigrants in
medium-sized cities.[63] Similar observations were made by Sam Bass
Warner, Jr., and Colin Burke.[64] The Cincinnati experience suggests
that the observations of Chudacoff and Warner and Burke were not
true of African Americans at mid-century. Even though blacks lived in
a multiracial residential environment during the antebellum period,

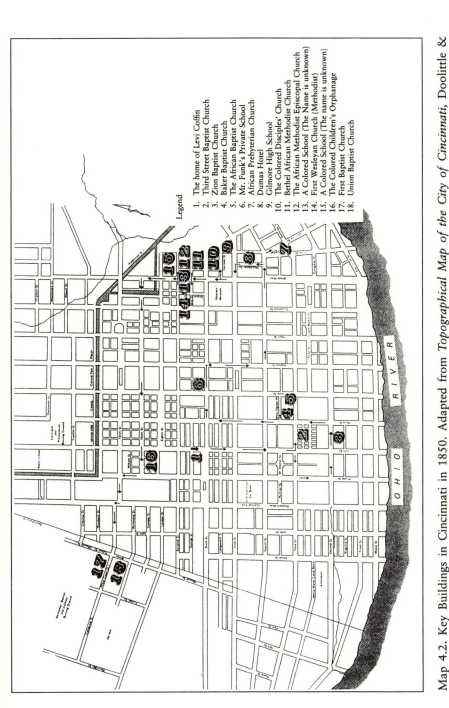

Legend

1. The home of Levi Coffin
2. Third Street Baptist Church
3. Zion Baptist Church
4. Baker Baptist Church
5. The African Baptist Church
6. Mr. Funk's Private School
7. African Prebyterian Church
8. Dumas Hotel
9. Gilmore High School
10. The Colored Disciples' Church
11. Bethel African Methodist Church
12. The African Methodist Episcopal Church
13. A Colored School (The Name is unknown)
14. First Wesleyan Church (Methodist)
15. A Colored School (The name is unknown)
16. The Colored Children's Orphanage
17. First Baptist Church
18. Union Baptist Church

Map 4.2. Key Buildings in Cincinnati in 1850. Adapted from *Topographical Map of the City of Cincinnati*, Doolittle & Munson, 1841, Cincinnati Historical Society; Charles Cist, *Cincinnati in 1841* (Cincinnati: Cist, 1841); Cist, *Cincinnati in 1851* (Cincinnati: W. H. Moore & Co., 1851).

the residential component was extremely important and played a decisive role in promoting the unity and cohesion necessary for the achievement of group solidarity and community formation.

The residential cluster is central to understanding the pre-ghetto black residential experience and to understanding how African Americans were able to overcome the effects of dispersal and internal divisions to build a community. In the antebellum city the residential cluster was the basic unit of residential organization. The unifying power of the cluster evolved from its heterogeneity. Clusters were formed without regard for differences in nativity, occupation, family and household type, age, and shade of color. The color issue, however, needs some qualification since there was a trend toward the segregation of blacks and mulattoes within the clusters. This trend was overshadowed by the fact that blacks and mulattoes lived near each other, with 73 percent of blacks sharing the same dwelling unit with mulattoes. The resulting social interactions strengthened communal bonds and facilitated the community formation process.

Thus within the residential clusters people from different backgrounds and various historic and everyday life experiences came into contact with one another. And it was here that the foundation of a strong community was laid.

The concentration of institutions also played a key role in community formation. The clustering of these institutions gave birth to a commons, which served as a hub that linked together the scattered African American population. Although dispersed across the city, the black residential clusters were still concentrated in two sections of Cincinnati, where they formed cluster-concentrations.

The cluster-concentrations created a critical mass of people in select parts of city, which, in turn, led to the formation of institutions in those locales. These institutions served as central places or meeting grounds for African Americans, regardless of where they lived in Cincinnati. Collectively they created a commons where people from across the city came together. In these shared institutions, a diverse people confronted similar problems and developed similar experiences, which reinforced shared values and united the population.

Notes

1. Carter G. Woodson, "The Negroes of Cincinnati Prior to the Civil War," *Journal of Negro History* 1 (Jan. 1916): 1–22; Gary B. Nash, *Forging*

Freedom: The Formation of Philadelphia's Black Community, 1720–1840 (Cambridge, Mass.: Harvard University Press, 1988); Leon F. Litwack, *The Negro in the Free States, 1790–1860* (Chicago: University of Chicago Press, 1961).

2. George A. Hillery, Jr., "Definitions of Community: Areas of Agreement," *Rural Sociology* 20 (Mar. 1955): 111–23.

3. Henry Louis Taylor, Jr., "Introductory Remarks: The Great Migration and Black Institution Building" (Paper presented at the Conference on Black Migration and the American City: Forging the African-American Community, Smithsonian Institution, National Museum of American History, Washington, D.C., 5–6 Feb. 1988); James Borchert, *Alley Life in Washington: Family, Community, Religion, and Folklife in the City, 1850–1970* (Urbana: University of Illinois Press, 1980), 100–142.

4. Thomas Bender, *The Community and Social Change in America* (New Brunswick, N.J.: Rutgers University Press, 1978), 6.

5. Roland L. Warren, *The Community in America*, 3d ed. (Chicago: Rand McNally, 1978), 37.

6. Borchert, *Alley Life*, 100–142; Gerald D. Suttles, *The Social Construction of Communities* (Chicago: University of Chicago Press, 1972), 21–43.

7. Bender, *The Community*, 8.

8. Kai T. Erikson, *Everything in Its Path: Destruction of Community in the Buffalo Creek Flood* (New York: Simon and Schuster, 1976), especially the introduction and part III, cited in Bender, *The Community*, 7.

9. Martin Buber, *Paths in Utopia* (London: Routledge and Kegan Paul, 1949), 145, cited in Bender, *The Community*, 7.

10. Robert A. Nisbet, *The Sociological Tradition* (New York: Basic Books, 1966), 47–48.

11. This point was particularly emphasized by the British anthropologist, J. Clyde Mitchell, who found that men and women in African cities remained within the bonds of community even though they lived in different parts of the city. These communities, he argued, were not locality based but were founded upon a very complex pattern of social interaction. Mitchell, "The Concept and Use of Social Networks," in *Social Networks in Urban Situations: Analyses of Personal Relationships in Central African Towns*, ed. J. Clyde Mitchell (Manchester, Eng.: Manchester University, 1969), cited in Bender, *The Community*, 49.

12. Historians agree that the residential environment plays a big role in shaping the everyday life and culture of urban blacks. However, most of what we know about the link between residential environment and community is based on studies of the black ghetto. Gilbert Osofsky, *Harlem: The Making of a Ghetto: Negro New York, 1890–1930* (New York: Harper and Row, 1963); Allen Spear, *Black Chicago: The Making of a Negro Ghetto, 1890–1920* (Chicago: University of Chicago Press, 1967); Kenneth Kusmer, "The Black Experience in American History," in *The State of Afro-American History: Past, Present, and Future*, ed. Darlene Clark Hine (Baton Rouge: Louisiana State University Press, 1986), 91–122.

13. Ira Berlin, "The Making of Americans," *American Visions*, Part 1 (Feb. 1987): 26–30; idem., "The Making of Americans," *American Visions*, Part 2 (Apr. 1987): 14–21.

14. Stephanie W. Greenberg, "Industrial Location and Ethnic Residential Patterns in an Industrializing City: Philadelphia, 1880," in *Philadelphia: Work, Space, Family and Group Experience in the Nineteenth Century*, ed. Theodore Hershberg (Oxford: Oxford University Press, 1981), 204–32.

15. Theodore Hershberg and Henry Williams, "Mulattoes and Blacks: Intra-group Color Differences and Social Stratification in Nineteenth-Century Philadelphia," in Hershberg, *Philadelphia*, 392–434; James Oliver Horton, "Shades of Color: The Mulatto in Three Antebellum Northern Communities," *Afro-Americans in New York Life and History* 8 (July 1984): 37–59. See also Ira Berlin, *Slaves without Masters: The Free Negro in the Antebellum South* (New York: Vintage Books, 1976), 195–98.

16. For a discussion of the concept of spatial dispersal and its relation to residential development, see Olivier Zunz, *The Changing Face of Inequality* (Chicago: University of Chicago Press, 1982), 40–59.

17. Charles Cist, *Cincinnati in 1851* (Cincinnati: W. H. Moore, 1851), 44; Leonard P. Curry, *The Free Black in Urban America: The Shadow of a Dream* (Chicago: University of Chicago Press, 1981), 56.

18. Henry Louis Taylor, Jr., "The Use of Maps in the Study of the Black Ghetto Formation Process: Cincinnati, 1802–1910," *Historical Methods* 17, no. 2 (Spring 1984): 44–57; Sam Bass Warner, Jr., and Colin B. Burke, "Cultural Change and the Ghetto," *Journal of Contemporary History* 4 (Oct. 1969): 173–87; Kathleen Neils Conzen, "Immigrants, Immigrant Neighborhoods, and Ethnic Identity: Historical Issues," *Journal of American History* 3 (Dec. 1979): 603–15; Zunz, *The Changing Face of Inequality*, 40–59.

19. See Henry Williams, "Appendix 2: Data Description," in *Philadelphia*, 503–20.

20. A two-step procedure was used to determine the location of the different residential areas and to delimit their boundaries. An examination of the 1850 U.S. manuscript census made it possible to pinpoint the residential concentrations of the different races, ethnic groups, and social classes. At this point, a correlation between the various population concentrations and the city's ward boundaries was observed. By making the residential areas correspond with the ward boundaries, it was possible to do both macro- and micro-level analysis of the residential areas. Rather than create artificial and arbitrarily selected residential areas, the goal of this project was to identify the city's actual residential areas, delimit their boundaries, and then analyze their internal structure. For a detailed description of this approach, see Taylor, "The Use of Maps," 44–58. See also Theodore Hershberg, "The Historical Study of Urban Space: Introduction," *Historical Methods Newsletter: A Special Issue: The Philadelphia Social History Project* 9 (Mar./June 1976): 99–105; Zunz, *The Changing Face of Inequality*, 40–59.

21. There is an abundant literature on the various methods of establishing the boundaries of residential areas. Since the early 1950s, for example, planning departments and citizen groups in a number of major cities have been dividing their cities into discrete neighborhoods for the purpose of planning. In 1980, for the first time, the U.S. Bureau of the Census provided neighborhood statistics for cities that had officially established neighborhood boundaries. We have applied these planning principles to the historic study of the city. Thomas Broden, Ronn B. Kirkwood, John Roos, and Thomas Swart, *Neighborhood Identification: A Guidebook for Participation in the U.S. Census Neighborhood Statistics Program* (Washington, D.C.: U.S. Department of Housing and Urban Development, 1980); Wendell Bell, "Social Areas: Typology of Urban Neighborhoods," in *Community Structure and Analysis*, ed. Marvin B. Sussman (New York: Crowell, 1959), 61–92.

22. Zunz, *The Changing Face of Inequality*, 40–59.

23. There was one large section of Cincinnati referred to by contemporaries as the Over-the-Rhine district. Although large numbers of Germans resided in the area, many other ethnic groups, along with blacks, lived there as well. We decided to use the term Over-the-Rhine to describe that broad residential section to the north of the Erie Canal and Liberty Street. Henry Louis Taylor, Jr., "On Slavery's Fringe: City Building and Black Community Development in Cincinnati, 1800–1850," *Ohio History* 95 (Winter–Spring 1986): 16–19.

24. In antebellum Cincinnati there was no rigid separation of commercial and residential space. William Pullen, "Map of the Business Portion of Cincinnati" (Cincinnati, 1863), Cincinnati Historical Society; W. H. Martin, "Map of Cincinnati for Fire Insurance Companies and Real Estate Agents," vols. 1 and 2 (Cincinnati, 1855). The Martin collection of maps identifies sixteen types of different structures, according to building materials and configuration. The maps also show the location and configurations of buildings, stores, dwelling units above stores, public institutions, churches, and factories. The maps make possible the detailed study of the land use structure and pattern of property development for antebellum Cincinnati.

25. Because street addresses were not recorded until the 1880 census, a two-step procedure for determining black residential locations was developed. In the first step, the names of blacks and their white neighbors were obtained from the manuscript census; in the second step, these individuals were looked up in the city directory, then their approximate addresses determined and plotted on an 1850 project base map. The 1850 Cincinnati city directories have two limitations that affected the mapping project, and they must be considered when interpreting the data. First, the city directories do not contain precise addresses. For example, the 1850 Williams City Directory indicated that Caleb Calloway, a black porter, lived on Pike between Third and Fourth streets. The city directory did not indicate on which side of the street Calloway lived, nor did it indicate where on Pike between Third and Fourth he resided. Thus the 1850 directory contains only approximate

addresses. See Henry Louis Taylor, Jr., "Spatial Organization and the Residential Experience: Black Cincinnati in 1850," *Social Science History* 10, no. 1 (Spring 1986): 45–69.

26. David M. Katzman, *Before the Ghetto: Black Detroit in the Nineteenth Century* (Urbana: University of Illinois Press, 1975), 53–80. The year 1850 is particularly important for the analysis of black residential clusters. First, by 1850 the commercial city had reached maturity, and the changes in this spatial structure that industrialization would produce following the Civil War had not yet taken place. Second, this is the earliest picture of the black residential cluster that can be taken. Prior to 1850 the census generally recorded only the names of household heads with summary data describing the age and sex structure of the household. Beginning in 1850, however, census marshals enumerated each member of the household separately and recorded specific information on each person's age, color, place of birth, school attendance, literacy, physical and psychological handicaps, and, for males, occupation. For African Americans, the census marshals also recorded shades of color (black or mulatto) among household members. This information makes possible, for the first time, a detailed study of the urban population. Although David M. Katzman and James Borchert have provided the most detailed descriptions of black residential clusters, their descriptions are for the years following 1870. By this time significant changes had already taken place in the structure of cities, changes that might also have affected the structure and organization of residential clusters. Borchert, *Alley Life*, 1–56.

27. This conclusion is based on an analysis of the white heads of households who lived in or adjacent to black residential clusters. The data set was derived from the U.S. Bureau of the Census, *The Seventh Census of the United States: Manuscript Census for Cincinnati and Hamilton County, 1850* (Washington, D.C.: National Archives Microfilm). See folder on "Residential Cluster Project," in Cincinnati Urban Studies Project Files, State University of New York at Buffalo, Center for Applied Public Affairs Studies, Center Archives.

28. The data on the residential clusters have been compiled in two data sets. The data set "1850 Cluster Sample Population: Black Cincinnati" is in a hard-copy format and contains the raw data taken from the 1850 manuscript census. A second data set, called Cinclust, 1850, was developed for analytical purposes. This data set is stored in the computer program DBase III+. The spreadsheet program Quattro was used in our analysis of the data. This information is also in a hard-copy data set called "Cincinnati's Black Clusters, 1850." All citations in this chapter will refer to "Cincinnati's Black Clusters, 1850," hereafter cited as "Black Clusters, 1850." Copies of all the data sets are housed at the Cincinnati Urban Studies Project, Center Archives.

29. "Black Clusters, 1850," 1.

30. Ibid., 20.

31. Women were overrepresented in the central business area, with 68 men living there versus 100 women, a difference of 32. In the other three resi-

dential areas the difference between men and women ranged between 8 and 14. It is assumed that most women were domestics, servants, cooks, and washerwomen. Since the elite was overrepresented in the central business area, a good number of the jobs available to women may have been located in this section, which would account for their overrepresentation. "Black Clusters, 1950," 9.

32. Ibid., 2.

33. A modified version of the family structure model developed by Andrew Billingsley and Paul Lammermeier was used in this study to analyze the family-household structure of the cluster population. The 1850 census did not specify the relations of household members. Whenever a man and woman who were about the same age had the same surname, we assumed that they were man and wife. If there were children in the household with the same surname as the household head and his assumed wife, it was assumed that these were the children of the "couple." It is not possible to determine if the other members of the household were relatives or boarders. Lammermeier got around this problem by listing people simply as relatives and/or boarders. We followed the same approach. We developed a list of the following types of family-household structures: simple nuclear (husband and wife), nuclear (father, mother, children), attenuated nuclear (father, children), attenuated nuclear (mother, children), and attenuated nuclear (mother, adult children). In the above three cases the family-household structures were coded differently: simple extended (husband, wife, relatives and/or boarders), extended (husband, wife, children, relatives and/or boarders), attenuated extended (father, children, relatives and/or boarders), attenuated extended (mother, children, relatives and/or boarders), single person (male), unmarried, and single person (female), unmarried. Andrew Billingsley, *The Black Family in White America* (Englewood Cliffs, N.J.: Prentice Hall, 1968); Paul J. Lammermeier, "The Urban Black Family of the Nineteenth Century: A Study of the Black Family Structure in the Ohio Valley, 1850–1880," *Journal of Marriage and Family* 8 (Aug. 1973): 441–89.

34. "Black Residential Clusters, 1850," 21–22.

35. Ibid., 21–22.

36. Ibid., 4.

37. Ibid., 4–5.

38. This impression is primarily based on a careful study of the Cincinnati city directories for the years 1840 and 1843. The occupations of women are sometimes listed in the directories. David Henry Shaffer, *The Cincinnati, Covington, Newport and Fulton Directory for 1840* (Cincinnati, 1840), 467-77; Charles Cist, *The Cincinnati Directory for the Year 1843* (Cincinnati, 1843), 441–45. See also Dorothy Sterling, ed., *We Are Your Sisters: Black Women in the Nineteenth Century* (New York: Norton Company, 1984).

39. "Black Clusters, 1850," 5.

40. U.S. Bureau of the Census, *Negro Population, 1790–1915* (Washington, D.C.: Government Printing Office, 1918), 221.

41. In four of the clusters (20%), the data were too limited to determine the influence of occupation on the organization of the residential environment. For example, in cluster 12 there were 4 households and 23 residents. Three laborers and one blacksmith lived in the cluster. Cluster 9 had 3 households and 13 residents. Three riverworkers, one cook, and one whitewasher lived in the cluster. "Black Residential Clusters, 1850," 9–20.

42. Ibid., 17–19.

43. Ibid., 20.

44. Ibid., 10–11.

45. Ibid., 20.

46. Henry Louis Taylor, Jr., "Spatial Organization," 45–69.

47. For a discussion of the family-household structures upon which this analysis was based, see Lammermeier, "The Urban Black Family," 453.

48. "Black Clusters, 1850," 1, 20.

49. Ibid., 21–22.

50. Ibid., 7–8.

51. Hershberg, "Mulattoes and Blacks," 392–434; Horton, "Shades of Color," 37–59; Berlin, *Slaves without Masters,* 195–98.

52. Horton, "Shades of Color," 37–59.

53. René Konig, *The Community,* translated from German by Edward Fitzgerald (New York: Schocken Books, 1968), 130.

54. James E. Blackwell, *The Black Community: Diversity and Unity* (New York: Harper and Row, 1975), 16.

55. Leon Festinger, Stanley Schacter, and Kurt Back, *Social Pressures in Informal Groups: A Study of Human Factors in Housing* (New York: Harper and Brothers, 1950), 155; Gunnar Boalt and Carl-Gunnar Janson, "Distance and Social Relations," *Acta Sociologica* 2 (1956/1957): 73–96; Berry Wellman and Barry Leighton, "Networks, Neighborhoods and Communities: Approaches to the Study of the Community Question" (Research Paper No. 97, Center for Urban and Community Studies and Department of Sociology, University of Toronto, August 1978); Barry Wellman, "The Community Question Re-Evaluated" (Research Paper No. 165, Center for Urban and Community Studies, University of Toronto, August 1987).

56. Festinger, Schacter, and Back, *Social Pressures,* 155.

57. There were 13 African Americans whose color could not be determined. The 63 percent is based on 525 African Americans in the sample population.

58. Chi Square is a frequently used test of significance in social science. It is based on the null hypothesis that there is no relationship between the two variables in the total population. The resulting operation is a set of frequencies that allows us to determine if there is a significant discrepancy between the observed conjoint distribution and the distribution we should have expected if the two variables were unrelated to one another. In essence we can determine if the relationship is statistically significant. Earl Babbie, *The Practice of Social Research,* 5th ed. (Belmont, Calif.: Wadsworth, 1989), 460–62.

59. See, for example, Lafcadio Hearn, *Children of the Levee,* O. W. Frost, ed. (Lexington: University of Cincinnati Press, 1957).

60. Howard P. Chudacoff, "A New Look at Ethnic Neighborhoods: Residential Dispersion and the Concept of Visibility in a Medium-Sized City," *Journal of American History* 60 (June 1973): 89.

61. Central place is a geographic concept that describes a place that provides services for a much broader region. See Brian J. L. Berry and Frank E. Horton, *Geographic Perspectives in Urban Systems* (Englewood Cliffs, N.J.: 1970), 192–244.

62. A variety of different sources, including dissertations and theses, were searched in order to secure a listing of organizations. The most important source was Cist, *Cincinnati in 1851.* Approximately forty organizations were identified. We were able to find locations for eighteen.

63. Chudacoff, "Ethnic Neighborhoods," 76–93.

64. Warner and Burke, "Cultural Change and the Ghetto," 173–87.

5

Nancy Bertaux

Structural Economic Change and Occupational Decline among Black Workers in Nineteenth-Century Cincinnati

The employment aspects of life in Cincinnati's black community are, and have always been, of utmost importance in understanding many other aspects of that life, including socioeconomic status, residential location, and educational attainment. Indeed, the occupational hierarchy is arguably the chief mechanism that creates and perpetuates the American version of the class system. Blacks who have been able to significantly increase their socioeconomic status have done so by breaking out of the occupations to which they have traditionally been confined. Occupational segregation by race, whereby blacks are concentrated in a limited number of job categories, has been a key factor in keeping blacks as a group at the bottom of the socioeconomic ladder.[1]

While the empirical existence of job segregation by race and its negative effects on blacks' economic status have been generally accepted, the cause of this segregation has been the subject of continuing debate. Some scholars insist that labor supply factors can explain the different occupational profiles of blacks and whites, arguing that "human capital" deficits of blacks, such as less (or lesser-quality) education, training, and work experience, have resulted in blacks' concentration in lower-paying, lower-prestige jobs. Other scholars pose various theories of racial discrimination, arguing that racist practices (emanating from employers, white employees, or from more impersonal labor market institutions) have kept blacks from achieving an occupational distribution similar to that of whites.[2]

Looking at the historical development of occupational segregation by race makes it abundantly clear that the human capital explanation is insufficient to account for nineteenth-century occupational trends. Other immigrant groups came to America with human capital endowments quite similar to those of blacks, yet were able to make substantially greater economic progress through their quicker access to a wider range of occupations. Racism and racial discrimination played an undeniable role in creating the low-paid, low-status occupational profile that continues to plague much of the black community today, and this is not difficult to document historically. What is more challenging is to identify the dynamics of this discrimination over place and time.

This chapter examines how structural changes in the economy of nineteenth-century Cincinnati intersected with trends in racism, immigration, and population growth to produce a clear pattern of occupational decline for the city's black community, in the context of continuing occupational segregation by race. Cincinnati's blacks had surely been at a disadvantage in the labor market from the city's earliest days, but in the late nineteenth century, when Cincinnati underwent the dynamic change from a preindustrial to an industrial economy, blacks' occupational status actually worsened.[3]

In the second half of the nineteenth century Cincinnati evolved from a preindustrial, commercially based "walking city" focused on its riverfront (1820s to the 1850s) to a sprawling, manufacturing-based industrial center (1860s onward). Industrialization, the bureaucratization of business firms, and investment in public services were major influences on the character of Cincinnati's economy in this era. These structural economic changes deeply affected the lives of both black and white workers, as they resulted in a changing distribution of job opportunities. Analysis of occupational trends shows that while many white workers, especially artisans, experienced job dislocation, white workers as a whole were able to take advantage of the new, "good" jobs that were created by industrialization.[4] Black workers, however, clearly occupied a deteriorating position in the labor force amid the dynamic economic shifts of the late nineteenth century; from 1860 to 1890 the more prestigious occupations that black men and women had managed to enter, such as barber and teacher, became less important in the black work force, while the low-status occupations of laborer and domestic servant increasingly dominated the occupational profile of Cincinnati's blacks. The occupations that blacks entered in greater and greater numbers were also the very occupations that whites were leaving for the better opportunities now available to them in the industrialized economy.

Moreover, this occurred amid a substantial decline in formalized racism, as many discriminatory barriers were eliminated through reforms in the legal arena. Thus what would appear to have been a period full of positive opportunities for blacks resulted in economic stagnation and decline for black workers. The new jobs generated by industrialization and the new legal climate created by post–Civil War reforms did not, in fact, produce an economic renaissance for Cincinnati blacks. This chapter will argue that a variety of increasingly informal discriminatory barriers, initiated by institutions as well as by employers and white workers, explains this apparent paradox. The current literature on occupational trends among blacks in post–Civil War America often contrasts events in the South (that is, the rise of the sharecropping system, Jim Crow laws, and so on) with those in the North (that is, discriminatory labor unions, the use of blacks as strikebreakers, and so on).[5] An examination of the complexities surrounding the occupational status of blacks in nineteenth-century Cincinnati, a borderland city, should enrich our understanding of the history of black workers during the dawning of the industrial age.

Looking at black workers in the nineteenth century also lays a foundation for considering both the achievements and frustrations of twentieth-century blacks. The post–World War II period has witnessed a major structural shift in the U.S. economy as our industrial, manufacturing-based economy continues evolving into a postindustrial economy centered on service and high technology. Once again, this structural change, which would appear to offer new opportunities for blacks to move forward economically, has also been taking place at a time when racist barriers appear to be falling, this time due to a variety of civil rights laws and affirmative action programs. Despite this situation, evidence suggests that these economic changes, while benefiting better-educated blacks, may be resulting in occupational decline for blacks as a whole.[6] Thus the story of black workers in the nineteenth century may help us to understand economic trends in the black community today.

Job Competition, Population Growth, and the Labor Market

Before the specific occupational structure of the black community in preindustrial and industrial Cincinnati is considered, the demographic context must be briefly sketched. Since workers are drawn from the overall population, population trends are important in understanding labor force trends.[7] Thus the pattern of black population growth, as well as the growth of the immigrant population, should be established. Labor force participation rates are also relevant in looking at the overall employment status of blacks.

In spite of the small percentage of blacks in nineteenth-century Cincinnati (less than 5 percent), the absolute size of Cincinnati's black population was one of the largest among northern cities throughout the century.[8] In the antebellum period Cincinnati was an obvious potential residence for freed or runaway slaves due to its location as the southernmost city in a free state; Kentucky, where slavery was legal, was across the Ohio River. This borderland status cut both ways: while Cincinnati was a hotbed of abolitionism during this era, its strong southern ties and heritage also contributed to frequent outbreaks of extreme racism, which sometimes caused declines in the growth of the black population. The most blatant example occurred in the late 1820s, when at least one thousand blacks (probably about half the blacks in Cincinnati at that time) were driven from the city by whites determined to enforce Ohio's previously inactive Black Laws. Ohio's Black Laws had been passed in 1804–07, and they required all blacks to register with local officials, show certificates of freedom, and post a bond of five hundred dollars to "guarantee good behavior." These laws also prohibited blacks from testifying against whites in court, holding public office, or serving in the military. Ohio's 1802 constitution had already denied blacks suffrage.[9]

While decennial census figures show a continual increase in the size of Cincinnati's black population during the nineteenth century (Table 5.1), the trend in the percentage of nonwhites (almost all of whom were black and mulatto) was U-shaped. Only after the Civil War did the proportion of blacks in the city's population begin slowly to rise. Even by the turn of the century, this proportion was still below the antebellum peak. This was due to the vast inflows of European immigrants, primarily German and Irish, that occurred in the antebellum era. While blacks outnumbered the foreign-born in 1825, by 1840 there were over twice as many foreign-born as black Cincinnatians, and in 1850 the ratio was over sixteen to one. While the proportion of blacks in the population never reached 5 percent in

Table 5.1. Population Characteristics of Cincinnati, 1825–1900

Year	White	Nonwhite	% Non-white	Foreign	Native	% Foreign
1825	14,887[a]	65[a]	4.2	509[b]	1,815[b]	21.9
1840	44,124	2,258	4.5	5,698[b]	6,594[b]	46.4
1850	112,198	3,237	2.8	54,541	60,558	47.2
1860	157,313	3,731	2.3	73,614	87,430	45.2
1870	210,335	5,904	2.7	79,612	136,627	36.8
1880	246,912	8,227	3.2	71,659	183,480	28.0
1890	285,244	11,684	3.9	71,408	225,500	24.0
1900	311,404	14,498	4.4	57,961	267,941	17.8

[a]Approximate figures.
[b]Figures for adult white males; total figures not available.
Sources: U.S. Bureau of the Census, Population of the United States, Eighth-Twelfth Census, 1860–1900; Steven J. Ross, Workers on the Edge (New York: Columbia University Press, 1985), 74.

the nineteenth century, the proportion of foreign-born grew to over 47 percent in 1850. After 1850 the immigration slowed dramatically, and the proportion of foreign-born fell for the rest of the century, although it was still nearly 18 percent in 1900. The presence of large numbers of first- and second-generation immigrants meant that black workers often faced stiff competition, even in low-status occupations. Competition with Irish-born workers was especially intense.[10] While Irish workers outnumbered black workers by seven to one in 1860; by 1890 the number of Irish-born and black workers was roughly equal (Table 5.2).

Labor Force Participation

An important indicator of the work status of a population is the labor force participation rate, which is defined as the proportion of the population that is in the labor force. In Cincinnati throughout the late nineteenth century, 1860–90, black labor force participation rates were higher than those for whites, 54.8 versus 47.2%, and women's rates were a fraction of those of men, roughly 15 to 20% versus 60 to 65% (Table 5.3). The labor force participation rates for men and for whites rose during the latter part of the nineteenth century, but the rates for women and nonwhites rose faster. The result was a labor force that was increasingly female, and increasingly nonwhite, based on the nonwhite labor force and the female labor force as a

Table 5.2. Cincinnati Labor Force by Place of Birth, Race, and Sex, 1860–90

Year[a]	U.S.	Germany	Ireland	Gr. Britain	White	Nonwhite
Total						
1860	17,660	21,940	12,640	2,860	59,220	1,760
1870	34,817	26,991	10,686	2,491	b	b
1880	62,826	24,117	7,843	2,106	b	b
1890	86,586	26,239	6,552	2,163	118,536	6,401
Females						
1860	3,820	3,020	3,560	540[c]	11,220	560[c]
1890	24,243	3,336	1,953	411	28,277	2,133
Males						
1860	13,840	18,920	9,080	2,320	48,000	1,200
1890	62,343	22,903	4,599	1,752	90,259	4,268
Percent of Labor Force That Is Female						
1860	21.6	13.8	28.2	18.9	18.9	31.8
1890	28.0	12.7	29.8	14.4	23.9	33.3

[a]Figures for 1860 are estimates based on a 5 percent random sample; figures on place of birth and race by sex were not published in 1870 or 1880; no data on nativity of the labor force were published in 1900.
[b]Data not available.
[c]Based on a very small sample size (27–28).
Source: U.S. Bureau of the Census, *Population of the United States, Eighth-Twelfth Census, 1860–1900.*

percent of the total labor force (Table 5.3). By 1890 about 28% of the Cincinnati labor force was either black, female, or both.[11]

The lower labor force participation rates of women were primarily due to women's unpaid work of caring for their families at home, which left them outside the official labor force. The higher labor force participation rates of blacks were due to a number of factors, most of which centered around the lower earnings of their families. Blacks began work at a younger age (which was related to their receiving fewer years of education); black workers were financially unable to retire as early as whites; and more black family members (especially women) were needed as workers in order to cover basic necessities.[12] Indeed, even when compared to other ethnic groups, black women's work rates appear high, based on figures showing how the proportion of female workers in the overall work force varied among different races and nationalities in 1860 and 1890 (Table 5.2).[13] The percentage of the labor force that was female was highest in the black

Table 5.3. Cincinnati Labor Force and Labor Force Participation
Rates by Race and Sex

Year[a]	White LF	LFPR (%)	Nonwhite LF	LFPR (%)	LF % Nonwhite
1860	59,220[b]	37.6	1,760[b]	47.2	2.9
1890	118,536	41.6	6,401	54.8	5.1

Year	Male LF	LFPR (%)	Female LF	LFPR (%)	LF % Female
1860	49,200[b]	59.8	11,780[b]	15.0	19.3
1870	60,842	57.2	17,081	15.6	21.9
1880	78,170	62.2[c]	22,284	17.2[c]	22.2
1890	94,527	65.2	30,410	20.0	24.3
1900	130,913	66.1	37,786	22.4	26.7

[a]Labor force figures by race were not published in 1870, 1880, and 1900.
[b]Labor force figures for 1860 are estimates based on a 5 percent random sample; the
nonwhite female labor force estimate derives from a small sample (*n* = 28).
[c]These figures are based on estimates of the Cincinnati population by sex derived
from actual figures on the Hamilton County population by sex.
Source: U.S. Bureau of the Census, *Population of the United States, Eighth-Twelfth
Census, 1860–1900.*

community. The Irish ran a fairly close second to blacks on this percentage, in accordance with their similarly low economic status. Native U.S., German, and English women were significantly less likely
to work.[14]

Black families' low earnings are especially sobering when their
higher labor force participation rates are considered; in effect, they
worked harder to earn less. Much of the reason for this phenomenon
lies in the very restricted nature of the occupations in which blacks
were generally employed. Moreover, as the city's economy developed,
blacks did not attain much upward mobility in the occupational
arena. In fact, the structural economic changes that occurred in the
late nineteenth century appear to have worked against, instead of
for, blacks.

The Preindustrial Racial Division of Labor

The city's black community developed during the period in which
Cincinnati was building its reputation as the mercantile center of the
West. Cincinnati's favorable location on the Ohio River in the steam-
boat era helped it become the fastest-growing city in the country dur-

ing the 1830s and 1840s. By the mid-1820s Cincinnati had one or two steamers a day stopping at its public landing. By 1830 Cincinnati was the economic leader of the West—the "Queen City." It was the distribution center for supplies destined for large parts of Ohio, Indiana, Kentucky, Illinois, and Missouri. Timothy Flint, the publisher of *Western Monthly Review,* reckoned in 1830 that Cincinnati was the central market town for one million people.[15]

For the early decades of the city's history, information on the actual occupations of black Cincinnatians participating in the labor force is somewhat spotty and impressionistic. The earliest descriptions of Cincinnati note that most black men labored on steamboats or on the riverfront, on internal improvement projects such as road and canal construction, and as common laborers in all areas of the city's economy. Some also worked as porters, messengers, shoeblacks, and vendors. Black women frequently worked as domestics. Certainly the experiences of black and white workers in Cincinnati had always been quite different. Dr. Daniel Drake, in his account of Cincinnati in 1815, wrote that the city's small number of blacks were "disciplined to laborious occupations" and "prone to the performance of light and menial drudgery." Around the same time, Cincinnati editor Timothy Flint referred to Cincinnati's borderland status when he noted that "the evils of slavery are not confined to the parts of the country where involuntary labour exists, but the neighborhood is infected. Certain kinds of labour are despised as being the work of slaves."[16]

Although the U.S. census did not collect information on occupations until 1850 (males) and 1860 (males and females), there are city directories that list occupations along with individuals' names. Data from the city directories should be used with great caution, since studies that cross-reference census and directory entries show that the early Cincinnati directories grossly undercounted blacks, transients, and the poor in general, while they completely excluded all working women who were not considered heads of household.[17] This obviously limits their usefulness for present purposes. For example, the directories failed to count domestic servants, who typically lived with their employers and were not considered household heads. Still the directories do give us some ideas about the occupational distribution available to blacks, and the most common occupations listed in directories continue to be important later in the century when census data are available. For instance, the 1836–37 directory listed 163 black household heads, 25 of whom were female. Among black males there were 28 laborers (20% of the black males listed), 24 boatmen and steamboat stewards (17%), and 22 barbers (16%). The black females were nearly all washerwomen (23, or 92%). Blacks listed in the 1840, 1842, and 1844 directories had similar occupational distributions.[18] From the limited information available, it would appear safe to conclude that in the commercial stage of Cincinnati's economy, job opportunities for blacks consisted of physical labor, much of which was centered around the riverfront and the provision of personal services to whites.[19]

It is clear that the restricted set of occupations available to blacks in preindustrial Cincinnati was strongly related to the many doors that were closed to blacks during this period. A variety of social institutions, including government, educational institutions, and trade unions, as well as private employers and white workers in general, worked to keep blacks out of the mainstream.

A black traveler to Cincinnati in 1827 reported that "I thought upon coming to a free state like Ohio I would find every door thrown open to receive me, but from the treatment I received by the people generally, I found it little better than in Virginia. . . . I found every door was closed against the colored man in a free state, excepting the jails and penitentiaries." Indeed, even the poorhouse was closed to blacks, as another of the provisions of the Black Laws mentioned earlier was that destitute, unemployed blacks were ineligible for poor relief.[20]

Blacks were heavily discriminated against in the educational arena. Black youths were barred from attending the public schools that had opened in 1829, and attempts to establish separate black schools were resisted. In 1830 the first ward "people of color petitioned the legislature that a school be opened for black children. When the legislature failed to respond positively, three abolitionists began teaching Black pupils in the East End. . . . Another abolitionist founded a school in the West End in the 1830s. Mob violence frequently kept scholars from attending these schools and the White teachers were refused accommodation in boarding houses." Although special private schools did operate for blacks intermittently over the early part of the nineteenth century, it was reported in 1845 that over half of Cincinnati's blacks were illiterate. In addition to being ineligible to attend public schools (even though many paid taxes), privately educated blacks were not permitted to enroll in professional schools such as the Cincinnati Medical College in 1837.[21]

The dramatic surge in German and Irish immigrants who settled in Cincinnati in the 1830s and 1840s had a significant impact on the local labor market. Woodson has argued that in antebellum Cincinnati the presence of large numbers of German and Irish immigrants willing to do menial labor greatly restricted job opportunities for black men: "Since the Negroes could not follow ordinary menial occupations there was nothing left them but the lowest form of 'drudgery,' for which employers often preferred colored women. It was, therefore, necessary in some cases for the mother to earn the living for the family because the father could get nothing to do." In 1838 Germans denounced a Cincinnati newspaper editor for his suggestion that blacks should be considered the equals of immigrant Germans, since they competed for the same jobs. The editor then modified his stance, stating that blacks should continue their monopoly on street sweeping and table serving.[22]

Inside and outside trade unions, the city's white workers were known to protest against working with blacks, especially when blacks were not in a subordinate position.[23] White protests were frequently rooted in the feeling "that it was a disgrace to work with Negroes." Blacks were reportedly denied membership in early trade unions, and the president of a local mechanics' association "was publicly tried in 1830 by that organization for the crime of assisting a colored youth to learn a trade." An incident from the 1830s illustrates the barriers faced by skilled black workers. A young cabinetmaker who had purchased his freedom in Kentucky came to Cincinnati to find work and succeeded in obtaining a position. "On entering the establishment, however, the workmen threw down their tools, declaring that the Negro had to leave or that they would. The unfortunate 'intruder' was accordingly dismissed."[24]

The "Colored" Job Market

In 1850 the U.S. census collected information on occupation by race, for male workers only, but did not publish summaries of this data. Recently scholars have summarized and analyzed the occupations of black men in 1850 by using data from manuscript returns. Consistent with the data from the earlier city directories, the top five occupations for black men in 1850 were (in order of frequency) boatman, barber, cook, laborer, and waiter. Together these five occupations accounted for two-thirds of all black male workers.[25]

By 1860 information on the occupations of black Cincinnati workers, by sex as well as race became available from the decennial U.S. census.[26] For most of the nineteenth century the census did not summarize occupations by race and sex, even at the national level, although the information was available on the original returns. For

1890 only, census volumes were published that summarize occupations by race and sex at the U.S. level and for the states and major cities, including Cincinnati. For 1860 I used an original data base consisting of a 5 percent random sample of all individuals listed as having occupations on the manuscript returns of the 1860 population census. The 1860 data were summarized for comparability to the 1890 figures,[27] and the overall size of the Cincinnati labor force by race and sex for 1860 and 1890 was calculated (Table 5.2).

The distribution of occupations by race and sex in 1860 illustrates the fact that there was more overlap in the occupations of whites and blacks of one gender than for males and females of the same race (Table 5.4). The same pattern is evident in the distribution of occupations in 1890 (Table 5.5). Thus in nineteenth-century Cincinnati, the occupations of black men and women followed the traditional "men's work" and "women's work" patterns.[28]

Cincinnati blacks of both sexes were disproportionately likely to hold the lowest-status occupations within these categories (Table 5.6). By 1860 black and white men and women occupied distinct occupational niches in the labor market (Table 5.4). In 1860 "laborer" was the most important occupation for both white and black males, but categories such as clerical/sales, traders and dealers, and the traditional crafts were more important for white males. Such categories accounted for about 40 percent of the white male labor force, but blacks were virtually excluded from these occupations. Black men were much more likely than whites to work at low-status jobs, such as dockworker and boatman, and in hotels, restaurants, and "miscellaneous" manufacturing and personal service.

Becoming a barber was the most prestigious choice available to more than 10 percent of black male workers. Writing in the 1920s, the black publisher Wendell P. Dabney described the black barbers of the mid-nineteenth century in sentimental terms: "In the early days colored men enjoyed a monopoly of the barber business. . . . Barber shops were the great places for gossip and the white customers were generally quite well informed as to the doings of Negro society. The patrons and barbers were very chummy in many ways. The Negro barber, as a workman, was an artist. The razor in his hands became an instrument that made sweet melody as it charmed away the grass that grew on facial lawns."[29] Small numbers of black men also found relative success in the field of catering, and some of the black stewards on steamboats were able to make a good living on the tips they received.[30]

Table 5.4. Proportion of Cincinnati Labor Force in Major Occupations by Race and Sex, 1860

	White Males (%)	Nonwhite Males (%)	White Females (%)	Nonwhite Females[a] (%)
Laborers	17.3	18.3	*	*
Other manufacturing	8.5	10.0	*	*
Clerical and sales	7.6	*	*	*
Traders and dealers	6.6	*	*	*
Carpenters	5.1	6.7	*	*
Steamboatmen and sailors	4.1	13.3	*	*
Other professional/ personal service	4.0	10.0	*	3.6
Boot and shoemakers	3.8	*	*	*
Drivers	3.7	*	*	*
Sewing trades	3.6	*	33.0	14.3
Iron and steelworkers	3.0	*	*	*
Masons and stonecutters	2.7	2.7	*	*
Coopers	2.5	*	*	*
Painters	2.4	3.3	*	*
Blacksmiths	2.0	*	*	*
Domestic servants	*	5.0	41.9	14.3
Launderers	*	*	11.2	53.6
Hotel and restaurant	*	6.7	2.3	10.7
Barbers and hairdressers	*	11.7	*	3.6
Total labor force	48,000	1,200	11,220	560

Note: A major occupation is defined as one containing greater than 2 percent of that nationality's labor force; estimates based on a 5 percent random sample of those listed with occupations on the 1860 census manuscript.
* = Contains less than 2 percent of that nationality's labor force.
[a]Based on a sample size of only twenty-eight.
Source: Manuscript of the 1860 U.S. population census for the city of Cincinnati, on microfilm at the University of Cincinnati Library.

Similarly, black and white women were concentrated in different areas of traditional "women's work." The majority of white females worked as domestic servants and in the sewing trades. In 1860, although significant proportions of black women worked at these occupations, they were much more likely than white women to be laundresses or hotel and restaurant workers (Table 5.6). Although none of the major occupational categories open to women were

Table 5.5. Proportion of Cincinnati Labor Force in Major Occupations by Race and Sex, 1890

	White Males (%)	Nonwhite Males (%)	White Females (%)	Nonwhite Females (%)
Laborers	10.3	36.6	*	*
Clerical and sales	9.9	*	8.1	*
Dealers and peddlers	6.4	*	*	*
Drivers	4.9	4.6	*	*
Painters	3.5	*	*	*
Carpenters	3.0	*	*	*
Boot and shoemakers	2.6	*	3.2	*
Iron and steelworkers	2.5	*	*	*
Sewing trades	2.4	*	29.9	6.4
Machinists	2.4	*	*	*
Printers	2.4	*	*	*
Messengers	2.2	4.4	*	*
Cabinetmakers	2.1	*	*	*
Blacksmiths	2.0	*	*	*
Servants	*	22.2	27.9	46.4
Barbers and hairdressers	*	3.5	3.5	*
Engineers and firemen	*	2.0	*	*
Launderers	*	*	4.0	37.6
Teachers	*	*	3.3	*
Textile mill operators	*	*	2.5	*
Housekeepers	*	*	2.4	2.9
Cigarmakers	*	*	2.2	*
Total labor force	90,259	4,268	28,267	2,133

Note: A major occupation is defined as one containing greater than 2 percent of that group's labor force.
* = Contains less than 2 percent of that group's labor force.
Source: U.S. Bureau of the Census, Statistics of the Population of the United States, Eleventh Census, 1890, 652–53.

well-paying or prestigious, the laundress category that black women dominated involved particularly heavy and tedious work.[31] Although no black women teachers showed up in the 1860 sample, a tiny group of them (less than 1 percent of the black female labor force) taught in the officially segregated black public schools from the 1850s to the 1870s under the direction of the prominent black leader Peter H. Clark.[32] The teachers of these schools were, of course, some of the most highly educated black workers in the city. Many had

Table 5.6. Detailed Occupations of 1860 Sample of Nonwhite Labor Force

Males (N = 60)	Females (N = 28)
Laborers = 11	Other professional/
10 laborers	personal service = 1
1 hod carrier	1 nurse
Other manufacturing = 6	Sewing trades = 4
5 firemen on steamboats	3 seamstresses
1 turner	1 dressmaker
Carpenters = 4	Domestic servants = 4
Steamboatman and sailors = 8	Laundresses = 15
3 deckhands	Hotel and restaurant = 3
2 boatmen	2 chambermaids
2 river hands	1 cook
1 steamboat hand	Barber = 1
Other professional/personal	
service = 6	
3 porters	
1 artist	
1 pantryman	
1 baggage master	
Painters = 2	
2 whitewashers	
Domestic servants = 3	
Hotel and restaurant = 4	
3 cooks	
1 waiter	
Miscellaneous[a] = 9	
1 bartender	
1 cabinetmaker	
1 blacksmith	
1 clergy (Baptist minister)	
1 shoemaker	
1 teacher	
1 sewing trades (tailor)	
1 trader/dealer (fruit dealer)	
1 watchman	

[a]Occupations containing less than 2 percent of total sample.
Source: Author's 5-percent sample of all respondents listed with occupations in 1860 manuscript census of population, Cincinnati, Ohio.

received their education in the city's black private schools, including the well-known and respected Gilmore High School.[33] In the early 1850s Cincinnati blacks had finally succeeded in their efforts to establish black public schools, after winning an extensive legal battle with the city administration that ended up in the Ohio Supreme Court. This struggle to establish public schools for black children in Cincinnati stands in marked contrast to the relative ease with which the city's German immigrants were able to attain German-speaking schools for their children.[34]

Examining 1860 census data on occupations typically held by other nineteenth-century ethnic groups shows that, as in the case of female labor force participation, the Irish were the most similar to blacks.[35] While U.S.-born men were likely to work in white-collar jobs such as clerical and sales occupations and German men in the sewing trades and as craftsmen, Irish men usually worked as laborers, boatmen, drivers, and hotel servants. While U.S.-born women with native-born parents often worked as teachers or bookbinders, those with foreign parents frequently did factory work. German women also worked as traders, dealers, and peddlers, and Irish women also worked as laundresses, hotel servants, and domestic servants. While the major inflows of Irish and German immigrants to Cincinnati occurred at the same time, the Irish were much slower to rise in the socioeconomic order than the Germans, due at least in part to the lower rates of literacy and capital ownership among Irish immigrants.[36]

In addition to occupational similarities, analyses of residential patterns tell us that "Irish and Negroes shared the Ohio river bottoms with wholesale houses and factories."[37] The physical proximity of blacks and Irish, combined with the fact that the two ethnic groups competed for many of the same low-paying jobs, frequently created conflict. The historian Steven J. Ross relates the following incident from the early months of the Civil War,[38] when Cincinnati's river trade was severely disrupted and violence erupted amid the hardships of unemployment among dockworkers: "Screaming 'Let's clear out the niggers,' Irish dock workers, angered by the attempts of black laborers to underbid them for jobs, initiated a two-day riot in July 1862, which left a trail of destruction that stretched from the city's docks into the black homes along the levee."[39] Several years later, however, the post–Civil War flurry of labor organizing led, at least temporarily, to a significant turnaround in the attitudes of black and Irish dockworkers, who "joined together in June 1866 and marched en masse to the city's docks to demand better pay for all."[40] In the long run, of course, this solidarity did not last, and workers of Irish descent fared much better than black workers. As we will see later, by the late nineteenth century Irish-born workers managed to show significant progress in their occupational distribution.

Although Cincinnati's black workers were clearly at a disadvantage with respect to other workers in the occupational structure of preindustrial Cincinnati, a comparison of their status with blacks in other cities shows that Cincinnati's blacks did relatively well during this period. Kenneth L. Kusmer has pointed out that in this era the fast-growing midwestern cities generally proved to be more economically hospitable to blacks than the older cities in the North or South (with the notable exceptions of the relatively flourishing black communities in antebellum New Orleans and Boston).[41] The occupational distributions of Cincinnati's black workers in 1860 look very similar to those of Detroit in the 1850–60 time frame.[42] Antebellum Cleveland, with its history of relative racial tolerance, produced an occupational distribution for blacks that was only slightly more favorable than that of Cincinnati.[43]

The Changing Structure of the Economy

Between 1860 and 1890 industrialization caused dramatic structural changes in the Cincinnati economy that had a negative impact on the jobs available to black workers. The economic focus of the city shifted from commerce to manufacturing, and Cincinnati became an important national player in the production of a variety of goods. By 1850 the labor force, capital, and transportation networks generated by Cincinnati's mercantile success had already helped make the city a manufacturing center of national importance—the 1850 census showed that while Cincinnati was the sixth largest city in the country, it was the nation's third largest manufacturing center.[44] After 1860, however, Cincinnati became increasingly reliant on manufacturing as an economic base due to the city's fall from regional commercial dominance.

By the eve of the Civil War, railroads had dramatically altered east-west trade routes, and the magic of Cincinnati's Ohio River location faltered. Although Cincinnati did build several railroads quite early (the first was completed in 1847), it failed to become part of any of the major east-west railroad routes that gained momentum beginning in the early 1850s. Private Cincinnati investors of the 1850s stayed away from railroads, since most of the early railroads failed to pay dividends. Contemporary observers blamed city leaders for lack of vision, claiming they did not invest enough money in railroads or invest fast enough. But the rise of cities like St. Louis and Chicago involved more than Cincinnati's mistakes. The railroad extended the boundaries of cultivation as it harnessed the power of steam for use on land. A Cincinnati historian pointed out that "railroads were effects as well as causes. Chicago benefited from railroads just as Cincinnati benefited from steamboats, and Chicago was building its trade on the agricultural productivity of the Mississippi Valley, just as Cincinnati had earlier profited from the productivity of its surrounding region."[45]

While Cincinnati's economy grew steadily throughout the nineteenth century, Cincinnati's reign as the Queen of the West was over, and the decline of the steamboat had a particularly noticeable effect on the occupations of black workers. As we have seen, a high proportion of black men worked in steamboat-related jobs such as boatman, fireman, and stevedore. Black men thus bore a disproportionate amount of the burden resulting from this economic dislocation. For example, by 1890 less than 2 percent of white or black men worked as steamboatmen; for white men this category had accounted for 4 percent of all jobs in 1860, while the figure for black men was 13 percent.[46]

The latter half of the nineteenth century was not, however, a period of general economic decline for the city as a whole. Although Cincinnati had to readjust, much new growth came from manufacturing and from investment in city utilities and transportation facilities. The city moved from booming growth to slow and steady growth.[47] The growth of manufacturing in late nineteenth-century Cincinnati took place in a diversified fashion, with the city playing regional or national roles in the production of carriages, furniture, boots and shoes, machine tools, soap, and pork products.[48]

This shift toward manufacturing was accompanied by substantial technological and organizational changes, which led to new workforce arrangements that usually did not include blacks. As the pace of industrialization accelerated in the 1870s and 1880s, the nature of the workplace for individual workers sharply changed. The antebellum workshop was transformed into the modern factory—the scale of individual businesses grew larger, production processes were reorganized, mechanization was increasingly utilized, and many jobs became more specialized. This transformation meant that many traditional craftsman jobs, which had been heavily dominated by white men, declined in importance. To save on labor costs, lower-paid white women and children were increasingly employed in many manufacturing establishments. Blacks, though, were rarely hired for these new factory jobs; thus they failed to benefit from one of the crucial work-force shifts that occurred in the transition from a preindustrial to an industrial economy.[49]

For white male workers, although the traditional crafts declined, the elite trade of machinist gained in importance, upwardly mobile jobs in the clerical and sales area increased, and the proportion of workers employed in common labor dropped dramatically (compare Tables 5.4 and 5.5). Many white males, then, were able to take advantage of the positive opportunities that arose in the industrializing, bureaucratizing firms of this era. Even the Irish, the group historically relegated to occupations most similar to those of blacks, registered occupational gains in the late nineteenth century. By 1890 significant proportions of Irish-born men and women held jobs as clerical and sales workers, traders and dealers, iron and steelworkers, blacksmiths, masons, policemen, and boot and shoemakers, while none of these categories were important for black workers.[50]

In contrast, the occupational status of black men appears to have unambiguously worsened. Blacks lost their hold in the relatively prestigious barbering business due to competition from white barbers. Dabney described this turn of events as follows: "White men came into the barber business. The Negro barbers laughed. More white men came. Less laughing. The white man brought business methods. He stood for the ridicule and kept working, quiet, easy, like the Boll Weevil in a crop of cotton. He gave new names to old things. Sanitary and sterilized became his great words, the open sesame for the coming generation. . . . Negro barber shops for white patrons melted away as snow before a July sun."[51] The occupations of messenger and driver were the only "new" job categories accounting for more than 2% of the black male work force. Furthermore, as white men shifted away from the occupation of laborer, black men increasingly became common laborers; by 1890 37% of black male workers were laborers, compared with 18% in 1860. During this period black men also became much more likely to work as domestic servants, which was, once again, an occupation that was declining in importance for the overall labor force; by 1890 22% of black male workers were servants, compared with 5% in 1860. By 1890, then, the majority of black men were employed as laborers or servants.

Likewise, in the female labor market, black women increasingly worked in jobs that white women were abandoning for the better opportunities available to them in the industrializing economy. The most important trend for white women workers was a decreased reliance on the occupation of domestic servant. Black women, however, showed a dramatic increase in this occupation; from 1860 to 1890 the proportion of black women employed as servants increased from 14 to 46 percent. By 1890 sizable numbers of white women moved into clerical and sales jobs, teaching posts, and factory jobs in the textile, boot and shoe, and cigar industries. Black women did not. In fact, even the small elite corps of black teachers in Cincinnati's segregated public schools declined in the late nineteenth century. The black school system was gradually absorbed into the white system following school desegregation legislation at the state level. In the process, most black teachers (as well as male principals) were phased out, and the influence of those who remained waned. The primary reason for the reduction in black teachers was that white parents and school officials would not allow them to teach classes that included white pupils. Similarly, black principals were not permitted to supervise white teachers.[52]

The overall pattern in late nineteenth-century Cincinnati was thus one of blacks increasingly moving into those occupations that became less important for whites, while being excluded from the new occupations that were gaining in importance for whites due to structural economic change. In effect, blacks were picking up job market leftovers. Other studies of black occupational status in the latter half of the nineteenth century in cities such as Cleveland, Detroit, and Milwaukee have reached similar conclusions.[53]

Part of the explanation for this phenomenon can be found on the supply side of the labor market.[54] On average, the black migrants of the post–Civil War period probably differed from earlier black settlers—they may have been less literate, less skilled, less familiar with an urban environment, or more likely to have worked in agriculture prior to migrating.[55] However, after having arrived in the city, they faced a variety of discriminatory practices that worked against upward occupational mobility for blacks, keeping them at the bottom of the economic ladder longer than white immigrant groups who had arrived with similar backgrounds.

Ironically, legal barriers to racial inequality in Ohio were being reduced in this period. In the three decades after the Civil War blacks were granted the right to vote, and the Ohio state legislature passed public accommodation laws, repealed the remaining vestiges of the Black Laws, and enacted legislation to give black children the opportunity to attend white public schools. Nevertheless, blacks continued to be excluded from many occupations by a variety of barriers that included the written and unwritten policies of companies, trade unions, and city government, as well as the racism of white employers and employees. Studies found that Cincinnati's racial tension, which had surely existed from the city's earliest decades, actually increased in these decades. In 1889 a local newspaper noted that the "color-line is everywhere."[56] As the political activism of blacks increased, so did the resentment of many white citizens. In addition, the extended economic depressions of the 1870s and 1890s brought unemployment and increased competition for jobs, a historical source of conflict between black and white members of the working class. In any event, the white community perceived the black migrants of the post–Civil War era in an increasingly unfavorable light.[57]

In the public sector blacks were barred from city jobs such as public health inspector and fireman on the grounds that the public, as well as fellow employees, would object to taking orders from blacks or working in close quarters with them.[58] The few remaining black teachers in the public schools were not permitted to supervise white children, and black principals were restricted to schools with all-black teaching staffs.[59]

Blacks were excluded by the constitutions or policies of nearly all trade unions, including the plasterers', carpenters', painters', and printers' unions. Even unions that admitted some blacks engaged in other discriminatory practices. In occupations such as hod carrier, blacks were organized into segregated locals.[60] Blacks were kept out of lucrative new trades, such as the plumbing and electrical trades, that arose from technological change and economic development. The historian David A. Gerber notes, "By the turn of the century only eight Cincinnati blacks were found in trade unions in the building trades; the majority were older men, most bricklayers, and of the latter all were said to be so light in color 'as not to be noticed among the sun-burned and brick-dust covered men.' At the same time, Cincinnati's bricklayers' locals refused to honor the traveling cards of visiting union-affiliated black bricklayers."[61] Significantly, there was only one black apprentice (a female) reported in the 1890 census.[62]

Increasingly, black business owners were patronized primarily by the small, relatively poor black community, as was the case in many other northern cities in the late nineteenth century.[63] Like the barbers discussed above, early black pioneers in the legal and medical professions had white patrons, but toward the end of the century they came to rely predominantly on black clients. This was a manifestation of the color line, but it also showed that the black community had become large enough to support a small number of black businesses and professionals.[64]

The exclusion of blacks from the growing number of white-collar jobs in the clerical and sales areas was particularly damaging, since these jobs generally offered upward mobility in the nineteenth century. These jobs required literate workers, and although thousands of black children attended the public schools from the 1850s on, there were only 58 black bookkeepers and clerks, 7 black sales workers, and 3 black stenographers in Cincinnati in 1890—altogether, a mere 1 percent of the black labor force.[65]

Conclusion: From Barbers and Teachers to Laborers and Servants

Cincinnati's growing black community faced a variety of discriminatory barriers in the nineteenth-century labor market, as well as in the educational system, which tended to confine black workers to relatively labor-intensive, low-paying, and low-status occupations. The result was a severe lack of occupational mobility in spite of the fact that black labor force participation rates were higher than those of whites.

Moreover, when structural economic forces changed Cincinnati from an antebellum commercial center to an industrial city of the late nineteenth century, blacks' occupational status actually worsened. They experienced job dislocation from the decline of the steamboat and were denied the better job opportunities generated in the process of economic development. They were increasingly displaced from the more desirable occupations they had managed to find niches in, such as barber and teacher, and were left with the declining job categories that were being deserted by white workers—laborer and servant.

This occurred despite the significant decline of legal, formalized racism in late nineteenth-century Ohio. It would appear that the more informal varieties of racial discrimination proved more than equal to the task of keeping blacks at the bottom of the occupational ladder. Although much of Cincinnati's foreign immigration occurred during the preindustrial era, the continuing presence of large numbers of first- and second-generation white immigrants allowed Cincinnati employers (who were sometimes actively encouraged in this by immigrants) to avoid hiring blacks for the new jobs created by the dynamic forces of industrialization.

Significant progress in the occupational rise of Cincinnati's blacks had to await the twentieth century, when labor shortages created by the world wars, combined with better educational opportunities and legal challenges to employment discrimination, finally gave blacks a degree of access to the better jobs that had been created by the industrialization process.[66] Even so, one may well ask whether this progress was too little, too late. As the U.S. economy shifts from an industrial to a postindustrial economy, many of the manufacturing-based jobs that blacks won after decades of struggle are the very jobs that are becoming obsolete.

Thus, as we near the end of the twentieth century, the labor market status of blacks remains troublesome. Occupations such as household servant, custodian, and restaurant worker remain all too common for black workers, and they clearly have their roots in the preindustrial nineteenth-century experience discussed above, while the industrial-era jobs that blacks belatedly gained access to are now on the decline. The substantial occupational achievements of middle-class blacks who have broken into fields such as public administration, education, medicine, and law have unfortunately been accompanied by a disastrous lack of progress in the labor market for the majority of blacks.[67] The nineteenth-century experience of Cincinnati blacks suggests that the United States' current structural economic changes cannot be relied upon to produce economic opportunities that benefit blacks, even when combined with a decline in formalized racial barriers. Continuing informal barriers based on race, as well as the cumulative effects of past discrimination, mean that conscious analysis and concerted action will be required to truly upgrade the occupational status of the black community as a whole.

Notes

1. For a brief summary of racial inequality in the contemporary U.S. labor economy, see National Urban League, *The State of Black America, 1992* (New York: National Urban League, 1992). For an economic analysis of how occupational segregation and job crowding can produce wage discrimination by race and sex, which results in economic benefits for white male workers, see Barbara Bergmann, "The Effect on White Incomes on Discrimination in Employment," *Journal of Political Economy* 79 (Mar./Apr. 1971): 294–313, and idem., "Occupational Segregation, Wages and Profits When Employers Discriminate by Race or Sex," *Eastern Economic Journal* 1 (Apr.–July 1974): 103–10.

2. For a short synopsis of economic theories of human capital and discrimination, see Howard M. Wachtel, *Labor and the Economy* (Orlando, Fla.: Academic Press, 1985), chapters 10 and 12. Some of the important works on economic theories of discrimination include the following: Gary S.

Becker's neoclassical formulation, *The Economics of Discrimination* (Chicago: University of Chicago Press, 1957), which emphasizes the role of individual racism on the part of employers and their white employees but predicts that the forces of market competition will eliminate discrimination over time, since employers who discriminate pay a premium for white workers and discriminatory practices should therefore be less profitable; Peter B. Doeringer and Michael J. Piore's institutional or "dual labor market" approach in *Internal Labor Markets and Manpower Analysis* (Lexington, Mass.: D.C. Heath Co., 1971), which emphasizes how labor market institutions work to keep blacks and whites in separate niches of the economy; and the more radical "political economic" theory utilized by Michael Reich in *Racial Inequality: A Political-Economic Analysis* (Princeton, N.J.: Princeton University Press, 1981), which puts racial discrimination in a class conflict perspective, arguing that employers as a class benefit from the lack of worker solidarity when they follow a "divide and conquer" strategy and encourage racial conflict between black and white workers.

3. For an analysis of this phenomenon at the national level, see William H. Harris, *The Harder We Run: Black Workers since the Civil War* (New York: Oxford University Press, 1982), especially chapters 2 and 3. For a general discussion of the impact on workers of the transition from a preindustrial to an industrial economy, see Melvyn Dubofsky, *Industrialism and the American Worker, 1865–1920* (Arlington Heights, Ill.: AHM Publishing, 1975), chapter 1.

4. See Steven J. Ross, *Workers On the Edge: Work, Leisure, and Politics in Industrializing Cincinnati, 1788–1890* (New York: Columbia University Press, 1985), for an excellent discussion of the often-negative impact of industrialization on Cincinnati's manufacturing workers.

5. See William Julius Wilson, *The Declining Significance of Race: Blacks and Changing American Institutions* (Chicago: University of Chicago Press, 1980), chapters 1–3 and Harris, *The Harder We Run*, chapters 1–2.

6. See Henry Louis Taylor, Jr.'s introduction to *African Americans and the Rise of Buffalo's Post-Industrial City, 1940 to Present* (Buffalo, N.Y.: Buffalo Urban League, 1991), for an analysis of how twentieth-century structural economic changes have affected the position of blacks in the Buffalo economy. "Where the Jobs Are Is Where the Skills Aren't," *Business Week,* 19 September 1988, reports that minorities have so far not benefited from the service economy since they are "stuck in the wrong jobs," with "too few in fast-growing jobs" (such as those in science, technology, engineering, and marketing) and "too many in slow-growing jobs" (such as low-level transportation and manufacturing jobs). See William B. Johnston and Arnold H. Packer, *Workforce 2000: Work and Workers for the Twenty-first Century* (Indianapolis: Hudson Institute, 1987), 89–91, 114–15, for a discussion of the uncertain prospects for improving the status of minorities in the U.S. labor market. This report identifies "integrating blacks and Hispanics fully into the workplace" as one of the six major challenges facing the American economy.

7. Throughout this chapter, the term "labor force" is used for convenience when referring to nineteenth-century work-force data. The modern concept of labor force includes the employed plus the "officially unemployed," which is defined as those available for work who have actively sought work in the recent past. Work-force statistics of the nineteenth century, however, were based on the concept of those with "gainful occupations," so that a person counted as a gainful worker may have been a retired or disabled worker or a discouraged worker at the time of the census, none of which are included in the modern definition of the labor force. On the other hand, employed nineteenth-century individuals who felt their employment was temporary might not have identified themselves as having an occupation. See the discussion in U.S. Bureau of the Census, *Historical Statistics of the U.S.* (Washington, D.C., 1975), 124.

8. For more discussion of black population trends in Cincinnati during this period, see Henry L. Taylor, Jr., "On Slavery's Fringe: City Building and Black Community Development in Cincinnati, 1800–1850," *Ohio History* 95 (Winter/Spring 1986): 5–33; Charles Cist, *Cincinnati in 1851* (Cincinnati: W. H. Moore, 1851), 46; and David A. Gerber, *Black Ohio and the Color Line, 1860–1915* (Urbana: University of Illinois Press, 1977), 14. Cincinnati's relatively large black community meant that Cincinnati led many other northern cities in the development of black religious, educational, and cultural institutions. Gerber, *Black Ohio*, 21–22.

9. See Marilyn Baily, "From Cincinnati, Ohio to Wilberforce, Canada: A Note on Antebellum Colonization," *Journal of Negro History* 58, no. 4 (Oct. 1973): 427–40; Carter G. Woodson, "The Negroes of Cincinnati Prior to the Civil War," *Journal of Negro History* 1 (Jan. 1916): 2–8; Richard C. Wade, *The Urban Frontier: Pioneer Life in Early Pittsburgh, Cincinnati, Lexington, Louisville, and St. Louis* (Chicago: University of Chicago Press, 1959), 223–29; Lyle Koehler, *Cincinnati's Black Peoples: A Chronology and Bibliography, 1787–1982* (Cincinnati: University of Cincinnati, 1986), 2; and Daniel Hurley, *Cincinnati: The Queen City* (Cincinnati: Cincinnati Historical Society, 1982), 48.

For a discussion of how the Ohio Black Laws affected blacks in Cleveland, see Kenneth L. Kusmer, *A Ghetto Takes Shape: Black Cleveland, 1870–1930* (Urbana: University of Illinois Press, 1976), 4–7. See David M. Katzman, *Before the Ghetto: Black Detroit in the Nineteenth Century* (Urbana: University of Illinois Press, 1973), 5–12, for a description of the effect of Michigan's Black Laws on Detroit's black community; in 1833 Detroit also experienced race riots over the issue of whether the Black Laws would be enforced, but the riots did not result in a major outmigration of blacks.

10. Gerber, *Black Ohio*, 62–63.

11. U.S. Census Office, *Report on the Population of the United States, Eleventh Census, 1890* (Washington, D.C., 1897), vol.1, pt. 2, 652–53.

12. Julie A. Matthaei, *An Economic History of Women in America: Women's Work, the Sexual Division of Labor, and the Development of Capitalism* (New York: Schocken Books, 1982), 120–40, and Alice Kessler-

Harris, *Out to Work: A History of Wage-Earning Women in the United States* (Oxford: Oxford University Press, 1982), 45–72.

13. Unfortunately, data on population by sex and ethnicity, which would allow the calculation of labor force participation rates for men and women by ethnic group, are not available in published reports.

14. Claudia Goldin's study of several southern cities in the same general time period found black women more likely to work for pay than white women, even when family income and other demographic variables were accounted for. Goldin speculated that this finding may support the hypothesis that black women's experiences as slaves resulted in different cultural attitudes about women and work. Goldin, "Female Labor Force Participation: The Origin of Black and White Differences, 1870 and 1880," *Journal of Economic History* 37, no. 1 (Mar. 1977): 87–108. For another statement on the effects of slavery on black women's attitudes toward work, see Matthaei, *Economic History of Women in America*, 133–36. In a comment to Goldin's work, Harold D. Woodman noted that the nature of nineteenth-century census data may lead researchers to understate the extent of unemployment. If black male unemployment rates were actually higher than estimated, this might mean that economic factors did offer a complete explanation for black women's higher labor force participation rates. Woodman, "Comment," *Journal of Economic History* 37, no. 1 (Mar. 1977): 109–12.

15. Hurley, *Cincinnati*, 22, 34; Wade, *The Urban Frontier*, 191, 196.

16. Wade, *The Urban Frontier*, 124, 223–24.

17. Theodore Hershberg, Alan Burstein, and Susan M. Drobis, "Record Linkage," *Historical Methods Newsletter* 9, nos. 2, 3 (Mar./June 1976): 139; Walter Glazer, "Cincinnati in 1840: A Community Profile" (Ph.D. diss., University of Michigan, 1968), 20–21.

18. Koehler, *Cincinnati's Black Peoples*, 21, 28–29.

19. This also appears to have been the case in the early economic history of other midwestern cities such as Cleveland and Detroit (in the case of these cities, the docks were located on Lake Erie and Lake Michigan instead of the Ohio River). See Kusmer, *A Ghetto Takes Shape*, 19 and Katzman, *Before the Ghetto*, 29.

20. Koehler, *Cincinnati's Black Peoples*, 8.

21. Ibid., 9, 11, 15, 20. In Detroit, although white resistance to black education was also in evidence, the city established a separate public school for black children at an earlier date than Cincinnati, and with somewhat less controversy. See Katzman, *Before the Ghetto*, 23–24. In contrast, the more racially liberal antebellum Cleveland had integrated public schools by the end of the 1840s. See Kusmer, *A Ghetto Takes Shape*, 16.

22. Woodson, "The Negroes of Cincinnati," 5; Koehler, *Cincinnati's Black Peoples*, 6, 20.

23. This type of discrimination has been noted by many scholars; for a good national overview of the subject, see the introduction to *Black Workers: A Documentary History from Colonial Times to the Present*, eds. Philip S. Foner and Ronald L. Lewis (Philadelphia: Temple University Press, 1989).

24. Woodson, "The Negroes of Cincinnati," 5–6; Koehler, *Cincinnati's Black Peoples,* 6, 20.

25. Patricia Mae Riley, "The Negro in Cincinnati, 1835–1850," (Master's thesis, University of Cincinnati, 1971); Henry L. Taylor, Jr., "Spatial Organization and the Residential Experience: Black Cincinnati in 1850," *Social Science History* 10, no. 1 (Spring 1986): 56–58.

26. Some caution should be expressed with regard to the census data on women's occupations. Many have commented on the underreporting of women workers by census takers. Valerie Kincade Oppenheimer, *The Female Labor Force in the United States* (1970; repr. Westport, Conn.: Greenwood Press, 1976), 10. Although this was more of a problem in agricultural areas, where women's farm labor was likely to be disregarded, it is also probable that some Cincinnati women who engaged in outwork (primarily clothing production) were not identified as having occupations.
    Given the importance of service occupations to the black work force, it is also interesting to note that census takers were given express directions to report all domestic servants under that general name, even if the interviewee reported a more specific occupation title, since "the organization of domestic service has not proceeded so far in this country as to render it worthwhile to make distinction in the character of work." This was completely opposite from the usual recommended procedure, whereby the census takers were instructed to get maximum detail in occupation titles. U.S. Bureau of the Census, *1870 Census,* "Directions to Census Takers," 19.

27. I developed this data base for my study of male and female workers in nineteenth-century Cincinnati. Nancy Elizabeth Bertaux, "Women's Work, Men's Work: Occupational Segregation by Sex in Nineteenth-Century Cincinnati, Ohio" (Ph.D. diss., University of Michigan, 1987). A random sample was taken from the original manuscript returns of the 1860 population census for the city of Cincinnati, available on microfilm at the University of Cincinnati Library. For each ward in the city, every twentieth person who was listed as having an occupation was placed into the sample. Individuals in the sample were originally given occupation codes of maximum detail; recoding was subsequently done to make occupations comparable to the categories used in later summaries published by the census office. The total number of observations in the sample is 3,049, including 2,400 white males, 561 white females, 60 black males, and 28 black females. See chapter 2 of Bertaux, "Women's Work, Men's Work," for further discussion of this sample.

28. This pattern has also been noted with regard to black workers in nineteenth-century Cleveland, Ohio. See Kusmer, *A Ghetto Takes Shape,* 19–21. Indeed, the same general result is found in modern studies at the national level. E. Almquist and J. Wehrle-Einhorn, "The Doubly Disadvantaged: Minority Women in the Labor Force," in *Women Working,* eds. A. Stromberg and S. Harkess (Palo Alto, Calif.: Mayfield Publishing Co., 1978), 80.

29. Wendell P. Dabney, *Cincinnati's Colored Citizens: Historical, Sociological, and Biographical* (New York: Negro Universities Press, 1970; originally published in 1926 by The Dabney Publishing Co.), 183–84.

30. Gerber, *Black Ohio*, 83–84; Dabney, *Colored Citizens*, 180–82; Woodson, "The Negroes of Cincinnati," 10.

31. Near the turn of the century, the work in Ohio commercial laundries was described as follows in a letter from a citizen to an Ohio state senator in support of restrictions on women's hours of work: "Laundresses are the most in need of the eight hour law, for they work every day from 7 A.M. to 6 P.M., and on especially busy days these hours are lengthened until 10:30, and this in a steamy atmosphere, with clothing and feet wet and all the time doing heavy work." Letter from Marcia Lucia Buckingham to the Honorable William Meinhardt, 26 Feb. 1910, manuscript collection of the Cincinnati Historical Society.

32. Listings of black teachers appeared in the *Annual Report of the Board of Trustees, Colored Public Schools of Cincinnati, 1857–73* (available at the Cincinnati Historical Society), showing from 4 to 10 female teachers and 4 to 7 male teachers and principals over the period. For an account of the career of Peter H. Clark, see Lawrence Grossman, "In His Veins Coursed No Bootlicking Blood: The Career of Peter H. Clark," *Ohio History* 86 (Spring 1977): 79–95. For references to the legal battle for black schools, see David Calkins, "Black Education and the Nineteenth-Century City: An Institutional Analysis of Cincinnati's Colored Schools, 1850–1887," *Cincinnati Historical Society Bulletin* 33 (1975): 161–71, and Koehler, *Cincinnati's Black Peoples*, 34–35.

33. Koehler, *Cincinnati's Black Peoples*, 29, 30, 32.

34. For descriptions of the efforts to establish black public education, see Calkins, "Black Education," 161–71 and Koehler, *Cincinnati's Black Peoples*, 34–35. For discussion of the establishment of German schools, see the *Annual Report of the Trustees and Visitors of the Common Schools of Cincinnati* (Cincinnati: n.p., 1840), 5, 18–19, and the *Annual Report of the Trustees and Visitors of the Common Schools of Cincinnati* (Cincinnati: n.p., 1841), 12–15.

35. This was also the case in many other nineteenth-century cities. For example, see Kusmer, *A Ghetto Takes Shape*, 19–22, and Katzman, *Before the Ghetto*, 44–45.

36. For a more complete discussion, as well as figures on occupation by nationality and sex, see chapter 2 of Bertaux, "Women's Work, Men's Work."

37. Zane L. Miller, *Boss Cox's Cincinnati: Urban Politics in the Progressive Era* (Chicago: University of Chicago Press, 1968), 4.

38. Other race riots occurred during 1862–63 in New York and Detroit and were at least partially motivated by the fear of actual or potential job competition from blacks. See Foner and Lewis, *Black Workers*, 5–6, and Katzman, *Before the Ghetto*, 44–48.

39. Ross, *Workers On the Edge*, 194–95.

40. Ibid., 197.

41. Kusmer, *A Ghetto Takes Shape*, 22–24.

42. Katzman, *Before the Ghetto*, 29–32.

43. Kusmer, *A Ghetto Takes Shape*, 19–22, 275–80. Kusmer uses an occupational index technique to assess the occupational status of Cleveland blacks in 1870. The index ranges from 100 for an all-professional work force to 700 for an all-servant work force, so that a higher index denotes lower occupational status. Using his method and categories, my Cincinnati data for 1860 yield occupational indexes that are only slightly lower than those of Cleveland blacks—618 versus 646 for black females, and 510 versus 526 for black males.

44. Hurley, *Cincinnati*, 56.

45. Ibid., 58, 60. See also the discussion of the westward shift of the corn belt from 1850 to 1870 in Stephen C. Gordon, "The City as 'Porkopolis': Some Factors in the Rise of the Meat-Packing Industry in Cincinnati, 1825–1861" (Master's thesis, Miami University, 1981).

46. See Table 4 and Gerber, *Black Ohio*, 64.

47. Miller, *Boss Cox*, 59–73 and 95–110. Although the steamboat faded rapidly as a viable transportation technology, the technology and skills that the production of steamboats had brought to Cincinnati was an important foundation for the growth of manufacturing in the city. Ross, *Workers on the Edge*, 76.

48. Bertaux, "Women's Work, Men's Work," 13–16.

49. For example, in the carriage and wagon industry, operations previously performed by skilled craftsmen were subdivided and simplified so that the training periods for workers went from months or years to days or weeks. The industry was thus able to employ women and children for over 40 percent of its work force. In the cigarmaking industry the major changes involved the introduction of machinery and the abandonment of traditional craftsmen's hand techniques, so that by 1880 36 percent of the industry's labor force consisted of women and children. Such innovations were often only possible with a larger scale of production; Ross reports that by 1880 half of the manufacturing labor force worked in factories employing one hundred or more workers. Ross, *Workers On the Edge*, 220–29.

50. By "significant" I mean occupations that contained greater than 2 percent of the Irish-born portion of the labor force. See Table 5 and Bertaux, "Women's Work, Men's Work," 87, 89.

51. Dabney, *Colored Citizen's*, 184–85. See Kusmer, *A Ghetto Takes Shape*, 75–76, and Katzman, *Before the Ghetto*, 116–17, for discussions of the similar decline of the black barbers in Cleveland and Detroit, respectively.

52. Calkins, "Black Education," 164.

53. See chapter 4 of Kusmer, *A Ghetto Takes Shape*; chapter 4 of Katzman, *Before the Ghetto*; and chapter 1 of Joe William Trotter, Jr., *Black Milwaukee: The Making of an Industrial Proletariat, 1915–45* (Urbana: University of Illinois Press, 1985).

54. For an economic study at the national level of how such human capital factors affected black-white earnings differentials, see James P. Smith, "Race and Human Capital," *American Economic Review* 74 (Sept. 1984): 685–98.

55. See Miller, *Boss Cox*, 30; Kusmer, *A Ghetto Takes Shape*, 67; and Daniel R. Fusfeld and Timothy Bates, *The Political Economy of the Urban Ghetto* (Carbondale: Southern Illinois University Press, 1984), 27–28.

56. Quoted in Miller, *Boss Cox*, 30.

57. Ibid., 31. See also chapter 3 of Kusmer, *A Ghetto Takes Shape;* chapter 3 of Katzman, *Before the Ghetto;* and Trotter, *Black Milwaukee,* 25–28, for discussions of similar experiences in Cleveland, Detroit, and Milwaukee, respectively.

58. Miller, *Boss Cox*, 30–31. See also Katzman, *Before the Ghetto,* 120–21, for the limited nature of city jobs available to Detroit blacks in this period.

59. See the listings of black teachers at the end of the *Annual Report of the Board of Trustees, Colored Public Schools of Cincinnati, 1857–1873* and the *Annual Report of the Trustees, Common Schools of Cincinnati, 1874– 1900;* Calkins, "Black Education," 164. One of the historically most common forms of occupational discrimination against blacks involves the situation where blacks and whites may work in the same organization (even side by side), so long as blacks are not above any whites in the job hierarchy—that is, they do not supervise whites. In a study of West Virginia coal miners in the early twentieth century, the economic historian Price Fishback concluded that "white tastes for discrimination are better described by a dislike for subordinance to blacks than by the Beckerian notion of dislike for physical proximity." Fishback, "Segregation in Job Hierarchies: West Virginia Coal Mining, 1906–1932," *Journal of Economic History* 44, no. 3 (Sept. 1984), 755.

60. Ross, *Workers On the Edge,* 212, 256, 262; Gerber, *Black Ohio,* 76.

61. Gerber, *Black Ohio,* 76, 303.

62. U.S. Census Office, *Report on the Population of the United States 1890,* vol. 1, pt. 2, 652–53. See also Katzman, *Before the Ghetto,* 124–26, and Kusmer, *A Ghetto Takes Shape,* 68–75, for information on union discrimination in other midwestern cities.

63. See Trotter, *Black Milwaukee,* 19; Katzman, *Before the Ghetto,* 129– 34; and Kusmer, *A Ghetto Takes Shape,* 77–78.

64. Gerber, *Black Ohio,* 80–81, 90–91, 310–18.

65. Ibid., 87; Koehler, *Cincinnati's Black Peoples,* 35–36; U.S. Census Offiice, *Report on the Population of the United States 1890,* vol. 1, pt. 2, 652–53. See Kusmer, *A Ghetto Takes Shape,* 78–80, for a discussion of the lack of black clerical workers in Cleveland at this time.

66. In a study of Cincinnati and other cities, the economic historian Warren C. Whatley has argued that twentieth-century black economic progress is attributable to the demand side of the labor market, noting that during the labor shortages of World War I, many firms that had previously hired no

blacks "learned" their value as workers. "Northern firms had to learn how to racially integrate their work forces and could do so only after having some concrete experience with black workers. Those firms that refused to hire blacks may have reinforced racial barriers, while those firms that employed blacks improved the future employment opportunities for other blacks." Whatley, "Getting a Foot in the Door: 'Learning,' State Dependence and the Racial Integration of Firms," *Journal of Economic History* 50, no. 1 (Mar. 1990): 43–66.

67. Human capital economists have asserted that the substantial economic gains experienced by educated blacks in the post–World War II period were primarily the result of educational gains. They give an optimistic forecast for the current generation of college-educated blacks, making the (heroic?) assumption that "salary increases and promotions will come at least as rapidly for the new black elite as for their white competitors." Nevertheless, they express concern for the "still-large black underclass," arguing that black economic progress after World War II "reflected hard-won, underlying achievements that enhanced black market skills, in the context of rapid American economic growth. Take away those underlying achievements and lose that growth, and black progress will stop." James P. Smith and Finis R. Welch, "Black Economic Progress after Myrdal," *Journal of Economic Literature* 27 (June 1989): 519–61.

6

Henry Louis Taylor, Jr.

City Building, Public Policy, the Rise of the Industrial City, and Black Ghetto-Slum Formation in Cincinnati, 1850-1940

Scholars of the black urban experience have firmly established the place of racism in the ghetto-slum formation process.[1] In a series of works written during the 1960s, Gilbert Osofsky (1963), Seth Scheiner (1965), August Meier and Elliott Rudwick (1966), and Allan H. Spear (1967) developed the standard theory of black ghetto-slum formation.[2] These historians argued that during the late nineteenth and early twentieth centuries black population growth, the institutional development of the black community, the activities of the real estate industry, and widespread urban change combined with a national rise in racist ideology to produce the black ghetto-slum. Racial hostility was the driving force behind this change process.

Although racism was the focal point of their theory, these scholars nevertheless indicated that other factors such as urban change and the operation of the housing market also played major roles in ghetto-slum formation. Writing in the 1970s, Theodore Hershberg and Kenneth L. Kusmer called upon historians to pay closer attention to the relationship between city building and the black urban experience.[3] Kusmer in particular urged scholars to study the role of city building (or structural forces, as he referred to it) in ghetto-slum formation. "Perhaps," Kusmer argued, "the most significant example of the effect of structural forces [in the black urban experience] is in the area of residential segregation. The historical development of the residential segregation of black Americans is a more complex process than is usually recognized, because in studying single communities, historians have ignored the impact of divergences in urban structure on the growth of ghettoization."[4] So, while the link between racism and residential segregation has been well documented, much less is known about the role that city building plays in ghetto-slum formation and about the relationship between the rise of an industrial city and the emergence of ghetto-slums.[5]

The purpose of this chapter is to determine the place of city building in black ghetto formation.[6] Specifically, it seeks to explain how the rise of the industrial city, the emergence of mass homeownership, zoning laws, building codes, city planning, and subdivision regulations led to the formation of a black ghetto-slum in Cincinnati. The rise of an industrial city was accompanied by the separation of land use by function and by the dramatic growth of homeownership and the emergence of a residential environment stratified on the basis of housing cost and type. The location of African Americans at the bottom of the economic ladder placed them at a disadvantage in the quest for good housing and neighborhood conditions. Thus in this new socioeconomic setting, homeownership and housing costs triggered a complex sorting and sifting process that gave birth to neighborhoods segregated on the basis of race and class. These forces, operating within the context of racial hostility, gave rise to the twentieth-century ghetto.

The main idea undergirding this hypothesis is that city building shapes the black residential experience, including ghetto-slum formation. The emphasis on city building is not meant to replace the standard theory of ghetto formation. Rather, it is to suggest a different but complementary way of understanding the formation of black ghettoes during the industrial city's rise.

Cincinnati was selected as a model city because it experienced the spatial changes characteristic of the evolving industrial city (growing differentiation by function, decentralization, and residential segregation based on class and race) and because Cincinnati in the teens and twenties became a national leader in the city planning and housing reform movements. Led by the Better Housing League, a citizens group founded in 1916, the city gained a national reputation for planning and housing reform. And in 1925 Cincinnati became the first large American city to adopt an official city plan.[7]

Before the Ghetto-Slum: The Commercial City and the Biracial Residential Environment

Although located in a "free" state, commercial Cincinnati was nevertheless a racist city in which blacks were subjected to tight social and occupational restrictions. The city, for example, was the site of bloody race riots in 1829, 1836, 1841, and 1862. Cincinnati blacks were prohibited by law from sitting on juries, testifying against whites in court, serving in the militia, attending public schools, securing relief, and being admitted to the poorhouse. They had to sit in segregated church pews and were buried in segregated graves in a potter's field.[8]

The color line also kept blacks tied to the bottom of Cincinnati's occupational ladder. The city's economy boomed during the commercial era. By 1850 Cincinnati had become the "Queen City of the West," the sixth largest city in the United States, the fourth largest manufacturing city in the country, and the leading commercial and manufacturing city in the Allegheny region.[9] This was Cincinnati's golden age.

Yet most black workers were confined to the lowest-paying jobs at the bottom of the job ladder. More than 80 percent labored as unskilled workers, as roustabouts on the docks, as stewards on the steamboats, and as washerwomen, domestics, servants, and cooks in the homes of white elites and in the city's hotels and boardinghouses. Against difficult odds, about 8 percent of black workers did manage to become blacksmiths, coopers, bricklayers, and carpenters. Nevertheless, both skilled and unskilled black workers were excluded from the city's rapidly expanding industrial base. Only about .76 percent of the city's blacks held factory jobs. A small black middle class did emerge during this period. About 6 percent of the black work force found jobs as clerks, shopkeepers, peddlers, traders, barbers, teachers, and businessmen.[10] Yet despite a few success stories, most blacks held low-paying menial jobs.

Although most blacks were poor, and white prejudice, discrimination, and hostility infiltrated every aspect of their lives, a black ghetto-slum did not form in commercial-era Cincinnati. A disproportionate number of blacks did live in alleys, apartments above stores, dilapidated wooden structures, and rickety tenements, but they still had white neighbors.[11] An examination of the residential location of

2,109 blacks, representing 66 percent of the African American population, showed that blacks did not live in homogeneous, racially segregated enclaves. Although concentrated in the eastern section of Cincinnati and along the waterfront, most blacks nevertheless lived in small clusters, lodged within white-dominated residential areas. Whites not only lived on every street where blacks resided but usually also outnumbered them. Even on those streets where blacks were most heavily concentrated, whites could be found living in large numbers.[12]

This situation, in most instances, had little to do with racial attitudes. White hostility, as previously mentioned, produced antiblack riots and omnipresent discrimination, but it did not produce residential segregation. The structure of the commercial city kept black ghettoes from forming. The population had no choice but to mix. Lack of adequate transportation systems, mixed patterns of land use, and the ubiquity of cheap housing led to the dispersal of both the immigrant and black populations.[13] Cincinnati's experience was not unique. Throughout the nineteenth century, in both the North and South, blacks lived in biracial residential areas; even in the most segregated locations blacks and whites lived adjacent to one another or shared the same dwellings.[14]

Rise of the Industrial City: Land Use Change and the Class-Stratified Residential Environment

Between the Civil War and the end of World War I, Cincinnati's commercial city was transformed into the spatially differentiated industrial city.[15] Although failing the quest for urban supremacy, Cincinnati still experienced substantial growth during the latter half of the nineteenth century. Industrialization, population growth, and a transportation revolution were the driving forces behind this growth and development. For example, the value of Cincinnati's manufactured products increased from $54 million in 1851 to $262 million in 1910, while its population increased from 115,435 in 1850 to 401,247 by 1920.[16]

Commercial Cincinnati formed in a six-square-mile basin surrounded by sharply rising hills. The Mill Creek Valley on the west and the Deer Creek Valley on the east were the only two entrances into the city. The hilly topography inhibited outward expansion, forcing most people to live in the basin area (Map 6.1). Cincinnati became a very crowded city. As late as 1870 only New York City was more congested.[17] In the 1880s and 1890s Cincinnati developed an

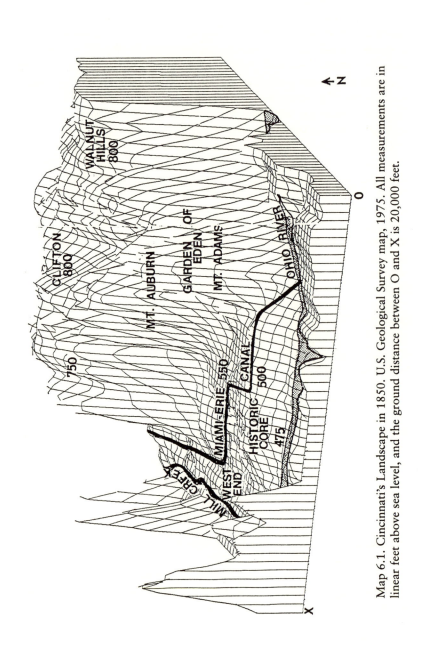

Map 6.1. Cincinnati's Landscape in 1850. U.S. Geological Survey map, 1975. All measurements are in linear feet above sea level, and the ground distance between O and X is 20,000 feet.

intraurban transportation system based on electric streetcars and inclines, a device that hoisted streetcars to the city's hilltops. Electrification of the intraurban transportation system made outward expansion possible while simultaneously tying the growing city together. By 1912 Cincinnati had 222 miles of track.[18] At the same time, through an aggressive annexation campaign the city extended its physical boundaries from six square miles in 1850 to fifty-two square miles by 1930. Collectively, these events facilitated the residential development of vast stretches of vacant land (Maps 6.2 and 6.3).[19]

The Industrial City Residential Environment

The emergence of Cincinnati as an industrial city involved not only growth and expansion but also a complex sorting-out process in which commercial, industrial, and residential forms of land use were separated from each other and then each internally reorganized. The industrial city, like the commercial city, had its own unique pattern of land use and its own unique residential environment.

Residential areas were not simply separated from other forms of land use. They were reorganized.[20] The industrial city residential environment was a highly stratified one in which neighborhoods were segregated by housing cost and type. The territorial expansion that took place with the rise of industrial Cincinnati gave birth to new neighborhoods located outside the basin.

In the commercial city most Cincinnatians had resided in the basin, where the residential environment was characterized by tenement buildings and a heterogeneous population. This was a renter-dominated setting in which the rich and poor, the native and foreign, white and African Americans lived within a stone's throw of each other.[21] It was also a place where dwelling units competed for space with factories, warehouses, office buildings, and railroad yards. In the late nineteenth and early twentieth centuries residential land use began to lose the competitive struggle for space as industrial and commercial expansion slowly transformed the basin into a land use conversion zone where new factories, buildings, alterations, renovations, and expanding railroad lines engulfed dwelling units. By 1900 the conflict between economic and residential development in the basin was making the area an undesirable place to live.[22]

At the same time, electrically powered streetcars and incline planes were making it possible for people to move out of the basin into new neighborhoods developing in other parts of Cincinnati. From about

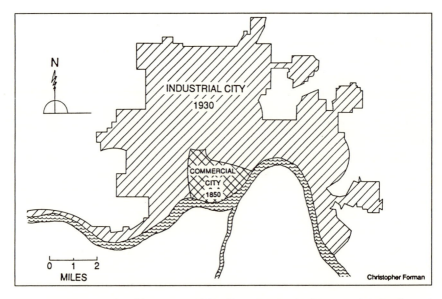

Map 6.2. Cincinnati, 1850 versus 1930. From James A. Quin, Earl Eubank, and Lois E. Elliott, *Population Changes: Cincinnati, Ohio, and Adjacent Areas, 1900-1940* (Columbus: Bureau of Business Research, Ohio State University, 1947).

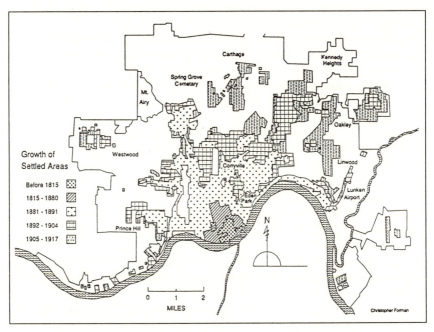

Map 6.3. Cincinnati, Growth from 1815 to 1917. National Archives, record group 31, n.d.

Table 6.1. Cincinnati's Basin Population by Race, 1860–1940

Year	Total Population	White	Black	Basin Population	% Total Population
1860	161,044	126,031	3,679	129,710	81
1870	222,139	136,693	4,630	141,323	64
1910	363,591	132,518	12,479	144,997	36
1920	401,247	98,776	19,776	118,520	25
1930	451,160	59,033	32,728	91,761	20
1940	455,610	45,859	37,227	83,086	18

Source: U.S. Bureau of the Census, Population of the United States, Eighth, Ninth,Thirteenth-Sixteenth Censuses, 1860, 1870, 1910–40.

1870 onward elite, middle-class, and higher-paid workers gradually moved out of the basin into Mt. Auburn, Mt. Hope, Mt. Harrison, Fairmont, Camp Washington, Cumminsville, Clifton, Clifton Heights, Corryville, Avondale, Walnut Hills, Mt. Adams, Mt. Lookout, Mt. Healthy, Hyde Park, Pleasant Ridge, Oakley, and other sections of Cincinnati City.[23] Between 1870 and 1940 the number of people living in the basin fell from 141,323 to 83,086, and the proportion of all Cincinnatians residing there dropped from 64 to 18 percent (Table 6.1).

These figures do not tell the complete story. The outmigration had a racial dimension. The majority of those moving out were white. This outmigration turned into a flood in the 1910–40 period, when 86,659 whites left and the proportion of all whites living there dropped to 11 percent. The historic core was no longer their primary residential location. According to the historian Zane L. Miller, those remaining were primarily low-income workers and small business-men "serving a clientele close to their home neighborhoods."[24] As whites moved out, blacks moved in. In the 1870–1940 period the black basin population increased by 704 percent. By 1940 about 67 percent of Cincinnati's black population resided in the core, which was rapidly becoming the primary residential location of African Americans (Table 6.1).

The movement of blacks into the basin and the movement of whites into the newly evolving valley and hilltop neighborhoods led to the growing residential segregation of African Americans. The index of dissimilarity developed by the sociologists Karl Taeuber and Alma Taeuber provides a measure of the growth of residential segregation in Cincinnati between 1850 and 1940.[25] An examination of computed indices of dissimilarity for this period shows that in

Table 6.2. The Index of Dissimilarity, Cincinnati, 1850, 1870–1940

Year	Index of Dissimilarity	Black Population	% Black
1850	0.375	3,731	2.31
1870	0.464	5,900	2.65
1910	0.465	19,639	5.40
1920	0.480	30,079	7.49
1930	0.657	47,818	10.59
1940	0.710	55,593	12.20

Source: U.S. Bureau of the Census, Population of the United States, Seventh, Ninth, Thirteenth-Sixteenth Censuses, 1850, 1870, 1910–40.

Cincinnati a biracial residential environment persisted until 1920. Between 1920 and 1940, however, residential segregation increased dramatically as whites fled the basin. In the seventy years between 1850 and 1920, for example, Cincinnati's index of dissimilarity increased slightly, from .375 to .480. But in the twenty years between 1920 and 1940 the dissimilarity index leaped from .480 to .710 (Table 6.2).

The Rise of Homeownership and the Class-Stratified Residential Environment

Those whites fleeing the basin were moving into new neighborhoods characterized by owner-occupied single-family dwelling units. By studying building permits issued for sixteen select years between 1908 and 1938, insight into this evolving residential environment can be obtained. The permits issued during the period provide information on the volume, type, and cost of residential construction in Cincinnati by census tract.[26]

The data show that the volume of residential construction skyrocketed in Cincinnati during the 1920s and late 1930s.[27] For instance, 82 percent (N = 11,176) of the 13,659 residential building permits issued for select years in the 1908–38 period were issued between 1923 and 1938.[28] Most of this building activity took place during the 1920s. Forty percent (N = 5,529) of the permits issued between 1923 and 1938 were issued in just three years, 1923, 1925, and 1928 (Table 6.3). Significantly, virtually all new residential construction took place outside of the basin. Between 1908 and 1938 only thirty-four, or .24 percent, of the 13,659 residential building permits issued were for the basin. And in the 1923–38 period there were only eighteen residential building permits issued for the basin.[29]

Table 6.3. New Residential Building Construction by Building Type, Cincinnati, 1923–38

Year	One-Family	Two-Family	Multiple-Occupancy	Total	% One-Family
1923	1,449	242	33	1,724	84.0
1925	1,499	272	38	1,809	82.8
1928	1,556	251	134	1,941	80.1
1930	735	90	58	883	83.2
1931	635	67	45	747	85.0
1932	262	34	9	305	85.9
1933	288	14	3	305	94.4
1934	204	8	2	214	95.3
1935	465	26	27	518	89.7
1936	808	58	65	931	86.7
1937	756	48	97	901	83.9
1938	700	85	109	894	78.2
Total	9,357	1,195	647	11,172	83.7

Source: James A. Quinn, Earl Eubank, and Lois E. Elliott, *Cincinnati Building Permits: Trends and Distribution, 1908–1938* (Columbus: Bureau of Business Research, Ohio State University, Special Bulletin, 1947), 26–34.

The single-family house was the predominant type of residential structure built during the period. Between 1923 and 1938 almost 84 percent of Cincinnati's new residential buildings were single-family dwellings (Table 6.3).[30] In most instances, single-family houses were owner-occupied units. This belief is supported by data on homeownership. Between 1900 and 1930 homeownership in Cincinnati increased by 204 percent as the number of families owning their homes leaped from 14,891 to 45,253 (Table 6.4).

Most of the new houses in Cincinnati's growing neighborhoods fell into the moderate-to-high-cost range. About 70 percent of the

Table 6.4. Number and Percent of Families by Tenure, 1900–1930

Year	Owner Families	Tenant Families	Unknown	% Owners
1900	14,891	56,384	2,244	20.3
1910	19,965	66,153	1,423	22.8
1920	30,266	75,092	881	28.5
1930	45,253	75,441	1,847	37.5

Source: Federal Housing Administration, Cincinnati Housing Inventory, vol. 2, Federal Reconstruction Corporation, National Archives, record group 31, box 11.

Table 6.5. Percentage of New Residential Construction by Value, 1908–38

Value	No.	%
$4,999 and under	4,179	30.59
$5,000 to 9,999	7,302	53.45
$10,000 to 19,999	1,797	13.51
$20,000 and over	378	2.76
Unknown	3	0.02
Total	13,659	

Note: Values are in constant dollars.
Source: James A. Quinn, Earl Eubank, and Lois E. Elliott, *Cincinnati Building Permits: Trends and Distributions, 1908–1938* (Columbus: Bureau of Business Research, Ohio State University, Special Bulletin, 1947).

new housing cost $5,000 or more, with 53.4 percent falling into the $5,000-to-$9,999 cost range (Table 6.5). Over time, the number of cheap housing units (under $3,000) under construction fell dramatically. For instance, in 1908 cheap houses accounted for 50.9 percent of all new housing construction. But by the 1920 building boom, housing in this cost range accounted for only 2 percent of new residential construction.[31] Cheap housing was not widely dispersed. Most of it was concentrated in the basin area, along the waterfront, and in a few sections of the Mill Creek Valley industrial district. Expensive housing, on the other hand, was located in the valley and hilltop neighborhoods, especially in the northern and eastern hilltop regions.[32]

The evolving industrial city residential environment did not replicate the mixed pattern of neighborhoods characteristic of the commercial city. Instead, for the first time, homogeneous neighborhoods began to appear. New houses were now commonly built only near houses of similar type and value.[33] Neighborhoods grew more uniform.[34] Before 1920 there were no building codes to regulate the construction of single-family dwellings, and there were no zoning regulations. Nevertheless, a system of regulation without law led to conformity in terms of the type and cost of houses appearing in different neighborhoods.[35] Cincinnati developers used a combination of deed restrictions and subdivision design to create neighborhoods segregated by housing type and cost.[36]

The neighborhoods evolving in the valley and hilltop regions became increasingly different from those in the basin. Indeed, the newer the residential district, the greater the proportion of single-family dwellings, the more expensive the housing, and the better the neighborhood conditions. Likewise, the older the residential district, the greater the proportion of multiple-family dwellings, the cheaper the housing, and the more deteriorated the neighborhood. Class had become the primary determinant of where people lived and the type of housing and neighborhood conditions available to them.[37] By 1930 Cincinnati's neighborhoods had been divided into three distinct types of residential districts: low-, moderate-, and high-rent (Map 6.4).[38]

The creation of a residential environment based on homeownership changed people's attitudes toward the living place. Buying and building a home took place in a market economy.[39] Before 1930 home buying was a risky financial journey.[40] Institutions required large down payments, charged high interest rates, and demanded the repayment of loans within a very short period, typically from two to five years.[41] So when a family used its savings to purchase a house, a big economic investment in the dwelling was made. This investment was risky[42] because rising or falling property values determined the home buyer's fate. Also, because few people could pay off their mortgage within two to five years, most counted on having it renewed again and again as needed.[43]

But mortgage renewal was not automatic. If a lending company believed that neighborhood conditions were declining and that housing values were depreciating, it might not renew the mortgage. If that happened, the home buyer might lose both the house and the money invested in it.[44] By building houses that maintained the class character of neighborhoods and by keeping out "bad" houses, factories, and businesses, home buyers maintained property values and protected the home investment. So maintaining property values and protecting the home investment became part of the cult of homeownership and "neighborhood culture," thereby transforming neighborhoods into "defended territories."[45]

Public Policy and the Rise of Mass Homeownership

The growth of neighborhoods in the valley and hilltop regions and the rise of mass homeownership transformed the housing reform movement in Cincinnati. In the 1865–1910 period reformers believed that the city's crowded and unsanitary tenements caused pauperism and family disorganization and thus represented a major threat to the basin as a residential environment. As early as 1865 the Cincinnati Relief Union, an association founded to aid the needy and worthy poor, argued that the "filthy" and "unhealthy" tenements threatened to contaminate "an otherwise healthy and prosperous city."[46]

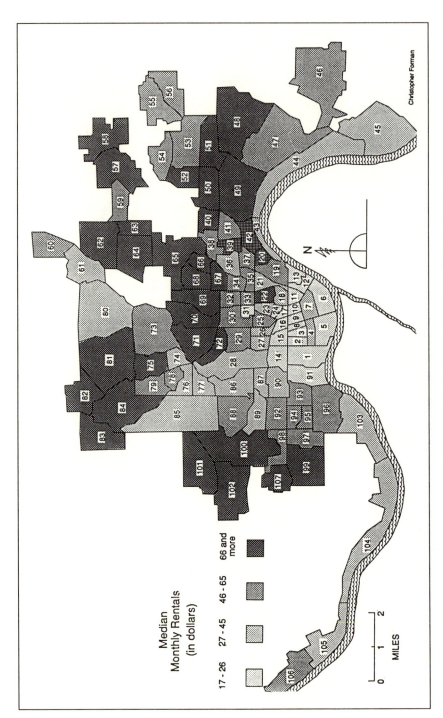

Median
Monthly Rentals
(in dollars)

17 - 26   27 - 45   46 - 65   66 and
                              more

N

MILES
0   1   2

Christopher Forman

Map 6.4. Cincinnati, Median Rentals by Census Tract, 1930. Public Health Federation.

Based on the notion that most Cincinnatians would continue to live in the congested basin, this view of residential development led to the emergence of a tenement reform movement centered on the use of building codes to regulate tenement buildings. The goal was to preserve the basin as a good residential environment by eliminating the tenement as a source of disease and social disorder.[47] The two most important organizations to emerge in the tenement reform epoch were the United Jewish Charities and the Associated Charities.[48] Both organizations pushed for passage and enforcement of tenement regulations. As a result of their activities, Cincinnati passed its first building code on August 15, 1898. The new law covered areas such as lot coverage, water closet accommodations, light shafts, and fire escapes.[49]

The reformers were not, however, happy with this building code. They wanted a stronger law. Yet in spite of support from groups such as the Union Bethel, the Elizabeth Gamble Deaconess Home, the Glen Industrial Home, the Mennonite Mission, and the Cincinnati City Council, the housing reformers did not achieve their goal of a tough building code until May 10, 1909. The new law greatly expanded the 1898 code. And most important, it made provisions for building code enforcement.[50]

The tenement house movement peaked with passage of the 1909 code. Outmigration from the basin and the growth of homeownership in valley and hilltop neighborhoods caused reformers to conclude that the basin was doomed as a good residential environment. This shift in thinking led to the creation of a new housing movement, one centered on the promotion of homeownership and the protection of new neighborhoods from an invasion of bad housing and factories and commercial enterprises.[51] The new movement called for an extension of building codes to single-family dwellings and the formulation of zoning laws, comprehensive city planning, and subdivision regulations.

The first sign of this new idea of residential development appeared in 1912 when the reform mayor, Henry Hunt, called for an active housing movement "to secure a real home for every man, woman and child in Cincinnati." He proposed the development of a rapid transit system to allow wage earners "more freedom in choosing their housing."[52] One year later the National Housing Association met in Cincinnati. Following a tour of the city, the delegates declared that Cincinnati's problem was one of the most serious in the cities west of New York. This conference stimulated interest in the need to develop a systematic approach to solving the housing problem by establishing an organization devoted exclusively to housing reform. Then on July 10, 1916, as a result of the efforts of the Woman's City Club, Max Senior, founder of the United Jewish Charities, and Courtenay Dinwiddie, secretary of the Anti-Tuberculosis League, the Better Housing League of Cincinnati (BHL) was founded. Max Senior was elected president, A. O. Elzner vice president, and Setty S. Kuhn treasurer.[53] The BHL became the leader of the new housing movement and ushered in a new era of housing reform in Cincinnati.

Initially the BHL's activities focused on tenement regulation. This changed, however, with the hiring of Bleecker Marquette, a close associate of Lawrence Veiller, the dean of restrictive tenement reform, on September 1, 1918. Marquette argued in a BHL report that one of the most striking shifts in the housing movement was the change in emphasis from "getting rid of slum conditions" to "providing decent shelter for the middle classes." He became the chief architect of Cincinnati's residential development strategy and the driving force behind its implementation.[54]

Under Marquette's leadership, the BHL's new residential development strategy was outlined in its first two published reports, appearing in 1919 and 1921. The 1919 report called for a revision of the city's building code so that it would cover the construction of one- and two-family houses. The league indicated that a revised building code would protect neighborhoods by keeping existing houses from deteriorating into slums. And in the 1921 report the BHL stated for the first time that the tenement was not an adequate type of dwelling unit and implied that homeownership represented the key to building a modern residential environment. "Any city's greatest asset is its homes. Tenement houses do not provide real homes, no matter how well constructed. They are not the best place for children to live in. . . . We must see to it that the single-family home habit is continued."[55]

In addition to a new building code, the BHL residential strategy called for the development of a comprehensive zoning law that would "divide the community into districts and protect residence neighborhoods against invasion by undesirable structures." The league's report stated, "It would be short-sighted policy to encourage the construction of small homes and to foster home ownership and at the same time fail to take every precaution to see to it that the residential districts are not properly protected."[56] The BHL acknowledged that some subdivisions were protected by restrictive covenants but indicated that such restrictions were unreliable and that only a comprehensive zoning system would protect neighborhoods from an invasion of bad housing, factories, and commercial buildings.[57]

The second report also indicated that homeownership was beyond the economic reach of "ordinary" workers. These wage earners could not afford new houses and "therefore the best that could be done would be to construct houses for those with a higher income with a view to relieving the pressure from the top." Thus, in stating its new approach to residential development, the BHL suggested that no new housing should be built in the basin. Rather, new dwelling units should be constructed in the valley and hilltop neighborhoods, and as people moved out of the basin their "old" housing could "trickle down" to lower-income groups.[58]

Simultaneously the BHL supported Cincinnati's nascent city planning movement. "Without a city plan there can be no successful solution to the housing problem," asserted the league.[59] The battle for a comprehensive city plan was led by Alfred Bettman, a Harvard-trained lawyer and one of the country's leading advocates of city planning, and the United City Planning Committee (UCPC), a citizen's group formed in 1915. The UCPC raised over one hundred thousand dollars for the preparation of a city plan, and in May 1921 the Technical Advisory Corporation, an urban planning consultant firm, was hired to conduct a preliminary city planning survey.[60]

As a result of these activities, Cincinnati enacted in 1924 a comprehensive zoning law.[61] The zoning law created three different types of residential areas. Residential class A reserved land exclusively for single-family homes, while class B permitted both two- and four-family detached housing. Class C allowed for the building of any type of family dwelling unit. The zoning law codified the city's emerging class-stratified residential environment and legally reinforced the economic walls separating the various residential districts. And in 1925 Cincinnati became the first American city to adopt an official city plan.[62]

During the 1920s the BHL also called for the development of subdivision regulations to control residential land use in Hamilton County. While building codes and zoning laws could protect neighborhoods in the city, the absence of land use controls in the county meant that the slums could spread to the suburbs by allowing speculators to create cheaply developed subdivisions.[63] During the 1920s and 1930s land speculators sometimes developed subdivisions without paved roads, sewage, water, and electricity.[64] Subdivision regulations would keep this from happening. The residential development strategy articulated by the BHL, the city planning advocates, and the other housing reformers guided Cincinnati's residential development process throughout the remainder of the industrial city era.

Formation of the Black Ghetto-Slum

As one-family homes were being erected and whites were being dispersed throughout Cincinnati's valley and hilltop neighborhoods, a black ghetto-slum was forming in the basin. Economic factors and the policies promoted by the BHL and the housing reformers played a big role in this. The emergence of a residential environment segregated on the basis of homeownership and housing cost coincided with the migration of thousands of southern blacks to Cincinnati. Between 1900 and 1940 the city's black population grew from 15,000 to 56,000, and blacks as a proportion of the total population jumped from 4 to 12 percent. The black population experienced its greatest rate of growth during the 1920s, when about 18,000 blacks moved to the city.[65]

Housing cost determined where most African Americans initially settled in Cincinnati. Most blacks labored in positions at the bottom of Cincinnati's occupational ladder.[66] Eighty-six percent worked as unskilled laborers and domestic and personal servants, as compared to 20 percent of native whites and whites with foreign or mixed parentage and 29 percent of immigrants (Table 6.6).[67]

Only a handful of blacks held positions at the top of the ladder. Blacks comprised, for instance, only 2 percent of professionals and 2 percent of proprietors, managers, and officials. And most black professionals (77 percent) were ministers, musicians, and teachers of music, not doctors, dentists, lawyers, judges, mechanical engineers, editors, and reporters. There were no black bankers, brokers, moneylenders, wholesale dealers, importers, exporters, city officials, or inspectors. The black middle class was very small, and its income base extremely fragile.

Occupational differences led to significant differences in the type of housing that black and white workers could afford.[68] African Americans, for the most part, could not afford to purchase homes in the formal housing market. They did not make enough money. In 1930, for instance, blacks owned only 1,126, or 2.49 percent, of the city's 45,085 owner-occupied dwelling units. Significantly, the handful of blacks who owned their homes owned the cheapest housing in Cincinnati. The median value of black owner-occupied housing was only $4,496 as compared to $7,464 and $8,003 for foreign-born and na-

Table 6.6. Rank-Ordered Distribution (Percent) of Select Occupations within Racial and Ethnic Groups in Cincinnati, 1920

Occupations	Rank	Native Whites	Foreign/ Mixed Parentage	Foreign-Born	Blacks
Professional	1	6.1	5.4	4.0	2.0
Proprietors, Managers, and Officials	2	9.0	12.2	16.2	2.3
Clerical	3	30.6	26.4	9.2	1.4
Skilled	4	20.3	21.4	27.0	3.4
Semiskilled	5	14.0	16.0	15.2	5.0
Unskilled	6	10.0	9.0	15.0	42.2
Domestic and personal	7	10.3	11.0	14.0	44.0

Note: Percents are for both males and females and do not include the category "Indians, Chinese, Japanese, and all others."
Source: U.S. Census Office, *Fourteenth Census, 1920* (Washington, D.C., 1922), vol. 4, 1081–84.

tive whites, respectively. Even more important, 26 percent of black owner-occupied housing cost under $3,000 as compared to 5 percent for both native and foreign-born whites. And 93 percent of the housing owned by blacks was valued at under $10,000 a year, while only 54 percent of the housing owned by whites fell below this figure.[69]

Most blacks living in Cincinnati were renters. And the data show that they occupied the cheapest rental housing in Cincinnati. In 1930 the median monthly rental for black-occupied dwelling units was $20 as compared to $27 and $28 for foreign-born and native whites. Moreover, 79 percent of the dwelling units occupied by blacks rented for less than $30 a month as compared to 56 percent for the foreign-born and 54 percent for native whites. The data are clear. Income and the economics of the housing market were central factors in determining what type of housing was available to African Americans and where in the city that housing was located.[70]

Low wages forced blacks to search for housing in the city's low-rent district, which was located in the West End of the basin, an area bounded by Court Street and the Ohio River and falling between Central Avenue and Freeman.[71] This is where the ghetto-slum formed (Map 6.5).[72] By 1930 more than thirty-thousand blacks, comprising 67 percent of the African American population, lived here.[73] No physical wall encircled the ghetto, but a wall of high rent did isolate blacks from their more affluent white neighbors.[74] Building codes,

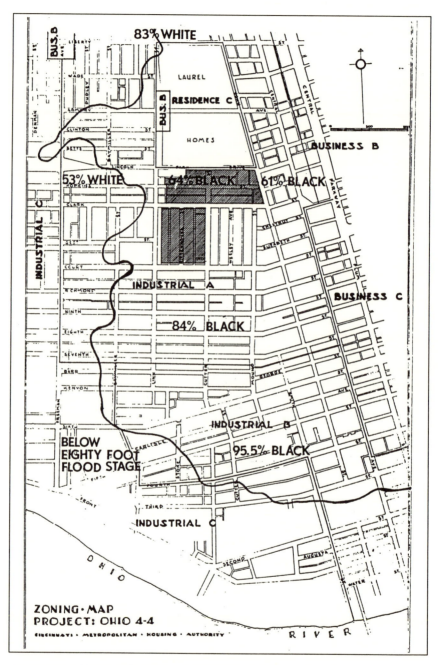

Map 6.5. Land Use Structure and Population Composition: The West End in 1930. Stanley Rowe Collection, Loan Application Project, Ohio 4-4, box 3, folder 1, Cincinnati Historical Society.

zoning laws, the 1925 city plan, and subdivision regulations reinforced this wall. In the 1920s and 1930s an informal housing market
existed that catered to the needs of low-wage workers. This market
emerged in the late 1800s and was fully developed by the 1920s. It
consisted of real estate speculators, building material companies,
banks, savings and loan companies, builders, and an army of carpenters all willing to help low-income workers build their own houses.[75]

This existence of this informal market meant that ambitious, determined low-income blacks could acquire or build cheap housing
in the valley and hilltop regions or in the suburbs.[76] For instance,
by 1930 blacks had developed residential areas in the suburbs of
College Hill (the Steele subdivision), Kennedy Heights, Wyoming,
Lockland, Woodlawn, and Hazelwood. In Cincinnati there were 6
census tracts outside with the basin in which 400 or more blacks resided (tracts 15, 21, 36, 37, 55, and 77), and there were 13 census
tracts outside the basin in which 100 to 399 blacks resided (24, 49,
54, 56, 58, 60, 62, 65, 69, 79, 80, 82, and 105). Approximately
13,542 African Americans lived in these 19 census tracts.[77] Many of
these blacks resided in inexpensive dwelling units. In some of these
neighborhoods, especially those located in the suburbs, the houses
were crudely constructed shacks located on poorly developed lots
with unpaved roads.[78]

The residents of these communities of homeowners were proud of
their neighborhoods. Housing reformers, however, had a different attitude. They believed that low-income black housing settlements represented a major threat to homeownership and to the development of
moderate- to high-rent neighborhoods. Standish Meacham, of the
BHL referred to them as "bad spots," which were potential slums. He
called, for example, the black Lockland suburb (Lincoln Heights)
"the ugliest collection of shacks I have ever seen." The director of
buildings for the city, Clifford M. Stegner, called these low-income
residential settlements a "menace to the city."[79]

Marquette, Stegner, Alfred Bettman, and other housing reformers
were particularly concerned that low-income black settlements such
as the communities in College Hill, Lockland, and Hazelwood would
lead to slums forming in the suburbs. In the 1920s and 1930s there
were virtually no residential land use regulations in Hamilton
County. In this setting, any type of subdivision could be developed,
and people could build any type of house. In the BHL's 1928 report
Marquette worried, "We find developing just outside the corporation lines potential slums which will eventually contain all of the
bad conditions we are fighting against now." The BHL called for the

establishment of a regional planning commission and for the development of subdivision regulations to promote "orderly growth" in the county.[80]

A central goal of the housing reformers was to confine low-income black workers to the basin by using building codes, zoning laws, subdivision regulations, and comprehensive city planning to outlaw cheap housing in other parts of Cincinnati and Hamilton County. Simultaneously, they planned to encourage higher-income whites to move out of the basin so that their old houses could trickle down to blacks. This strategy was advanced in 1924, when black leaders and members of the Cincinnati Community Chest asked the BHL to develop a plan for addressing the worsening black housing problem.

The BHL told blacks and their supporters that "it is impossible to build houses directly for the colored people because the facts show that their wages are insufficient to pay the cost of present-day construction." The BHL then suggested that friends of African Americans should be encouraged to invest their money in the building of new houses for whites. "This," the BHL indicated, "while not relieving colored families directly would tend to relieve them indirectly by drawing white families out of the district now occupied for the most part by colored people."[81] Confinement in the basin and trickle-down housing were to become the cornerstones of the housing reformers' strategy for dealing with the black housing problem.

The BHL even tried to keep blacks from escaping to white-dominated neighborhoods on the fringe of the basin. When realtors started to rent and sell to blacks dwelling units in the white working-class neighborhood of Mohawk-Brighton, the BHL tried to stop the practice because of the "outbursts of violent feeling and bitterness." The BHL asked its visiting social workers and housekeepers to persuade blacks not to move into the neighborhood, and intensified its efforts to find "room for the expansion of colored people . . . without this scattering into white neighborhoods."[82]

The real estate industry and white homeowners also tried to keep blacks concentrated in the basin. For example, in the 1920s the Cincinnati Real Estate Board mandated, "No agent shall rent or sell property to colored people in an established white section or neighborhood and this inhibition shall be particularly applicable to the hilltops and suburban property."[83] Jacob G. Schmidlapp said that when he tried to build low-income housing for blacks in Avondale, "Whites in the neighborhood objected to us renting to colored tenants although we had bought the plot from a colored man and his people were living on each side of the lot."[84]

Also the housing reform movement conducted a massive public relations campaign to win support for its housing program. The goal of the campaign was to "arouse the public to the serious housing plight of the poor" by creating "a graphic picture of the conditions under which our underprivileged families are compelled to live." This campaign consisted of public speeches, newspaper articles, and a moving picture. The blighting effect of bad housing and the need to contain it in the basin were the central themes of this campaign. Since most blacks lived in bad housing and since their housing situation was considered the worst in the city, the public relations campaign may have exacerbated racial animosity.[85]

These urban policies trapped most blacks in the basin and transformed the ghetto into a slum.[86] They forced blacks to live in a volatile land use conversion zone where housing units were being demolished to make way for economic development. The 1925 city plan zoned most of the basin for commercial and industrial development. This meant that blacks had to build their community in a poor residential environment, an unstable setting characterized by omnipresent construction and demolition.[87] For instance, in sixteen select years between 1908 and 1938, 29.3 percent of the 1,990 new factories, offices, service shops, and amusement places constructed in Cincinnati were built in the basin. In the same period, 47.5 percent (N = 1,638) of the 3,449 buildings demolished in Cincinnati were located in the basin. The most intense period of residential displacement occurred between 1924 and 1934 when 1,169 residential buildings, housing more than 3,514 families, were demolished. Between 1920 and 1935 the black basin population jumped from 19,776 to 39,042.[88]

Black population growth and the ongoing consumption of residential land by factories, stores, shops, office buildings, rail spurs, and passenger and freight terminals led to the deterioration of housing and neighborhood conditions in the basin.[89] For example, between 1934 and 1935 the number of basin dwelling units classified as good by the Department of Buildings decreased from 7,561 to 5,836, while the number of dwellings classified as very bad, bad, and fair increased from 5,812 to 7,462.[90] Congestion, poor living conditions, inadequate health care delivery, low wages, and the concentration of social and health problems in the basin made the black ghetto-slum a very undesirable place to live.[91] Yet the policies promoted by the BHL and the housing reform movement made escape to Cincinnati's white-dominated valley and hilltop neighborhoods difficult.

Conclusion

Cincinnati's biracial residential environment persisted until 1920. But during the decades of the 1920s and 1930s residential segregation increased dramatically. It was in this period that the ghetto-slum took form. The growing segregation of blacks coincided with the emergence of a housing reform movement based on the promotion of homeownership and the protection of residential districts from an invasion of bad housing and factories and commercial building. Housing reformers believed that homeownership and homogeneous (class-stratified) neighborhoods were central to the building of a modern residential environment. To protect neighborhoods from nonconforming patterns of land use and to encourage homeownership, they used building codes, zoning laws, and subdivision regulations.

These public policies, combined with the practices of the real estate industry and white homeowners, kept most blacks out of the new, white neighborhoods developing in Cincinnati's hilltop and valley districts and segregated them in the basin area. Blacks and whites began to live in two very different types of neighborhoods. Most whites now lived in neighborhoods dominated by single-family, owner-occupied dwelling units, characterized by open space and amenities. Blacks, on the other hand, lived in the tenement-dominated low-rent district, where they shared residential space with factories, buildings, and the railroads. In Cincinnati public policies and the building of a modern residential environment contributed to the formation of a black ghetto-slum. The city-building process played a prominent role in ghetto-slum formation.

Notes

1. In this study the term "ghetto" is used to define a residential area that is dominated (80 percent or more of the population) by a racial or white ethnic group and that contains at least 60 percent of that group's total population. The term "ghetto-slum" is defined the same way, except that it is also characterized by bad housing, a dilapidated physical environment, and the concentration of social problems. Thus a series of spatially differentiated residential clusters containing varying proportions of the black population and bad housing would not necessarily qualify as either a ghetto or a ghetto-slum.

2. Gilbert Osofsky, *Harlem: The Making of a Ghetto: Negro New York, 1890–1930* (New York: Harper and Row, 1963); Seth Scheiner, *Negro Mecca* (New York: New York University Press, 1965); August Meier and El-

liott Rudwick, *From Plantation to Ghetto* (Urbana: University of Illinois Press, 1966); Allen Spear, *Black Chicago: The Making of a Negro Ghetto, 1890–1920* (Chicago: University of Chicago, 1967), 6. These scholars were writing in the 1960s during the height of the civil rights movement; their emphasis on integration and racial hostility was no doubt influenced by this movement. There have been several excellent reviews of the literature on black urban history. See, for example, Kenneth L. Kusmer, "The Black Experience in American History," in *The State of Afro-American History: Past, Present, and Future,* ed. Darlene Clark Hine (Baton Rouge: Louisiana State University Press, 1986), 91–122; Joe William Trotter, Jr., *Black Milwaukee: The Making of an Industrial Proletariat, 1915–1945* (Urbana: University of Illinois Press, 1986), 265–91.

3. Theodore Hershberg, "The New Urban History: Toward an Interdisciplinary History of the City," in *Philadelphia: Work, Space, Family, and Group Experience in the Nineteenth Century,* ed. Theodore Hershberg (Oxford: Oxford University Press, 1981), 3–35; Kusmer, "The Black Urban Experience," 91–122.

4. Kusmer, "The Black Urban Experience," 107–8.

5. A number of urban studies have shown that both the pace and timing of black ghetto formation is related to city size, region, and the emergence of an industrial city. T. J. Woofter, *Negro Problems in Cities* (New York: Doubleday and Doran, 1928; repr., Negro Universities Press, 1969); Homer Hoyt, *The Structure and Growth of Residential Neighborhoods* (Washington, D.C.: Government Printing Office, 1939); Robert C. Weaver, *The Negro Ghetto* (New York: Harcourt, Brace and Company, 1947); Gilbert Osofsky, "The Enduring Ghetto," *Journal of American History* 55 (Sept. 1968): 243–55.

6. The term "city-building process" is based on the idea that the city is a built environment. It is based on the study of the city as a dependent variable. The concept refers, then, to decisions and activities that lead to the physical, technical, economic, social, and political development of urban areas. Based on this conceptualization, the city is a dynamic, constantly changing place. And at every stage in its development, the city is characterized by a specific type of economy, transportation system, and ecological complex (structure and form). So, then, the city is built as a result of a complex interplay among economic, technological, and social forces. See Hershberg, "The New Urban History," 3–35; Roy Lubove, "The Urbanization Process: An Approach to Historical Research," *American Institute of Planners* 33 (Jan. 1967): 33–39; Eric E. Lampard, "American Historians and the Study of Urbanization," *American Historical Review* 67 (Oct. 1961): 49–61.

7. For an in-depth study of the housing reform movement in Cincinnati, see Robert B. Fairbanks, *Making Better Citizens: Housing Reform and the Community Development Strategy in Cincinnati, 1890–1960* (Urbana: University of Illinois Press, 1988).

8. Carter G. Woodson, "The Negroes of Cincinnati prior to the Civil War," *Journal of Negro History* 1 (Jan. 1916): 1–22; Richard C. Wade,

"The Negro in Cincinnati, 1800–1830," *Journal of Negro History* 39 (Jan. 1954): 43–57; Leonard Harding, "The Negro in Cincinnati, 1860–1870: A Demographic Study of a Transitional Decade" (Master's thesis, University of Cincinnati, 1965); Samuel B. Matthews, "The Black Educational Experience in Nineteenth-Century Cincinnati, 1817–1874" (Ph.D. diss., University of Cincinnati, 1985); Charles Thomas Hickok, *The Negro in Ohio, 1802–1870* (New York: AMS Press, 1975, reprint); Henry Louis Taylor, Jr., "On Slavery's Fringe: City Building and Black Community Development in Cincinnati, 1800–1850," *Ohio History* 95 (Winter–Spring 1986): 5–33.

9. Charles Cist, *Cincinnati in 1851* (W. H. Moore, 1851); Steven J. Ross, *Workers on the Edge: Work, Leisure, and Politics in Industrializing Cincinnati, 1788–1890* (New York: Columbia University Press, 1985).

10. To study the black occupational structure in Cincinnati I organized data on 915 black male workers (derived from the 1850 manuscript census and from a master's thesis by Patricia Riley) and placed the data in a file entitled "Cincinnati Black Worker Data File, Wards 1–12, 1850." See Patricia Riley, "The Negro in Cincinnati: The Black Experience, 1835–1850" (Master's thesis, University of Cincinnati, 1964), 53–76; Woodson, "The Negroes of Cincinnati," 1–22.

11. Data on the types of dwellings in which blacks lived were derived from the collection of Martin Fire Insurance maps. These maps identify sixteen different types of structures according to building materials and structural configuration and also show the location and configuration of buildings, stores, dwelling units above stores, public institutions, churches, and factories. Studying these maps in relation to the location of blacks in the city sheds light on the type of housing that blacks occupied. W. H. Martin, *Map of Cincinnati for Insurance Companies and Real Estate Agents,* vols. 1 and 2. The Martin collection features one of the earliest insurance maps, and the only known copy is located at the Cincinnati Historical Society.

12. To determine where blacks lived in Cincinnati, the residential location of the entire black population for 1850 was determined and plotted on a map. To overcome the limitations of the index of dissimilarity (a popular method used to measure residential segregation), I used the 1850 census to make a microlevel (street) analysis of the black residential pattern. U.S. Bureau of the Census, *The Seventh Census of the United States, 1850: Manuscript Census for Cincinnati and Hamilton County* (Washington, D.C.: National Archives Microfilm), reel 6, roll 690: 1044–51, 986–1011, 1018–41, 1034–36. For a detailed description of this approach, see Henry Louis Taylor, Jr., "Spatial Organization and the Residential Experience: Black Cincinnati in 1850," *Social Science History* 10, no. 1 (Spring 1986): 45–69. For a description of the index of dissimilarity, see Karl Taeuber and Alma Taeuber, *Negroes in Cities: Residential Segregation and Neighborhood Change* (New York: Atheneum, 1969).

13. Sam Bass Warner, Jr., and Colin B. Burke, "Cultural Change and the Ghetto," *Journal of Contemporary History* 4 (Oct. 1969): 173–187.

14. Leonard P. Curry, *The Free Black in Urban America, 1800–1850* (Chicago: University of Chicago Press, 1981).

15. The Cincinnati experience was typical. Most of the cities in the northern commercial belt underwent change during this period. The change process has been well documented. See, for example, Sam Bass Warner, Jr., *The Urban Wilderness: A History of the American City* (New York: Harper and Row, 1972).

16. U.S. Bureau of the Census, *The Thirteenth Census of the United States Taken in Year 1910*, vol. 1, *Population, 1910, General Report and Analysis* (Washington, D.C.: Government Printing Office, 1913), 80–81; James A. Quinn, Earl Eubank, and Lois E. Elliott, *Population Changes—Cincinnati, Ohio and Adjacent Areas, 1900–1940*, Research Monograph No. 47 (Columbus: Bureau of Business Research, Ohio State University Press, 1947), 14. Most of the territorial expansion of Cincinnati took place between 1850 and 1910. A series of maps by H. M. Waite shows the quantitative changes in the city's spatial structure. Waite, *Topographical Survey, City of Cincinnati, 1912* (Washington, D.C.: 1912). These maps show the entire area of Hamilton County and its existing level of urban development. See also Richard Rhonda, "Urban Transport and the Expansion of Cincinnati, 1858–1920," *Cincinnati Historical Society Bulletin* 35 (Summer 1977): 131–43; Richard M. Wagner and Roy J. Wright, *Cincinnati's Streetcars: Horsecars and Steam Dummies* (Cincinnati: Wagner Car, 1968).

17. U.S. Department of the Interior, Census Office, *U.S. Ninth Census, 1870*, vol. 1, *Statistics of the Population of the United States*, 598.

18. Wagner and Wright, *Cincinnati Streetcars;* idem., *Cincinnati Streetcars: No. 2: The Inclines* (Cincinnati: Wagner Car, 1968); Rhonda, "Urban Transport," 131–43.

19. Zane L. Miller, *Boss Cox's Cincinnati: Urban Politics in the Progressive Era* (New York: Oxford University Press, 1968), 6.

20. While the general features of the process of urban change have been well documented, much less is known about the reorganization of the residential environment that accompanied the emergence of the modern American city. Some works have dealt with various aspects of the change process, including housing, but none, to my knowledge, have focused exclusively on the residential environment, with discussions of the specific changes that took place and the social and behavioral significance of these changes. See, for example, Sam Bass Warner, Jr., *Streetcar Suburbs: The Process of Growth in Boston, 1870–1900* (Cambridge, Mass.: Harvard University Press and M.I.T. Press, 1962); Robert H. Wiebe, *The Search for Order: 1877–1920* (New York: Hill and Wang, 1967); Olivier Zunz, *The Changing Face of Inequality: Urbanization, Industrial Development, and Immigrants in Detroit, 1880–1920* (Chicago: University of Chicago Press, 1982).

21. There were only five thousand homeowners in Commercial Cincinnati. Cist, *Cincinnati in 1851*, 73.

22. This conflict between economic and residential development in the basin will be discussed later.

23. Quinn, Eubank, and Elliott, *Population Changes*. This monograph provides a detailed look at population movement in Cincinnati by census tract. It contains a number of excellent maps that show population movement and housing characteristics.

24. Miller, *Boss Cox*, 15.

25. The index of dissimilarity is a comparative measure of the citywide distribution of blacks and whites. It is based on the assumption that uneven distribution between the races is equivalent to their separation in geographic space. The index is simple to calculate and straightforward in its interpretation: Let the index of dissimilarity be $S1$ and let n be the total number of spatial units in the city; let P be the city's total population and Pi be the population in the ith spatial unit. Let G be the total population of the group under study and gi be the number of individuals in that group in the ith spatial unit. Then the index of dissimilarity is:

$$I = 1/2 \frac{n\,Pi - gi\,gi}{i = 1\,P -_. G\,G}$$

Using this formula, the index of dissimilarity for Cincinnati was computed. For an analysis of the problems involved when using this methodology, see Taylor, "Black Cincinnati," 46–69; Taeuber and Taeuber, *Negroes in Cities*.

26. Cincinnati's Buildings Department was authorized to issue permits for the construction or demolition of buildings within the city limits. For each permit the department requested certain information: the purpose of the building, the location of the building, the type of construction, and the proposed height of the building. To trace trends in buildings in Cincinnati, the University of Cincinnati's Department of Sociology obtained records of building permits and demolitions for the following sixteen years: 1908, 1910, 1918, 1920, 1923, 1925, 1928, and 1930–38. These data provide an accurate picture of trends in building for Cincinnati and its various subdivisions. Evidence of a permit application does not prove that the actual construction or demolition took place, but it was rare for such applications to be made without full intent to construct. Except for unusual circumstances, then, we can assume that these applications represent actual constructions or demolitions. In addition to the data on select years between 1908 and 1938, the Federal Reconstruction Corporation examined the volume of residential construction in Cincinnati, and its data base provides information on building permits for each year between 1921 and 1940. James A. Quinn, Earl Eubank, and Lois E. Elliott, *Cincinnati Building Permits: Trends and Distribution, 1908–1938* (Columbus: Bureau of Business Research, Ohio State University, Special Bulletin, 1947); Federal Reconstruction Corporation, "Building Permits, City Proper, Cincinnati, Ohio, 1916–1945," Federal Reconstruction Corporation, box 11, record group 31, National Archives.

27. There was a residential building boom throughout the United States during this period. Most of the cities in the manufacturing belt experienced substantial increases in their housing stock. David M. Blank, *The Volume of*

Residential Construction, 1889–1950 (New York: National Bureau of Economic Research, Studies in Capital Formation and Financing, Technical Paper 9, 1954); Robert G. Barrows, "Beyond the Tenement: Patterns of American Urban Housing, 1870–1930," *Journal of Urban History* 9 (Aug. 1983): 395–420.

28. Quinn, Eubank, and Elliott, *Building Permits,* 35.

29. Ibid.

30. The Cincinnati experience was consistent with national trends. For example, by 1920 80 percent of all residential structures built in the United States were single-family dwelling units. Blank, *The Volume of Residential Construction,* 69; Barrows, "Beyond the Tenement," 395–420.

31. Quinn, Eubank, and Elliott, *Building Permits,* 35.

32. Ibid., 40. See Map 3, which shows the percent of the total number of residential building permits by census tracts and by cost of construction for the 1908–38 period.

33. Miller, *Boss Cox,* chapters 1–3; Cist, *Cincinnati in 1851,* 268–70; Willard Glazier, *Peculiarities of American Cities* (Philadelphia: Hubbard Brothers, 1983), 121–25; U.S. Bureau of the Census, *Twelfth Census of the United States, 1900: Population* (Washington, D.C.: Government Printing Office, 1902), 654–55, 708; idem., *Sixteenth Census of the United States, 1940: Population and Housing: Statistics for Census Tract: Cincinnati, Ohio and Adjacent Areas* (Washington, D.C.: Government Printing Office, 1942), 4–39; "Aid the Home Builder," 18–19; *The Citizen and the Taxpayer,* 4.

34. U.S. Bureau of the Census, *Report on Vital and Social Statistics, Cincinnati, Ohio, Eleventh Census, 1890* (Washington, D.C.: Government Printing Office, 1892), 182–97; University of Cincinnati Department of Sociology, "Table Showing the Computed Combined Median Rental and Derived Representation Income for Cincinnati, 1930" (based on Table 10 of the Federal Census Tract Tabulation, 1930), Census Tract Data Center, box s.28.24, Archive and Rare Book Department, University of Cincinnati; Warner, *Streetcar Suburbs,* 153; Miller, *Boss Cox,* chapters 1–3.

35. As early as the 1830s Cincinnati had developed some rather primitive types of zoning codes. For example, wooden buildings were not allowed in the business section of the city. It was not until 1924, however, that the city had its first modern, comprehensive zoning law. Cist, *Cincinnati in 1851,* 71–73; Cincinnati, *Zoning Ordinance,* June 1933, p. 26, Stanley Rowe Papers, box 3, folder 6, Cincinnati Historical Society. Sam Bass Warner, Jr., posits that investors in this period sought to protect their heavy personal financial commitment to the home-building process by seeking conformity in architectural style and cost in the types of houses being constructed in a given neighborhood. Warner, *Streetcar Suburbs,* 117–52.

36. Developers in cities across the country made great use of subdivision design and deed restrictions to determine the socioeconomic character of their developments. Indirect control could be accomplished by manipulating the physical design and layout of subdivisions. To evaluate Cincinnati, plats and deeds were examined for select areas of Mt. Auburn, Corryville, Clifton,

Avondale, and Walnut Hills. The subdivisions selected for analysis were located along major arteries. While no evidence of deed restrictions in these areas was found, it was clear that the design and layout of the subdivisions would have kept low-income groups from buying lots. Also, one of the lawyers that assisted in the research indicated that because the selected areas were high-income neighborhoods, deed restrictions were not really needed to keep blacks out. The analysis of the subdivision designs supports his theory. At the same time, Bleecker Marquette indicated that sometimes deed restrictions were used to keep low-income groups out of neighborhoods. Hamilton County Auditor's Plat, Book 214, Hamilton County Recorder's Office, Cincinnati, 6; Better Housing League, *Housing Progress in Cincinnati: Second Report,* July 1921, 29 (pamphlet); Patricia Burgess Stach, "Deed Restrictions and Subdivision Development in Columbus, Ohio, 1900–1970, *Journal of Urban History* 15 (Nov. 1988): 42–68.

37. Cincinnati was not a big ethnic city. Between 1890 and 1920 Cincinnati's foreign-born population dropped from 24 to 11 percent. But even in those cities with large ethnic populations, class became the driving force behind the organization of the residential environment. U.S. Bureau of the Census, *Thirteenth Census, 1910* (Washington, D.C.: Government Printing Office, 1913), 854–55, cited in Miller, *Boss Cox,* 14; Zunz, *The Changing Face of Inequality,* 286–370.

38. Zane L. Miller referred to these three areas as the circle, zone, and hilltop. Miller, *Boss Cox,* chapters 1–3. The low-rent district was found in the historic core, or basin, area; the moderate-rent district was situated in the industrial corridor that stretched up the Mill Creek Valley and the Norwood Trough; and the high-rent district was located on the Cincinnati hilltops. Public Health Federation, "Median Rentals: Based on the 1930 Federal Census Tract: Showing Four Classification Groups by Census Tract, Cincinnati, Ohio" (map); Federal Housing Authority, "Statistical and Economic Survey, Cincinnati, Ohio" (map, n.d.), State University of New York at Buffalo, Center for Applied Public Affairs, map collection, Archives. Although no date is given on the FHA map, it was probably done in 1935. The map is highly detailed and breaks the city down into a number of small units. Each unit contains the following information: median rental group, median value of one-family structures, number of dwelling units, median year built, percentage of owner-occupied units, percentage needing structural repairs or dilapidated, percentage without private baths, and percentage occupied by blacks. This highly detailed map leaves no doubt about the class nature of the residential environment. See also Cincinnati Department of Buildings, "Number of New Residence Buildings Constructed, 1914–32," Cincinnati Model Homes Papers, box 61, folder 7, Cincinnati Historical Society (CHS); idem., "The Value of Building Construction, 1913–1932," Cincinnati Model Homes Papers, box 62, folder 6, CHS.

39. Hoyt, *Residential Neighborhoods;* Homer Hoyt, *One Hundred Years of Land Values in Chicago* (Chicago: University of Chicago, 1933); Blank, *The Volume of Residential Construction;* Warner, *Streetcar Suburb;* Daniel D.

Luria, "Wealth, Capital, and Power: The Social Meaning of Homeowner-ship," *Journal of Interdisciplinary History* 7 (Autumn 1976): 261–82; Zunz, *The Changing Face of Inequality;* John Bodnar, Roger Simon, and Michael Weber, *Lives of Their Own: Blacks, Italians, and Poles in Pitts-burgh, 1900–1960* (Urbana: University of Illinois Press, 1982), 153. Robert G. Barrows argues that a clear correlation existed between homeownership in a given community and the percentage of families borrowing from local build-ing and loan associations. Barrows, "Beyond the Tenement," 416; Richard O. Davies, "One-Third of a Nation: The Dilemmas of America's Housing, 1607–1970," in *The National Archives and Urban Research,* ed. Jerome Fin-ster (Athens: Ohio University Press, 1970), 41–55.

40. The New Deal policies changed the nature of home finance and sought to make home buying a more secure economic investment. U.S. De-partment of Labor, "The Wage Earners' Problem of Home Mortgage and Home Ownership" (pamphlet) (Washington, D.C.: Women's Bureau, 1934), 1–27.

41. The data on interest rates for mortgages and the length of mort-gages were derived from the Hamilton County mortgage books for the period between 1923 and 1933. The books are located at the Hamilton County courthouse in Cincinnati. Data on interest rates were obtained for ninety-one cases. In most instances the rate of interest was about 7 percent per annum. Every time the loan was refinanced, though, the borrower had to pay refinance charges as well as additional interest rates. This meant that the actual cost of borrowing money was much higher than the published rates of interest. In Cincinnati the length of the mortgage term generally ranged from four months to four years, and no mortgage term lasted longer than seven years. See, for example, Theresia Krody and John Krody, *Mort-gage Book 1456,* Hamilton County Courthouse, Recorders Office, 33–34; Elsie P. Creuty and Otto Creuty, *General Index Book,* series 7, book 49, Hamilton County Courthouse, Recorders Office, 153. See also Depart-ment of Labor, "The Wage Earners," 1–27; Warner, *Streetcar Suburbs;* Bodnar, Simon, and Weber, *Lives of Their Own;* Zunz, *The Changing Face of Inequality.*

42. Roger Starr, *Housing and the Money Market* (New York: Basic Books, 1975).

43. See Antonio Saving and Loan Company, "Report of the Executive Committee," 22 Apr. 1929, ms. 717, vol. 9, Cincinnati Historical Society.

44. The terms of the mortgage contracts make clear the dangers of fore-closure. See Harry Briner, *Mortgage Book 1456,* 378, Hamilton County Courthouse, Recorders Office; Anna E. Meisman, *Mortgage Book 1246,* 7; Department of Labor, *Wage Earners,* 1–27.

45. The idea of neighborhoods as defended territories is central to the work of Gerald D. Suttles, *The Social Construction of Communities* (Chi-cago: University of Chicago Press, 1972); James Borchert, *Alley Life in Washington: Family, Community, Religion, and Folklore in the City, 1850–1970* (Urbana: University of Illinois Press, 1980), 100–142.

46. *Sixteenth Annual Report of the Cincinnati Relief Union,* cited in Fairbanks, *Making Better Citizens,* 13.

47. The historian Robert B. Fairbanks has a different but complementary interpretation of this period. Fairbanks interprets the reformers' actions in terms of housing and community, while I interpret their actions in terms of residential development. Consequently, Fairbanks is primarily concerned with housing developments in the basin and big housing projects such as public housing and the New Deal Greenbelt housing program. My concern, on the other hand, is with the development of moderate-to-middle-income neighborhoods outside the basin and the efforts of the reformers to contain low-cost housing in the basin. Fairbanks, *Making Better Citizens.*

48. The Anti-Tuberculosis League played a major role in the tenement reform movement as well. But it did not emerge as a real force until after 1909, when the movement's emphasis shifted from the passage of a tough tenement law to enforcement of the existing code.

49. Fairbanks, *Making Better Citizens,* 100.

50. Ibid., 23.

51. "Good" and "bad" housing and neighborhood conditions had very specific meanings in Cincinnati during the opening decades of the twentieth century. The housing leaders defined the housing problem as a problem of community, not merely one of shelter, safety, sanitation, and family privacy. The disintegration of the physical environment and the psychological disorganization that followed resulted from poor people living in a residential environment characterized by mixed land uses, an extremely heterogeneous and mobile population, and an absence of formal social organizations. The worst of such chaotic settings produced slum dwellers: apathetic, anomic, and alienated individuals with an inhibited capacity for development as citizens. Ironically, blacks defined good housing and neighborhoods in similar terms. They defined bad and good housing both in terms of the quality of the dwelling unit as well as the stability and quality of life inside the neighborhood. Robert B. Fairbanks and Zane L. Miller, "The Martial Metropolis: Housing, Planning, and Race in Cincinnati, 1940–55, " in *The Martial Metropolis: U.S. Cities in War and Peace,* ed. Roger W. Lotchin (New York: Praeger, 1984), 197–98.

52. Fairbanks, *Making Better Citizens,* 26.

53. Bleecker Marquette, "The History of Housing in Ohio" (Paper presented at the Conference of Ohio Housing Authorities, Youngstown, Ohio, 9 June 1939, 4), BHL Papers, box 10, folder 30, Archives and Rare Books Department, University of Cincinnati (UC); idem., *Ten Years of Housing Work in Cincinnati, 1928,* BHL, 1928 (pamphlet), 3–4, BHL Papers, Archives and Rare Books Department, UC.

54. Robert B. Fairbanks, "Housing the City: The Better Housing League and Cincinnati, 1916–1939," *Ohio History* (Spring 1980): 156–80; BHL, "Housing Progress in Cincinnati: Second Report," July 1921, 4, BHL Papers, Archives and Rare Books, UC. By the phrase, "getting rid of slums," Marquette was probably referring to improving conditions within the slum

area, not "slum clearance and community redevelopment financed by phi-
lanthropists or public funds." When Marquette made this statement he was
emphasizing the shift from tenement house reform to the building of single-
family homes for higher-paid workers and the middle classes. This entire
BHL report centers on three themes: the housing shortage, tenement house
reform, and the building of single-family houses and homeownership. Marquette stresses that the building of single-family homes and homeownership
are the most important aspects of the housing reform movement. Also he
indicates that the tenement reform movement is important but secondary
to homeownership.

55. In the league's 1928 report on housing, Marquette indicated that as
early as 1918 the BHL realized that its original objective to "improve conditions in the tenement house district was too circumscribed." Marquette,
Ten Years of Housing Work, 13; Fairbanks, *Making Better Citizens,* 32;
BHL, "Housing Progress in Cincinnati," 27–28; Julian A. Pollak, President
of BHL, to C. J. Livingood and Mary Emery, 24 Apr. 1922, BHL Papers,
Cincinnati Historical Society.

56. BHL, "Housing Progress in Cincinnati," 29.

57. Ibid.; Bleecker Marquette to Alfred Bettman, 7 Dec. 1920 BHL Papers, CHS; BHL, "Report of the Committee on Zoning Ordinance," 11 Dec.
1923, BHL Papers, box 6, folder 41, Archives and Rare Books, UC.

58. BHL, "Housing Progress in Cincinnati," 9; Julian, W. A., M. W.
Mack, A. O. Elzner, Alfred Bettman, Edward P. Moulinier, letter, 28 July
1917, BHL Papers, CHS; Minutes, Housing Committee, BHL, 30 Dec.
1921, 19 Jan. 1922, 25 Jan. 1922, 8 Mar. 1922, BHL Papers, box 1, folder
4, Archives and Rare Books, UC.

59. BHL, *Houses or Homes: First Report of the Cincinnati Better Housing League, Cincinnati 1919,* BHL Papers, Archives and Rare Books, UC, 23.

60. Bleecker Marquette, *Housing, Health, and Other Things* (Cincinnati:
Bleecker Marquette, 1972), 57–59. Bettman organized the United City Planning Committee and convinced C. M. Bookman, head of the Community
Chest, to allow the UCPC to use the chest as a vehicle for raising money for
the city plan survey by allowing people to designate a Community Chest do-
nation as a gift to the city. The Technical Advisory Corporation was hired by
the city council to conduct the survey.

61. Marquette, "The History of Housing in Ohio," 5.

62. Cincinnati City Planning Commission, *The Official City Plan of Cincinnati, Ohio* (City Planning Commission, 1925), 50–53. The 1925 city plan
refined and further developed the 1924 zoning law.

63. BHL, "Housing Progress in Cincinnati," 31; Marquette, *Ten Years of
Housing Work,* 20; City Planning Commission, *Rules of the City Planning
Commission for the Subdivision of Land* (Cincinnati: City Planning Com-
mission, 1929), 5.

64. Henrietta Maria Smith, "Black Suburbia Versus the Stereotype of
Suburbia: The History of Lincoln Heights, Ohio" (Master's thesis, University of Cincinnati, 1967); Rhoza A. Walker, "Housing as an Educational

Problem for Negroes in Cincinnati" (Master's thesis, University of Cincinnati, 1940). Actually, the practice of creating cheaply developed subdivisions for low-wage workers started in the late nineteenth century. Zunz, *The Changing Face of Inequality,* 129–76.

65. U.S. Bureau of the Census, *Negro Population in the United States: 1790–1915* (New York: Arno Press and the New York Times, 1968), 93; idem., *Sixteenth Census of the United States, 1940: Population and Housing: Statistics for Census Tracts: Census Tracts: Cincinnati, Ohio, and Adjacent Areas* (Washington, D.C.: Government Printing Office, 1942), 4–5.

66. With few exceptions, historians have generally failed systematically to study the black occupational structure. The position of blacks in the economy has usually been studied in isolation from other white groups, and scholars have too readily accepted the U.S. Census Bureau's classifications of jobs, which tend to hide more than they reveal. Using a classification scheme developed by Alba M. Edwards and Kenneth L. Kusmer, the occupations tabulated by the census in 1920 were categorized under subheadings ranked from 1 (the highest category) to 7 (the lowest). This rank-ordered classification scheme made it possible to construct a hierarchical model of Cincinnati's occupational structure and to determine the location of blacks—vis-á-vis native whites, whites with foreign or mixed parentage, and foreign-born whites—within that structure. I also analyzed the place of blacks and whites in the occupational structure by using the census bureau's classification scheme. This method allowed me to measure the importance of industrial jobs to Cincinnati blacks. A combination of these two methods provides a more complete picture of the occupational experience of blacks. The study is based on an analysis of 136,977 male and female members of Cincinnati's work force. See "Appendix 1: A Note on the Analysis of Occupational Data," in *A Ghetto Takes Shape: Black Cleveland, 1870–1930,* ed. Kenneth L. Kusmer (Urbana: University of Illinois Press, 1976), 275–80.

67. U.S. Bureau of the Census, *Fourteenth Census, 1920* (Washington, D.C.: Government Printing Office, 1922), 4, 1081–84. The totals do not include the category "Indians, Chinese, Japanese, and all others." See also the data set, "Blacks and the Cincinnati Occupational Structure, 1900–1930," Center Archives, Center for Applied Public Affairs Studies, State University of New York at Buffalo.

68. A detailed study of housing conditions among blacks, which was based on the Real Property Inventories first conducted by the Civil Works Administration, the Federal Emergency Relief Administration, and the Works Projects Administration, shows that in every city in which data were available significant differentials in the ability to purchase and rent housing existed between blacks and whites. Richard Sterner, *The Negro's Share: A Study of Income, Consumption, Housing and Public Assistance* (New York: Harper and Brothers, 1943).

69. Federal Housing Administration, Cincinnati Housing Inventory, "Owner-Occupied, Non-Farm Dwellings by Value and Racial Classes, 1930," vol. 2, Federal Reconstruction Corporation, National Archives,

record group 31, box 11. See Zunz, *The Changing Face of Inequality,* for an explanation of the formal housing market concept.

70. Federal Housing Administration, Cincinnati Housing Inventory, "Tenant-Occupied, Non-Farm Dwelling Units by Rental Value and Racial Classes, 1930," vol. 2, Federal Reconstruction Corporation, National Archives, record group 31, box 11.

71. Some scholars have suggested in their studies that income was not a central factor in the segregation of blacks. All of these studies focus on developments relating to the post–World War II black community, and it is questionable if the insights of these scholars can be extended backward. These studies are methodologically flawed anyway. To begin with, they use a single-factor approach that ignores the internal causes of ghetto-slum formation. Consequently they argue that since poor blacks and poor whites do not live in racially mixed areas, therefore economics does not play a major role in residential segregation. A host of other studies make a different argument. These studies point to the fact that significant income differentials exist between blacks and whites, and that national surveys show that significant differences exist between blacks and whites in terms of neighborhood preference. Blacks prefer living in neighborhoods that are 50 percent black, while whites prefer living in neighborhoods that are from 0–30 percent black. Since there are no magical ways to reach these favored proportions, the quest of blacks to reach their 50 percent preference could lead to significant clustering. Moreover, studies also show that the socioeconomic levels among blacks determine the types of neighborhoods that they are likely to move into. Indeed, even within black residential areas, there is stratification by class. Thus, economics—in terms of income, household wealth (assets), and equity (in housing)—when linked to the social preferences of blacks represents the major cause of residential segregation. See John F. Kain, "The Influence of Race and Income on Racial Segregation and Housing Policy," in *Housing Desegregation and Federal Policy,* ed. John M. Goering (Chapel Hill: University of North Carolina Press, 1986), 99–138; John Kain and J. Quigley, *Housing Markets and Racial Discrimination: A Microeconomic Analysis* (New York: Columbia University Press, 1975); and Taeuber and Taeuber, *Residential Segregation.* For an indepth critique of Kain and the scholarly literature relating to the link between income and residential segregation, see W. A. V. Clark, "Residential Segregation in American Cities: A Review and Interpretation," *Population Research and Policy Review 5* (1986): 95–127; Kathryn P. Nelson, "Recent Suburbanization of Blacks: How Much, Who, and Where" (U.S. Department of Housing and Urban Development, Office of Policy Development Research, report, Washington, D.C., 1979).

72. During the period in which blacks were moving into Cincinnati, thousands of whites were moving out. This outmigration created a geographical area containing large numbers of cheap housing units. The concentration of cheap housing is the historic condition that made ghetto-slum formation possible. See the *Sanborn Fire Insurance Maps of Cincinnati,*

1904 (uncorrected) (New York: Sanborn Map Co., 1904); Quinn, Eubank, and Elliott, *Population Changes,* 14–15; ibid., "Map 6: Dwelling Units: Percent of Dwelling Units Built Before 1900, Cincinnati, Ohio, By Census Tracts," and "Map 7: Dwelling Units: Percent of Dwelling Units Built Before 1919, Cincinnati, Ohio, by Census Tracts." A number of scholars have concluded that low incomes forced blacks to live in the low-rent district. Sterner, after an exhaustive study of national housing conditions in the 1930s, concluded, "In the first place, segregation is seldom complete. It is at least easier for Negroes to move around in slum areas than in more desirable sections, and most Negroes cannot afford to live in places other than slums anyway." Sterner, *The Negro's Share,* 209. Contemporaries of Sterner also concluded that most blacks could not afford to live outside the slum. Woofter, *Negro Problems;* Hoyt, *Residential Neighborhoods.* See also William M. Tuttle, Jr., *Race Riot: Chicago in the Red Summer of 1919* (New York: Atheneum, 1982); Anthony Jackson, *A Place Called Home: A History of Low-Cost Housing in Manhattan* (Cambridge, Mass.: M.I.T. Press, 1976); John Oliver and Alfred D. Price, *Housing New York's Black Population: Affordability and Adequacy* (Albany, N.Y.: The African American Institute, 1988).

73. Analysis of Population by Census Tracts (map), Stanley Rowe Collection, Loan Application Project, Ohio 4-4, box 3, folder 1, Cincinnati Historical Society; James A. Quinn, Earl Eubank, and Lois E. Elliott, *Cincinnati Population Characteristics by Census Tracts, 1930–1935* (Columbus: Ohio State University, 1940), 35.

74. Public Health Federation, "Median Rentals: Based on 1930 Federal Census" (map).

75. See *Mechanic Lien Book 51,* 27 Sept. 1927, 474; *Mechanic Lien Book 39,* 28 May 1929, 368. These records are located in the Hamilton County Recorders Office in Cincinnati. The mechanic lien books are an important source on the building activities of low-income blacks. They point out companies that were suing homeowners for nonpayment of contracts. These suits provide insight into who was constructing homes and lending money to these low-income homeowners, as well as information on subcontractors who helped blacks in the construction of their homes. A study of these records provided information on the wide variety of institutions and individuals from whom blacks secured mortgage monies.

76. Zunz, *The Changing Face of Inequality,* 170–76; Roger D. Simon, *The City-Building Process: Housing and Services in New Milwaukee Neighborhoods, 1880–1910* (Philadelphia: The American Philosophical Society, July 1978).

77. Department of Sociology, "Tables Showing No. Negroes by Sex, No. and Percent for Cincinnati Census Tract: 1930 (Total population of each tract, all classes, based on Federal Census, Census Tract)," University of Cincinnati Library, Archives and Rare Books, S.28.27.22. This file contains data on the population movement of black Cincinnatians from 1930 to 1970. There are both typescript and handscript data, and there are maps showing the population movement and population concentrations during this period.

78. Not all of these settlements were neighborhoods of poor blacks. For instance, Walnut Hills had a concentration of middle-income blacks. Burdette and Melrose Avenues, in particular, had large clusters of middle-class blacks. And middle-class blacks also built good homes in the suburb of Wyoming. But in most locations, blacks built or occupied cheaply constructed housing. For an excellent description of black neighborhoods in Cincinnati and the outlying suburbs in the 1930s, see Walker, "Housing as an Educational Problem."

79. C. M. Stegner, "The Menace of the City," n.d., Stanley Rowe Papers, box 5, folder 5, Cincinnati Historical Society; Myron D. Downs, "Planning the Redevelopment of the Slum Area of Cincinnati" (Speech presented at the Cincinnati Engineer's Club, 20 Sept. 1934, Stanley Rowe Papers, box 3, folder 1, CHS; *Cincinnati Post*, 17 Feb. 1940, 18 Feb. 1940, Urban League Papers, Housing Committee, 1941–44, box 16, folder 6, CHS.

80. Marquette, *Ten Years of Housing Work*, 19–20.

81. Better Housing League, *Minutes*, Special Committee on Negro Housing Problem, 4 Feb. 1924, BHL Papers, box 1, folder 4, Archives and Rare Books, UC.

82. Minutes, BHL Board of Directors, 7 Oct. 1924, BHL Papers, box 1, folder 4, Archives and Rare Books, UC.

83. *Cincinnati Union*, 14 May 1921, p. 1.

84. Jacob Schmidlapp, *Low-Priced Housing for the Wage Earner* (New York: National Housing Association, 1919), 5.

85. "Lights and Shadows in Cincinnati" (Public Meeting Held in Emergy Auditorium, 21 Apr. 1924, BHL Papers, Archives and Rare Books, UC.

86. The zoning plan articulated in the 1925 city plan divided the city up into five basic residential areas: low-rent tenements, new higher-class apartment houses, lowest-cost one- and two-family houses, new one- and two-family houses with ample open space about them, and the best one-family houses. A combination of market forces, building codes, and subdivision regulations was then used to help enforce these zoning ordinances. The upshot was a confinement policy that made it difficult for blacks to leave the low-rent district. A close examination of the Public Health Federation's map of median rentals based on the 1930 census shows that they succeeded. Planning Commission, *City Plan*, 50–53; Public Health Federation, "Median Rentals"; BHL, Committee on the County Zoning Bill, Minutes, 5 Mar. 1939 and BHL, Meeting of the Committee on County Zoning," Minutes, 5 Nov. 1940, BHL Papers, box 6, folder 22, University of Cincinnati Special Collections.

87. The entire basin, or historic core, was zoned for industry and business, with all types of industries and businesses concentrated in the area. Most of the West End was zoned for industrial B usage, while the Waterfront, East End, and the Court Street area were zoned for industrial A usage. The central business district was zoned for business B, while the Central Avenue area was zoned for business A. City Planning Commission, *Official City Plan Map*, Cincinnati Historical Society; City Planning Commission,

Cincinnati Master Plan Studies: Industrial Areas (City Planning Commission, 1946); Harry J. Mohlman, "Statement Presented to the Urban Redevelopment Commission, State of Ohio," 28 Dec. 1945, Stanley Rowe Papers, box 5, folder 1, CHS.

88. Department of Sociology, Federal Census Data, Negro and Total Population of Cincinnati by Census Tract, 1935 (handscript), Archives and Rare Books, UC, S.28.27.33.

89. To determine the combined effects of the railroad, industry, and business on the West End, a series of land use maps was studied. E. Robinson, *Atlas of Cincinnati, 1883–84* (Philadelphia, 1884); Sanborn Fire Insurance Maps of Cincinnati, 1904 (corrected and uncorrected). The 1904 Sanborn maps have been corrected to 1930; Noe, "Industrial Maps," 1900, 1920, 1940, CHS; Taylor, "The Use of Maps," 44–58.

90. Cincinnati Metropolitan Housing Authority, *Supporting Data: Application for a Low-Rent Housing Project,* Exhibit 11-A, Stanley Rowe Papers, box 3, folder 4, CHS. This exhibit shows the Department of Buildings classification of residential buildings in the basin area.

91. Ernest Grunwald, "The West End: A Preliminary Ecological Survey of an Area in Cincinnati" (Master's thesis, University of Cincinnati, 1936); Stegner, "The Menace of the City," 5.

7

ROBERT B. FAIRBANKS

Cincinnati Blacks and the Irony of Low-Income Housing Reform, 1900–1950

Cincinnati blacks suffered from inadequate housing long before the so-called "Negro housing crisis" appeared during and after World War I. In fact, a recent study of mid-nineteenth-century Cincinnati concluded that local blacks "occupied the worst land and housing" in the city.[1] And although by the turn of the century Cincinnati had greatly expanded in population and size from its walking city days, the plight of the Queen City's blacks had improved but little. Observing housing conditions in the streetcar city during 1913, the city health officer J. H. Landis lamented, "In Cincinnati it is almost impossible for a colored man to secure decent quarters for his family." These conditions bothered the officer, who felt that blacks "are respectable, law abiding and industrious but because of race prejudice are compelled to live in the slum districts."[2]

Cincinnati blacks faced discrimination in other areas too. Most of the city's hotels, restaurants, and saloons barred blacks, while theater managers seated them in segregated quarters. Enterprising blacks experienced equally humiliating conditions in their quest for vocational or professional training. Neither the city's medical schools nor its Ohio Mechanics Institute admitted them. Most local unions also closed their doors to blacks. As a result, they remained on the bottom rung of the city's economic ladder. Racism worked against local blacks in many ways and created what the historian Thomas Philpott has called a "color line" that limited both economic and residential mobility.[3]

Even the efforts of white tenement reformers at the turn of the century often adversely affected blacks. By 1900 many of the city's middle- and upper-class citizens had abandoned their old homes in the basin (a four-square-mile area that had composed the old walking city) to poor urban newcomers interested in locating near the expanding industrial and commercial sections of the city where work opportunities abounded. The large slums that resulted from this remarkable population turnover frightened many who left and spurred them to promote "reform" organizations concerned with ordering and regulating what they perceived as the chaos of the slums. Tenement reform emerged as one of the most important movements to come out of this anxiety about the slums. Local civic, philanthropic, religious, and health organizations joined together to promote a new tenement code out of fear that poorly built and maintained tenements encouraged bad morale, poor health, and improper morals. After a long struggle in May 1909 the city strengthened its tenement regulations as part of a broader building code.[4]

Enforcement of those regulations negatively affected blacks in several ways. It depleted the city's already-limited housing stock by eliminating the city's worst housing but doing little to promote new housing. Since blacks lived in the city's most dilapidated tenements, their housing came under the most careful scrutiny of tenement regulators, who often ordered expensive repairs (sometimes passed on to the tenants in higher rents) and occasionally vacated irredeemable dwellings.[5]

Tenement regulation also discouraged the construction of inexpensive tenement houses, thus further limiting black housing opportunities in the basin. According to the Cincinnati Real Estate Board in 1917, "Very few tenement-houses had been erected in the basin of the city" after the new tenement code because it had "increased the cost of building and maintenance of this property to such an extent that the rent received from such property does not pay a fair return on the investment."[6]

Although tenement regulation proved the most important legacy of Progressive era tenement reform, some effort was directed at building "model tenements" for the poor. Yet such undertakings were handicapped by what Philpott has called the "business creed" of housing developers. The tenets of that creed were simple—"housing was a commodity for private enterprise to provide at a profit," and if model tenements were to succeed, they would have to return a profit of not less than 5 percent to their investors. Completely philanthropic endeavors never seemed to have been considered by Cincinnati reformers since they viewed such housing as detrimental to both the marketplace and the tenant. Tenement reform in Cincinnati prior to 1915, then, was clearly limited by the color line and the business creed. But it also was shaped by a definition of housing problems that focused on the dangers posed by deteriorated, congested, and unsanitary buildings.[7]

Jacob G. Schmidlapp's early efforts at model housing reflected this preoccupation with the dwelling place. Schmidlapp, a wealthy Cincinnati businessman and philanthropist, became interested in the city's housing problem, particularly its black housing problem, while serving as a trustee for the McCall Colored Industrial School. Schmidlapp decided to experiment with model housing after discovering the appalling conditions in which many of the school's students lived. Between 1911 and 1914 he constructed ninety-six units of housing for both whites and blacks—and located them all outside the congested basin. Schmidlapp erected simple and affordable working-class housing with the hope that other capitalists would follow his example. His first venture, two-family houses with separate entrances and a backyard, contained individual baths, indoor toilets, and gas heat. Despite his concern for needy blacks, however, Schmidlapp only built twelve of the first fifty-six units he completed for them.[8] The color line and the business creed had clearly limited his efforts. His Chapel Hill project, located in a black neighborhood in Walnut Hills, provided four three-family dwellings. These "prison-like tenements" on the southeast corner of Park Avenue and Chapel Street contained a washtub and other conveniences not usually found in black housing. Schmidlapp built another project for blacks on Fredonia and Whittier streets, but angry neighborhood whites in the racially mixed area forced him to exclude blacks from the completed dwellings.[9]

Schmidlapp's concern with inadequate black housing led him in 1914 to form the Model Homes Company. He convinced other prominent Cincinnatians to join in his housing effort and raised five hundred thousand dollars. With that money the Model Homes Company developed a large-scale housing project for blacks on Syracuse Avenue in Walnut Hills, located outside the city's congested basin area. Like other Schmidlapp ventures, this 188-unit project was expected to provide a 5 percent return to its investors.[10]

Unlike earlier Schmidlapp housing ventures, however, Washington Terrace focused on the neighborhood rather than merely the dwelling

place. Developed along a "community plan," the project would provide a wholesome neighborhood environment, producing not only
physical and moral betterment but also civic improvement. This massive reconstruction of the tenants' physical and social world would
free them from the dangers of social disorganization, physical disease,
and neighborhood deterioration—all characteristics of the slum. Furthermore, in their new setting blacks would be able to learn the
middle-class values of hard work and participatory democracy. Indeed, Schmidlapp's concern with making better citizens led him to re-
quire tenants to join community clubs that would be "responsible for
caring for the place and for the conduct of its members." To encourage group activities Schmidlapp built a two-hundred-seat assembly
hall, which residents could use for religious, educational, and civic
meetings. Around the buildings Schmidlapp enhanced the landscape
and designed playgrounds to create a "cheerful surrounding."[11]

The Washington Terrace project, then, differed from earlier Cincinnati housing reform efforts. It defined housing not simply as
dwelling space but as a package of amenities—such as play space,
neighborliness, and shared commercial conveniences—that created
some type of neighborhood "culture." This new approach to housing, emphasizing neighborhood community rather than individual
dwelling units, would dominate Cincinnati housing reform efforts
until the 1950s. Although blacks were the first to benefit from this
new definition of the housing problem in Cincinnati—they ultimately
would suffer under the new orientation of the reformers.

Cincinnati, like many other northern cities, experienced unprecedented black migration during World War I. Rural southern blacks
flooded into the city after 1915, lured by the Queen City's economic
opportunities stimulated by a war-induced boom economy. By 1920
the city's black population had increased nearly 2½ times what its
size had been in 1890. Many of the black newcomers crowded into
three wards of the once-aristocratic West End and found accommodations in mansions now divided up into small tenement apartments. Between 1910 and 1920 the black population in that section
of the old walking city almost doubled, rising from 8,647 to 17,209.
Blacks were particularly concentrated in the lower West End near the
Ohio River.[12]

The combination of virtually no new building during the war and
increased black and white migration to the city resulted in extreme
congestion in basin neighborhoods. That congestion, in turn, attracted greedy speculators who bought West End tenements, raised
rents, and then sold them for artificially high prices. Blacks suffered

the consequences. Between 1918 and 1922 rents tripled for some buildings. These high costs, as well as the very real shortage of dwelling units for blacks, promoted some extraordinarily congested buildings. In 1923 the Better Housing League (BHL) found a three-room flat at 1131 Hopkins Street that somehow accommodated twenty blacks. It also discovered a twelve-room tenement house on George Street that housed ninety-four blacks.[13]

In response to the housing shortage, many West End families took in relatives or friends. Others, attempting to supplement their meager incomes, rented rooms to strangers. A survey conducted during the postwar housing crunch found that 740 black families in those three wards took in at least one lodger. More than 160 black families housed three or four lodgers nightly.[14]

The combination of high congestion, poor sanitation, and improper maintenance of these old dwellings yielded severe health problems. Black mortality rates were double that of Cincinnati as a whole. Conditions deteriorated to such a low that when the noted public health official Dr. Haven Emerson visited Cincinnati's West End in 1923, he told the city's Public Health Federation, "You could not produce a prize hog to show at the fair under conditions that you allow Negroes to live in this city. Pigs and chickens would die in them for lack of light, cleanliness and air."[15]

Local reformers readily acknowledged the severity of the black housing problem in the West End, and when conditions failed to improve even after the Post–World War I housing crunch for whites had ceased, they created a Special Committee on Negro Housing. That committee developed several strategies for combating the black housing problem. First it focused on education and regulation. Hoping to teach the rural black migrants good housekeeping practices, the special committee recommended that the Better Housing League increase its staff of visiting housekeepers from six to fifteen. The BHL, established as the city's housing reform organization in 1916, had instituted its visiting housekeeper program in 1918 at the request of real estate agents. The realtors persuaded the BHL to create a program to teach urban newcomers the principles of better housekeeping because they thought that ignorant black tenants comprised the root of the city's housing problem. Now the special committee recommended that the Community Chest increase its financial allotment to the BHL so it could employ more of its friendly visitors.[16]

The committee also requested that the city hire more housing inspectors and encouraged investors to make additional deposits in building and loan association accounts to provide much needed

capital for building homes. In addition the Special Housing Committee sponsored a contest and offered a $500 prize for the best house
that could be constructed for less than $5,500. Finally it asked local
capitalists to invest an additional $500,000 in the Cincinnati Model
Homes Company so that organization could build more new housing. None of these strategies were carried out, however. Even the
housing contest failed to elicit appropriate entries.[17]

The inability to raise new capital for the Model Homes Company particularly distressed the housing reformers, who firmly believed that "the present situation" could not be "relieved materially
without the construction of more homes." Although the Model
Homes Company had erected 402 dwelling units between 1914 and
1919, including 213 low-cost housing units for blacks, it remained
practically dormant after World War I. The combination of Schmidlapp's death in April 1919 and the highly inflated housing costs after
the war limited the company's activity. Inflation particularly inhibited the company's building program. A flat constructed in 1915
for $1,400 could not be duplicated in 1925 for anything less
than $3,750.[18]

When the company finally constructed an "experimental" three-
unit building in 1923, the consequences of high building costs became very evident. Rents for a four-room flat in Washington Terrace
went for $11 per month in 1915. Eight years later, a four-room flat in
the new building rented for $35, a price much too expensive for all
but a few of the city's blacks. As a result, company officials decided
that any new housing it built at this time would be erected for whites,
since most blacks could not afford the high rents brought on by inflated construction costs. Building for whites might still benefit
blacks, according to Model Homes officials, by drawing whites out of
the basin and opening up more opportunities there for blacks.[19]
About the same time, the Model Homes Company initiated a program that it hoped would more directly help blacks. In 1926 the company acquired a tenement on Carr Street in the lower West End,
remodeled it, and rented it to blacks. According to its 1927 annual
report, this ten-unit dwelling proved only a "limited success." Indeed,
the Carr Street unit was the company's only black unit with excessive
vacancies. The explanation for this was simple, according to company officials. Blacks wanting and willing to afford Model Homes accommodations simply did "not want to live in the West End
Bottoms."[20] The ambitious poor wanted out of the basin slum and
would not be satisfied with just a better dwelling—they wanted
better neighborhoods.

The rising costs of the 1920s also adversely affected those blacks lucky enough to live in Model Homes' other projects. The Model Homes Company raised rents 25 percent in 1924 because maintenance costs continued to increase, and the company remained committed to the business creed of housing. The decision of the local tax appraiser in 1926 to more than double the assessment of Model Homes Company properties also affected rents for the buildings.[21]

The Special Committee on Negro Housing and the Model Homes Company were not the only participants involved in housing betterment during the 1920s. That decade witnessed a variety of activities concerned in part with improving the city's housing. Over the next twenty years Cincinnati would gain national renown for its commitment to better housing through effective planning and housing leadership. The Cincinnatians Alfred Bettman and Ladislas Segoe gained national prominence in the planning profession, while BHL's head, Bleecker Marquette, became a respected figure in national housing circles.[22]

All three adopted the Washington Terrace approach to Cincinnati's housing needs by defining the problem as inappropriate neighborhood community rather than merely inadequate shelter. As a result, they abandoned the notion that good housing could exist in the congested basin and focused on promoting good housing outside that area. Regulation remained a part of this new housing movement, but it too reflected the new goals of neighborhood betterment. Tenement codes were supplemented by comprehensive zoning and master planning as a way to protect and encourage the development of better neighborhoods for the entire city. Unlike the reform emphasis at the turn of the century, which attempted to eradicate the worst kind of housing conditions and only regulated slum dwellings, the 1920s movement promoted citywide housing guidelines to protect Cincinnati from future slums. For instance, the city's master plan of 1925, drawn up largely through the efforts of Bettman and Segoe, provided a model of a good subdivision layout and identified the elements that made up good neighborhood community.[23]

The new town of Mariemont, developed on the eastern outskirts of Cincinnati by Mary Emery, provided the city's greatest monument to the neighborhood community emphasis of the 1920s. This development combined neighborhood communities with commercial and recreational opportunities in an attempt to create in its residents a sense of identity and involvement in community affairs. High housing costs and discriminatory practices, however, prevented blacks from experiencing the benefits of this model suburban town.[24]

As the housing emphasis gradually changed from eliminating or improving deteriorating tenement dwellings to promoting good community housing, blacks benefited little. Not only did they fail to see any of this community housing be built for them in the 1920s, but the whole notion of community housing became equated with homogeneous neighborhoods, thus reinforcing the color line. The slum in the 1920s was defined not merely as dilapidated dwellings inhabited by poor people but as an environment characterized by heterogeneity of peoples, shelters, and land uses. Such a setting lacked "an established cultural pattern which could serve as a guide for the overt actions of the community." As a result, groups, individuals, and families in slums lost "their identity" and lived "various social patterns" without "any purposeful objective." The response to this "problem" in the 1920s was to push homogeneous neighborhood settings based on shared social, economic, or racial characteristics.[25]

This concern with homogeneous neighborhood community, as well as the emphasis on providing good housing for the entire metropolitan area, helps explain why planning and housing activists reacted so negatively toward black efforts to find better housing during the 1920s. When blacks started moving into the predominantly white Mohawk-Brighton area of the basin due to the blockbusting efforts of white realtors, the BHL moved swiftly to stop this "scattering in white neighborhoods." League officials instructed its visiting housekeepers to persuade house-hungry blacks to avoid Mohawk-Brighton, fearing that such a movement would not only promote racial tension but also facilitate the rapid deterioration of a neighborhood through race mixture.[26]

Ambitious blacks, seeking to leave the social pathology of the West End, faced similar disapproval from housing and planning activists when they started building cheap housing on unimproved subdivisions on the fringes of metropolitan Cincinnati just north of suburban Lockland. Because this black suburban housing violated the accepted norms of good neighborhood housing, as well as middle-class aesthetic standards, BHL officials called this black push for better housing "a momentous problem" and sought county zoning legislation to halt the future spread of these "suburban slums."[27]

Housing officials had enough power to thwart black initiatives for additional housing, but they proved impotent to carry out their own plans for additional good black housing. The Model Homes Company, for example, had accumulated sufficient capital during the 1920s to construct another large-scale project for Cincinnati's black wage earners. Model Homes officials decided to develop a Washington Terrace–type project for blacks since building costs had leveled off by 1929 and blacks continued to face serious housing shortages in the city. They purchased a site adjacent to an already-established black enclave in West College Hill in suburban Cincinnati, but threats and protests from nearby white communities forced the company to abandon its plans and sell the site.[28] The Model Homes Company stood ready to build a large-scale project for blacks outside the basin even after the stock market crash, but it failed to find a vacant land site acceptable to Cincinnati whites.[29]

Some new housing opportunities did occur for blacks as a result of the Great Depression, however. The nation's economic collapse stimulated a local and national movement for federally supported slum clearance and low-income housing for urban America. Unlike the Model Homes Company, which had attempted to build close to the city's periphery, the Depression movement focused on the redevelopment of the urban core. Throughout the 1920s local housing reformers had avoided such a strategy for two reasons. First, since they defined good housing on a neighborhood scale, the high costs of land acquisition and slum removal seemed prohibitive for large-scale projects. Second, the reformers believed the city's core was destined for nonresidential use as the city's commercial and industrial base expanded. By the end of 1929, however, they questioned these assumptions. Now it appeared that the process of "natural growth" had slowed to a halt and the West End would remain a slum unless some "outside" help was forthcoming.[30]

This new view led Cincinnati groups such as the BHL, which had earlier opposed federal intervention, now to support federal efforts for expensive slum clearance and public housing in the basin. Only then could the city's most disordered area be tamed and local residents persuaded to live there by the lure of decent housing.

The Planning Commission, under the direction of Alfred Bettman and Myron Downs, conducted an intensive investigation of the basin's social, economic, and physical characteristics. Its findings led to a plan calling for the redevelopment of a 145-block area in the city's urban core. According to the plan, the "hopeless slum" in the north and west central basin area should be razed and redeveloped around neighborhood community settings arranged as sixteen "superblocks." These settings would encourage a sense of neighborliness and provide plenty of open space and recreational opportunity. Superblock development attempted to create the same type of setting for "community development" that both Washington Terrace and Mariemont had promoted. Good housing under this formula meant good neighborhoods. And these planned settings would not only produce healthy tenants but also help promote civic-minded citizens anxious to participate in the larger community.

A significant omission appeared in the redevelopment plan, however. The city's worst slum area, the lower West End (census tract 5), was not included. Reformers viewed this area, which contained the city's most dilapidated buildings, its worst criminals, and its sickest citizens, as irredeemable because of its complex land mix and the enormous poverty and "hardened" attitudes of its residents. It also happened to be 95 percent black.[31]

The city's redevelopment plan guided the local public housing program and helps explain why the city's neediest (and blackest) area received no housing projects. It does not totally explain, however, why the city's initial public housing program provided so little housing for the city's black population. When the all-white Cincinnati Metropolitan Housing Authority (CMHA) first submitted a proposal to the Public Work Administration's (PWA) Housing Division in 1933, it requested the redevelopment of six superblocks in the West End. Four of those six blocks were in white areas and were scheduled for whites-only public housing. The CMHA also requested a "suburban black project north of Cincinnati," in an effort to clean up the "suburban slum" areas that had bothered housing officials during the 1920s. Later, in 1934, when officials resubmitted the application for basin slum clearance and public housing, the city secured permission to build approximately 1,400 units for white families and 600 units for blacks.

Landowners from the racially mixed area scheduled for slum clearance and black public housing thwarted government plans when they refused to sell their land at what the PWA thought a reasonable cost. This forced the PWA to purchase land in a nearby area undergoing racial change but still considered part of the white West End. As a result, officials designated the city's first public housing venture, Laurel Homes, as a whites-only project. A large public uproar from the black community eventually pressured the CMHA into allocating part of that project to blacks on a segregated basis, but it opened less than one-third of the units for blacks.[32]

Several reasons appear to explain why the CMHA developed its unusual priority system, which gave the fewest housing units to the city's neediest people. First was the problem of rents. Slum clearance and redevelopment were costly. The neighborhood community plans for PWA public housing provided low-density housing on expensive central city land. Land acquisition and demolition costs, along with the project's design, which provided for open spaces, added greatly to developmental costs. And since rents provided a means of repaying loans made to cover much of those costs, they were relatively high for low-income residents. Although officials eventually modified the PWA program, during the planning stages the CMHA initially projected rent for Laurel Homes as high as twenty-one dollars per month. Only 9 percent of the blacks living in the basin paid such rent as compared to approximately 21 percent of the basin's whites. This might have influenced the CMHA in its decision to allocate twice as many units for whites.[33]

Another reason that the CMHA allocated more public housing to whites may have been tied to the concept of the "deserving poor." Housing reformers believed that many tenants in the city's slums were deserving poor, either urban newcomers with no other place to live or residents temporarily down on their luck. One of the reformers' chief goals was to separate these deserving poor from the vicious, or undeserving, poor of the slums because they believed that continued residency in the chaotic slum setting, along with long-term contact with those permanent slum dwellers, might adversely affect the deserving poor. By moving them into good citizen-building communities, housing reformers hoped to save or rehabilitate those just starting to show the effects of slum life. Public housing, then, provided more than mere shelter and was an effort at social engineering. Apparently local reformers thought that more deserving whites lived in the basin than deserving blacks. Or possibly they may have felt that Cincinnati blacks had been exposed to the pathology of the basin slums longer and would therefore be harder to rehabilitate. Simply put, reformers may have thought it judicious to avoid the neediest tenants and concentrate on "saving" the clearly salvageable.[34]

Finally, the color line played a role in the CMHA's decision. The first slum site chosen was located in a section of the West End still considered white, and turning it over to blacks might have caused hard feelings and opposition among white basin dwellers. Indeed, the PWA Housing Division had developed a "neighborhood composition rule," which stated that a public housing project should reflect the population characteristics of the area in which it was built. Since public housing was so new and controversial, local advocates did not want to do anything—such as displacing whites for black housing—that might antagonize the public.

Congress passed the Housing Act of 1937 as the PWA constructed Laurel Homes. Shortly after President Roosevelt signed the bill, the CMHA secured three public housing projects for Cincinnati from the newly created United States Housing Authority (USHA). Not only would the CMHA be permitted to develop a slum clearance project for blacks in the West End but the USHA authorized it to erect two other projects on vacant land outside the basin—one for blacks and one for whites. The Lincoln Court slum project for blacks, planned for the area immediately south of Laurel Homes, sparked a new round of controversy. Many realtors and landowners in the lower West End, anxious to increase property values, thought that the city's next slum clearance project should be located there, rather than in the less-deteriorated central West End area. They correctly argued that the lower West End was the city's worst slum area.[35] But because public housing focused on community and citizen rehabilitation rather than merely providing safe and sanitary shelter, the CMHA passed over the nearly all-black and desperately poor area because of high land costs and the undesirability of many of its "undeserving residents."

High land costs imposed by the community development strategy nearly thwarted Lincoln Court's development. Work on the project stalled when land and building costs exceeded the USHA's limits. Meanwhile white resistance also halted the planned vacant-land housing project for blacks. As a result, the first public housing projects in Cincinnati built under the Housing Act of 1937 were the vacant-land projects of Winton Terrace and English Woods. Both admitted whites only.

The CMHA's announcement of its intention to build its first two projects under the Housing Act of 1937 for whites only produced a storm of protest from both house-hungry blacks and unhappy white realtors. The former clearly felt betrayed and challenged the sincerity of the CMHA. The latter believed that public housing should only be built for the city's most deteriorated basin slum areas, where it might help depressed property values.

Eventually the USHA modified its requirements so Cincinnati could have its all-black West End public housing project. This action came none too soon because black housing continued to deteriorate, and vacancies for blacks remained scarce. Indeed, by 1939 the amount of black housing available for occupancy was 1.3 percent of the total stock. Normal vacancy rates usually ran about 5 percent.[36]

In many ways, however, the redevelopment of the Lincoln Court site simply compounded the housing shortage. The clearance of the area dislocated 1,030 black families at a time when there were only 205 suitable vacancies in the city for blacks. When completed, it produced a net increase of 38 units. Many of those displaced by the project were ineligible for public housing because of inadequate income. More than 600 displaced families on relief were neither eligible for public housing nor able to find relocation housing easily. The CMHA eventually rehoused them by convincing tenement owners in racially mixed areas to turn out their white tenants and rent to blacks. Landlords agreed when they were reminded that they could charge higher rents to blacks.[37]

The city's neediest blacks were barred from Lincoln Court, as had been the case for Laurel Homes. Although many of the moral and social requirements that had been imposed on applicants for Laurel Homes had been dropped for Lincoln Court, the relatively high rents and minimum income requirement clearly limited who could live there. The wartime setting further complicated Lincoln Court's occupancy. The CMHA agreed to give black war workers first priority in moving into Lincoln Court in order to receive a needed allocation of building supplies from the War Productions Board. Even black workers outside the basin were admitted to Lincoln Court before residents displaced by the slum project. Throughout the war the CMHA allowed defense workers with incomes exceeding the maximum limits set by the USHA to remain in the project.[38]

Public housing during the 1930s and 1940s, then, did not address the problem of insufficient shelter for the city's neediest. Rather it was built to reward the ambitious but moderately poor black family that wished to avoid the pathology of the slum but could not because of conditions beyond its control. Given the limited housing opportunities for this group of blacks, this was no small achievement.

But the irony of the situation was, nevertheless, very real. Reformers who embraced the negative approach to housing betterment through tenement regulation at the turn of the century focused exclusively on the poor. This negative approach to housing betterment eliminated the city's worst housing, which unfortunately was the only kind many black Cincinnatians could afford. By the 1930s, however, when housing reform embraced a more positive approach to addressing the city's housing needs through the building and promotion of good neighborhoods, the city's neediest citizens—its poorest blacks—were ignored. Even worse, slum clearance projects displaced many blacks, and CMHA officials barred them from living in the new public housing due to minimum income requirements.

Public housing policy changed again in the 1950s, this time opening up opportunities for the city's poorest blacks, although the government never built enough projects to meet their need. By this time, however, the enthusiastic and energetic leadership that had characterized the housing movement in the 1930s had waned. Housing professionals and management experts replaced committed reformers as the force behind public housing. Balanced ledgers and maintenance needs supplanted citizen making as the main concern of these new "housers." This limited vision, along with curtailed financial assistance from the federal government, eventually transformed the city's housing projects into its newest slums.

In some ways the policy of the 1950s and 1960s resembled the much earlier strategy emphasizing elimination rather than construction because the urban redevelopment and highway building projects of this era often destroyed the city's poorest neighborhoods. Little was done to guarantee that those displaced would find better neighborhoods. As a result, bulldozers razed the city's most dilapidated slum areas, worsening the housing shortage, which led to overcrowding and slum formation in other parts of the city as the private real estate market proved totally incapable of providing good housing for needy blacks. And the new public housing policy abandoned ambitious blacks, who had once benefited from community-oriented public housing projects, to the whim of a racist private housing market. Such developments, unfortunately, had their payoff in 1967 when black rioting occurred in the city's new slum of Avondale.

Notes

1. Henry Louis Taylor, Jr., "The Use of Maps in the Study of the Black Ghetto-Formation Process: Cincinnati, 1802–1910," *Historical Methods* 17 (Spring 1984): 54.

2. Discussion, "Housing in America," in *Proceedings of the National Housing Association*, vol. 3 (New York, 1913): 203.

3. Frank W. Quillan, "The Negro in Cincinnati," *Independent* 68 (Feb. 1910): 399–403; Thomas Philpott, *The Slum and the Ghetto: Neighborhood Deterioration and Middle-Class Reform, Chicago, 1880–1930* (New York: Oxford University Press, 1978), 117–19.

4. Associated Charities of Cincinnati, *Twenty-second Annual Report, 1901–2* (Cincinnati, 1902), 8–9; Robert B. Fairbanks, *Making Better Citizens: Housing Reform and the Community Development Strategy in Cincinnati, 1890–1960* (Urbana: University of Illinois Press, 1988), 17–23.

5. William Devou, a major tenement owner in the lower West End, constantly battled tenement reformers and inspectors about ordered improvements that would force him to raise rents beyond the ability of his impoverished black tenants. Devou was often criticized by housing officials

as being selfish and parochial because he did not see the larger picture of how his tenements affected the whole city. *Houses or Homes? First Report of the Cincinnati Better Housing League* (Cincinnati, 1914), 21–22.

6. *William's Cincinnati Directory, June 1917* (Cincinnati: William's Directory Company, 1917), 17.

7. Philpott, *Slum and Ghetto*, 204–5.

8. Fairbanks, *Making Better Citizens*, 34–36; Douglas G. Knerr, "Housing Reform and Benevolent Capitalism: Jacob G. Schmidlapp and the Cincinnati Model Homes Company, 1911–1920," *Queen City Heritage* 43 (Summer 1985): 28.

9. Louis A. Cornish to Jacob G. Schmidlapp, 21 Mar. 1916, Model Homes Company Files, Cincinnati Historical Society (CHS); Harris Ginberg to W. R. Clark, 13 Sept. 1921, Model Homes Company Files.

10. Jacob G. Schmidlapp, *Low-Priced Housing of Wage Earners* (New York: National Housing Association, 1916), 1–8; Schmidlapp, "Housing Reform," 6 Nov. 1915, Jacob G. Schmidlapp Papers, Urban Studies Collection, Archival Collection of the University of Cincinnati; Report, Annual Meeting of the Model Homes Company, April 1919, Schmidlapp Papers.

11. Jacob G. Schmidlapp, untitled paper, 6 Nov. 1919, Schmidlapp Papers.

12. The city's black population in 1890 was 11,655 and jumped to 30,079 in 1920. U.S. Bureau of the Census, *Report on Population of the United States at the Eleventh Census: 1890, Part I* (Washington, D.C., 1892), 942; idem, *Fourteenth Census of the United States Taken in 1920*, vol. 3, *Population* (Washington, D.C., 1922), 792; idem, *Thirteenth Census of the United States Taken in 1910*, vol. 3 (Washington, D.C., 1912), 427.

13. Fairbanks, *Making Better Citizens*, 63–65.

14. *The West End Problem: First Annual Report. Shoemaker Health and Welfare Center* (Cincinnati, 1927), 24.

15. Quoted in *The Housing Situation Today: Report of the Better Housing League, 1925* (Cincinnati, 1925), 2.

16. Minutes, Special Committee on the Negro Housing Problem, 4 Feb. 1924, Better Housing League (BHL) Papers, Urban Studies Collection, Archival Collection of the University of Cincinnati; "Lights and Shadows," BHL Papers; Bleecker Marquette, "A Discouraging Situation in Cincinnati," *Housing Betterment: A Journal of Housing Advance*, Feb. 1925, 98.

17. "Lights and Shadows," BHL Papers; Minutes, BHL Board of Directors, 9 Dec. 1924, BHL Papers; Special Committee on the Negro Housing Problem, 4 Feb. 1924, BHL Papers.

18. Fairbanks, *Making Better Citizens*, 66.

19. Minutes, BHL Board of Directors, 7 Oct. 1924, BHL Papers.

20. Harris Ginberg, "Interesting Facts about Model Homes and Their Tenants," *Housing* 20 (Mar. 1931): 70.

21. Minutes, BHL Board of Directors, 10 Oct. 1922; 27 Apr. 1926, BHL Papers.

22. Fairbanks, *Making Better Citizens*, 5–7.

23. Cincinnati City Planning Commission, *The Official City Plan of Cincinnati, Ohio* (Cincinnati: City Planning Commission, 1925), 50.

24. Fairbanks, *Making Better Citizens,* 49–51.

25. Manuel C. Elmer, "Social Service for the Slum: What Constitutes a Slum?" in *Slums, Large-Scale Housing and Decentralization,* ed. John M. Gries and James Ford (Washington, D.C.: President's Conference on Home Building and Home Ownership, 1931), 322–23.

26. Minutes, BHL Board of Directors, 7 Oct. 1924, BHL Papers.

27. BHL Report, "New County Subdivisions," Nov. 1928, 1–5, Stanley Rowe Personal Papers, Mariemont; Minutes, BHL Board of Directors, 19 Apr. 1928, BHL Papers; Henry Louis Taylor, Jr., "The Building of a Black Industrial Suburb: The Lincoln Heights, Ohio, Story" (Ph.D. diss., State University of New York at Buffalo, 1979), 190–94.

28. Minutes, BHL Board of Directors, 17 Oct. 1929, BHL Papers.

29. Ginberg, "Interesting Facts about Model Homes," 70.

30. Fairbanks, *Making Better Citizens,* 52–54, 71–72.

31. Ibid., 82–83; Bleecker Marquette, Memorandum on Census Tract 5 as a site for housing redevelopment, 14 May 1935, Rowe Papers.

32. Fairbanks, *Making Better Citizens,* 86–87, 124–31.

33. Cincinnati Metropolitan Housing Authority (CMHA), Memorandum on Rents, 20 Aug. 1934, Rowe Papers. For a similar experience in Cleveland, see Christopher G. Wye, "The New Deal and the Negro Community: Toward a Broader Conceptualization," *Journal of American History* 59 (Dec. 1972): 628.

34. For a clear articulation of this attitude, see the Cincinnati building commissioner Clifford M. Stegner's "The Menace of the City" (typescript), Rowe Papers, Cincinnati Historical Society. My interpretation differs from that of John F. Bauman, who sees public housing as a way station or foothold for the working class on its way to homeownership. I see it as a training center for homeownership and good citizenship. Bauman, *Public Housing, Race, and Renewal: Urban Planning in Philadelphia, 1920–1974* (Philadelphia: Temple University Press, 1987), 52.

35. Edward Richter to Horatio B. Hackett, 27 Mar. 1935, Record Group 196, National Archives.

36. Howard B. Myers, "Survey of Vacancies in Dwelling Units of Cincinnati, Ohio," Feb. 1941, Rowe Papers, CHS; Housing Committee of the Division of Negro Welfare, 20 Oct. 1943, Cincinnati Urban League Papers, CHS.

37. Albert C. France, "Report on the Relocation of Tenants for Lincoln Court Slum Clearance Project," 28 Oct. 1941, CMHA Papers, CHS.

38. Minutes, BHL Board of Directors, 17 Dec. 1942, BHL Papers; *Fifteenth Annual Report of the CMHA,* 1948.

8

ANDREA TUTTLE KORNBLUH

James Hathaway Robinson and the Origins of Professional Social Work in the Black Community

In Cincinnati, as in many other northern cities, the early twentieth century brought with it both a growing number of African American urban dwellers and attempts to organize the black community to meet the needs of both newcomers and longtime citizens of the city. Pioneer black sociologists and social workers of this era developed theories and programs to help them better organize families and communities and to provide for improved employment opportunities, housing, health, recreation, and education. Acutely aware of racial discrimination, they sought the reformation of a prejudiced judicial system and improved race relations. This work, often initiated by branches or affiliates of the National Urban League, characteristically began with a survey of conditions in the black community. In Cincinnati the Council of Social Agencies (CSA) funded such a survey by a young black sociologist, James Hathaway Robinson. This study of Robinson's education, his survey, and his plan for social work in Cincinnati's African American community, provides a detailed illustration of how these early professional social workers described the nature of the problems facing the black community and how they sought to use social science to solve these problems. For Robinson and his contemporaries, improved race relations did not mean the racial integration of individuals but rather the development of black institutions and their influence in the larger, pluralistic community.[1]

James Hathaway Robinson, educated at Fisk, Yale, and Columbia, was hired by the Cincinnati Council of Social Agencies in 1917 to make a survey of black migration to the city and of the housing conditions of the black community. The survey, and Robinson's subsequent recommendations for social work in the city's black community, guided the council's work for the next thirty years.[2] Robinson developed a two-pronged attack on the problems facing the black community. He described two distinct but interconnected tasks: organizing the black community internally and then making that community, as a group, an equal participant in the larger metropolitan community. He ranked programs for both of these areas as equally important and said they needed to be pursued simultaneously. Both Robinson and the Negro Civic Welfare Committee (NCWC), which he created, said the programs should develop social welfare services for the black community and build interracial goodwill and understanding by emphasizing the equality of blacks as a cultural group and their desire for equal services. These programs included, but were not limited to, the hosting of the first national conference on interracial goodwill, held in Cincinnati in 1925, the regular celebration of Race Relations Sunday, and annual interracial dinners.[3]

This strategy for improving black-white relations in northern urban society in the 1920s, 1930s, and 1940s can be viewed as one manifestation of the concept of "cultural pluralism." In those years this idea gained favor with Americans interested in explaining how American society was, or ought to be, organized. Cultural pluralism appeared to provide a way to a talk about America as one country—one culture—composed of a series of equal, or potentially equal, subunits variously defined as regions, racial and ethnic groups, occupational or professional groups, and gender-based groups.[4] Thus social welfare organizers in Cincinnati, as in other cities, sought to develop comprehensive organizations representative of all the groups in the city. It was as members of groups, not as individuals, that citizens ought to seek representation. These social welfare advocates envisioned a pluralistic community based on cooperation among a diverse variety of groups and the coordination of their activities.[5]

In Cincinnati in 1913 the Council of Social Agencies began putting together such a pluralistic and representative body. The CSA took as its responsibility the centralization of the city's private and public social work activity, and to this end it organized investigations of social conditions, initiated new agencies, and conducted an annual joint fund-raising campaign for affiliated agencies. In 1916 the Associated Charities, an umbrella group of Protestant social service agencies, joined the joint fund-raising efforts of the CSA. The Bureau of Catholic Charities followed in 1917, and in 1918 the United Jewish Social Agencies added its forces to the CSA. Agencies serving immigrants, such as the Immigrant Welfare Committee and the Santa Maria Institute (which was devoted to meeting the needs of the city's Italian community), also belonged to the CSA. In 1917 the CSA's fund-raising included two agencies that served the African American community—the Walnut Hills Day Nursery and the Home for Colored Girls.[6] Unlike the Bureau of Catholic Charities or the United Jewish Social Agencies, however, no coordinating body existed to centralize the work of those social service agencies serving the African American community. As a first step toward including the black community, the CSA undertook an investigation of what it referred to as the "Negro Problem" and hired James Hathaway Robinson to make a survey of black migration to Cincinnati and the local housing situation facing the black community.[7]

James Hathaway Robinson was probably the Cincinnatian best suited to directing the council's survey of black life. The son of an ex-slave, Robinson was born in 1887 in Sharpsburg, Bath County, Kentucky. He attended school in Winchester and Lexington, Kentucky, and at the age of nineteen enrolled at Fisk University. During his last year at Fisk, the school added a new department of social science devoted to the study of race relations. George Edmund Haynes, a black sociologist who in 1910 had cofounded the Committee on Urban Conditions Among Negroes (which in 1911 became the National Urban League), headed the new department. From Fisk, Robinson went to Yale, where he received his masters degree and completed his residency requirements for a Ph.D. in sociology in 1914. The National Urban League awarded Robinson a fellowship to attend the graduate school of Columbia University to study sociology and social service in 1914–15. In the fall of 1915 he moved to Cincinnati, where he settled into a black neighborhood in Walnut Hills and began teaching sixth grade at the Douglass School.[8]

Robinson told Wendell P. Dabney, a newspaper editor and chronicler of black Cincinnati, that he had turned down offers to teach at Fisk, Strait, Morehouse, Georgia State, and Nalden in order to come to Cincinnati, but he did not describe what had attracted him to the Queen City.[9] It should be noted, however, that at that time Cincinnati's African American community was an object of interest to black scholars of national repute. For example, the first issue of the premier volume of the *Journal of Negro History,* published in January 1916, carried an article by Carter G. Woodson titled, "The Negroes of Cincinnati Prior to the Civil War."[10]

By the time that Robinson began teaching at Douglass,[11] it was the only remaining all-black public school left in Cincinnati from the nineteenth-century "Colored School" system.[12] All the black children in the city did not attend Douglass, but the school did have an all-black teaching staff and the largest single concentration of black students in the district. And the year before Robinson began to teach at Douglass, Jennie Davis Porter, who taught at Douglass from about 1900 to 1914,[13] left her position at the Walnut Hills school and began her campaign to develop for the West End a "separate" public school (Harriet Beecher Stowe School) dedicated to the interests of black students in this most rapidly growing black neighborhood in the city.[14]

The Douglass School where Robinson began his teaching career was impressive—a new building had been constructed in 1910 by the school board at a cost of $167,871. The building included fifteen classrooms, an auditorium, gymnasium, library, lunchroom, open air room, neighborhood club room, boys' and girls' shower rooms, manual training and domestic science rooms, laundry room, model flat and sewing room, and seats for eight hundred pupils. In 1913 the board's annual report contended that Douglass School was "one of our finest modern school buildings and perhaps the best equipped in the city for industrial training."[15] But while the board emphasized the industrial training offered students at Douglass, the faculty of thirty-two also included specialists in kindergarten work, German, music, writing, art, and physical education.[16]

The Douglass School attracted national attention, and R. H. Leavell, a journalist for the *Outlook,* a national magazine that called itself "an illustrated weekly journal of current events," visited the school during the First World War to discover "what the Negro asks of white America in the ways of a fighting chance to win democracy." At the main entrance to the Douglass School, Leavell reported, hung "four huge placards that confront the visitor." These proclaimed the following slogans: "Self-Control; Self-Reliance; Self-Respect; and Race Pride!" Leavell noted that the example of Douglass School represented "the chance to teach the world the supreme truth that democracy means, not the wiping out of racial personality, but rather the cherishing of racial difference and the enabling of diverse stocks for the enrichment of us all." Leavell also argued that black parents preferred to send their children to Douglass rather than to racially mixed schools, and that "the colored community is overwhelmingly in favor of the separate school."[17]

The journalist did not devote much space to an examination of the regular school day; instead he concentrated his report on the ways in which the school functioned as a community center. In the evenings the school offered nightly sessions of "The Rough House," a supervised program for such activities as basketball and boxing. This resulted, Leavell thought, in the development of teamwork and democratic spirit rather than the formation of "tough gangs," which could result in an undirected "overflow of vitality." The school also provided quiet evening entertainment, such as checkers and "crokinole," as well as a community branch of the public library. A night school made training available in academic and industrial subjects and offered gym classes for men and women. Douglass School also provided space for many neighborhood clubs—"clubs for house servants, for factory girls, for young men, for girls in high school, and for girls in the University."[18]

When Robinson arrived at Douglass School, Francis M. Russell was the principal, and he had held the position since 1909. Russell, born in 1879 in Knoxville, Tennessee, attended the University of Cincinnati, where he received his B.A. in 1904 and his M.A. in 1906. A member of the African Methodist Episcopal Church, the Masons, and the Alpha Phi Alpha fraternity, Russell taught in black public schools in two Kentucky cities just across the Ohio River. First a teacher at Covington High School (1904–5), he went on to become a principal in Newport, Kentucky (1905–9) before going on to Douglass. In 1914 Russell became one of the twelve first members of the board of trustees of the privately supported Cincinnati Colored Industrial School, which had been established in that year.[19]

Russell also played a role in the establishment of the Ninth Street Branch (Colored) of the Young Men's Christian Association (YMCA). In 1913 this black branch of the YMCA opened at Seventh and Plum streets. The Ninth Street building, erected in 1915 with the financial support of the Chicago philanthropist Julius Rosenwald, opened in 1916. Russell served as one of the twelve original members—all black—of that branch's Committee of Management. Along with the creation of this all-black branch came a change in the YMCA's organizational structure. The minutes of the YMCA of Cincinnati for December 21, 1916, record a "change in organization to the so-called metropolitan basis, which places in the hands of a Committee of Management for each branch, including [the] Central [branch], the responsibility for the work of each branch with a common treasurer and Board of Directors, the members of the committee being appointed by the President of the Board." By 1919 the black physician Dr. William T. Nelson had become, according to the historian of the Cincinnati YMCA, "the first Negro to be named a member of any YMCA Metropolitan Board of Directors." The new organizational structure thus allowed both for a separate black branch and a racially integrated leadership body composed of representatives from all branches in the city.[20]

Leavell noted in his article that eleven out of the twenty-eight Douglass teachers he surveyed came from the South. In fact, most came from the North, and several of them came from families that had lived in Cincinnati for generations and composed the Queen City's black aristocracy. Amelia C. Taylor, a second-grade teacher at Douglass, and her sister, Hettie G. Taylor, a first-grade teacher, were descended from pioneer citizens of Cincinnati—William and Amelia Beckley.[21] E. Camille Friason, who taught third grade, was the daughter of Harry H. Friason and Lucy Armstrong. Mr. Friason was born in 1866 in Cincinnati, the son of Augustus, a fireman, and Elizabeth. He attended the Cincinnati public schools and Gaines High School, which opened in 1866 and served as the city's only high school for black students and was an important training ground for future teachers until 1887, when the state legislature tried to eliminate segregated schools. A Republican and a Mason, Friason was also the treasurer and steward of Brown Chapel African Methodist Episcopal Church in Walnut Hills. He held a variety of jobs, including a term as a clerk in the county recorder's office, as an inspector in the Improvement Department of the Waterworks and in the Engineer's Department, and as an assistant city paymaster.[22]

Neola E. Woodson who, along with Camille Friason, taught third grade at Douglass, was also descended from an old Cincinnati family. Her parents were Cassie Guthrie Woodson and Jessie J. Woodson, and her paternal grandparents, Jesse and Patsy Ann Woodson, lived in Cincinnati when her father was born in 1861. Like Friason, Jesse Woodson had attended public school and Gaines High School. He was a trustee of the Brown Chapel A.M.E. Church and belonged to the Knights of Pythias Lodge No. 32 and F.& A.M. St. John Lodge No. 8. A trustee of the Board of the Colored Orphan Asylum for twelve years and the Home for Aged Colored Women (established in 1891), Jesse Woodson also was a member of the Committee of Management of the YMCA and a member of the NAACP, established in 1915. Woodson had a forty-year career with the U.S. Postal Service as a letter carrier. His daughter, Neola, the Douglass teacher, received her B.A. from the University of Cincinnati. Neola Woodson married James Hathaway Robinson in 1916.[23]

Douglass School and its faculty were intimately involved in the history of Cincinnati and in the development of leadership for the African American community. This institution and its faculty had ties to the separate nineteenth-century colored school system and such old community institutions as the Brown Chapel A.M.E. Church and the Home for Aged Colored Women, both, like Douglass, in Walnut Hills. The school and its faculty also participated in the new developments of the early twentieth century, such as the movement to establish school social centers and the creation of new all-black branches of existing institutions, such as the Ninth Street branch of the YMCA and the Harriet Beecher Stowe School. In 1915 when James Hathaway Robinson arrived at Douglass School it was perhaps the largest center of organized black community activity in the city. Robinson's two-year stay there provided him with employment, a spouse, and an insider's understanding of Cincinnati's African American community.[24]

Francis Russell, the principal at Douglass, may have been responsible for the CSA's hiring of Robinson to make the survey. Russell, as a member of the board of managers of the black Ninth Street YMCA, would have known of both Robinson's training in sociology and the desire of social welfare groups to study the condition of Cincinnati's black community. In at least one account, the Ninth Street YMCA is given credit for the existence of the organization Robinson founded: the historian of the Cincinnati YMCA notes that Robinson's organization emerged from the Ninth Street branch Employment and Welfare Department.[25] The general secretary of the Cincinnati YMCA who oversaw the creation of the Ninth Street branch was Alfred Guitner Bookwalter, who also served as the YMCA representative to the CSA. Bookwalter became an active organizer for the NCWA and served as its first chairman.[26] Bookwalter was also a member of the CSA's Centralized Budget Committee.[27]

The idea for the Negro Civic Welfare Association may have come from the Ninth Street branch of the YMCA, but the money for the survey was raised by the CSA. In the fall of 1916 the CSA's Central Budget Committee noted that "the entire colored situation seems to [be] in a chaotic state in Cincinnati." To remedy this the budget committee recommended earmarking $5,000 "to secure a comprehensive plan" for work in the black community.[28] The CSA's January 1917 fund drive included solicitations for a "Special Fund for Colored Work," describing the need as follows: "The work among the colored people is so much disorganized that many givers have requested a complete reorganization of this work. The Central Budget Committee did not allow any increases in organizations doing work among the colored people, but estimate that the reorganization will cost $5,000."[29]

A. G. Bookman, of the YMCA and the CSA, announced the CSA's plan to survey the "Negro Problem" in May 1917, and Robinson released his preliminary results in July of that year. He chronicled the reasons new migrants gave for leaving the South, their religious and economic backgrounds, the housing conditions they found in the Queen City, and the programs of the social service agencies that tried to serve their needs. Robinson argued that the primary cause for the migration of massive numbers of southern blacks to the North was economic. Out of 40 migrants, 27 said they had come North for better wages, 6 for "better privileges," 5 "to better condition," 2 because of "bad treatment" in the South, and 1 "just took a notion." These statistics, Robinson wrote, "corroborate a mass of evidence from other sources that the movement is primarily economic." He outlined specific economic causes in the South—low wages, high prices, "the disadvantages of the crop-lien system," flood destruction, and the boll weevil. On the northern end of the equation, a scarcity of labor had been created by both the expansion of industry and the dearth of foreign immigrants. "At this moment," Robinson wrote, "came the labor agents from the North, offering the negro wages of which he had never dreamed, and privileges of which he had only read in the Constitution." Once the movement began, enthusiastic letters home from early migrants helped "to swell the numbers."[30]

Cincinnati played a unique role in what Robinson referred to as "this great folk wandering," for he suggested that the Queen City served "as a junction where migrants from different points in the South are distributed to other points in the North, rather than as a terminus." Cincinnati, Robinson thought, was too near the South from which the migrants were fleeing and did not offer "the attractive wages" that could be found in northern cities like Cleveland, Chicago, and Pittsburgh. "As a gateway to the South," he said, "many pass through but most of them make their way to Northern Ohio, Michigan, Illinois, Pennsylvania and New York." Robinson made a one-week study of the migrants arriving in Cincinnati on the four trunk line railroads that served the city. The largest number arrived on the L & N, the next largest on the Southern, then the B & O. The fourth railroad, the C & O, said Robinson, carried "so few as to be almost a negligible factor." Of the 980 migrants who arrived in Cincinnati during the survey period, 314 had tickets to Cincinnati, while 666 were ticketed to points beyond. Of the 125 who arrived on the B & O, 70 were ticketed for Cincinnati, while 55 went on. Robinson thought that many of those who initially planned to stay in Cincinnati left. He estimated that 30,000 migrants had passed through Cincinnati in the past twelve months but that only about 4,000 had settled in the city.[31]

For these newcomers to the city the most pressing problem was adequate housing. Employment was not an immediate problem, for Robinson thought the migrants were either absorbed into the common labor market or "sent to other fields almost as soon as they arrive[d]." But only a few shabby houses in the most crowded districts of the city were available. In addition, he reported the "almost universal" tendency to charge black tenants higher rents. Robinson mentioned the work of a group called the Joint Housing Committee, which advertised its efforts to find housing for the newcomers with three hundred real estate salesmen, but still had more applications for houses than what it could provide.[32]

In addition to his concern with the final destinations of the migrants, Robinson also investigated their religious and economic backgrounds. "The colored man from the South," he noted, "is a church-going man, and his presence is going to strengthen and animate the negro religious life of the city in no small measure." Of the 218 migrants he questioned, 146 belonged to a church: 87 were Baptists, 56 Methodists, and 3 he identified as "Holy." Many of the newcomers, Robinson said, had been property owners in the South, had had bank accounts there, and had worked at the same places for many years. "Some," he added, "had recommendations of a high order." "Here and there," he added, "was found also a professional man, usually a doctor or minister, and when asked why he was going North, one of them replied that he was following his practice."[33]

James Hathaway Robinson presented his final survey results and the program he had developed to the CSA's board early in January 1919,[34] but he thought his work had significance beyond the borders of Cincinnati. He reported to his fellow social workers on his survey at the National Conference of Social Work's Forty-sixth Annual Session held in Atlantic City, New Jersey, June 1–8, 1919, in a conference session titled "The Negro and the Local Community."[35] In his presentation Robinson characterized Cincinnati as "a northern city with a southern exposure, a gateway between North and South used alike by fugitive slave and freeman of yesterday and migrant of today in their quest of Utopia." To the black, he said, Utopia was a place "where a man is a man," a place that is "seemingly a much sought after but ever fleeting if ever existing Land of Nowhere."[36]

For more than a century, Robinson said, the North and the South had been meeting and discussing what should be done with blacks in a dialogue that treated the black as "an innocent bystander." Now, with the creation of the CSA's Negro Civic Welfare Association, blacks themselves could finally play an active role in these discussions. As an example of this new cooperation he pointed to the first project of the Negro Civic Welfare Association—the survey. Financed by the CSA, the survey had the endorsement of "many important colored organizations in the city." But more important, he noted, the black organizations did more than simply lend their stamp of approval to the survey, they helped to conduct it. "Heads of institutions, business men, and housekeepers," said Robinson, opened their doors for investigation, librarians "rendered valuable assistance," and "every conductor on the four southern railroads converging here kept a daily record of the migrants from the South destined for the city." Paid survey workers conducted house-to-house investigations assisted by the "voluntary services" of social workers. Also, 357 public schoolteachers conducted twenty thousand telephone interviews, "collecting a mass of data" that, Robinson said, "would have been physically impossible to obtain otherwise."[37] The survey was truly a community undertaking.

Robinson said the survey yielded several results. It helped to point out problems, teach about the work of social service agencies, create citywide interest, and provide the facts about conditions that would serve as "leverage in re-adjusting the situation." Part of Robinson's understanding of the current situation was based on a historical knowledge of Cincinnati's treatment of its black inhabitants. Although Ohio had never been a slave state, he wrote, "from the earliest days of its statehood there began to grow up a set of laws creating a separate status for the Negro." In 1887 the Arnett Law made the Black Laws illegal, but Robinson found the effect of this legislation "not entirely salutary." With the passage of the Arnett Law, Robinson claimed, an important by-product of the separate black institution—strong African American leadership—disappeared. In the three decades after the law went into effect, the old generation of capable leaders died out. Then came "the influx of hordes from the South, white and colored, the one usually hostile and the other too often the less progressive type." Conditions in the city, he said, went from bad to worse.[38]

Robinson estimated that the city's current black residents numbered between thirty and forty thousand. Since 1910 the population had more than doubled, and Cincinnati blacks were now, he said, "primarily of southern birth." The black population of the city was "not a normal social group" demographically, for there were few children or old people and "an unduly large number of persons in the prime of life." Robinson claimed that many of the problems of the group could be traced to the large number of "male floaters," a term that apparently referred to young men not anchored in family life. Robinson also expressed concern about the geographical dispersion of the black population, suggesting that people living "in widely separated communities" but "facing essentially the same handicaps" found themselves "unable to join hands in the common cause of self-betterment."[39]

Robinson thought that the working conditions of Cincinnati blacks—limited in the main to "common labor at common laborer's pay"—prevented the black worker from developing or striving, "for much of the incentive is lacking." "The same necessity that forces him to accept the least desirable jobs at the poorest pay," Robinson said, "also forces him to eat the poorest food and wear the shabbiest clothes; to live in the most unsanitary houses in the filthiest slums where he meets vice, poverty, disease, despair, death." In a similar way, the community's abhorrent housing conditions were both physically unsafe and a danger to the stability of the black family. Robinson described two-thirds of the families he studied as "proper" blood-kinship families. The remaining one-third seemed to be forced by economic conditions to become part of a new and nontraditional social unit. "Is the Negro family in the large city becoming less a group of people who live together because related by blood and bound by common traditions," he asked, "and more an unrelated group forced together by high rents, low wages and the scarcity of houses available to them?"[40]

In examining the education available to the children of African American families, Robinson found that black children attended not only the 2 all-black schools but all of the 59 elementary schools in the city. In the previous six years seventy-four black students had graduated from high school, a figure that Robinson thought compared "poorly with the record in other cities," although he added that many of those graduates had taken further training. A small but growing number of black students was graduating from the university, and Robinson noted that "the correspondence between this number and the increasing demand for teachers is suggestive." Robinson thought many students dropped out of school before graduating from high school because education did not seem to broaden the limited opportunities for employment.[41]

In his survey of employment opportunities, Robinson looked particularly at the problems of common laborers and the barriers to industrial work, but he also investigated the economic life of other segments of the black community. The black business community was not large, and, he found, it tended to be dominated by the small shops run by such entrepreneurs as undertakers, barbers, tailors, cobblers, beauticians, druggists, insurance men, grocers, caterers, newspaper editors, real estate agents, and printers. The professional class, on the other hand, was "of considerable numbers" and included doctors, dentists, lawyers, ministers, teachers, and social workers. Even among this more successful group, however, Robinson pointed out that "various handicaps prevent the development of men of wide reputations."[42]

In a category he labeled "organizations chiefly of the Negro's creation" Robinson listed 54 churches and missions, 84 fraternal societies, 22 federated clubs, 35 "other societies worthy of note," and "nearly a dozen" philanthropic institutions. All of these, Robinson noted, "seem to bespeak a powerful instinct for organization," an instinct that had been hampered from its fullest expression by "lack of experience, vision and other handicaps."[43] He thought the black community had the potential to organize to meet its needs; it seemed only to lack leadership.

In his description of the social problems facing the black citizens, Robinson stressed the causal role of discrimination. The city had, he said, "a southern racial relationship" that brought with it discrimination not only in employment opportunities but also in amusements. "Not only do hotels, restaurants and soda fountains refuse to serve him," Robinson reported, "but moving picture houses and private parks refuse to admit him; theaters segregate and often embarrass him." With limited exceptions, no schools, hospitals, or clinics allowed African Americans to train or practice as nurses or doctors. The black crime rate was 23 percent of the total rate, although the black population was only 7 percent of the total population. Robinson suggested that "a noticeable factor in this rate is prejudice." "The presumption," he argued, "is invariable against the Negro and he is often arrested and sentenced where others would be excused." In a similar manner Robinson charged the press with giving "undue publicity to his weaknesses, foibles and crimes," while seldom mentioning black accomplishments and virtues " 'because they lack news value' to a misinformed public."[44]

Robinson also surveyed and evaluated the work of the social agencies concerned with the black situation. Eleven black agencies devoted themselves to work with black clients, and eight white agencies included "special departments and workers objectively dealing with [their] problems." Robinson reported that some of the black agencies were more efficiently managed than others, but all "have played an important role in the development of business experience, social vision and group consciousness." Perhaps the biggest problem was a lack of centralized leadership. There was, he lamented, no agency "at work with executive powers and a city-wide interest, viewpoint, purpose or propaganda to make effective any remedial recommendations that are made."[45]

On the basis of these criticisms, Robinson developed a program for future work that began with "a federation of forces" that would "unify purpose, harmonize spirit and promote efficiency." Robinson described the CSA as "a financial federation," of which the NCWA was a department charged with coordinating "the work among colored people." The new federation of black social service agencies included three child-care institutions, two homes for the aged, two homes for young women, a YWCA and a YMCA, and "the colored departments" of eight white agencies. Additionally, new agencies devoted to "community music and recreation," he added, would serve "not merely as ends in themselves" but also to "stimulate interest in the work-a-day features of this city-wide program." The main features of the coordinating division were social service planning, institutional efficiency, financial campaigns, civics, and central case conferences. An advisory group would be created, composed of individuals representing "groups ably advised on the Negro problems." The members would include black doctors, lawyers, ministers, and social workers.[46]

Finally, Robinson planned "a great experiment in Negro organization" based in the churches. Church federation, Robinson reported, had not been a success in Cincinnati, which suffered from "rampant" denominationalism and "the common interests which really exist have been overshadowed by smaller differences." He did not propose trying to federate the churches on a "religious basis"; instead his goal was the federation of the auxiliary societies or social service departments of local churches with "a common interest in social service." If that plan was successful, Robinson planned to expand the program to include clubs and fraternal societies. "Fundamentally,"

Robinson stressed, "there is no reason why a group of people with common ills, common interests and a common destiny could not be made to forget small differences and unite, not in religious work or fraternal work as such, but in social and civic work which is our concern."[47]

Robinson's plan for social work in the black community did not take as a starting point the individual problems faced by those less fortunate people who needed the assistance of social agencies. He did not suggest that those people, who lacked adequate housing, employment, or education, had failed because of some lack of moral rectitude or social or cultural defects or problems in character. Instead he pointed the finger at larger social forces—such as the shift from a rural agricultural life to an urban industrial one and the family stress caused by inadequate income and housing—problems against which a single individual could do little. His hope for the future improvement of the condition of the African American people lay in organizing the institutions that served the community into a coherent whole, and organizing among individuals a sense of belonging to a community. His concerns reflected a feeling that the African American community needed more and better leadership and stronger institutions, however. Robinson also expressed a concern about the geographic dispersion of the city's black residents—the lack of a coherent black residential community, which seemed to him necessary for joint action. For Robinson, the stimulation of group consciousness and the development of organizations provided a route to improve the conditions faced by black Cincinnatians.

Robinson called for self-organization of group consciousness among the city's black people and for a campaign of education among white people. Racial discrimination, Robinson thought, was based in white people's ignorance of black life. "The Negro lives by himself," Robinson said, "works by himself and when sick suffers by himself in the colored ward." When he dies, "he is buried by himself whether in a colored cemetery or the colored section of the Potter's Field." This separation meant that others learned little of the black citizen's life, little of his "aspirations, handicaps, disappointments." The whites' lack of familiarity with black people led them to frequently distort facts and misunderstand the aims and motivations of African Americans. Instead of advocating residential and social integration, however, Robinson contended that the white community should be taught the positive aspects of black life and culture. Such teaching of African American culture could become part of the program of social welfare agencies.[48]

Robinson was not alone in this effort to educate the white community about the culture of black Cincinnatians. Wendell P. Dabney, for example, in his preface to *Cincinnati's Colored Citizens* (1926), explained that by setting forth the history and achievements of Cincinnati's black people, he would provide information that would "go far to eradicate much of the prejudice . . . that owes its origin to the ignorance or superficial knowledge of our white citizens." Dabney suggested that he had "strayed far from the cold, formal, stereotyped historical volume in efforts to show the soul as well as the body of a people, who are so little known, so little understood and, for so many years, so much oppressed because of such misunderstanding."[49]

By the early 1920s Robinson and his Negro Civic Welfare Association (changed to Committee in 1921) had become an integral part of Cincinnati's social welfare planning apparatus. Robinson reported on this growing cooperation between the NCWC and other agencies in a summary of his agency's accomplishments between 1919 and 1921. After completing the survey of black conditions in 1917, the NCWA turned its attention to coordinating and developing social work in the black community. This included encouraging white agencies to expand their work into that community with the use of black social workers, improving the "financial basis" of the all-black agencies, and upgrading the "personnel of the workers in the colored field." The NCWA also began using community centers to educate the public, drawing it "into a clearer and deeper appreciation of the social service program." The NCWA undertook fund-raising for the Community Chest in the black community and initiated direct social service activities "with a view of turning them over later to other agencies."[50]

Robinson's program of combining social service organization with a campaign to build understanding about the African American condition and appreciation for black culture provided a framework for the work of the NCWA and its successor organizations for the next thirty years. In the 1920s Robinson and the NCWC set the groundwork for the development of special programs for African Americans in public recreation and public health. Like the NCWC, the Division of Negro Recreation, which was a component part of the Cincinnati Recreation Commission created at the inception of the commission in 1927, not only made sociological studies of the needs of the black community but also developed special programs to meet those needs in the areas of athletics, drama, and music.

Just as Robinson enlisted the aid of the black community in making his survey in 1917, so professional black recreation and cultural

workers in the 1920s, 1930s, and 1940s relied on the black community as well. One example of this was the annual Negro music festivals of the 1930s and 1940s. Organized by a community advisory
group under the aegis of the Cincinnati Public Recreation Commission, these events celebrated black musical culture and brought to
Cincinnati nationally prominent performers, such as Paul Robeson,
to sing in the city's parks. In the public health arena the Shoemaker
Health and Welfare Center, established by Robinson, provided both
health care to the black residents of the West End and clinical practice opportunities for black nurses and doctors at a time when they
were excluded from practicing in white hospitals. Throughout the
1920s, 1930s, and 1940s this model of combining the provision of
social welfare programs with the organization of the black community guided African American social work. The Negro Civic Welfare
Committee in 1935 became the Division of Negro Welfare of the
Council of Social Agencies (1935–49). Throughout the years and
the name changes, however, Robinson's vision of how to organize the
black community remained constant. Only in the late 1940s did it begin to change as racial integration, rather than community self-
development, became the tactic for racial advancement. In 1949 the
Division of Negro Welfare became the Cincinnati Urban League,
making formal an implicit connection that had existed since Robinson began his work in 1917 but also making a step toward a new direction, the civil rights movement of the 1950s and 1960s.[51]

Notes

1. Nancy J. Weiss described the early history of this movement in *The National Urban League, 1910–40* (New York: Oxford University Press, 1974),
documenting the work of the national organization, which she characterized
as relying on "conciliation, persuasion, diplomacy, and polite protest." Arvarh E. Strickland told the story of one Urban League branch in his *History
of the Chicago Urban League* (Urbana: University of Illinois Press, 1966).
He described the Urban League's task as "orienting the new migrant to urban life." Kenneth L. Kusmer, in *A Ghetto Takes Shape: Black Cleveland,
1870–1930* (Urbana: University of Illinois Press, 1976), suggested that the
Cleveland Urban League affiliate, the Negro Welfare Association, was handicapped by its orientation, which "focused on the failure of the individual
rather than the injustices of the social system." The Cincinnati Negro Welfare Association is a different case. Cincinnati's pioneer professional social
workers did not limit their concern to the problems of new migrants. Rather

they sought to organize the entire black community—and to organize it through establishing coordination and cooperation among the agencies serving local African Americans.

2. Robinson's survey and its results no longer exist, but he presented a summary of his work in a Cincinnati social service publication and at the 1919 session of the National Conference on Social Work. See *Social Service News: "A Magazine of Human Helpfulness"* 1: 7 (July 1917): 100–101; "The Cincinnati Negro Survey and Program," in *Proceedings for the National Conference on Social Work at the Forty-sixth Annual Session Held in Atlantic City, New Jersey, June 1–8, 1919*, 523–31. After the completion of the survey, the Council of Social Agencies hired Robinson to create and head its Negro Civic Welfare Association (established in 1919). This body over the years was variously called the Negro Civic Welfare Committee (1921–35), the Division of Negro Welfare of the Council of Social Agencies (1935–49), and, after 1949, the Cincinnati Urban League. The papers of these organizations for the years 1921 to 1975 can be found in the Urban League of Greater Cincinnati Collection at the Cincinnati Historical Society.

3. For more on the interwar interracial goodwill movement, see Andrea Tuttle Kornbluh, "The Bowl of Promise: Cincinnati Social Welfare Planners, Cultural Pluralism and the Metropolitan Community, 1911–1952" (Ph.D. diss., University of Cincinnati, 1988), 33–149.

4. See Henry D. Shapiro, "The Place of Culture and the Problem of Identity," in *Appalachia and America: Autonomy and Regional Dependence*, ed. Allen Batteau (Lexington: University of Kentucky Press, 1983), 131–33, for the argument about region and racial or ethnic groups. For the idea of occupational- or professional-based culture in these years, see Zane L. Miller, "Pluralizing America: Walter Prescott Webb, Chicago School Sociology, and Cultural Regionalism," in *Essays on Sunbelt Cities and Recent Urban America*, Robert B. Fairbanks and Kathleen Underwood, eds. (College Station: Texas A&M University Press, 1990): 173–74, n.9. For the gender-based culture of the 1920s, 1930s, and 1940s, see Andrea Tuttle Kornbluh, *Lighting the Way: The Woman's City Club of Cincinnati, 1915–1965* (Cincinnati: Woman's City Club, 1986), 97–102. Harold Cruse in *Plural But Equal: A Critical Study of Blacks and Minorities and America's Plural Society* (New York: William Morrow, 1987), 67, suggests a distinction between "separate but equal" and pluralism: "Philosophically, 'separate but equal' is, in the normative sense, 'unequal' only if in social practice it is the governing intent to make separateness politically, economically, and socially unequal, which of course makes such practices immoral. Thus, separateness, which is not immoral, became segregation, which *is* immoral because it was not the intent to make separate equal." For Cruse removing the legal sanctions of imposed segregation would give separateness "the potential of achieving quality in its own right."

John Higham, *Strangers in the Land: Patterns of American Nativism, 1860–1925* (New York: Atheneum, 1970), 304, mentions cultural pluralism briefly but discounts its effect. He attributes what he calls a "radically new theory of American nationality in defense of minority cultures" to Horace Kallen, a theory that "argued that true Americanism lay in the conservation and actual fostering of group differences, not in melting them down or 'contributing' them." Higham added, however, "At the time his doctrine of cultural pluralism made little impression outside of Zionist circles."

5. Historians of twentieth-century social work tend to ignore social work in the black community in the 1920s, 1930s, and 1940s, beginning that story with the 1960s. For example, James Leiby devotes a chapter of his book *A History of Social Work in the United States* (New York: Columbia University Press, 1978) to the years 1900–1919 (pp. 136–62) and discusses settlement houses, the National Council of Charities and Corrections, the YMCA and YWCA, and the Red Cross, but does not mention the National Urban League. Leiby finally talks about black Americans, but not their organizations, in a chapter covering the years 1967–72 (pp. 316–39). Walter I. Trattner, in *From Poor Law to Welfare State: A History of Social Welfare in America* (New York: Free Press, 1974), follows the same pattern. Even scholars who write about a more restricted time period of social welfare history do not include the social work by and for African Americans. Clarke A. Chambers, in *Seedtime of Reform: American Social Service and Social Action, 1918–1933* (Minneapolis: University of Minnesota, 1963), devotes one full sentence to the work of the National Urban League. Roy Lubove, *The Professional Altruist: The Emergence of Social Work as a Career, 1880–1930* (Cambridge, Mass.: Harvard University Press, 1965), argues that the council of social agencies and community chest movement was "the ultimate in bureaucratization," but he does not mention black social welfare work and how it might have been affected by this move to centralize social work. To be fair to historians of American social welfare, they have generally concentrated their efforts on explaining a process they see as moving from nineteenth-century philanthropy, through settlement houses and community chests, to the New Deal and the welfare state. They have chronicled changes in methods, from reform to case work, and have not concentrated their efforts on the inclusion of different groups in the social welfare network. This angle of vision has had the strange result of giving us histories of social welfare that ignore black individuals and organizations more than the contemporary social welfare workers did. The problem is compounded by the fact that those historians who concentrate on black social work tend to look at it as a history of institutions such as the Urban League or as black community studies, missing the complex interaction between black and white social service agencies.

6. "Amounts Budgeted by Years and by Agencies," chart in Community Chest of Cincinnati and Hamilton County, *The First Twenty Years, 1915–1935* (Cincinnati: Community Chest of Cincinnati and Hamilton County, 1935).

7. "Survey of Negro Problem," Cincinnati *Enquirer,* 26 May 1917, 2.

8. Wendell Phillips Dabney, *Cincinnati's Colored Citizens: Historical, Sociological, and Biographical* (1926; repr., New York: Negro Universities

Press, 1970), 220; Joseph J. Boris, ed., *Who's Who in Colored America: A Biographical Dictionary of Notable Living Persons of African Descent in the United States, 1928–29* (New York: Who's Who in Colored America Publishing Corp., 1929), 314; *Who Was Who in America*, vol. 4; *1961–68*, 801–2; Nancy J. Weiss, *The National Urban League, 1910–1940* (New York: Oxford University Press, 1974) 30, 41–46; *Fisk University Catalog, 1910–1911*, 42, Fisk University Archives; *Yale Class History, 1912*, 275, xerox copy included with letter to author from Judith Ann Schiff, chief research archivist, Yale University Library, 11 December 1985. For more on the Urban League Fellowship programs, see Eugene Kinckle Jones, "National Urban League," *Opportunity: A Journal of Negro Life* (Jan. 1925): 13. My attempts to reconstruct James H. Robinson's life benefited from the assistance of Frances Forman, reference librarian, Cincinnati Historical Society, and Elaine Hughes, assistant head of reference, Walter C. Langsam Library, University of Cincinnati.

9. Dabney, *Colored Citizens*, 220.

10. In 1915 Carter G. Woodson published *The Education of the Negro Prior to 1861*, which also included references to Cincinnati. C. G. Woodson was born in Virginia and raised in West Virginia. See Sister Anthony Scally, *Carter G. Woodson: A Bio-Bibliography* (Westport, Conn.: Greenwood Press, 1985).

11. Douglass was named after the famous abolitionist Frederick Douglass in 1902. Before that time it was known as Elmwood Place School or the "Walnut Hills Colored School." The Cincinnati *Times-Star*, 25 April 1940, credits Grace Slade, a teacher at the school, with the suggestion for renaming the school. The Cincinnati public schools began a general switch from numbered to named schools in 1902. See Public Schools of Cincinnati, *Seventy-third Annual Report of the Public Schools of Cincinnati for the School Year Ending August 31, 1902*, 48, Cincinnati Historical Society; *Cincinnati Public Schools Directory, 1915–16* (Cincinnati: Board of Education, 1916), Cincinnati Historical Society.

12. In 1849 the Ohio legislature authorized the creation of free schools for black children, but Cincinnati city and school officials argued that it was unconstitutional to allow black men to vote in elections of school board trustees. For the following three years the school authorities refused to turn over to the black community the funds to maintain the schools. But a court decision in 1852 upheld the constitutionality of the legislation and required a pro rata share of the funds be placed "at the command of a board elected by the colored people." In 1874 the colored school board was abolished, and in 1887, with the passage of the Arnett Bill, separate colored schools as a class were abolished and black children were formally allowed to attend white schools. By 1902 Douglass School and a "one-room colony" were the only remaining separate black schools. See John B. Shotwell, *A History of the Schools of Cincinnati* (Cincinnati: The School Life Company, 1902), 455–56, 459–60. See also David A. Gerber, *Black Ohio and the Color Line, 1860–1915* (Urbana: University of Illinois Press, 1976), and David Lee

Calkins, "Black Education and the Nineteenth-Century City: An Institutional Analysis of Cincinnati's Colored Schools, 1850–1887," *Cincinnati Historical Society Bulletin* 33, no. 3 (1975): 160–73.

13. Cincinnati Public Schools, *Annual Reports, 1900–1901 to 1915–16.*

14. For Porter's description of her program, see Jennie D. Porter, "The Problem of Negro Education in Northern and Border Cities" (Ph.D. diss., University of Cincinnati, 1928). Porter's program for the creation of new all-black schools drew severe criticism from Wendell P. Dabney, who noted that "public sentiment seemingly condones the violation of state laws relative to separate or segregated schools." He suggested that white people generally favored separate schools as being more effective ways to teach subserviency, and they claimed that black supporters of such schools did so "through selfishness, ignorance or cowardice . . . as the easiest method of getting colored teachers appointed." See Dabney, *Colored Citizens,* 149.

15. Cincinnati Public Schools, *Eighty-fourth Annual Report, Year Ending August 13, 1913* (Cincinnati, 1914), 182.

16. *Cincinnati Public Schools Directory, 1915–16,* 42.

17. R. H. Leavell, "What Does the Negro Want? The Answer of the Douglass Public School," *Outlook,* 29 Aug. 1919, 605–6.

18. Leavell, "What Does the Negro Want?," 604–6.

19. Dabney, *Colored Citizens,* 243, 419, 211. Dabney refers to Russell as the "second colored graduate of the University of Cincinnati" on page 419.

20. Dabney, *Colored Citizens,* 419; Harry Senger, *The Story of the Young Men's Christian Association of Cincinnati and Hamilton County, 1853–1953* ([Cincinnati]: Parthenon Press, n.d. [1953]), 89, 90. Other original Committee of Management members included Dr. W. T. Nelson, Morris S. Walton, Washington Simms, Thomas J. Monroe, Eugene H. Simms, Horace Sudduth, W. B. Young, Richard Connelly, John J. Taylor, G. W. Hays and Dr. N. C. Vaughn. YMCA, Minutes, 21 Dec. 1916, YMCA Administrative Office, Cincinnati.

For an account of the connection between the Negro Welfare Association in Cleveland (like the Cincinnati Negro Civic Welfare Association, it was the black social work component of the Council of Social Agencies) and the formation of a black YMCA in Cleveland, see Kusmer, *A Ghetto Takes Shape,* 265–66. Kusmer notes that the Cleveland Negro Welfare Association's Community House, created in 1919, became the black branch of the YMCA in 1921, with little adverse comment about the creation of a separate institution. For the story of the origins of the black Chicago YMCA (the Wabash Avenue YMCA), see Allan M. Spear, *Black Chicago: The Making of a Negro Ghetto* (Chicago: University of Chicago Press, 1967), 100–101. Spear describes only limited contemporary criticism of the project as "Jim-Crowism" and notes that most Chicago blacks "heartily approved of the idea." Julius Rosenwald pledged the black community of Chicago $25,000 if it could raise another $50,000 for the new establishment. Once this was underway Rosenwald expanded his offer to every black community in the United States. Chicago was thus the prototype for the black YMCA. Spear identifies the black YMCA as part of a "separate Negro community with civic institutions, businesses, and political organizations of its own." He does not describe a change in organizational form of the YMCA like the one that accompanied the organization of the Cincinnati black branch and allowed representatives of the black branch to join the citywide leadership body of the YMCA.

21. Dabney, *Colored Citizens,* 281. According to Dabney, the Taylor sisters' mother, Mary E. Beckley Taylor, born in Cincinnati in 1845, had been educated in the Cincinnati public schools and was active in the Methodist Episcopal Church. Her civic involvement included the presidency of the Ladies' Aid Society, the Home Missionary Society, the Lincoln Lyceum of Union Chapel Church, and the Board of Lady Managers of the Colored Orphan Asylum. Four of her daughters became teachers in the Cincinnati schools.

22. Dabney, *Colored Citizens,* 273; Shotwell, *A History of the Schools,* 458–59.

23. Dabney, *Colored Citizens,* 270. Other Douglass teaching staff members included Jennie Austin (physical education teacher) and Mary Lee Tate (art teacher), both of whom graduated from the University of Cincinnati in 1911. Lyle Koehler, *Cincinnati's Black Peoples: A Chronology and Bibliography, 1787–1982* ([Cincinnati]: Privately printed, 1986), 105.

24. Contemporary observers in the 1920s and 1930s noted the importance of black educational institutions. Alain Locke, in *The New Negro* (New York: Albert and Charles Bonie, 1925; repr., New York: Atheneum, 1983), included both an article on Howard University by the sociologist Kelley Miller and an article on Hampton and Tuskegee by Robert R. Moton. Edwin R. Embree, in *Brown America: The Story of a New Race* (New York: The Viking Press, 1932), 137, suggests the importance of Howard University, Fisk University, Meharry Medical School, Atlanta University, and Dillard University, arguing that "the most significant strategy in Negro education now is the strengthening of the four great centers [Washington, D.C., Nashville, Atlanta, and New Orleans] of higher learning." To put the role of the Douglass School into context it would be nice to have an assessment of the role of black public primary and high schools in these years as well. In certain instances even those schools that were not colleges or universities seemed to serve as intellectual centers in the same way. For example we should know more about the M Street High School (which became Dunbar High School) in Washington, D.C., and the Lincoln High School in Philadelphia. Among the literary figures who taught at M Street was Jessie Redmon Fauset, novelist, poet, and educator.

25. Senger, *The Story of the YMCA of Cincinnati,* 93.

26. Dabney, *Colored Citizens,* 222.

27. [Council of Social Agencies], "Sentiment and Business Management Have Joined Hands," [1915] pamphlet, Pamphlet Collection, Cincinnati Historical Society.

28. "Report of the Sub-Committee of the Budget Committee of the Council of Social Agencies," undated [1916] typescript, 8, Henry Bentley Papers, Cincinnati Historical Society, box 14, folder 9. The report notes that the CSA received requests for increased funding from the Colored Girls Home and

from the Anti-Tuberculosis League for funds to establish a branch in the West End to undertake work "among the colored patients." The budget committee declared it did not fund these requests, for the work had not been coordinated. "While we appreciate the necessity of an increase in the amount expended upon this and other colored charities," the report argued, "we believe that it would be well to secure a comprehensive plan before increasing the expenditures of separate organizations on this work."

29. Council of Social Agencies, "1917 Pledge Blank for 24 Social Service Organizations," Pamphlet Collection, Cincinnati Historical Society. On the fund-raising activities of the Council of Social Agencies in 1917, see Kornbluh, "The Bowl of Promise," 165–69. Such surveys of black urban life were common in the teens. Between 1911 and 1914 George Edmund Haynes, for example, made preliminary studies on the conditions of life among black people in Nashville, Pittsburgh, Philadelphia, and Newark. In 1917 he published *The Negro Newcomer to Detroit, Michigan.* See Butler A. Jones, "The Tradition of Sociology Teaching in Black Colleges: The Unheralded Professionals," in *Black Sociologists: Historical and Contemporary Perspectives,* ed. James E. Blackwell and Morris Janowitz (Chicago: University of Chicago Press, 1974), 143.

30. *Social Service News,* 100.

31. Ibid.

32. Ibid.

33. *Social Service News,* 100–101. People of both races were developing programs to meet the needs of these newcomers, and Robinson singled out for praise the Model Homes Company, which provided low-cost housing for workers. The Park Street A.M.E. Church offered several services, including providing the newcomers with a temporary home and a social worker who met the trains and directed the migrants to "their proper places." The Baptist Ministers' Alliance and St. Andrew's Episcopal Church had similar programs.

Most important of the social programs developed to meet the needs of the southern newcomers, however, was the recently established (1919) Negro Civic Welfare Committee (NCWC) of the Council of Social Agencies. Robinson reported that the NCWC had a biracial executive committee composed of nineteen blacks and thirteen whites. The NCWC maintained an office and a staff of three workers at the Ninth Street YMCA and, Robinson said, had "taken upon itself the task of making a scientific survey of conditions among negroes in Cincinnati." Working in cooperation with the Better Housing League, the NCWC was finding better homes for the migrants and "planning a co-operative block system by which they may be visited in their homes with friendly advice and helpful information." "With both races working together," Robinson concluded, "and guided by the scientific spirit for accuracy in information and economy in effort, this organization ought to do much toward bettering the racial situation in Cincinnati."

34. A Cincinnati *Enquirer* story reported that the CSA planned to "take up the negro situation from all its angles" and that the CSA intended to

"stimulate interest, and intelligent co-operation on the part of the negroes" in the areas of housing, sanitation, education, and recreation. To this end the CSA planned to sponsor the creation of new agencies "to care for the physical and moral needs of negro communities." The CSA additionally expressed hope that "all work carried on by separate organizations will be coordinated through the adoption of the recommendations of this report." See Cincinnati *Enquirer,* 11 Jan. 1919, 14.

35. His fellow speakers included Helen B. Irvin, speaking on Negro women in industry, George E. Haynes on "Negro Labor and the New Order," and R. R. Wright, Jr., on "What Does the Negro Want in Our Democracy?"

36. Robinson, "The Cincinnati Negro Survey," 523.

37. Ibid., 524–25.

38. Ibid., 525.

39. Ibid.

40. Ibid., 525–26.

41. Ibid., 526.

42. Ibid., 525.

43. Ibid., 526–27.

44. Ibid., 527.

45. Ibid., 528.

46. Ibid., 530.

47. Ibid.

48. Ibid., 530.

49. Dabney, *Colored Citizens,* 4–5. Among the scholars whom Dabney thanks in this preface are Arthur A. Schomburg, "president of the Negro Academy, famous Bibliophile, Connoisseur and Collector of Negro Literature and Art," and Alain Le Roy Locke, "a product of Harvard, Oxford, and Berlin Universities, winner of Rhodes Scholarship, author of *The New Negro.*" Ibid., 5.

50. "Service Report of the Negro Civic Welfare Committee of the Council of Social Agencies (Development thru two years)," typescript, Urban League Papers, Cincinnati Historical Society.

51. Accounts of both these programs in public health and public recreation can be found in Kornbluh, "The Bowl of Promise." For the Shoemaker Health and Welfare Center, see 268–309; for the Negro music festivals, see 370–80.

9

CHARLES F. CASEY-LEININGER

Making the Second Ghetto in Cincinnati: Avondale, 1925–70

The study of black urban history has emphasized the processes that led to the formation of black ghettoes during the World War I era, when thousands of southern blacks poured into northern industrial centers. The ghettoes that emerged during that period reflected the massive migration of African Americans from the South to the North and from farm to city. Indeed, the rise of the black ghetto signaled the beginning of a new period in northern urban development and of the black urban experience.[1]

The Second World War triggered another massive outmigration of southern blacks, which led to the formation of much larger ghettoes in most northern cities.[2] These second ghettoes made African Americans an even more important element in the residential and political development of northern urban areas. Central cities became increasingly identified as residential enclaves for blacks and poor whites, while the suburban ring that surrounded them became characterized as residential havens for more affluent, mostly white populations. The rise of a second black ghetto, then, ushered in yet another stage in the development of the northern city and in the development of the black urban experience. With the exception of Arnold Hirsch's study of Chicago, however, there have been no book-length investigations of the processes that led to the formation of the post–World War II black ghetto. This is perplexing since the black ghetto rebellions of the 1964–68 period played a central role in the ferment that inspired the emergence of black urban history and the study of the northern black urban experience.[3]

This chapter is an attempt to understand the making of a portion of the post–World War II inner-city black ghetto in Cincinnati. That ghetto took shape between 1945 and the early 1960s, a period of changing attitudes toward race and of a transformation in the racial and economic distribution and composition of the city's population.[4] Between 1940 and 1970 Cincinnati's black population increased from 55,593 (12 percent of the total) to 125,070 (28 percent), an increase of 226 percent. During the same period the white population of the city decreased by 52,671, 12 percent of the 1940 white population. Part of the decrease in the white population of the city was directly attributable to migration from the city to the new suburbs developing outside the city limits. Between 1955 and 1960 a net total of 44,145 white Cincinnatians moved from the city to outlying locations within the Cincinnati Standard Metropolitan Statistical Area (SMSA). Though the trend slowed somewhat in the next decade, a net total of 27,445 white city dwellers sought refuge in the suburbs of the metropolitan area between 1965 and 1970. During the same two five-year periods a net total of only 5,309 blacks left the central city, 1,576 between 1955 and 1960 and 3,733 in the five years leading up to 1970.

Concurrent with the rapid migration of whites out of the central city and the rapid increase in black population, slum clearance and superhighway construction decimated the city's black West End ghetto. Between 1940 and 1970 the population of the West End, and of Mohawk-Brighton to the north of it, fell from 62,363 to 17,068, and the black population fell from 37,369 to 16,509. The confluence of these and other forces led to the formation of Cincinnati's second black ghetto.[5] This chapter focuses primarily on the Avondale section of that ghetto, census tracts 34 and 65–69 (Map 9.1).

Cincinnati's First Black Ghetto: The West End

Cincinnati's first black ghetto took shape during the 1920s in the West End, one of the city's oldest neighborhoods. This area lay to the west and northwest of the central business district. During the 1910–40 period it absorbed most of the city's new black population, thus breaking the old pattern in which blacks lived in relatively small concentrations in enclaves both in the old basin area close to the Ohio River and in the newer hilltop neighborhoods. By 1940 64 percent of

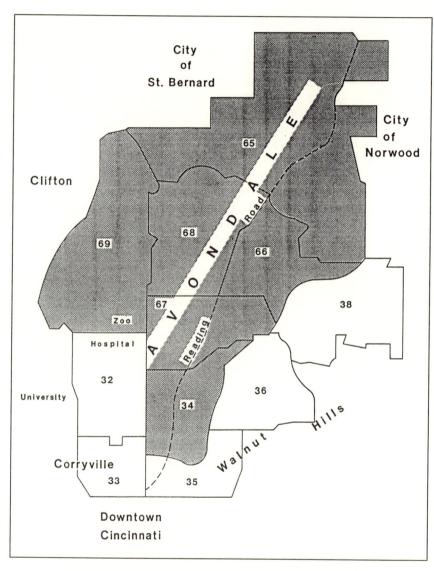

Map 9.1. Avondale and Vicinity. U.S. Census Bureau, 1970.

Cincinnati's black population lived in the West End, an area then 74 percent black. Though middle-class blacks lived in the West End, the small land area of that neighborhood and the extreme shortage of housing there made it difficult for them to escape the slum conditions that enveloped much of the neighborhood. Thus the ghetto was racially homogeneous, but heterogeneous with respect to class.[6]

Decrepit and deteriorating housing conditions made the West End the object of attack by housing reformers and city planners, who first hoped to eliminate it as a residential site, and failing that to build there new and lower-density segregated housing for some of its residents while dispersing the rest to other segregated locations.[7]

As Robert B. Fairbanks points out (see chapter 7), Cincinnati's planners and housing reformers developed segregated housing schemes because they had a certain vision of the nature of neighborhood and community. Prior to World War II good housing practices required the residential segregation of people with differing backgrounds and social mores. Both blacks and poor whites, the reformers argued, lacked the appropriate skills to function well in an urban setting. If they scattered into better neighborhoods, they would carry blight with them. Until such time that housing reformers and social workers could impart the skills necessary to live in a modern urban community, the most appropriate place for blacks and poor whites to live was planned and supervised housing projects. The incorrigible poor were believed best isolated and left in their decaying neighborhoods, tended to by charity, social workers, the police, and the courts.[8] Following the war, this segregationist vision began to break down but continued in part to inform the efforts of Cincinnati city planners and some of their allies in housing reform.

Escaping the West End

Prior to World War II the same decrepit and deteriorating housing conditions attacked by the planners and housing reformers bred a desire among many black West Enders to escape. Some moved into older black enclaves within the city, especially into the Walnut Hills black community. Walnut Hills had long contained one of the city's most important black areas, which a 1925 Cincinnati Chamber of Commerce survey identified as a "higher type of Colored settlement."[9] This community extended into an adjacent small portion of South Avondale.[10] After World War II the Walnut Hills–South Avondale black community became a nucleus of the second black ghetto in Cincinnati.

In 1940 Avondale was a largely white, middle-class neighborhood that contained pockets of poor whites and three small black enclaves. The Avondale section of the Avondale–Walnut Hills black community lay entirely in census tract 34 and encompassed the largest black settlement in Avondale (Maps 9.1 and 9.2). Slightly less than half (46 percent) of Avondale's black population lived in tract 34, which was 20 percent (945) black. Twenty-three percent of the tract's census blocks contained 97 percent (243) of its black households. As in the mid-1920s, this hilltop black community contained more prosperous citizens and better housing than the West End slum ghetto. Eighty-one percent of the black labor force in tract 34 found employment outside of publicly funded work relief projects, compared to 60 percent in the West End. Eighteen percent owned their own homes, while only 2 percent did so in the West End. And while nearly 50 percent of black housing in tract 34 needed major repairs or lacked a private bath, 87 percent of the blacks in the West End occupied such housing (Map 9.1).[11]

Two other Avondale black enclaves contained another 40 percent of Avondale's black households, and in equal proportion. A small enclave occurred just north of the Cincinnati Zoo in tract 69 (Map 9.1). Black households along Rockdale Avenue east of Reading Road comprised the third enclave, which provided homes for more prosperous blacks, doctors, teachers, and Pullman car porters, who in the mid-1920s became the first of their race to live in the area.[12]

The Beginnings of the Second Ghetto

The period between 1945 and about 1960 proved critical in the development of the second ghetto. Starting about 1945, blacks, faced with extremely low vacancy rates in traditional black areas and with an increasing population, began to move into housing previously occupied by whites in Avondale tracts 34 and 67 as well as into other traditionally white areas of the city. By 1960 all three of Avondale's prewar black settlements had expanded so that they now formed one large black area, and whites lived only on the periphery of the neighborhood (Maps 9.1 and 9.2). Similar changes in the racial makeup of other contiguous neighborhoods occurred simultaneously. Together these new black areas formed Cincinnati's second black ghetto.

Several factors contributed to the growth of the Avondale portion of this ghetto between World War II and 1970. Prewar segregation, the failure to eliminate the West End slums and provide adequate housing for its black population, and a large influx of new

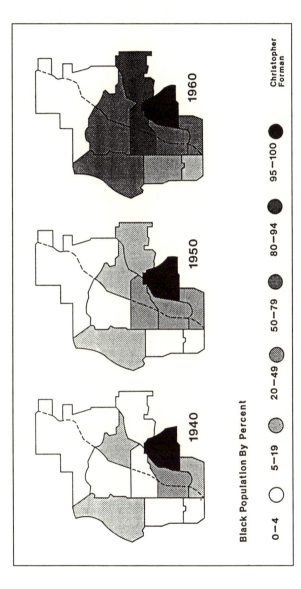

Black Population By Percent

0—4 ◯ 5—19 ◯ 20—49 ◉ 50—79 ◉ 80—94 ⬤ 95—100 ⬤

Christopher
Forman

Map 9.2. Racial Change in Avondale. U.S. Census Bureau, 1940, 1950, 1960.

blacks—22,600 between 1940 and 1950—played a crucial role in the postwar formation of the city's second ghetto. By 1943 vacancies in black areas dropped to around one-third of 1 percent. This extreme pressure on the housing stock, in combination with new conditions, broke down old patterns of residential segregation and replaced them with new ones.[13]

The new factors included white migration to areas away from the central city, increased prosperity among blacks, the easing of racial restrictions on real estate mortgages, and a new willingness by a few real estate agents to sell and rent to blacks in previously all-white areas. Among the earliest areas to expand was the Walnut Hills–South Avondale black community. By 1950 it occupied parts of seven census tracts (34–38 and 67) and had expanded into Evanston, a neighborhood to the east of Avondale and north of Walnut Hills. This nascent ghetto contained 12,056 blacks, 40 percent of the total population of the seven tracts. Despite its increase in size and population, the percentage of the city's black population in this area remained the same (15.4 percent) as in the smaller area encompassed by the 1940 settlement (Maps 9.1 and 9.2). White migration to the suburban hinterland apparently made the black occupation of these new areas possible. Between 1940 and 1950 the population of Hamilton County outside Cincinnati increased from 166,377 to 219,954. Of that increase, whites made up fully 98 percent (50,270).[14]

In the late 1940s, as part of the birth of this new ghetto, the black areas along Rockdale Avenue and in tract 34 expanded and merged as white residents began to abandon the area. Before 1950 the expansion of the black population in Avondale was limited entirely to tracts 34 and 67. By 1950 tracts 34 and 67 contained 2,765 blacks, 26 percent of the population of those two tracts and 77 percent of Avondale's black population (Maps 9.1 and 9.2). Forty-seven percent of the census blocks in tracts 34 and 67 contained 93 percent (756) of their black households. Nevertheless, only 39 percent of the households in this area were black.[15] By the mid-1950s, however, blacks lived in a large portion of Avondale from the Forest–Rockdale Avenue corridor southward. While the new ghetto had not reached its fullest extent, its existence had been assured.[16]

Census data for 1950 suggest that those in better economic circumstances led the black influx into Avondale. Tract 67, which had a higher percentage of residents of a year's duration or less (48 percent) than tract 34 (17 percent), also had higher rates for blacks in the categories of employment, professionals and managers, median income, housing costs, and good housing conditions. Black employment in tract 67 surpassed that in tract 34 (93 percent compared to 84 percent), and only 9 percent of tract 34 blacks worked as professionals or managers, while 14 percent did so in tract 67. Median income, at about $1,500 in tract 34 compared to approximately $2,000 in tract 67, reflected this difference. Renters in tract 67 paid far more in rent, $43.69 per month, than in tract 34, $27.17. Housing conditions in tract 67 also reflected the better circumstances of its black inhabitants. Only 14 percent of black housing there lacked a private bath or appeared dilapidated in contrast to tract 34, where fully one-third fell below this good housing standard (Map 9.1).[17]

Though tract 34 apparently still served as a haven for blacks in better circumstances than those in the West End, the economic position of blacks in tract 34 compared to that of West End blacks had slipped since 1940. The percentage of professionals and managers and the rate of homeownership indicated that blacks in tract 34 still maintained greater economic health than those in the West End, where only 4 percent worked at these jobs and 2 percent owned their own homes. Perhaps the major difference between the old ghetto and tract 34 lay in the quality of housing; 74 percent in the West End lacked a private bath or appeared dilapidated. Despite these positive indicators, other factors indicated a slip in relative economic health. The median income for black families in tract 34 fell in the middle of the range found in West End tracts, and unemployment equaled that in the older ghetto.[18]

Blacks moving into formerly all white sections of Avondale in the postwar period faced several difficulties. Though some lending institutions eased racial restrictions on mortgage money, many lenders still refused to provide financing to blacks or would only provide it in areas already black. Ads in newspapers often designated the race of those to whom property was available, and the local white real estate board still subscribed to a national code of real estate ethics that effectively placed a prohibition on introducing blacks into white neighborhoods. Those blacks who managed to find homes outside the old ghettos often faced hostility from the remaining whites.[19]

Some of the tension resulted from the activities of unscrupulous real estate agents. Such agents became known as blockbusters for their ability to cause racial change in a neighborhood in a very short time. Blockbusters used a variety of tactics to pressure whites in a targeted area to offer their homes for sale. The panic that resulted from the activities of these agents contributed to changing Avondale from white to black. In several situations where tension developed as neighborhoods underwent racial change, members of the Cincinnati

Mayor's Friendly Relations Committee (MFRC) intervened to help calm people's fears and to attempt to stabilize the neighborhood. Nevertheless, black newcomers sometimes required police protection for themselves and their property. Furthermore, the MFRC achieved, at best, only a temporary stability in a few of the areas in which it worked.[20]

While it is clear that blockbusting played a part in the rapid racial change in Avondale during this period, it has proven difficult to obtain more than a handful of documentable accounts of blockbusting in the available sources and to establish that unethical real estate brokers played a major role in Avondale's story. Indeed, real estate agents interviewed for this study who operated in Avondale during this period disagree with each other rather strenuously about this point. It is worth noting, however, that whatever role real estate agents, unscrupulous or otherwise, played, they could not have "turned over" Avondale without a rapidly growing supply of new housing available to whites, a rapid increase in black population, and a general agreement, at least among whites, that countenanced racially segregated neighborhoods.

City Planning and the Second Ghetto

At the same time that South Avondale's black population began to mushroom, Cincinnati's city planners, housing reformers, and parts of the business community renewed their attack on the city's housing problems.[21] The Cincinnati metropolitan master plan of 1948 and its supporting studies were central elements in these efforts. Though Cincinnati's second ghetto had begun to develop in the late 1940s and early 1950s before many of the master plan's goals could be implemented, two of its most important goals eventually played critical roles in the consolidation of the new ghetto. One of these goals called for leveling most of the basin's slums and replacing them with lower-density private and public housing and with light industrial and commercial districts in sections separate from the housing. The other goal of the master plan that would affect Avondale was a network of limited-access superhighways linking all parts of the metropolitan area. Both the slum clearance program and the highway construction program required clearing a major portion of the West End. Without the successful completion of these two goals, planners, housing reformers, and business interests believed that the city would stagnate and suffer economically.[22]

Because both the highway building program and the redevelopment of the basin involved the elimination of thousands of units of housing and the displacement and relocation of huge numbers of people, city officials and housing reformers began to plan in the late 1940s and early 1950s for new housing. They hoped that a multifaceted approach would meet the housing needs of those to be displaced. New privately built housing in the suburban hinterland would empty older housing near the basin and make it available to those who could afford to live in private-sector housing. Public housing built on vacant land in several parts of the metropolitan area and on a small portion of the cleared land in the basin would house those at the other end of the financial spectrum. Housing that was operated not for profit or for limited profit by organizations interested in housing reform and constructed with the help of government subsidies would serve those in between. The city would enforce zoning and housing codes in order to prevent the spread of decay as the slum dwellers moved into new areas.[23]

Execution of these relocation housing plans proved more difficult than their authors had hoped. By 1955, on the eve of construction of the expressway through the West End and the start of the first slum clearance project there, little of the proposed housing had been built. Public pressure by whites who feared blacks living close to them severely limited the ability of the Cincinnati Metropolitan Housing Authority (CMHA) to build public housing. What little the CMHA could build, rapidly filled with blacks, thus creating new segregated neighborhoods. Private plans to provide low-cost subsidized housing largely failed due to high cost. Private builders produced most of the new construction in the metropolitan area in single-family houses at prices well above the means of people living in the basin slums. By the mid-1950s this new construction helped ease the housing shortage for the white middle class and those whites being displaced from expressway and slum clearance sites, but not enough older housing filtered down to blacks to ease their housing shortage.[24]

In the mid-1950s, contemporaneous with the failure of Cincinnati's relocation housing programs, city officials and housing reformers began to be concerned by the spread of blight into the older hilltop neighborhoods as large numbers of blacks and poor whites poured into housing vacated by the white middle class. Many of these newcomers, strapped for money and desperate for housing, occupied their new apartments and houses at a higher density than the previous residents, leading, at least in the opinion of some, to the deterioration of those neighborhoods. Zoning and housing code enforcement seemed unable to deter decay.[25]

Among the several neighborhoods affected, south and central Avondale attracted particular attention. Planners and reformers noted that they still had a large supply of good housing stock worth preserving. The evidence indicates the planners intended urban renewal efforts in Avondale to preserve private-sector housing for blacks displaced from slum clearance sites. Important city officials defended segregated housing and thus presumably favored channeling black relocatees to black or changing neighborhoods. From 1948, when the master plan was issued, through 1959, no Cincinnati city officials concerned with housing (other than members of the MFRC) stated for the record, as far as I could determine, that they believed in racial residential integration. On the contrary, in 1959 the head of Cincinnati's Department of Urban Development, the local agency in charge of urban renewal, in a statement to the press, defended placing segregated black relocation housing in Avondale and in other black or changing areas. And in 1961 the chief of the city's housing bureau, in his annual report to the city manager, spelled out how whites might defend their neighborhoods from blacks seeking housing there.[26]

In addition, by the mid-1950s the portion of Avondale chosen for rehabilitation, parts of tracts 34, 67, and 69, had attracted a substantial black population. During the next four years slum clearance, as planned, displaced thousands of blacks from the West End. By 1960, when the city issued its renewal plan for Avondale, only the northernmost census tract in Avondale remained below 50 percent black.[27]

Though the renewal plan itself did nothing overt to channel more blacks into Avondale, several subsidized housing projects proposed for Avondale intended to do just that. Plans for these housing projects specifically designated them for people displaced from urban renewal sites. In at least two cases city officials linked them with the need to house West Enders, the majority of whom were black. Three other proposed relocation housing projects intended for Avondale sites were openly designated for blacks.[28]

In addition to conserving Avondale's housing stock, planners and the business community also worried about the proximity of the growing ghetto to the University of Cincinnati and Cincinnati's major complex of hospitals. To protect these institutions and the potential supply of good used relocation housing in Avondale, city planners began in 1956 to develop an urban renewal plan for an area that encompassed parts of Avondale and of Corryville, a neighborhood that lay south of Avondale and adjacent to both the university and the hospitals.[29]

When completed in 1960, the Avondale-Corryville General Neighborhood Renewal Plan (A-C GNRP) set standards for rehabilitating residential property and planned for urban renewal experts to provide assistance to homeowners trying to meet those standards. In addition the plan proposed public improvements designed to increase the desirability of the neighborhood as a residential area and intended to encourage private developers to upgrade the three main shopping areas. Furthermore, the plan recognized the need of the university and the hospitals to expand into previously residential areas.[30]

The Consolidation of the Ghetto

By 1960 Avondale's population reflected the destruction of the old West End ghetto, a large increase in black population citywide, and continued white migration to suburban Hamilton County. Cincinnati's black population increased by 30,500 during the 1950s, rising from 15 percent to 22 percent of the total at the same time that the city's white population decreased by 32,448. During this same period the black population in the West End decreased by 15,000. Thus in 1960 roughly 45,000 more blacks lived in areas of Cincinnati outside the West End than in 1950. At the same time the suburban population (Hamilton County outside of Cincinnati) increased from 219,954 to 361,550, but of that increase only 2 percent (3,004) was black. Avondale, with 56 percent of its population now black and home to 18 percent of the city's blacks, had become part of a new deteriorating black ghetto (Map 9.2). Over the decade, black population in the neighborhood increased by over 16,000 individuals, all of it in tracts 34 and 66–69. Simultaneously, total population in those tracts increased by 16 percent, reflecting the greater crowding noted by housing officials over the previous five or six years.[31]

Blacks were not evenly scattered throughout the neighborhood. This growing ghetto encompassed a large contiguous area of Avondale, including the three original enclaves. Only 2 percent of tract 65 residents were black, while elsewhere in the neighborhood blacks made up 69 percent of the population. One-half of the census blocks in tracts 34 and 66–69 contained 80 percent or more black-occupied dwelling units. Another 23 percent contained greater than 80 percent white units. The remaining blocks had more mixed populations (Map 9.1).[32]

Census data indicate a slip during the 1950s in housing quality in tracts 34 and 66–69 (Map 9.1). In 1950 these tracts had one-third the rate of poor housing of the rest of the city. In 1960 those same tracts had one-half the rate of poor housing for all of Cincinnati. But despite the relative drop in housing quality over the decade, Avondale south of tract 65 still provided a refuge for blacks in better-than-average economic condition. Black median income in those tracts ranged from a low of $3,800 to a high of $4,800, compared to $3,250 for blacks citywide. Several other indices of economic health, including the proportion of professionals and managers in the work force, rates of homeownership, and median value of owner-occupied housing, all indicated that black Avondale, particularly tracts 66, 68, and 69, remained better off than black Cincinnati as a whole. Furthermore, tract 68, which had the highest percentage of newcomer blacks, 66 percent over the previous two years, also had for Avondale blacks the highest rents, value of owner-occupied housing, proportion of professionals and managers, and owner-occupants as a percentage of black-occupied one- and two-unit buildings (Map 9.1). Apparently, then, in the late 1950s middle-class blacks led the way for the black advance into Avondale.[33]

The Failure of the Avondale-Corryville Renewal Plan

Despite the relative economic health of black Avondale and despite years of planning, urban renewal plans for Avondale-Corryville immediately ran into trouble. The housing rehabilitation aspects of the program eventually failed because of the rapidly changing population, the high cost of residential rehabilitation, the lack of money and initiative from financially strapped residents within the project area, and insensitivity on the part of the staff charged with executing the plan. Instead, the renewal plan provided a vehicle for the expansion of the hospitals and the university within the renewal area. Little of the federal and city money spent on the project went directly to housing rehabilitation. The city sacrificed more than half of Corryville's housing stock to institutional expansion, and the University of Cincinnati dormitory space accounted for over half the new housing units constructed in the project area by 1970 when the renewal program ended. Indeed, new construction funded by the program provided only twenty-eight units for non-elderly, low-income families and individuals.[34]

The Evolution of a New Ideology of Race and Housing

During the 1950s a new ideology began to unfold that saw benefits for both individuals and the public at large from residential racial integration. The unfolding of that ideology was closely linked in Cin-

cinnati with its urban renewal efforts. As had Cincinnati city plan
ners before the war, the authors of the master plan of 1948 believed
in segregated neighborhoods.[35] Their belief in the appropriateness of
segregated communities informed much of the work of the planners
through the late 1950s. The failure of relocation housing plans
throughout the 1950s, spreading slums in Avondale and elsewhere,
escalating racial tension as old black enclaves expanded into formerly
white areas, and difficulties with the Avondale-Corryville urban renewal program in the early 1960s led some city officials to link the
success of urban renewal with racial residential integration. Before
the planners began to reexamine their beliefs, however, some housing
reformers began to question the value of residential segregation, and
by the mid-to-late 1950s they began to work for residential racial integration as a way to provide good housing for the city's blacks and
to empty the slum whose housing conditions had so concerned them
for most of the century.[36]

The growing support for racial integration also found expression
in neighborhood organizations. In 1959 and 1960 two biracial organizations formed in Avondale in response to chaotic racial change
and deteriorating housing. The first formed in early 1959. The Crescent Civic Association, centered around North and South Crescent
avenues in north central Avondale, attempted, but failed, to stabilize
the area it claimed to represent. By the early 1960s blacks occupied
much of the Crescent neighborhood, and owners had cut up many
formerly single-family homes into apartments and rooming houses.

In early 1960 following the failure of the Crescent Civic Association, another group formed in Avondale to encourage the stable development of an integrated neighborhood in the North Avondale
school district (which included most of the Crescent area). While the
Crescent Civic Association did not explicitly state its support for
racial integration, its biracial character implied that it accepted such
a neighborhood. The North Avondale Neighborhood Association
(NANA), however, stated its support for residential racial integration
from its beginning in its bylaws and other public declarations. NANA
did ultimately prove helpful in assisting the transition of its primarily
middle-class neighborhood from white to racially mixed in some
areas.[37]

By the early 1960s support for residential racial integration
reached the highest levels in Cincinnati's urban renewal agency. In
late 1960 Charles Stamm, longtime head of Cincinnati's Department
of Urban Development, estimated that those blacks displaced by slum
clearance could be relocated with relative ease if they could be placed

in the existing good housing scattered throughout Cincinnati. By taking this stand, Stamm reversed his earlier defense of racially segregated housing.[38]

As support for integrated housing grew, its advocates proposed
several laws and ordinances at both the local and state level to ban
real estate sales practices believed to enforce residential racial segregation. The first of these ordinances came before the Cincinnati city
council in early 1962. While substantial support apparently existed
on the council for some sort of legislation banning blockbusting, it
failed to pass any sort of fair housing legislation during this period.
Most members of the council argued that only statewide laws would
be effective and that local ordinances might exacerbate the trend toward a black and poor city surrounded by wealthier white suburbs. A
state fair housing law did garner considerable support among politicians statewide as early as 1962, but it was not until 1965 that the
Ohio General Assembly passed such a statute.[39]

The passage of this statute signaled the coalescence among housing
activists and some public officials of a new ideology about race and
housing that stood in sharp contrast to earlier attitudes. Before World
War II, slum dwellers, according to the theorists, caused blight by
their nature and habits, and thus good housing practices required
that neighborhoods be segregated on racial and economic lines to
protect better neighborhoods and to allow housing officials to exercise proper control over poor and black neighborhoods. After the
war this ideology began to break down, though it informed the master plan of 1948 and a number of other planning and urban renewal
schemes. By the mid-1950s housing activists implicitly separated race
from the cause of blight by calling for racial residential integration as
a tool in the fight against slums. Racial integration, they believed,
might be a way of providing relocation housing to make way for slum
clearance.

By the mid-1960s those who propounded the new ideology argued
that those who denied individuals the right to live where they chose
committed a moral wrong. Furthermore, they contended that blacks
and poor whites did not cause slum conditions. Rather, poverty and
racial segregation caused slums, personal degradation, racial alienation, and continued poverty. Thus it was in the public interest to
provide blacks and poor whites with the means and opportunity to
escape slums and ghettos and to live in neighborhoods integrated
both by race and class. The alternative, racial and economic residential segregation, led to "physical decay of neighborhoods, deepening
racial alienation and pyramiding public expense."[40]

Despite a growing agreement by housing activists and some public officials with laws intended to ban racial discrimination in housing, resistance to such laws and to racial residential integration remained powerful forces. Indeed, Cincinnati civil rights activists argued that some members of the city council, while supporting a state law, opposed a local fair housing ordinance because they feared alienating local white voters. In addition, the Ohio fair housing law was relatively weak. The state law exempted owner-occupied one- and two-family buildings, which represented the majority of sales. In addition, the law required that only bona fide home seekers could file complaints, which inhibited civil rights groups from helping implement the law. Making matters worse, enforcement rested with a relatively ineffective Ohio Civil Rights Commission (OCRC). OCRC staff proved inept, if not obstructive, and complainants experienced long delays in having their cases heard.[41]

Resistance to fair housing existed at the federal level as well. Proponents of federal fair housing legislation experienced several defeats before they obtained the housing portions of the Civil Rights Act of 1968. Indeed, only the emotional outpouring in the wake of Martin Luther King, Jr.'s assassination enabled them to persuade Congress to pass such a law. But while that law was somewhat stronger than the Ohio law, Cincinnati civil rights activists still found it difficult to force compliance.[42]

Fair housing legislation failed to help substantial numbers of blacks leave the ghetto for at least three reasons. These included lack of income on the part of many blacks, continued racial antipathy by both blacks and whites, and continued racial housing discrimination. Income was a major problem. Of 19,065 housing units scheduled for destruction by slum clearance and highway construction by 1966, two-thirds were occupied by nonwhites. To make matters worse, at least half the black population could not afford to buy any of the 45,800 new dwelling units built for sale in the metropolitan area between 1950 and 1958. Even for those with adequate income, discrimination confined most black home buyers to areas in which the houses were forty or more years old. These carried higher down payments, shorter mortgage periods, and higher maintenance requirements that tended to force the monthly shelter costs to levels as high or higher than those for whites in the same income bracket. The rental situation was little better. The cost of the private portion of the 14,600 new rental units put up in the period also exceeded the means of many blacks. Most of the people who were being displaced by renewal or public works were not even able to afford the proposed

2,200 units of federally subsidized relocation housing assigned to developers by 1960.[43] In addition to overt discriminatory practices that a law might ban as well as financial restrictions, one report on the situation argued, attitudes on the part of both blacks and whites would restrict the growth of an open housing market. Thus, the author noted: "There is indeed considerable evidence that a substantial majority of both white and Negro families hesitate to expose themselves to the uncertainties and emotional hazards that accompany any departure from the conventions that govern race relations. . . . A Negro family must have extraordinary fortitude and courage to risk the cold stares, the slights, rebuffs and outright insults that may be its reward for shopping for houses outside the accepted areas."[44]

But even for blacks with adequate income and the fortitude to seek housing in white areas, open housing legislation largely failed. Local civil rights activists documented widespread patterns of discrimination in housing in violation of both state and federal legislation throughout the late 1960s and 1970s.[45]

Thus, though some blacks lived outside the densest ghetto by 1970, most remained trapped in largely black areas (Map 9.3). Fifty-one census tracts combined contained only 1 percent of Cincinnati's black population. Thirty-six tracts had populations over 99 percent white, and another thirty-six census tracts that were 50 percent or more black contained 76 percent of Cincinnati's black population. This latter set of thirty-six tracts formed two large groups and four smaller clusters of black population. The West End ghetto (tracts 1–5 and 8) plus tracts 14 and 15 just to the north still contained a population 97 percent black, which comprised 15 percent (19,062) of the city's African Americans. The central business district and an adjacent neighborhood, Over-the-Rhine, separated the burgeoning second ghetto from the older one. The newer ghetto encompassed twenty-one tracts with an African American population of 59,767— 83 percent of the general population of the area and 48 percent of the city's blacks. Two clusters in the Millcreek Valley (tracts 76, 77, and 86.02, and tract 80) each held about 5,500 blacks (79 and 75 percent black respectively). Two other clusters with about 4,000 African Americans each occurred in Kennedy Heights (tract 58, 58 percent black) and Madisonville (tract 55, 62 percent black) (Map 9.3).[46]

While the pre–World War II ghetto contained blacks of all classes in close proximity, the second ghetto took on a new form. Prior to World War II, public policy and racial antipathy had largely confined blacks in Cincinnati to two relatively small geographic areas, the West End and Walnut Hill–South Avondale. In 1940 these two areas

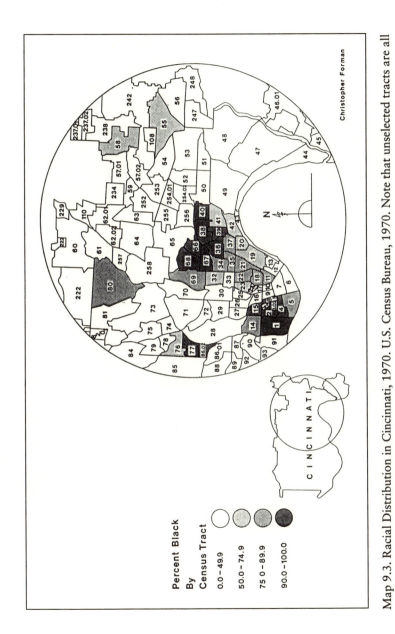

Christopher Forman

Map 9.3. Racial Distribution in Cincinnati, 1970. U.S. Census Bureau, 1970. Note that unselected tracts are all within the 0.0–49.9 percent range.

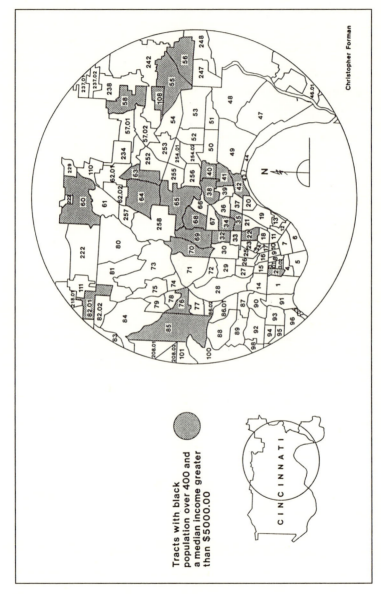

Tracts with black
population over 400 and
a median income greater
than $5000.00

CINCINNATI

Christopher Forman

Map 9.4. Black Median Income in Cincinnati, 1970. U.S. Census Bureau, 1970. Note that unselected tracts
do not meet the population/income requirement.

accounted for 80 percent of Cincinnati's black population. While good housing existed in both of these communities, their small geographic extent made it difficult for blacks who could afford quality housing to escape close proximity to slum conditions. By 1970 stratification on the basis of income had developed in the now vastly expanded ghetto. Relatively high income allowed some African Americans to move outside the areas of heaviest black concentration. Nine of the twenty-three tracts with black median income over $5,000 lay outside those areas greater than 50 percent black. Only one of these higher-income tracts (tract 82.01), however, occurred at a distance from the postwar ghetto (Map 9.4).[47]

Though racial residential segregation in Cincinnati is no longer openly sanctioned by official governmental policy, it is still enforced by real estate practices, economic discrimination, and racial animosity. At best, the new ideology of racial integration has allowed a few blacks with adequate incomes and fortitude to escape the ghetto entirely. Most, however, remain in a new type of ghetto much larger than the old, and now stratified by income.

Notes

1. For a more detailed discussion of the issues raised in this chapter, see Charles F. Casey-Leininger, "Making the Second Ghetto in Cincinnati, Avondale, 1925–70" (Master's thesis, University of Cincinnati, 1989).

2. It is not clear if second ghettoes formed in western cities. For example, Douglas Henry Daniels argues that prior to 1940 no ghettoes existed in San Francisco. A similar argument was posed by Lawrence B. DeGraaf with regard to Los Angeles. See Douglas Henry Daniels, *Pioneer Urbanites: A Social and Cultural History of Black San Francisco* (Philadelphia: Temple University Press, 1980); Lawrence B. DeGraaf, "The City of Black Angels: Emergence of the Los Angeles Ghetto, 1890–1930," *Pacific Historical Review* 39 (Aug. 1970): 323–52.

3. For the development of pre–World War II ghettoes, see Arna Bontemps and Jack Conroy, *Anyplace But Here* (1945; repr., New York: Hill and Wang, 1966); August Meier and Elliott Rudwick, *From Plantation to Ghetto*, 3d ed. (New York: Hill and Wang, 1976); John H. Bracey, August Meier, and Elliott Rudwick, eds., *The Rise of the Ghetto* (Belmont, Ca.: Wadsworth Publishing Co., 1971); Gilbert Osofsky, *Harlem: The Making of a Ghetto: Negro New York, 1890–1930* (New York: Harper and Row, 1966); Allan H. Spear, *Black Chicago: The Making of a Negro Ghetto, 1890–1920* (Chicago: University of Chicago Press, 1966); George C. Wright, *Life Behind a Veil: Blacks in Louisville, Kentucky* (Baton Rouge: Louisiana

State University Press, 1985); Kenneth L. Kusmer, *A Ghetto Takes Shape: Black Cleveland, 1870–1930* (Urbana: University of Illinois Press, 1976); Thomas Lee Philpott, *The Slum and the Ghetto: Neighborhood Deterioration and Middle-Class Reform, Chicago, 1880–1930* (New York: Oxford University Press, 1978); David A. Gerber, *Black Ohio and the Color Line, 1860–1915* (Urbana: University of Illinois Press, 1976); Joe William Trotter, Jr., *Black Milwaukee: The Making of an Industrial Proletariat* (Urbana: University of Illinois Press, 1986); James R. Grossman, *Land of Hope: Chicago, Black Southerners, and the Great Migration* (Chicago: University of Chicago Press, 1989); and Kenneth L. Kusmer, "The Black Urban Experience in American History," in *The State of Afro-American History,* ed. Darlene Clark Hine (Baton Rouge: Louisiana State University Press, 1986). For the postwar period, see Arnold R. Hirsch, *Making the Second Ghetto: Race and Housing in Chicago, 1940–1960* (New York: Cambridge University Press, 1983); and Kenneth T. Jackson, *Crabgrass Frontier: The Suburbanization of the United States* (New York: Oxford University Press, 1985).

4. For the purpose of this discussion, I define a black ghetto as an area of the city that is substantially or primarily occupied by blacks. Ghettoes often contain a substantial part, if not the majority, of a city's black population and, while predominantly poor, may contain a population diverse in socio-economic characteristics and religious affiliation. Black ghetto areas have generally formed around one or more smaller centers of black population that grew by accretions along their edges and by coalescence, where two or more areas were initially involved.

5. U.S. Bureau of the Census, *Population and Housing: 1940 Statistics for Census Tracts Cincinnati, Ohio and Adjacent Areas* (Washington, D.C.: Government Printing Office, 1942), 4; idem, *1960 Census of Population and Housing: Census Tracts, Cincinnati, Ohio-Kentucky,* 15, 70; idem, *1970 Census of Population and Housing: Census Tracts, Cincinnati, Ohio-Kentucky-Indiana,* P1–P2, P10–P11, P97–P98.

6. Zane L. Miller, *Boss Cox's Cincinnati: Urban Politics in the Progressive Era* (New York: Oxford University Press, 1968), 14–15, 28, 30–31, 251 n. 8; U.S. Bureau of the Census, *Thirteenth Census of the United States Taken in the Year 1910,* vol. 3 (Washington, D.C., 1913), 426–27; idem, *Sixteenth Census of the United States: Population and Housing: 1940, Statistics for Census Tracts, Cincinnati, Ohio and Adjacent Area* (Washington, D.C., 1942), 4; James A. Quinn, Earl Eubank, and Lois E. Elliott, *Population Characteristics by Census Tracts: Cincinnati, Ohio: 1930 and 1935* (Columbus: Bureau of Business Research, Ohio State University, 1940), 35–37. In 1910 Cincinnati wards 16–18 included the West End as well as some adjacent areas. In 1930 and 1940 census tracts 1–5 and 8 comprised the West End. The correlation between wards and tracts is only approximate.

7. Robert B. Fairbanks, "Better Housing Movements and the City: Definitions of and Responses to Cincinnati's Low-Cost Housing Problems, 1910–1954" (Ph.D. diss., University of Cincinnati, 1981), 2–3, 55–56, 106–7, 128–30; City Planning Commission, *The Official City Plan of Cincinnati, Ohio* (Cincinnati, 1925), 51–52.

8. Fairbanks, "Better Housing Movements," 130, 180, 208–9, 294, 312–14, 330–31.

9. Technical Advisory Corp., *Cincinnati Industrial Survey* (Cincinnati: Chamber of Commerce, 1925), vol. 3, sec. 9, 5–6; Miller, *Boss Cox*, 31.

10. Quinn, Eubank, and Elliott, *Population Characteristics*, 35–38.

11. U.S. Bureau of the Census, *Sixteenth Census of the United States, 1940: Housing, Block Statistics* (Washington, D.C., 1942), 5–6, 18–19, 32–34; idem, *Census Tracts, 1940*, 4, 51–52, 54, 74–75.

12. U.S. Bureau of the Census, *Block Statistics, 1940*, 5–6. Tracts 66 and 67 each contained one of the two census blocks that encompassed the Rockdale Avenue area. Wendell P. Dabney, *Cincinnati's Colored Citizens: Historical, Sociological, and Biographical*, 383; Donald Spencer to author, 23 Oct. 1984 (interview).

13. U.S. Bureau of the Census, *Census Tracts, 1940*, 4; idem, *United States Census of Population, 1950: Cincinnati, Ohio Census Tracts*, 7; Arnold Walker, "Prejudice and the Church," in Division of Negro Welfare, "Minutes of the Board of Trustees" (Cincinnati, n.p., 15 Nov. 1943), Urban League Collection, Box 3, File 2, Cincinnati Historical Society.

14. Spencer interview; Helen Ehodin to author, 30 Oct. 1984 (interview); Robert Sachs to author, 30 Mar. 1984, 6, 13 Apr. 1984 (interview), University of Cincinnati Library, Department of Archives and Rare Books; Ethel Edwards, *Ringside Seat on Revolution* (Cincinnati: Psyche Press, 1972), 35; Allen L. Bivens, "Housing Migration of Black Cincinnatians in the 1950s and 1960s" (Master's thesis, University of Cincinnati), 51–52; U.S. Bureau of the Census, *Census Tracts, 1950*, 9, 11; idem, *Census Tracts, 1940*, 4; idem, *United States Census of Population: 1950, Vol. 2: Characteristics of the Population, Part 35, Ohio*, 159; idem, *Sixteenth Census of the United States: 1940, Population, Vol. 2: Characteristics of the Population, Part 5*, 578.

15. U.S. Bureau of the Census, *Census Tracts, 1950*, 7, 9, 11; idem, *Block Statistics, 1950*, 16–30.

16. Spencer interview; U.S. Bureau of the Census, *Census Tracts, 1950*, 9, 11; Edwards, *Ringside Seat on Revolution*, 45–50.

17. U.S. Bureau of the Census, *Census Tracts, 1950*, 44–46.

18. Ibid.

19. Better Housing League of Cincinnati, "Minutes of the Board of Trustees" (n.p., 18 Feb. 1952), BHL Collection, University of Cincinnati Libraries, Department of Archives and Rare Books; *Cincinnati Daily Enquirer*, 4, 18, 25 Apr. 1954, classified ads, houses for sale; Ehodin interview; Spencer interview; Sachs interview; Rose Helper, *Racial Policies and Practices of Real Estate Brokers* (Minneapolis: University of Minnesota Press, 1969), 201.

20. Spencer interview; Sachs interviews; Ehodin interview; Barbara Hadden to author, 17 Oct. 1984 (interview); Marvin and Gerry Kraus to author, 18 Oct. 1984 (interview); Edwards, *Ringside Seat on Revolution*, 44–48; Mayor's Friendly Relations Committee, "Minutes of the Board of Trustees," Cincinnati, 9 Apr., 14 May 1953, 10 Feb., 13 Oct. 1955, 20 Feb. 1958,

Cincinnati Human Relations Commissions Collection, University of Cincinnati Libraries, Department of Archives and Rare Books; idem, "Annual Report for 1954" (n.p., 1955), 3; idem, "Annual Report for 1954—Proposed Outline," typescript (n.p., n.d.); idem, "Annual Report for 1955" (n.p., 1956), 3.

21. This analysis largely ignores the political issues that developed around urban renewal in Cincinnati, not because they were unimportant, but because I couldn't look at all aspects of the story. In addition, I found other parts personally more interesting. It is, however, useful to note that neither I nor Robert B. Fairbanks found prior to about 1960 the kind of self-interested city planning by downtown and institutional interests that Arnold R. Hirsch found in Chicago. In fact, Fairbanks argues convincingly that planning in Cincinnati in this era largely focused on metropolis-wide solutions to the city's problems rather than on the narrow interests of one group or another. No doubt an analysis of the political side of city planning and ghetto making in this era would broaden our understanding. Indeed, evidence presented later in this chapter suggests that during the 1960s interests associated with the University of Cincinnati and neighboring medical facilities used urban renewal to further their own narrowly conceived ends at the expense of the surrounding communities, including Avondale. Unfortunately, the details of how the university and the medical center complex acted together or separately remain unexplored. See Robert B. Fairbanks, *Making Better Citizens: Housing Reform and the Community Development Strategy in Cincinnati, 1890–1960* (Urbana: University of Illinois Press, 1988), chapter 10; Hirsch, *Making the Second Ghetto*, chapters 4–5.

22. Zane L. Miller, *Suburb: Neighborhood and Community in Forest Park, Ohio, 1935–1976* (Knoxville: University of Tennessee Press, 1981), 9–15; Cincinnati City Planning Commission, *The Redevelopment of Blighted Areas* (Cincinnati, 1951), 10–11, 13–16; idem, *Residential Areas* (Cincinnati, 1946), 12, 121; idem, *The Cincinnati Metropolitan Master Plan and Official City Plan of the City of Cincinnati* (Cincinnati, 1948), 65–67; Citizens Development Committee (CDC), "Minutes of the Board of Trustees," Cincinnati, 8 Feb. 1952, 1–2, CDC Collection, Cincinnati Historical Society; BHL, "Annual Report for 1951" (n.p., 1952).

23. Cincinnati City Planning Commission, *Residential Areas*, 12, 121; idem, *Communities: A Study of Community and Neighborhood Development* (Cincinnati, 1947), 47; idem, *Master Plan of 1948*, 65–67; Action, Inc., "Report to the Subcommittee on Housing and Urban Renewal of the Citizens Development Committee," in CDC, *Bulletin* 18:1 (Cincinnati, Feb. 1961), CDC Collection, Cincinnati Historical Society; Cincinnati City Planning Commission, *Blighted Areas*, 23–27; BHL, "Annual Report for 1952," 1953, 4–7; CDC, "Housing Program for Hamilton County for 1952–1954," in "Minutes of the Housing and Urban Redevelopment Committee" (n.p., 19 Mar. 1952); Miller, *Community in Forest Park*, xxviii–xxix, 19–21; Fairbanks, "Better Housing Movements," 386–37, 397–99, 404–6. The CDC was a group of local business elites that concerned itself from the mid-

1940s through at least the 1960s with slum clearance and urban renewal and, where it impinged on these, Cincinnati's black housing problem.

24. Fairbanks, "Better Housing Movements," 386–87, 397–99, 400–406; *Cincinnati Daily Enquirer,* 25 July 1952, 3; MFRC Board of Trustees minutes (n.p., 10 June 1954); Office of the City Manager, Division of Urban Redevelopment, "An Estimate of Housing Needs, Cincinnati, Ohio, 1955–1959, for Families Displaced through Governmental Action, etc." (Cincinnati, 1955), 14–16.

25. BHL Board Minutes, 25 Sept. 1952, 22 Dec. 1953, 27 May, 16 Dec. 1954, 26 May 1956, 27 Sept. 1956; Housing Bureau, "Annual Report to the City Manager, 1956," in Office of the City Manager, "Annual Reports, 1956" (Cincinnati, 1957), 275; Department of Urban Renewal, "A Preliminary Report to City Council on the Undertaking of Surveys and Plans for Renewal Area #3" (Cincinnati, 7 Sept. 1956), 1–3, 6–7.

26. Department of Urban Renewal, "A Preliminary Report to City Council on the Undertaking of Surveys and Plans for Renewal Area #3" (Cincinnati, 7 Sept. 1956), 1–5; *Cincinnati Post and Times-Star,* 26 May 1959, 2; "Housing Bureau Annual Report for 1960," in "Annual Reports to the City Manager" (Cincinnati, 1961), 292.

27. Action, Inc., "Report," in CDC, *Bulletin* 18:1 (Cincinnati, Feb. 1961), CDC Collection; U.S. Bureau of the Census, *Census Tracts, 1960,* 18, 20.

28. Cincinnati City Planning Commission, *Blighted Areas,* 25–27; idem, "An Interim Report on the Avondale-Corryville Renewal Project UR-3" (Cincinnati, Aug. 1958), 3, 10–12, 16–18; BHL, "Page-A-Month," No. 205, Sept. 1958; *Cincinnati Daily Enquirer,* 19 May 1959, 5-B.

29. Anthony J. J. Rourke, "Rourke Report of 1956" (Cincinnati, Office of the City Manager, 1956); idem, "Rourke Report of 1959" (Cincinnati, CDC, June 1959), R6-R8; "Preliminary Report for Renewal Area #3," 1; Cooper, Alvare, and Harkins, City Planning Consultants, "Consultants' Preliminary Report: Avondale-Corryville Renewal Area" (Cincinnati: City Planning Commission, 22 May 1957), sec. 7.

30. City Planning Commission, "Avondale Corryville General Neighborhood Renewal Plan" (Cincinnati, Dec. 1960), 2–3, 12–14, 18–19, 21–22, 27, 32, 39–51; Department of Urban Development, "Urban Renewal Plan: Avondale-1 Corryville, Ohio R-6" (Cincinnati, Apr. 1961), 16–18.

31. U.S. Bureau of Census, *Census Tracts, 1960,* 15–18, 20; idem, *Census Tracts, 1950,* 7–10, 11.

32. U.S. Bureau of the Census, *Census Tracts, 1960,* 18, 20; idem, *United States Census of Housing: 1960, City Blocks: Cincinnati, Ohio* (Washington, D.C., 1961), 11, 24–25.

33. U.S. Bureau of the Census, *Census Blocks, 1950,* 3–4; idem, *Census Blocks, 1960,* 11, 24–25; idem, *Census Tracts, 1960,* 70, 71–74, 96, 98–99.

34. Elizabeth Wood, "A Report to the Department of Urban Development on the Rehabilitation and Conservation in the Avondale-Corryville Area, Cincinnati, Ohio" (New York: Management Services Associates, Inc.,

Dec. 1962), 3–5, 27; Rowland E. Dietz, "To: John G. Vaughn. From: Rowland E. Dietz" (n.p., n.d.), 1960 Minutes of the Board of Trustees file, BHL Collection; Christopher J. Gibbons, Raymond G. Tessemer, Jr., *From Housing Rehabilitation to Neighborhood Development* (Cincinnati: Department of Urban Development, Sept. 1972), 64–67.

35. Cincinnati City Planning Commission, *Master Plan of 1948*, 10–11.

36. Urban League of Cincinnati, "1948–1958 Summary of Activities" (n.p., n.d.); MFRC, "Minutes of the Board of Trustees," 10 Feb. 1955; BHL, "Page-a-Month," No. 204, (n.p., June–July 1958); *Cincinnati Daily Enquirer*, 20 May 1969, 8-A.

37. Gary P. Kocolowski, "The History of North Avondale: A Study of the Effects of Urbanization upon an Urban Locality" (Master's thesis, University of Cincinnati, 1971), 47–53, 59–60, 63, 67–71; Office of the County Recorder, Hamilton County Ohio, Title Transfer Records for 703–752 South Crescent Avenue, Cincinnati; Cincinnati City Directories, 1958–1962; Petition from the residents of North and South Crescent avenues, Alter Place, Eaton Lane, and Greenwood Avenue; Cincinnati City Planning Commission, Zoning File for North Crescent Avenue, 1933–1963; North Avondale Neighborhood Association, "Bylaws," 4 Oct. 1960, in association's office archives; U.S. Bureau of the Census, *United States Census of Population and Housing: 1970, Census Tracts, Cincinnati, Ohio* (Washington, D.C., 1972), P13.

38. BHL, "Minutes of the Board of Trustees," 11 Nov. 1960.

39. MFRC, "Minutes of the Board of Trustees," 16 May 1962, p. 2, 23 Jan. 1963, p. 1, 27 Feb. 1963, p. 2, 11 Sept. 1963, p. 2, 23 Oct. 1963; BHL, "Minutes of the Board of Trustees," 19 Apr., 18 May 1962; "Summary of Ohio Fair Housing Law," unsigned typescript, box 58, file 24, BHL Collection.

40. George Schermer, "A Background Paper for the Greater Cincinnati Conference on Equal Opportunity in Housing" (Cincinnati: The President's Committee on Equal Opportunity in Housing, 1964), 1, appendix, 6–7, box 58, file 23, Cincinnati Housing Rights Commission (CHRC) Collection; BHL, "Minutes of the Board of Trustees," 19 Mar. 1964.

41. State of Ohio, *Legislative Acts*, vol. 131, Ohio Revised Code, sec. 4112.01-.08 (1965), 980–990; "Summary of Ohio Fair Housing Law," CHRC Collection, box 58, file 24; "Housing Bill Has Negligible Effect," *Cincinnati Daily Enquirer*, 3 Apr. 1968, Housing Opportunities Made Equal (HOME) Collection, University of Cincinnati Libraries, Department of Archives and Rare Books, US-82–5, box 3, file 3; HOME Board Minutes, 12 Dec. 1966, HOME Collection, US-82–5, box 1, file 19; HOME, Minutes of the "Brainstorming" Committee, 28 Feb. 1967, HOME Collection, US-82–5, box 1, file 20, 1; "Case 4, Notes of M. Smudski, HOME," 21–28 Feb. 1967, HOME Collection, US-82–5, box 1, file 20, 1; "HOME's Observations Re: Housing since the Riots," HOME Collection, US-82–5, box 1, file 77, 3; HOME, "Discrimination in Housing: Busch, Estelle and Arthur," Feb. 1969, HOME Collection, US-82–5, box 2, file 17.

42. Paul K. Conklin, *Big Daddy from the Pedernales: Lyndon Baines Johnson* (Boston: Twayne Publishers, 1986), 218–19; HOME, "Federal Fair Housing Laws and HOME's Activities" (n.p., n.d.), HOME Collection, control file.

43. Schermer, "Equal Opportunity in Housing," appendix, 4–5; Martin Meyerson, "The Background to Relocation in Cincinnati," 12 Feb. 1960, 1, 3–4, in CDC, "Minutes of the Housing and Urban Renewal Committee," 24 Feb. 1960, appendix, CDC Collection.

44. Meyerson, "The Background to Relocation," 10.

45. "Housing Bill Has Negligible Effect," *Cincinnati Daily Enquirer*, 3 Apr. 1968, HOME Collection; HOME Board Minutes, 12 Dec. 1966, HOME Collection; HOME, Minutes of the "Brainstorming" Committee; "Case 4, Notes of M. Smudski, HOME" (Smudski's notes on the case list the client only as "Miss P."); "HOME's Observations Re: Housing since the Riots"; HOME, "Discrimination in Housing: Busch, Estelle and Arthur"; "Apartment Discrimination Probed," *Cincinnati Post*, 27 Dec. 1972, 41; idem, "HOME Testing Report—Summer 1972," HOME Collection, US-82–5, box 1, file 80; idem, "Final Report Housing Opportunities Made Equal Testing Project, June 25 thru September 14, 1973," HOME Collection, US-82–5, box 1, file 81; idem, "HOME Testing Project, 1975, Final Report," HOME Collection, US-82-5, box 1, file 82.

46. U.S. Bureau of the Census, *Census Tracts, 1970*.

47. Ibid., Bureau of the Census, *1970 Census of Population and Housing, Census Tracts, Cincinnati Standard Metropolitan Statistical Area* (Washington, D.C.: U.S. Government Printing Office, 1972), P1–P16, P105–P111.

10

ROBERT A. BURNHAM

The Mayor's Friendly Relations Committee: Cultural Pluralism and the Struggle for Black Advancement

In the aftermath of the Detroit race riot of 1943, cities and states across the country rushed to form race relations or intergroup relations committees for the purpose of reducing interracial hostilities. Though this was a national phenomenon of some significance, it has been little studied by scholars.[1] Those who have considered the subject tend to address it in two ways. First, they assess the goals and activities of the committees that were formed in the 1940s from the perspective of the civil rights movement of the 1960s. This has led to interpretations that criticize these committees for failing to take militant action toward ending discrimination against blacks and improving the conditions under which they lived.[2]

The second approach sees the establishment of these committees as a response to interracial tension caused by the Second World War. According to this argument, the war acted as a causative factor, in part by dramatizing fundamental contradictions between American ideals and American social realities. Nothing indicated this better than the fact that the United States fought the war in the name of democracy but used segregated troops to do so. Similarly, the prevalence of employment discrimination in war industries highlighted the unequal social status of blacks. Moreover, those who hold this view point out, the mass migration of southern blacks to western and northern cities during the war led to more frequent contact between whites and blacks in those cities and placed great strain on urban resources. This development supposedly precipitated interracial tension and violence, which, in turn, led contemporaries to establish race relations and intergroup relations committees.[3]

Though domestic tension during the war provided an impetus for forming these committees, an examination of one of them, the Mayor's Friendly Relations Committee (MFRC) of Cincinnati, suggests that it was a product of the contemporary tendency to see society as divided into various racial, religious, and ethnic groups, each possessing its own culture, which had a deterministic effect on the individual members of the group. This pluralistic vision yielded, among other things, a broad intercultural understanding movement between 1915 and 1954 that aimed to promote tolerance for cultural group diversity within American society.[4] As part of that movement, the MFRC functioned, first and foremost, to minimize tension between groups—tension that stemmed from racial, religious, and ethnic prejudice—in hopes of preventing violent outbreaks. This goal required that the committee address the issues of prejudice and discrimination as the underlying causes of group conflict. Although blacks were the main targets of prejudice and discrimination, the pluralistic vision dictated that the MFRC consider the problems of all groups and show partiality to none. Thus, in its early years the MFRC self-consciously avoided taking an advocacy role for the rights of blacks or any other single racial, religious, or ethnic group. Nonetheless, as an official arm of the city government charged with reducing intergroup tension and promoting intergroup harmony as matters of public policy, the MFRC helped provide a climate in which Cincinnati blacks could pursue their struggle for civil rights.[5] Indeed, the initiative for forming the MFRC came from the city's black leaders, who believed that improving intergroup relations would benefit the members of their race.

In the wake of the Detroit race riot, a delegation of blacks met with Republican Mayor James G. Stewart on July 8, 1943, to discuss measures to "lessen any likelihood of similar trouble in Cincinnati."[6] The delegation included Harold Snell, executive director of the local NAACP; Sadie Sammuels, an elementary schoolteacher and NAACP member; William Lovelace, an adult probation officer for the Common Pleas Court and NAACP member; and Arnold B. Walker, executive director of the Cincinnati Community Chest's Division of Negro Welfare.[7] They suggested that the mayor arrange a meeting with "newspapers, church leaders, union leadership, educational directors of radio stations, chamber of commerce officials, OCD officials, etc.," and select a representative "cross section" of those attending to sit on a "citizens committee on unity." They also considered it crucial for this committee to be "independent politically" so it could "demand protection for the minorities." The mayor thought that the idea of forming such a committee was a "good suggestion" and said he would name a "small group of civic leaders" to implement it.[8]

Mayor Stewart's slow response to the concerns of black leaders, however, suggested that he felt no great sense of urgency.[9] After allowing three months to lapse, he finally held a meeting for the purpose of forming an intergroup relations committee on October 7, 1943. This meeting was attended by representatives of the Division of Negro Welfare, B'Nai B'rith, the Council of Churches, the Public Recreation Commission, the CIO, Catholic Charities, the Chamber of Commerce, and the Frontiers Club (a black men's club consisting of businessmen and professionals devoted to community service).[10] All those who spoke at the meeting, including the mayor, placed their aims in the context of the war effort by claiming that they sought to make democratic ideals function at home as well as abroad.[11] At the same time there was general agreement that the proposed committee should be made "permanent."[12] Thus, while wartime concerns and conditions played a significant role in the establishment of the MFRC, from the outset Cincinnati leaders envisioned a committee that would continue to function after the war's end, an indication that they did not see their action as merely a response to wartime problems. Moreover, the conferees showed their inclination to think in pluralistic terms by suggesting that the committee "should go even further than dealing with interracial problems and accept the problems of religious, economic and other social groups."[13] It was also agreed that the mayor should be responsible for appointing the members of the committee and for presenting the entire plan to the city council to get its official backing. The Cincinnati City Council passed a resolution authorizing the creation of the committee on November 17, 1943. The resolution declared, "Whereas, America is made up of many diverse groups with varying viewpoints and different beliefs . . . the hope of both the present and future of our republic is that . . . we shall work together in harmony and without prejudice, hate, or intolerance."

As for Cincinnati, the resolution expressed the belief that "conflicting problems" between "various groups could be solved upon the basis of friendship rather than hostility." To achieve this the resolution authorized the mayor "to appoint a committee to be known as the Friendly Relations Committee, representing the various racial, industrial, religious, and other groups, for the purpose of studying the problems connected with the promotion of harmony and tolerance, and [for] working out community problems . . . and [by] acting as an advisory committee for their solution."[15]

The resolution was significant because, first, it gave the MFRC official status, and thus identification with the city government. Second, it clearly asserted a pluralistic view by repeatedly referring to society as being divided into groups and by basing the committee's structure and function on that same notion. And finally, by limiting the services of the MFRC to that of an advisory committee and to the study of problems, the resolution also limited its role. Without any enforcement powers, the MFRC had to rely on its ability to persuade people to change their prejudiced views and discriminatory practices.

The committee was to be composed of one hundred members, although the number sometimes fluctuated slightly due to resignations and new appointments. Members sat as representatives from various civic and social clubs, religious denominations and organizations, social agencies, black organizations, newspapers and radio stations, labor organizations, business and industry, the public schools, and colleges and universities. By forming a relatively large committee and basing appointments on organizational affiliation, those active in the planning of the MFRC hoped to achieve broad representation in order to reach the "essential roots of the community" and to ensure the participation of all groups.[16] The appointments to the MFRC also indicated a desire to recruit people of some stature, as members normally headed the organizations or institutions they represented. This served to increase the rate of turnover on the committee because each time a represented organization elected a new president or chairperson that person usually replaced his or her predecessor as a member of the MFRC.[17] Between 1943 and 1946 167 people were appointed to the committee. Forty-nine were women, at least ten were blacks, and at least nine were Jews. As for the occupational makeup of the committee, social workers, educators, clergymen, doctors, lawyers, and businessmen predominated.[18]

The committee first met on December 23, 1943, and unsurprisingly issued a statement announcing that it would not function as a black advocacy group. "We are not working for the welfare of any one group," declared the committee, "but are fostering improvements in conditions, interrelations, and interplay of personalities which will safeguard the rights of all citizens."[19] And the MFRC did engage in various types of intergroup relations activities. In 1945, for instance, it helped with the resettlement in Cincinnati of Japanese Americans who had been victimized by the federal government's wartime policies. The MFRC also worked to promote "religious toleration" by participating in and sponsoring events designed to bring people with different religious backgrounds together.[20] But the committee spent most of its time on the problems that divided whites and blacks. These problems warranted close attention not only because they were most obvious and pervasive but also because they seemed most likely to spark racial violence.

The kind of crisis the infant MFRC feared developed on the night of June 5, 1944, when a group of between fifty to one hundred "men and boys" stoned a Mt. Adams home occupied by two black families who had moved into the downstairs apartment that day. The crowd threw "hundreds" of rocks and stones, which destroyed all the doors and windows and tore out the fittings of the first floor stovepipe. The two black families, reportedly the "first Negro residents" on the street, were persuaded by the police to spend the night elsewhere as a safety precaution.[21]

The situation heated up again three days later as several hundred people staged a demonstration outside the Mt. Adams home of Mrs. Cortland Bennett, a white woman who had publicly criticized the participants in the house stoning. According to Bennett's fourteen-year-old daughter, the police did nothing to disperse the demonstrators, who vented their anger by hanging an effigy of her mother. Police Lieutenant Chester Swillinger, however, claimed that the patrolmen at the scene had responded with caution for fear of provoking further hostilities.[22]

The Mt. Adams incidents caught the MFRC and the police unprepared. The MFRC took essentially no action on either incident, which indicated not a lack of concern, but the inability of a rather large and cumbersome committee, which met only once a month, to deal with emergency situations that arose without warning. The events in Mt. Adams put the MFRC in an unenviable position by simultaneously exposing its weaknesses and emphasizing the need for action. The MFRC experienced pressure from the city's safety director, Gordon Scherer, who came before the executive board on July 13, 1944, to urge its members to step up their efforts. For his part, Scherer said he had taken "all steps possible" to "quell disturbances that may arise" by making "connections" with the State Guard and the Federal Protective Service and by ordering patrolmen to "lean over backwards" to avoid prejudice.[23] Scherer in a speech delivered before the Civic Club on September 19, 1944, recognized the "racial issue" as an old problem that "never has been handled" because "white people" had "ignored" it.[24]

In an effort to address the problem, Scherer established a Race Relations Detail within the Cincinnati Police Department during the winter of 1945. The Race Relations Detail was to be called upon to deal specifically with race-related disturbances. Lieutenant Stanley R. Schrotel, a white officer who would become chief of police in 1951, headed this special unit, which also included one white officer, Henry Sandman, and one black officer, Robert Wilson. The fact that the Race Relations Detail and the MFRC shared office space in city hall brought them in almost daily contact with each other and ensured a close working relationship.[25] The MFRC also took action that would make it a more responsive body by hiring Marshall Bragdon in the summer of 1945 to serve as executive secretary of the committee. Bragdon, a native of Minneapolis and a graduate of Wesleyan University, came to Cincinnati from Springfield, Massachusetts, where he had been the literary critic for the *Springfield Republican*.[26] He was brought to the attention of the MFRC, however, through his writings and lectures on behalf of the so-called "Springfield Plan," an educational program initiated in 1939 by the Springfield public schools that enlisted the support of the entire community for the purpose of diminishing "group antagonisms" and promoting "democratic citizenship."[27] As a full-time employee of the MFRC, Bragdon's position enabled and required him to keep up on the issues and events relevant to the functions of the committee on a day-to-day basis, as well as to plan, direct, and help carry out its activities.

With Bragdon in office, the MFRC faced another potential racial crisis in 1946. On August 19, 1946, four black men stopped a young white couple who were driving through Cincinnati's predominantly black West End en route to Price Hill, a white neighborhood, and allegedly raped the woman while holding her escort at gunpoint.[28] Cincinnati whites, especially those living in Price Hill, reacted to the incident with outrage. Claiming that his own daughters had been "threatened by Negroes," the Price Hill attorney John Scanlon demanded the "right to carry arms."[29] The Eastern Hills Lions, a Price Hill club, offered the "services" of its members to "help" police "protect our women folk." With the specter of vigilantism presenting itself, the Price Hill Civic Club called for a "mass meeting" to be held on August 22.[30]

The MFRC acted to head off the threat of violence surrounding the meeting by making "personal contacts with ministers, civic leaders and others who could strike a note of common sense and moderation." On the day of the meeting the MFRC also met to discuss emergency strategy and could report that its contact people had already "revised the situation so that the Price Hill meeting was unlikely to take a racial turn."[31] This assessment proved correct: those who attended the meeting directed their scorn less against blacks than against city officials and police for failing to provide protection at the West End approaches to Price Hill.[32] To further direct attention away from the race issue, the MFRC issued a statement to the press asking Cincinnatians to refrain from blaming an "entire neighborhood or racial group" for "individual misdeeds." That the committee felt the need to encourage citizens not to associate individual criminal behavior with cultural group affiliation attested to their proclivity to see individual behavior as culturally determined. The statement also urged citizens to look beyond the crime of rape and see the need to aid West End blacks who lived under "deplorable conditions which breed poverty, disease, despair and crime."[33]

The prompt response of the MFRC, however, was only part of a concerted effort to diffuse racial tension and reduce the possibility of violence. The acting city manager, John Ellis, released statistics on rape that showed that the problem was not racial in nature nor confined to the West End. Gordon Scherer, now a member of city council, and Bleeker Marquette, executive secretary of the Better Housing League, also attempted to play down the race issue by publicly announcing their belief that slum conditions in the West End fostered crime. Black organizations issued a joint statement offering their "complete cooperation to those seeking to apprehend the criminals and bring them to justice."[34]

The effectiveness of these statements may be judged by the fact that the violence many feared never materialized. But whether or not these efforts proved the deciding factor, they did win praise from the *Ohio State News*, a Columbus-based black newspaper, which reported that both white and black "community leaders" in Cincinnati responded to the "dire threats against the community's Negroes" by taking "action on an unprecedented scale."[35]

After the crisis had subsided, the MFRC began to examine the factors that tended to fan racial flames and to seek preventative measures. The committee concluded that the local press and radio heightened tensions by their "injudicious and even hysterical" reports of the crime. Acting on this view, Marshall Bragdon and Judge Robert Gorman, who sat on the MFRC executive board, arranged a meeting in mid-September with the publishers Robert Ferger of the *Cincinnati Enquirer* and Hulbert Taft of the *Cincinnati Times-Star.*

When confronted with the issue, both Ferger and Taft agreed that the race label was an "integral part of the story" and therefore appropriate. Taft did, however, express his disapproval of the repeated use of the word "Negro" in the reports and pledged to see that it did not happen in the future. Ferger gave his assurances that similar crimes would be reported "sympathetically." In addition to gaining these concessions from Taft and Ferger, the MFRC entertained its own plan for countering racially inflammatory reporting. It proposed to secure advance support from "highly influential and key individuals who would be ready on the shortest notice to publish a statement counseling moderation, orderly democratic procedures, [and] fair play."[36]

While the West End rape proved the most threatening immediate problem the MFRC had to face in its early years, the committee was constantly called upon to address other racial incidents. Of these, charges of brutality and other forms of abuse against blacks by Cincinnati policemen received the most public attention. This issue came up at an MFRC board meeting on April 18, 1946, when board member Arnold B. Walker suggested that policemen should be provided with "training in minority problems" and the "techniques needed to meet them." In addition, he recommended that district officers call on the Race Relations Detail with greater frequency. Responding to Walker, the city safety director, Oris Hamilton, who also sat on the MFRC board, voiced his reluctance to institute race relations training for fear that the cop on the beat might come to consider himself an "expert" and try to deal with situations he could not handle. Hamilton also claimed that Walker was wrong to suggest that the police were not referring racial matters to the Race Relations Detail.[37]

Due to "many instances" of "violent and brutal treatment," however, the local NAACP "declared war on police brutality" in August 1946 by issuing a public statement charging Cincinnati law enforcers with "anti-Negro attitudes." According to the statement, the Police Trial Board, a body within the police department that heard complaints against officers, rarely returned judgments of guilty. The NAACP recommended "public trials" for officers, "colored" representation on the Police Trial Board, and "race relations" training for police.[38]

On December 31, 1946, the city manager, Wilbur N. Kellogg, further inflamed the sense of injustice felt by blacks by announcing that he found "no reason" to censure the two detectives involved in the case of Nathan Wright.[39] In late November, Wright, a black ministerial student, had been stopped for questioning by the two detectives, and afterward he accused them of using "abusive and threatening" language toward him.[40] Wright's case came before the city council law committee on January 6, 1947, and two witnesses testified that the detectives did not use abusive or threatening language in their questioning. The city manager, who attended the hearing, said that none of the testimony had persuaded him to change his original decision not to take action against the detectives.[41]

In its January 1947 board minutes, the MFRC referred to the Wright case as "our most publicized headache." This short phrase conveyed much about the attitude of the committee. Though the MFRC hoped to see an end to police misconduct and supported race relations training for officers, it thought that the publicity surrounding the Wright case contributed to racial tension and therefore represented another obstacle to the promotion of tolerance among groups. This view predominated on the MFRC not only in response to the Wright case but in response to any divisive issue confronting the committee, which normally preferred to work quietly behind the scenes. Nonetheless, the MFRC believed that some positive signs emerged out of the Wright case. The case, asserted the MFRC, helped develop better "cooperation and consultation" between police and "leading citizens" within the black community, and it led Safety Director Hamilton to promise that in the future police training would include information on "human relations."[42]

At best, the optimism of the MFRC proved premature. Many of the same issues involved in the Wright case resurfaced with the case of Haney Bradley, a black man who was beaten by two policemen and charged with disorderly conduct in June 1947. Judge William D. Alexander, who heard Bradley's case, dismissed the disorderly conduct charge and asserted that "there was no cause for the officers to beat this defendant."[43] Despite the ruling of the court, Safety Director Hamilton announced in August that the police department hearing on the Bradley case led him to conclude that there was "no reason" to take "disciplinary action" against the officers.[44]

Hamilton's announcement prompted disgruntled representatives of the Council of Churches, the NAACP, the Woman's City Club, the Jewish Community Council, and the West End Civic League to send a joint letter to the city council, which planned to review Bradley's case. The letter criticized police procedure on the grounds that the hearing was "held in secret" and that Bradley's counsel and "other interested persons" were not "permitted to attend." In addition, it charged Safety Director Hamilton and the chief of police with acting primarily to "protect" the officers while showing "little interest in social attitudes and tensions in the community."[45]

The MFRC decided not to sign the letter, though encouraged to do so by executive board member Richard Bluestein, who lent his signature as a representative of the Jewish Community Council. The MFRC board minutes did not state the reason for not endorsing the letter, but the decision attested to the committee's disposition to avoid taking a definite stand in the interest of impartiality. In this case, however, Bluestein "urged" the MFRC to take "some action," which prompted Marshall Bragdon to suggest providing instruction in "race relations" for the "rookie" officers then in training.[46] As a result, the MFRC brought in the New York University psychology professor Howard Lane, who had worked with the Detroit Police Department, to give a talk to the young officers in early October.[47] Lane's presentation, however, was a one-time event, thus leaving unresolved the question of instituting race relations training as a regular part of police instruction.

The city council reviewed the Bradley case in November and cleared the two policemen of brutality charges. But it also called for public hearings of citizen complaints against officers, "conferences" between the police and the black community, and race relations training. The MFRC expressed its willingness to help "implement" the conferences and the training "if called upon" to do so, thus leaving the initiative to the police department. In September 1948, however, approximately eight months after the city council hearing, the MFRC lamented the fact that the police had taken no action toward beginning either the conferences or the training.[48] The lack of effort on the part of the police department should perhaps not have been surprising given the evidence of racism among some of its upper echelons. For instance, during the Bradley hearing it was discovered that Assistant Police Chief William C. Adams had hung on his office wall a cartoon that depicted "the body of a gorilla and the head of a Negro Man" and carried the caption, "Us'ns Brutalized."[49]

Police brutality represented only one manifestation of the prejudice and discrimination that permeated Cincinnati society. In Cincinnati no hospitals would provide convalescent care for blacks or accept them into nurses' training programs. Neither the Cincinnati Conservatory of Music nor the local carpenters' and bricklayers' unions admitted blacks.[50] Restrictive covenants effectively prevented blacks from living in certain areas. In addition, blacks were discriminated against at public pools, skating rinks, the Coney Island Amusement Park, and restaurants.[51]

In October 1945, some Cincinnati blacks and whites set out to change these conditions by forming the Citizen's Committee for Human Rights (CCHR), which became a Congress of Racial Equality

(CORE) affiliate.[52] The CCHR challenged discriminatory policies directly by sending its members out in interracial groups to eat in the major downtown restaurants. By December 1945 blacks were eating at over ten such restaurants on a regular basis. While it appears that this visitation campaign met with few problems at most establishments, the manager of the Mills Restaurant proved hostile to change. He tried to discourage black customers by "embarrassing them and by openly predicting 'trouble' from white patrons."[53]

Believing that the manager was attempting to incite racial conflict, Arnold B. Walker brought the matter before the MFRC executive board on November 15, 1945, asking for "clarification of the permissible role of the Police Race Relations Detail in such situations." Lieutenant Schrotel, the head of the detail, asserted that the police had "virtually no power except where a law had actually been violated."[54] The manager of Mills did not deny blacks service, which would have been a violation of the Ohio law, but tried to intimidate them into going elsewhere.[55] Mayor Stewart, who was present at the meeting, said that although he regretted "prejudice and discrimination," such problems "could not be reached by law but by gradual education of public opinion."[56] Indeed, the law proved ineffective because juries would not convict those charged with discrimination. For instance, a Cincinnati jury deliberated a full "five minutes" before acquitting Happy Watson, a waitress employed by Graeters Ice Cream Store, on charges that she refused service to several blacks in July 1946. Moreover, no Cincinnatian had ever been convicted under the law though numerous cases had been tried.[57]

Some MFRC board members "expressed disappointment" concerning the reluctance of the police to involve themselves in cases of restaurant discrimination, but others accepted it and took the position that the problem more appropriately came within the jurisdiction of the MFRC than the police. Marshall Bragdon suggested that Claude Courter, an MFRC executive board member and the superintendent of the Cincinnati public schools, should be "empowered" to appoint a "small committee" to monitor the "situation," but "no formal action was taken."[58] The unwillingness of the MFRC and police to take decisive action made Walker feel like he was "fighting a losing battle,"[59] but he continued to pressure the MFRC. On December 20, 1945, he requested that the committee hold a conference with representatives of the Citizen's Committee for Human Rights, the NAACP, and the Division of Negro Welfare to "discuss the next stage of the current restaurant-visiting campaign by Negroes and to foster the most peaceful possible solution of the frictions and difficulties incident to the visitation." This caused a stir among MFRC board members, several of whom "emphasized that our Committee must not take sides in the controversy, nor even appear to; that our effectiveness lay in consultation with all parties concerned." With its position established, the executive board passed a motion authorizing Marshall Bragdon to meet with the aforementioned organizations as an "impartial conciliator" and to confer with the restaurant managers as well.[60]

Though neither the board minutes nor reports indicate what resulted from these meetings, the stance of the MFRC on restaurant discrimination said much about its workings. By stressing that its role was limited to impartial mediation, the MFRC reaffirmed its function as a committee formed to "promote tolerance" among various groups, which, as conceived by its creators and members, prohibited it from advocating the rights of blacks as a separate group.

The same views characterized the attempts of the MFRC to deal with employment discrimination. Of all the issues that needed attention in 1944, the MFRC put top priority on "adequate and continuing employment," which it considered the "most effective insurance for improving relations among races, among religious groups and between labor and management."[61] Given this view, in April 1944 the executive board requested that John Baker, chairman of the MFRC industrial relations committee and director of the War Manpower Commission in Cincinnati, begin studying postwar employment prospects and problems with special emphasis on job opportunities for blacks and women. On August 23, 1945, Baker reported that since VJ day "reconversion employment" had begun and that "some firms" were hiring more blacks than they had during the war. Thus he found the employment picture in Cincinnati to be "much brighter than anticipated." This, however, seemed to hold true for men only because Baker expected unemployment to rise among both black and white women.[62]

Although Baker saw reason for optimism, at least with respect to job prospects for black men, racially discriminatory hiring practices remained a problem in Cincinnati. In March 1945 the federal Fair Employment Practices Committee (FEPC) held hearings on discrimination cases against the Crosley Corporation, the F. H. Lawson Company, the Baldwin Company, the Streitmann Biscuit Company, and Victor Electric Products. During the hearings spokespersons for the companies defended their practices by claiming that white employees would walk off the job if forced to work with blacks.[63] This was not an unfounded concern. In June 1944 about fifteen thousand white workers at the Wright Aeronautical Corporation had gone on strike when the company attempted to integrate its machine shop.[64] Other so called "hate strikes" occurred in 1945 at Delco Products and the Lunkenheimer Company. To deal with such problems, in May 1945 the MFRC pledged to seek the cooperation of the War Manpower Commission and the FEPC in "anticipating situations of racial tension by determining in advance which plants contemplate adopting policies of complete utilization of manpower" (that is, integration). Upon identifying such companies, the MFRC planned to offer management and labor unions its "services," which consisted of providing "educational material, speakers and other mediums to prepare" for integration.[65]

The MFRC also began meeting with companies that had initiated integration programs in order to collect information that might prove useful in convincing other companies to do the same. The MFRC conferred with Stacy Brothers Gas Construction Company, Cambridge Tile Manufacturing, Schaible Manufacturing, and Pressler's Cafeteria, each of which began hiring blacks either because of a "manpower shortage" or at the "insistence" of the FEPC. These companies claimed that, while white workers at first voiced "opposition," integration resulted in "no particular difficulty." In addition, the MFRC met with Cincinnati Milling Machine officials, who said their company hired blacks as a matter of "policy" but "limited Negro employees to definite job categories and restricted upgrading."[66]

When approaching companies about black employment, the MFRC, in accordance with its desire to minimize any tensions associated with racial issues, favored gradualism and discretion. In large measure, the committee placed its hopes for increasing the "quality of Negro employment" on meetings between local employers and Homer Lunken, an MFRC executive board member and vice president of the integrated Lunkenheimer Company.[67] Lunken seemed the appropriate person to undertake such a mission because those he met knew they would not be "put on the spot." Lunken believed that employers who feared "trouble" from their employees should not be pushed along "too quickly," thus a "gradual give-and-take" characterized his meetings.[68] By April 1947, approximately six months after Lunken began conferring with businessmen, he had achieved "heartening progress though on a small scale."[69]

While the MFRC approached employment problems with caution and apparently met with little success, some black Cincinnatians adopted a more aggressive style. In 1946 the West End Civic League, "a Negro job seeking group," began approaching the white owners of businesses in the predominantly black West End in hopes of persuading them to hire black workers.[70] The members of the West End Civic League used diplomacy first, but if that failed they resorted to picketing and distributing handbills outside those businesses that practiced discrimination. After having been subjected to such tactics, the owners of Stein Department Store and Laurel Cleaners called on the MFRC for help. Marshall Bragdon responded by bringing the disputing parties together for negotiations.[71] Bragdon, however, did not particularly like the role he played in these meetings because he felt it put the MFRC in the "middle of a crossfire." He also disliked the pressure tactics of the West End Civic League. Nonetheless, he recognized black employment needs and considered it the "duty" of the MFRC to serve as an "impartial yet sympathetic channel." The negotiations achieved some success: both owners agreed to hire one black worker. Considering Bragdon's discomfort with his role, he was relieved that neither the West End Civic League nor the businessmen accused the MFRC of "unfairness."[72]

That same year the West End Civic League also pressured the Central Five Cents to One Dollar Store into hiring four blacks, which prompted all the white saleswomen to quit. To Bragdon this substantiated his judgement about West End Civic League tactics. He felt that "if the developments had not come so fast, we and other parties interested in the situation might have averted this exodus."[73]

The MFRC viewed its meetings with businessmen to discuss discriminatory hiring practices as an educational endeavor. The MFRC hoped to persuade people to change their behavior by changing their attitudes through education. While virtually every activity of the committee contained an educational element, it also sponsored a variety of programs and events designed solely for that purpose.

In September 1944, for example, the MFRC sponsored its first Friendly Relations Week, which became an annual event. During Friendly Relations Week the MFRC solicited the organizations represented on the committee and all racial and religious groups to participate in programs designed to promote the virtues of tolerance.[74] Friendly Relations Week illustrated two points about MFRC educational programs: they were targeted to reach a broad spectrum of the population and intended to reduce tension between different groups. When Theodore M. Berry requested in August 1944 that the committee sponsor a race relations institute, the executive board thought that such an "institute should not be confined to racial discussions."[75] The MFRC attempted to resolve this matter by including in its Friendly Relations Week program an "Institute on

Propaganda, Housing and Jobs" to address the problems faced by blacks.[76] The same kind of issue surfaced again during preparations for Friendly Relations Week in 1946. The MFRC publicity committee proposed to promote the event using the slogan "Lets be Friendly" accompanied by a photograph of a black hand and a white hand clasped together. This set off a debate because, in Marshall Bragdon's opinion, such a photo would give the "erroneous impression that the Friendly Relations Committee is preoccupied solely with the Negro-White problem."[77] The committee finally decided to hold a photo contest and leave "it to the photographers to seek pictorial instances of understanding."[78]

In 1948 the MFRC was the local sponsor of the Freedom Train, a privately funded event initiated by U.S. Attorney General Tom C. Clark, who thought it would be a good idea to send some of the most famous documents in American history across the country by train and allow the public to view them as a means of promoting "better citizenship."[79] The Freedom Train stopped in Cincinnati August 6–7, and an estimated ten thousand people turned out on the first day.[80]

While busy preparing for the Freedom Train during the summer of 1948, the MFRC also engaged in a budget dispute with the city council. The disagreement developed after the council finance committee refused to grant a supplement to the 1948 MFRC budget to pay proposed cost of living increases for the staff. Councilman Charles P. Taft suggested that the MFRC search for "outside" funding if it insisted on raising salaries. This did not please most of the executive board members, who thought that the city should pay "adequate salaries" if it "recognized the need for MFRC." They also voiced the concern that dependence on outside funds might "bias" the "operation" of the committee.[81]

After some wrangling back and forth, the council agreed to the budget supplement in October.[82] But it also proposed to alter the relationship between the city and the MFRC. The committee had existed as an arm of the city government and received its funds out of the mayor's budget. The council wanted to change all this by paying the MFRC $15,000 in a "lump sum" to perform "certain specific services for the city" on a contract basis. Some executive board members expressed reservations about this plan because they considered it crucial that the committee retain its identification with the city so as not to undermine its official status.[83] Despite such worries, the new setup was established in January 1949. Marshall Bragdon assured those concerned about the committee's official status that it was "still the Mayor's committee." The mayor would continue to appoint members, and there would be "little overt change so far as the general public is concerned."[84] As part of the new arrangement the MFRC incorporated as a not-for-profit organization on January 11, 1949.[85]

Incorporation and the new relationship to the city, however, did not change the functions of the MFRC, or its approach to solving problems. The committee continued in its preference for working behind the scenes and chose not to take any stand that in the view of the members might be interpreted as showing partiality toward blacks as a group or lead to confrontations that might increase racial tension. And, of course, the general problems remained the same—prejudice and discrimination against blacks.

The efforts of the MFRC to combat racial prejudice and discrimination bore the marks of the basic ideas from which the committee sprung. The tendency to view society as divided into different groups resulted in the creation of a committee designed to hear the complaints of all groups but not take sides in disputes between them. Thus the MFRC would not take an advocacy role for the rights of blacks or any other single racial, religious, or ethnic group. In essence, the committee intended to treat all groups equally. Treating all groups equally, however, implied that they were in fact equal, yet most of the problems addressed by the MFRC could be attributed to the unequal social status of blacks. During its early years the MFRC never seemed to recognize this contradiction between the assumptions under which it operated and social reality. But it must be remembered that the primary purpose of the MFRC was to reduce tension between groups in hopes of preventing violent upheaval. This function required that the committee work toward ending prejudice and discrimination, but it also dictated the approach to such work. The fear of taking any action that might increase tension resulted in the adoption of a cautious and gradualistic approach, which limited the role the MFRC would play.

To expect the MFRC or the similar committees that were formed in other cities during the 1940s to take the kind of militant action advocated in the 1960s is to ignore the notions that prevailed in the United States during the second quarter of the twentieth century. The pluralistic mode of thought rested on the premise that cultural group affiliation determined the character of individuals, a premise that posited the group as the basic unit of social concern, and one that supported a separate but equal doctrine in social relations. The MFRC did not challenge the conventional wisdom but, rather, reflected it. In a period that tended to view society as pluralistic, the central problem became how to get the diverse groups that comprised the city to

cooperate in the interest of securing the welfare of the city as a whole.
This depended, among other things, upon the maintenance of some
measure of "toleration" for racial, religious, and ethnic diversity and
the prevention of intergroup conflict. Not until the emergence in the
1950s of a new mode of thought, one that placed primacy on the
autonomous individual rather than the group, did the notion of
cultural group determinism come under serious attack for inhibiting
autonomous individuals in their pursuit of self-advancement and
self-fulfillment.[86]

Notes

1. According to a study conducted by the Social Science Institute of Fisk
University, there were at least 224 race relations or intergroup relations committees in the United States by the end of 1944. The Fisk study examined 166
of these committees and found that 13 were national, 2 regional, 16 state,
and 135 local. In addition, the study also noted that only 32 of the 166 committees were "official action committees," which meant that they had been
appointed by "mayors, city councils, boards of supervisors, governors, or
state legislatures." The rest were citizens' committees and had no official status. Of the 151 state and local committees examined, 130, or 86 percent,
were located in the North and 21, or 14 percent, were located in the South.
Moreover, only 2 of the southern committees enjoyed official status. Though
it did not state how many, the Fisk study also indicated that some of the
country's 224 committees had been in existence prior to the Detroit race riot.
This suggests a need to look beyond the riot and wartime tension in order to
explain the creation of these committees. See "Programs for Action on the
Democratic Front," *A Monthly Summary of Events and Trends in Race Re-
lations* 2 (Aug.-Sept. 1944): 23–32. Also see Lester B. Granger, "A Hopeful
Sign in Race Relations," *Survey Graphic* 33 (Nov. 1944): 455, and Robert C.
Weaver, "Whither Northern Race Relations Committees?" *Phylon* 5 (Third
Quarter, 1944): 208.

2. Harvard Sitkoff, "Racial Militancy and Interracial Violence in the Sec-
ond World War," *Journal of American History* 58 (Dec. 1971): 678–79;
Neil A. Wynn, *The Afro-American and the Second World War* (New York:
Holmes and Meier Publishers, 1976), 108; Byron Richard Skinner, "The
Double 'V': The Impact of World War II on Black America" (Ph.D. diss.,
University of California, Berkeley, 1978), 141–42; Patricia L. Adams,
"Fighting for Democracy in St. Louis: Civil Rights during World War II,"
Missouri Historical Review 80 (Oct. 1985): 73–74. For a more sympathetic
interpretation, but one that also views the race relations and intergroup re-
lations committees created in the 1940s from the perspective of the civil
rights movement, see Howard Allan Droker, "The Seattle Civic Unity Com-

mittee and the Civil Rights Movement, 1944–1964" (Ph.D. diss., University
of Washington, 1974). For an account that charges black leaders during the
Second World War with following a "conservative approach to the solution
of racial problems," see Lee Finkle, "The Conservative Aims of Militant
Rhetoric: Black Protest during World War II," *Journal of American History*
60 (Dec. 1973): 692.

3. Sitkoff, "Racial Militancy and Interracial Violence," 670–71, 678:
Skinner, "The Double 'V,' " 108, 119, 124, 130, 141; Wynn, *The Afro-
American and the Second World War*, 60, 108; Howard A. Droker, "Seattle
Race Relations during the Second World War," *Pacific Northwest Quarterly*
67 (Oct. 1976): 163–69.

4. For a discussion of the urban dimension of this phenomenon, see Andrea Tuttle Kornbluh, "The Bowl of Promise: Social Welfare Planners, Cultural Pluralism, and the Metropolitan Community, 1911–1953" (Ph.D. diss.,
University of Cincinnati, 1988), and idem, "Women's City Club: A Pioneer
in Race Relations," *Queen City Heritage* 44 (Summer 1986): 21. For an account that grapples with the notion of cultural pluralism as it applied during
the World War II period, see Phillip Gleason, "Americans All: World War II
and the Shaping of American Identity," *Review of Politics* 43 (Oct. 1981):
483–518.

5. Such a climate was rather different than the one that prevailed in the
South, where public policy, as identified with the existence of de jure segregation, and public attitudes served to discourage civil rights activism during
the 1940s. On the differences between the North and the South regarding the
issue of segregation, see Gunnar Myrdal, *An American Dilemma: The Negro
Problem and Modern Democracy* (New York: Harper and Brothers, 1944),
579–580, 599–603; Richard Polenberg, *One Nation Divisible: Class,
Race and Ethnicity in the United States Since 1938*, Pelican History of the
United States, vol. 7 (New York: Viking Press, 1980; repr., 1981), 25–29;
Richard Kluger, *Simple Justice: The History of Brown v. Board of Education
and Black America's Struggle for Equality, 1954–1980* (New York: Hill and
Wang, 1981), 5, 8. On the relative difficulties of engaging in civil rights activism in the North and South during the 1940s, see Thomas R. Brooks,
*Walls Come Tumbling Down: A History of the Civil Rights Movement,
1940–1970* (Englewood Cliffs, N.J.: Prentice Hall, 1974), 41; August Meier
and Elliott Rudwick, *CORE: A Study in the Civil Rights Movement, 1942–
1968* (Urbana: University of Illinois Press, 1975), 23, 26–27, 34–36.

6. *Cincinnati Times-Star,* 9 July 1943.

7. *Cincinnati Post,* 4 Jan. 1979; newspaper clippings on William
Lovelace, Newspaper Obituary Collection, Cincinnati Historical Society.
William Lovelace was the first black to be elected, in 1965, as a municipal
court judge in Cincinnati.

8. "Conference with the Honorable James Stewart, Mayor of Cincinnati," 8 July 1943, 1–2, Urban League of Greater Cincinnati Papers (hereafter cited as ULGC), box 24, folder 6, Cincinnati Historical Society,
Manuscripts Collection; *Cincinnati Times-Star,* 9 July 1943.

9. Though the mayor did not seem particularly alarmed, the recommendations presented to him by black leaders reflected a fear that race riots might erupt in Cincinnati. In this regard, the Division of Negro Welfare of the Cincinnati Community Chest received numerous inquiries from nervous citizens, prompting Arnold B. Walker to examine the issue of race riots in the August 1943 edition of the *Division of Negro Welfare Bulletin*. Walker asserted that he did not believe Cincinnati would experience a race riot but warned his readers not to become "complacent" because there was evidence of "interracial pressure generated by wartime conditions." In particular, he noted that a "great" number of whites from the "hill section of Kentucky, Tennessee," and other "southern areas" had migrated to Cincinnati seeking employment in war industries. He considered these people a "problem" because of his feelings that they brought southern racial prejudices with them and thus contributed to the racial tension that existed in the city. While the potential for conflict seemed to exist in the changing composition of the population, Walker claimed that certain factors that had contributed to rioting in Detroit did not exist in Cincinnati. Compared to Detroit, which had "mushroomed to large proportions," Cincinnati experienced slower growth. Nor had an "organized movement" to suppress blacks developed in Cincinnati "as in Detroit." Nonetheless, in Walker's view, the "dangerous fact" about racial violence was that it often began over some "trivial incident" rather than from a "broad movement or trend that can be checked." Arnold B. Walker, "Will There be a Race Riot in Cincinnati?" *Division of Negro Welfare Bulletin* (Aug. 1943): 1–2, 5, ULGC, box 24, folder 6.

10. "Notes on Mayor Stewart's Committee," 7 Oct. 1943, 1, ULGC, box 24, folder 5; "What The Frontiers Club is:—," (n.d.), 1, ULGC, box 13, folder 6; *Ohio State News,* 6 July 1946.

11. "Notes on Mayor Stewart's Committee"; *Cincinnati Post,* 8 Oct. 1943; *Cincinnati Times-Star,* 8 Oct. 1943.

12. Unsigned letter to Mayor Stewart, 10 Nov. 1943, ULGC, box 24, folder 5.

13. *Cincinnati Enquirer,* 8 Oct. 1943.

14. "Notes on Mayor Stewart's Committee."

15. Cincinnati City Council Resolution, 17 Nov. 1943, Cincinnati Human Relations Committee Papers (hereafter cited as CHRC), box 67, folder 4, University of Cincinnati Libraries, Rare Books and Archives; Cincinnati, *City Bulletin,* 17 (23 Nov. 1943): 2.

16. Statement by the Cincinnati Friendly Relations Committee, 30 Dec. 1943, 1, CHRC, box 7, folder 1; memorandum from William A. A. Castellini to Mr. Johnson, 3 Jan. 1944, 1, CHRC, box 7, folder 1.

17. MFRC board minutes, 24 May 1945, 1, CHRC, box 4, folder 2.

18. MFRC rosters, CHRC, box 6, folder 1.

19. "Mayor Stewart's Friendly Relations Committee," 23 Dec. 1943, 1–2, ULGC, box 24, folder 5.

20. MFRC board minutes, 15 Mar. 1945, 1, CHRC, box 4, folder 2; idem, 20 Dec. 1945, 1, CHRC, box 4, folder 2; idem, 16 Nov. 1944, 1, CHRC, box 4, folder 1; idem, 24 Dec. 1944, 1, CHRC, box 4, folder 1.

21. *Cincinnati Times-Star,* 10 June 1944; *Cincinnati Post,* 6 June 1944; *Cincinnati Enquirer,* 6 June 1944.

22. *Cincinnati Times-Star,* 10 June 1944.

23. MFRC board minutes, 13 July 1944, 2, CHRC, box 4, folder 1.

24. *Cincinnati Times-Star,* 19 Sept. 1944; *Cincinnati Post,* 19 Sept. 1944.

25. *CIO SUN,* 2 Feb. 1945; Arnold B. Walker, "Race Relations in Metropolitan Cincinnati," 1 Mar. 1945, 1, ULGC, box 39, folder; newspaper clipping on Stanley Schrotel, Newspaper Obituary Collection, Cincinnati Historical Society.

26. MFRC board minutes, 23 Aug. 1945, 1, CHRC, box 4, folder 2, "MFRC Monthly Reports," 23 Aug. 1945, 1–6, CHRC, box 6, folder 1; *Cincinnati Enquirer,* 11 Jan. 1987.

27. Biographical notes on Marshall Bragdon, 1955, 1, CHRC, box 25, folder 8; Clarence I. Chatto and Alice L. Halligan, *The Story of the Springfield Plan* (New York: Hinds, Haydon and Eldredge, 1945), vii, xiii. Also see Alexander Alland and James Waterman Wise, *The Springfield Plan* (New York: The Viking Press, 1945).

28. *Cincinnati Enquirer,* 20 Aug. 1946.

29. *Cincinnati Times-Star,* 21 Aug. 1946.

30. *Cincinnati Enquirer,* 21 Aug. 1946.

31. MFRC board Minutes, 22 Aug. 1946, 1, CHRC, box 4, folder 3.

32. *Cincinnati Post,* 23 Aug. 1946.

33. *Cincinnati Enquirer,* 23 Aug. 1946.

34. *Cincinnati Post,* 23 Aug. 1946; *Cincinnati Enquirer,* 23 Aug. 1946.

35. *Ohio State News,* 7 Sept. 1946.

36. MFRC board minutes, 19 Sept. 1946, 1, CHRC, box 4, folder 3. It should be noted that the third Cincinnati daily, the *Cincinnati Post,* refrained from race-labeling the story.

37. MFRC board minutes, 18 Apr. 1946, 2, CHRC, box 4, folder 3.

38. *Cincinnati Post,* 19 Aug. 1946; *Ohio State News,* 3 Aug. 1946.

39. *Cincinnati Times-Star,* 31 Dec. 1946.

40. *Cincinnati Enquirer,* 1 Jan. 1947.

41. *Cincinnati Post,* 3 Jan. 1947.

42. MFRC board minutes, 16 Jan. 1947, 1, CHRC, box 4, folder 4.

43. *Cincinnati Enquirer,* 11 July 1947.

44. *Cincinnati Enquirer,* 22 Aug. 1947.

45. Letter to the city council relating to the Bradley case, n.d., 1–3, ULGC, box 4, folder 7.

46. MFRC board minutes, 9 Sept. 1947, 3, CHRC, box 4, folder 4. Bluestein's personal correspondence indicated that he was frustrated by the committee's unwillingness to act. Letter from Solomon Andhil Fineberg to Richard Bluestein, 13 Feb. 1946, Jewish Community Relations Committee Papers, box 26, folder 3, Hebrew Union College, American Jewish Archives.

47. MFRC monthly reports, 3 Sept.–6 Oct. 1947, 3, CHRC, box 6, folder 4; MFRC board minutes, 14 Oct. 1947, 2, CHRC, box 4, folder 4.

48. Letter from G. Barret Rich, of the Racial Amity Committee, to division members, 14 Nov. 1947, ULGC, box 4, folder 7; MFRC monthly

reports, 3 Feb., 3 Mar. 1948, 1–2, CHRC, box 6, folder 3; MFRC board minutes, 21 Sept. 1948, 2, CHRC, box 4, folder 5.

49. *Cincinnati Post,* 18 Dec. 1947.

50. Arnold B. Walker, "Race Relations in Metropolitan Cincinnati," 28 Mar. 1948, 6, ULGC, box 39, folder 3; MFRC board minutes, 11 July 1946, 1, CHRC, box 4, folder 3; idem, 22 Nov. 1946, CHRC, box 4, folder 3; *Cincinnati Post,* 6 Aug. 1948.

51. MFRC board minutes, 14 Oct. 1947, 4, CHRC, box 4, folder 4; idem, 19 Sept. 1946, 2, CHRC, box 4, folder 3; *Cincinnati Times-Star,* 19 Feb. 1946; Arnold B. Walker, "Race Relations in Metropolitan Cincinnati," 31 Oct. 1944, 6, ULGC, box 39, folder 2.

52. Meier and Rudwick, *CORE,* 44, 58.

53. Walker, "Race Relations in Metropolitan Cincinnati," 31 Oct. 1944, 3, and 3 Dec. 1945, 4, ULGC, box 39, folder 3; MFRC board minutes, 15 Nov. 1945, 2, CHRC, box 4, folder 2.

54. MFRC board minutes, 15 Nov. 1945, 2.

55. Walker, "Restaurant Fight in Cincinnati," n.d., 3, ULGC, box 40, folder 10. An Ohio law passed in 1884 and amended in 1894 stipulated that "all persons" were "entitled to the full enjoyment of the accommodations, advantages, facilities, and privileges of inns, restaurants, eating houses, barber shops, public conveyances on land, water, theatres and all other places of public accommodations and amusement." As quoted in Frank U. Quillin, *The Color Line in Ohio* (Ann Arbor: George Wahr, 1913), 104.

56. MFRC board minutes, 15 Nov. 1945, 2.

57. *Cincinnati Enquirer,* 27 May 1947; *Ohio State News,* 20 July 1946; *Cincinnati Post,* 6 Aug. 1948.

58. MFRC board minutes, 15 Nov. 1945, 2.

59. Walker, "Race Relations in Metropolitan Cincinnati," 3 Dec. 1945, 5.

60. MFRC board minutes, 20 Dec. 1945, 2, CHRC, box 4, folder 2.

61. MFRC monthly reports, May 1944, 1, CHRC, box 6, folder 1.

62. MFRC board minutes, 21 Apr. 1944, 2, CHRC, box 4, folder 1; idem, 23 Aug. 1945, 2, CHRC, box 4, folder 2.

63. *CIO Sun,* 23 Mar. 1945. Also, see *Cincinnati Enquirer,* 28 Feb. 1945.

64. Robert B. Fairbanks and Zane L. Miller, "The Martial Metropolis: Housing, Planning, and Race in Cincinnati, 1940–55," in *The Martial Metropolis: U.S. Cities in War and Peace,* ed. Robert W. Lotchin (New York: Praeger Publishers, 1984), 196.

65. MFRC monthly reports, May 1945, 1, 4, CHRC, box 4, folder 6.

66. Ibid., 2–3.

67. MFRC board minutes, 24 Oct. 1946, 1, CHRC, box 4, folder 3; MFRC monthly reports, July 11, 1946, 1, CHRC, box 6, folder 2.

68. MFRC board minutes, 24 Oct. 1946, 2, CHRC, box 4, folder 3.

69. MFRC board minutes, 8 Apr. 1947, 1, CHRC, box 4, folder 4. Unfortunately, the minutes did not provide any specific details about Lunken's "progress."

70. MFRC board minutes, 18 Apr. 1946, 1, CHRC, box 4, folder 3.

71. Ibid., 4 June 1946, 2.

72. MFRC monthly reports, 4 June 1946, 4, CHRC, box 6, folder 2.

73. Ibid., 11 July 1946, 1.

74. MFRC board minutes, 14 Aug. 1944, 1, CHRC, box 4, folder 1.

75. Ibid.

76. *Cincinnati Post*, 23 Sept. 1944.

77. MFRC board minutes, 21 Feb. 1946, 1–2, CHRC, box 4, folder 3.

78. Ibid., 21 Mar. 1946, 2.

79. Ibid., 8 June 1948, 2.

80. *Cincinnati Post*, 7 Aug. 1948.

81. MFRC board minutes, 13 July 1948, 1, CHRC, box 4, folder 5; ibid., 3 Aug. 1948, 1.

82. Ibid., 12 Oct. 1948, 1.

83. Ibid., 28 Dec. 1948, 1.

84. Ibid.

85. MFRC board Articles of Incorporation, 11 Jan. 1949, 1–3, CHRC, box 67, folder 4.

86. For a fuller discussion of this new mode of thought, see Zane L. Miller and Bruce Tucker, "The New Urban Politics: Planning and Development in Cincinnati, 1954–1988," in *Snowbelt Cities*, ed. Richard M. Bernard (Bloomington: Indiana University Press, 1990), 91–106.

11

NINA MJAGKIJ

Behind the Scenes:
The Cincinnati Urban League,
1948–63

"You can holler, protest, march, picket, demonstrate, but somebody must be able to sit in on the strategy conferences and plot a course. There must be the strategists, the researchers, and the professionals to carry out a program. That's our role," said Whitney M. Young, Jr., in 1964 as executive director of the National Urban League.[1]

During the 1950s and 1960s American society underwent tremendous changes as African Americans waged an aggressive fight for their civil rights. Scholars of the civil rights movement have focused largely on the well-publicized activities of the Congress of Racial Equality (CORE), the National Association for the Advancement of Colored People (NAACP), the Southern Christian Leadership Conference (SCLC), the Student Nonviolent Coordinating Committee (SNCC), and the charismatic role of Martin Luther King, Jr.[2] Sit-ins, protest marches, freedom rides, picket lines, and boycotts in the South have attracted the attention of most scholars, while only little consideration has been given to civil rights activities in the North. Has this single-minded focus on the civil rights battles of the South caused us to miss a vital struggle taking place in the North?

This chapter examines the efforts of the Urban League to improve race relations in Cincinnati during the turbulent years of the civil rights movement. While the struggle in the South received much media coverage, the Cincinnati Urban League utilized a behind-the-scenes, or nonconfrontational, approach as a strategy for social change. Considering confrontation dysfunctional, the Urban League resorted to quiet negotiations at the office level rather than activism oriented toward maximizing the visibility of racial inequality. This chapter examines the use and effectiveness of the league's technique in the fields of employment, education, and recreation from 1948 to 1963.

The Cincinnati Urban League (CUL) was founded on September 24, 1948.[3] A major concern of the league during its initial years was the development of job opportunities for Cincinnati's steadily increasing black population.[4] In 1948 one-half of Cincinnati's companies with more than 1,500 employers did not hire African Americans, in part because unions excluded them from their ranks, while some companies employed African Americans exclusively in menial positions.[5] In the early 1950s, for example, the local telephone company employed almost 3,000 Cincinnatians, of whom no more than 50 were black, all of them "confined exclusively to labor categories."[6]

Immediately after its inception the league began to serve as mediator between black workers and the Queen City's business community. As early as December 1948, the CUL developed a program of industrial relations headed by Francis L. Dowdell, a graduate of the Atlanta University School of Social Science and Wilberforce University.[7] The industrial relations program under Dowdell became the focus of CUL activities during its early years. Dowdell consulted with business and industry, labor organizations, and public and private agencies and urged them to hire African Americans and upgrade opportunities based on merit.[8] Moreover, the industrial secretary recruited qualified African Americans and prepared them for placement "in newly created work situations."[9] In the five-year period between 1948 and 1953 the CUL made 523 so-called pilot placements. Each participant was "handpicked" to assure that desegregation would occur gradually and in a nondisruptive manner.[10]

Illustrative of the league's technique were its first attempts at desegregating the work force of Cincinnati's department stores. In early September 1948 the league approached the Shillito department store about the employment of African Americans as sales personnel. The league encountered opposition, however, and Executive Secretary Joseph A. Hall "concluded that the time was not quite ripe for such a move."[11] Nevertheless, Hall and Dowdell decided to start work on the problem by establishing close relations with the people in power. In the case of the Shillito department store, they were able to get support from its vice president, Fred Lazarus III, whom they placed on the board of the league.[12] The move was successful, for soon thereafter Shillito officials began discussing with the league the upgrading of qualified African Americans already employed by the store. As a result Shillito hired its first black salesperson. Dowdell concluded "the whole job was executed through the establishing of such close relationship with Fred Lazarus himself."[13]

Soon other stores followed Shillito's example. In early 1949 Dowdell reported that Ben's Department Store, with a total of 32 employees, had 11 African Americans who worked in service, general clerical, and sales capacities, while Max Clothing Store employed 9 African Americans out of a total of 19 employees.[14] In 1950 Dowdell reported that "some progress has been made. . . . three of the largest downtown department stores already have employed Negro girls as fur storage, stock and information clerks."[15]

Throughout the 1950s the league continued its program of industrial relations but also utilized its negotiation technique to desegregate and to prevent the further segregation of Cincinnati's educational and recreational facilities. In the fall of 1952 Betty Donovan, a *Cincinnati Post* reporter, sought the help of the league in the case of the three black children of the Graham family. The principal of Springmeyer School had for over three years refused to admit the Graham children and had referred them to schools in other districts. These schools also denied admission, though, because the Grahams lived in the Springmeyer district. Consequently, the children failed to attend school for one year. Then the Addyston School agreed to accept them but did not provide schoolbus transportation. After Donovan's phone call, Executive Secretary Hall visited the Grahams and confirmed Donovan's story. He then went to see Springmeyer's principal, who assured Hall that the problem was not racially motivated but one of transportation, as "schoolbus facilities could not be arranged for them [the Graham children]."[16]

Nothing came from this meeting, and on October 9, 1952, Hall called Springmeyer's principal to point out the "urgency of the Graham problem . . . in view of possible unfavorable news coverage."[17] Hall's use of this subtle pressure yielded a partial success. On October 28, the president of the Board of Education of Green Township informed Hall that all children involved in the controversy would be picked up by the Addyston School bus beginning November 1.[18]

In the Graham case Hall utilized the behind-the-scenes technique developed by the Industrial Relations Department to address educational problems of Cincinnati's black population. Instead of arousing masses, Hall appealed initially to the moral conscience of officials in key positions. If this approach failed to secure cooperation, Hall resorted to the use of subtle pressure by pointing to the possible negative effects of publicity. It was obvious, however, that the league was not prepared to intervene further and compromise its behind-the-scenes role.

Meanwhile the league began to play an active role in the desegregation of Coney Island, Cincinnati's major amusement park. In January 1952 members of the NAACP and the Cincinnati Committee on Human Rights (CCHR), an affiliate of CORE, began picketing the amusement park in protest of its exclusion of African Americans.[19] In March the CCHR decided to desegregate Coney Island during the upcoming season.[20] Initially the organization hoped to secure a conference with the park management. When this failed, members of the CCHR continued picketing outside Coney Island's downtown office at Sixth and Main while others tried to enter the park.[21] At the end of July Cincinnati's city council formed a committee to look into the racial policy of Coney.[22] In the fall the committee asked the league for help in assembling information about the situation in amusement parks in other areas of the United States. Hall wrote letters to all Urban League affiliates asking for data concerning the racial policies of private amusement parks in preparation for a possible contact with Coney Island officials.[23]

In 1953 the CCHR continued its activities against Coney Island, and as a result the State Conservation Department canceled a wildlife exhibit at the amusement park.[24] In addition, the issue was brought to the courts by the NAACP. On July 2 and 4, Ethel Fletcher, a black member of the NAACP, tried to enter Coney Island, but park officials denied her admission.

At the same time, Edward L. Schott, the president of Coney Island, became increasingly concerned with a possible economic loss due to these activities and contacted Dorothy Dolbey of the Mayor's Friendly Relations Committee (MFRC).[25] Dolbey referred him to Joseph A. Hall, and on November 19 Schott took the initiative and discussed the matter with Hall. Schott initially expressed fears that desegregating the park would lead to financial losses and spark a violent public reaction, "particularly on the parts [sic] of the few white hoodlums whom he knows frequent the park."[26] Despite these concerns, Schott called Hall in December requesting information about other amusement parks.[27]

After looking through the material Hall had gathered during the previous year, Schott met with Hall on January 21, 1954. Schott did not oppose opening the park to African Americans except for the use of Moonlight Gardens, the park's ballroom. Hall suggested that "there should not be a public announcement" of the desegregation of the park and contended "that quiet handling would be a better procedure."[28] At the end of the meeting, to secure Schott's continued confidence and cooperation, Hall assured him that their contacts were strictly off the record.[29]

Despite the apparent ease with which Schott agreed to desegregate the park, problems occurred soon afterward. At the opening of the 1954 season of Coney Island, members of the CCHR attempted to enter the park but were denied admission. By that time, too, the court case initiated by the NAACP had aroused increased publicity.[30] Throughout the court controversy negotiations between the CUL and Coney Island came to a standstill. While the league and Coney officials remained "friendly," they did not discuss "the issues."[31]

In July 1954 Ethel Fletcher was awarded an injunction against the park, allowing her to enter Coney Island.[32] The ruling applied only to her, though, and not to African Americans in general. In protest, Cincinnati ministers from various churches drew up a petition asking the park to stop its Jim Crow policy.[33] This attracted widespread publicity and was followed by another attempt by NAACP members to enter the park. In August 1954 an interracial group consisting of fifty adults and children was denied admission.[34] Public pressure grew when sixty-five clergymen issued a "Statement of Concern" urging a change in the admission policy of the park.[35]

The park's management, aroused by the publicity the court case and the resulting activities had caused, feared economic loss and eventually expressed a willingness to engage in negotiations to secure a peaceful desegregated opening for 1955. In a meeting with Hall, the park managers expressed their interest "in a solution to what could be, if not carefully planned, a serious race relations problem at the time of the 1955 park opening."[36] They agreed with Hall that "publicity, further demonstrations and fanfare were unwise in contrast to a quiet, unpublicized well-planned job".[37]

Schott proposed a "step-by-step" procedure desegregating all facilities except the pool and Moonlight Gardens in 1955. Explaining the proposal, Schott, Kiely, and Wachs claimed that "any withdrawal on the part of regular clientele would throw the park into financial reverses" because the pool and dance hall represented the "heart operations" of the park.[38] Hall reluctantly gave in. "I can see your point," he said, "and am inclined to go along with you; yet I must point out that a sound procedure would be a complete open policy once and for all."[39] Hall then suggested that Coney Island officials prepare the 1955 opening in cooperation with local civil rights groups. The park managers balked, characterizing members of some of the groups as "troublemakers." Instead they demanded to discuss the question among themselves and then call a meeting with the Urban League, the NAACP, and park representatives.[40]

The meeting never took place, however, because the park managers opposed the NAACP's insistence on involvement of groups other than the Urban League.[41] The NAACP in the meantime had combined forces with the Jewish Community Relations Committee (JCRC) and the Civil Liberties Union in order to convince the city manager, C. A. Harrell, to withhold Coney's operating license.[42] Schott rejected the intervention of these civil rights groups: "We do not propose to have Mr. Berry [NAACP] or Mr. Posner [JCRC] tell us how to run Coney Island."[43] Five days later the city safety director, Oris E. Hamilton, approved Coney's license.[44]

In April 1955, following the confrontation with the NAACP, the JCRC, and the Civil Liberties Union, Schott asked Hall for support of "a quiet opening" of Coney Island. Except for the general admission of African Americans the park's racial policy remained vague, as the management decided "not to do any specific planning relative to the swimming pool and dance pavilion until such a time a problem presents itself."[45] Hall conferred with Webster Posey, president of the local NAACP, and both agreed that the NAACP "will set up controls so that those who attend the park will be handpicked for a period."[46] Moreover, the league and the NAACP agreed to organized efforts so that "non-whites should arrive singly or in pairs."[47] After the park opening on April 30, 1955, biweekly contacts between Hall and park officials continued. While African Americans in numbers from six to twenty-five attended the amusement park, no hostile incidents were reported.[48] Only once did the park manager have to remove signs posted some distance from the park that read "Niggers don't go to Coney."[49]

Throughout the first month after the opening Hall inquired periodically about the pool policy, but Schott and the park manager, Ralph G. Wachs, remained noncommittal. Finally, on July 4, 1955, George Johnson, a black park visitor, challenged Coney's pool policy by taking a swim. The pool manager and Wachs discussed the matter with Johnson and persuaded him to withdraw from the pool. Johnson left the park without any further disturbances and the incident received no publicity in the local press.[50]

In addition to the continued segregation of the pool and dance hall, the admission of interracial groups remained a problem. Some Cincinnati companies, such as Gruen Watch, Fashion Frock, and General Electric, asked Hall about the possibility of having "mixed personnel picnics at Coney." But Schott believed it inexpedient and advised Hall to wait until later that year or until 1956.[51]

Hall's confidential behind-the-scenes negotiations prepared the way for an agreement prior to the opening of the park in 1955. To prevent economic loss through racial violence, Coney Island's management agreed to admit African Americans, and the league and the NAACP promised careful timing and selection of visitors. But the 1955 policy was only a partial victory for the league. As long as the pool and the dance hall remained segregated, Coney Island was "still unfinished business" and sure to arouse public opinion in the future.[52]

Four years later, in 1959, the pool and dance hall problem surfaced again. This time, however, the league was less successful in negotiating with Coney officials. In July, Margaret Riley informed Hall that her son and a group of friends had been denied admission to a rock and roll concert at Moonlight Gardens. Switchboard operators at the park and at Coney's downtown office had told her that African Americans would not be welcomed at Moonlight Gardens. Hall then called upon Schott, stressing "the legal implications of park representatives denying anyone the right to use a facility that is publicly advertised."[53] Schott claimed to be unaware of the specific problem but pointed out that rock and roll concerts had indeed caused "some disorder" in the past.[54] Moreover, Schott admitted that he did not like African Americans attending such concerts because of the "trouble potential in the teenage gathering."[55] Believing that the time was not right for desegregating Moonlight Gardens, Schott nevertheless agreed to think about the matter and to discuss the problem with other park officials.[56]

Three days later Schott informed Hall that the management had decided "not to consider an open policy" at the dance hall.[57] Schott, until then very cooperative, excitedly complained that Coney Island "was being focused on while other parks . . . did not even allow non-whites on their grounds."[58] Hall, eager to maintain cooperation with Schott, responded that he had inquired just "to point to possibly sound planning."[59] Schott had grown impatient, however, and ended the conversation abruptly. Hall informed Riley about the conversation and advised her about legal actions she could take, but he left the decision to her.[60] After four months of no contacts, Hall took the initiative and wrote Schott a letter assuring him that his "whole interest in Coney Island over a period of time has been progress from a race relations point of view rather than conflict."[61]

Despite earlier successes with the management of Coney Island, the incident of 1959 illustrates the major shortcoming of the league's approach. The success of its cautious behind-the-scenes technique depended largely on the cooperation of the white establishment. If mediation failed, the league, unwilling to sacrifice its good relationships with many key people in the community, was not prepared to intervene further.

Two years later the amusement park once more became the focus of civil rights attention. This time, however, the league was not only mediator between the black community and white park officials but also between the various civil rights groups involved in the struggle for Coney's desegregation. On April 29, 1961, a black couple sent by the Congress of Racial Equality was refused admission to Moonlight Gardens. Schott, "excited and disturbed," called Hall, indicating his "refusal to talk with CORE and NAACP officials."[62] Hall believed this to be "a decided mistake" and urged Schott to talk to the groups in question.[63]

But, as the conversation later revealed, the roadblock was not Schott, who had been ill for several months, but Wachs, who in the meantime handled the park.[64] Wachs, "fearful of economic loss, troublemakers, and the future of the park," had refused to see CORE members.[65] This, Hall observed, had led to "mutual dislike which has only made both CORE and NAACP more determined."[66] Throughout the following two months, Hall maintained close contact with Wachs. Although he cooperated, Hall noticed that Wachs, who in the past had displayed little or no willingness to accept an open policy, showed "no conviction as to the rightness" of desegregated facilities.[67]

Shortly after the dance hall incident of April 29, Eugene Martin, the cochairman of CORE, informed Hall that his organization had devised a plan to make use of the pool and dance hall during the 1961 season and asked the league for cooperation.[68] Throughout May CORE and the NAACP picketed the park, leading to the arrest of twenty-seven black and white women and men for "trespassing and disorderly conduct."[69] On May 20 and 25 members of both groups attempted to use Coney's pool. According to William F. Bowen, president of the NAACP, sixteen members went to Coney and "six of the group were arrested on trespass warrants filed by the park police."[70] The park manager, Wachs, claimed that no violence was involved and said that the groups were ejected because they had "blocked the turnstiles at the pool."[71]

At this point, Coney officials "acceded to [the] demonstrations" and agreed to a conference with representatives of local civil rights groups.[72] The subsequent meeting on May 27, 1961, resulted in a decision for joint action to desegregate all facilities starting May 30. Explaining the decision, Schott declared, "For 75 years Coney Island has made available to the people of this area the finest amusement park in the world. We intend to continue that service. With reference to recent events which have received some publicity I wish to say that any person whose motives are only to use the facilities we provide and who is prepared to conduct himself properly will be admitted to any part of the park."[73]

The desegregation of Coney Island was publicized as a significant victory for the NAACP and CORE.[74] But the league, although not present during the crucial May meeting, played an important role in the desegregation of Coney Island. Since 1952 Hall had carefully timed his negotiations with park officials, gaining their confidence and cooperation. Hall utilized this mutual trust to ask for, but never to demand, desegregation. Moreover, he never threatened park officials with publicity and was willing to accept partial victories rather than to make no progress at all. As a result Coney officials admitted African Americans to the amusement park although they continued to exclude them from the pool and the dance hall.

Nevertheless, as the 1959 incident showed, the league's success depended on the cooperation of the white establishment and pressure from activist groups as well.[75] Coney Island's management sought the help of the league only after civil rights groups had begun picketing the park. Fear of negative publicity and possible economic losses compelled park officials to open negotiations with the Urban League. The final struggle over Coney's desegregation also illustrates that new forces gained momentum in the late 1950s and early 1960s. Less patient than the CUL, these civil rights activists rejected the league's gradualism and its behind-the-scenes approach and increasingly resorted to boycotts, sit-ins, protest marches, and picket lines in order to accelerate desegregation.

Not only Coney Island, but Cincinnati's business community at large, became the target of these groups. In April 1960 several African Americans began picketing Cincinnati's Woolworth store to expose the chain's Jim Crow policy in the South.[76] In fall 1962 civil rights activists gathered outside the Hamilton County courthouse and sang hymns, protesting against discriminatory treatment of African Americans in the South.[77] It was not until 1963, however, that "Cincinnati awoke to a cold, hard reality."[78]

In June 1963 several demonstrations involving violence occurred at school construction sites exposing discriminatory practices in the building trades. Between July 2 and 4, 1963, police chief Stanley Schrotel reported that African Americans had assembled in crowds, used vulgar language, and interfered with officers making arrests.[79] Marshall Bragdon, director of the MFRC, characterized the situation as one of "growing pains," while Schrotel called it "potentially explosive."[80]

Many Cincinnatians may have agreed with the *Cincinnati Enquirer,* which was startled by what seemed the sudden awakening of racial unrest. In the fall of 1963 it asked, "What's wrong? Why are the Negroes protesting? Isn't all that discrimination and segregation the South's worry? What are all these meetings and pronouncements about? Why the demonstrations, the picketing, the boycotting, here in fair-minded Cincinnati?"[81] City officials and the CUL, however, were not taken by surprise and had prepared a course of action. Beginning in June 1963, several conferences were held involving the city manager, the city solicitor, the director of safety, the chief of police, the fire chief, the executive director of the MFRC, and the league.[82] The goal of these meetings was to establish guidelines for the police in handling nonviolent, direct-action demonstrations.

The CUL, the only organization representing African Americans, took an active role in shaping the police guidelines in the interest of black protesters. Chief Schrotel proposed that the "primary responsibility of the police division is to protect life, and property."[83] Joseph A. Hall was successful in adding the word "liberty" to the phrase.[84] Moreover, Hall added to Schrotel's outline a sentence stating that "the demonstrators and the opposition must be protected in the public's interest."[85] Thus despite the CUL's rejection of nonviolent direct action, the league indirectly aided civil rights activists through its negotiations with city officials.

Hall explained his action by pointing out that the CUL did not reject methods other than negotiations: "Our behind-the-scenes work is just one way to handle the problem. . . . We know the other groups and other techniques also are needed. We don't claim any prior rights in the work in behalf of equal opportunity for all."[86] In fact, as the Coney Island case showed, the league profited from the pressure exerted by civil rights groups.[87] Businessmen trying to avoid becoming targets for militant desegregationists turned to the CUL for help in desegregating their businesses gradually.[88] They sought the help of the league because it offered confidentiality, thereby avoiding publicity that might have incited the population. Moreover, while other groups that fostered desegregation underwent continuous changes in leadership, Hall represented a consistent negotiation partner. In this light, the follow-up service the league provided was of special importance. The league not only opened new job opportunities for skilled African Americans, it also helped to overcome adjustment problems blacks and whites faced in their new employment situation.

The effectiveness of the league's behind-the-scenes technique is difficult to assess. The league was able to secure the confidence and support of many influential white citizens who favored the organization's gradual approach over radical changes and who were willing to make at least partial concessions. Moreover, the league was able to maintain cooperation with white citizens even in times when communication between key officials and civil rights groups had broken down. Thus the league became an important link between civil rights activists and the white establishment.

Nevertheless, the league's quiet diplomacy was effective only when the white decision-makers were willing to cooperate. Moreover, as the struggle for the desegregation of Coney Island showed, quiet negotiations were most successful when combined with either direct action or at least the threat of such. Without the use of economic and political pressure the league's behind-the-scenes strategy lacked an important force. The league was afraid to exert pressure lest it lose its standing, but unless it pushed, it had little leverage.

The limitations of the league's approach became obvious during the late 1950s and early 1960s. African Americans no longer asked for concessions but publicly demanded social justice and democracy. Moreover, the passage of the Civil Rights Act in 1964 and the establishment of an Equal Employment Opportunity Commission made the league's gradualistic behind-the-scenes role seem outmoded.

Notes

1. "United Funds, Community Chests and the Urban League: A Vital Campaign Matter for Community Leaders," 1964, in Urban League of Greater Cincinnati Records, box 2, no. 6, Cincinnati Historical Society, Cincinnati, Ohio (hereafter cited as CUL Papers).

2. Some of the more recent example illustrating this trend are Taylor Branch, *Parting the Water: America in the King Years, 1954–1963* (New York: Simon and Schuster, 1988); David J. Garrow, *Bearing the Cross: Martin Luther King, Jr., and the Southern Christian Leadership Conference* (New York: William Morrow, 1986), *The FBI and Martin Luther King, Jr.: From "Solo" to Memphis* (New York: W. W. Norton, 1981); Robert J. Norell, *Reaping the Whirlwind: The Civil Rights Movement in Tuskegee* (New York: Knopf, 1985); Aldon Morris, *The Origins of the Civil Rights Movement: Black Communities Organizing for Change* (New York: The Free Press, 1984); Stephen B. Oates, *Let the Trumpet Sound: The Life of Martin Luther King, Jr.* (New York: Harper and Row, 1982); Clayborne Carson, *In Struggle: SNCC and the Black Awakening of the 1960s* (Cambridge, Mass.: Harvard University Press, 1981); Harvard Sitkoff, *The Struggle for Black Equality* (New York: Hill and Wang, 1981); and William H. Chafe, *Civilities and Civil Rights: Greensboro, North Carolina, and the Black Struggle for Freedom* (New York: Oxford University Press, 1980).

3. "The Urban League of Greater Cincinnati" (1953), CUL Papers, box 44, no. 4.

4. The CUL believed that the black population of the city had risen from 51,700 in 1947 to 68,000 in 1948. Charlotte Ayers to Richard R. Jefferson, Department of Research, National Urban League, 31 Dec. 1947, CUL Papers, box 45, no. 3; *Annual Report* 1948, CUL Papers, box 2, no. 5.

5. *Annual Report* 1948, CUL Papers, box 2, no. 5; and Francis L. Dowdell to James A. Pawley, Industrial Secretary, Washington, D.C., Urban League, 4 Apr. 1950, CUL Papers, box 18, no. 1.

6. Dowdell to David L. Glenn, assistant director, Industrial Relations Department, Baltimore Urban League, 25 Aug. 1952, CUL Papers, box 18, no. 1.

7. *Annual Report* 1948, CUL Papers, box 2, no. 5; and Dowdell to E. Shelton Hill, industrial secretary, Portland Urban League, 7 Aug. 1951, CUL Papers, box 18, no. 1. Dowdell claimed, "As goes the Industrial Relations Department so goes our Urban League program."

8. "Community Health and Welfare Council, 1956–61," CUL Papers, box 8, no. 3.

9. Ibid.

10. "The Urban League of Greater Cincinnati" (1953), CUL Papers, box 44, no 4; and Joseph A. Hall to Whitney M. Young, Jr., industrial secretary, St. Paul Urban League, 27 Oct. 1949, CUL Papers, box 17, no. 6.

11. Dowdell to Margery T. Ware, Community Organization Secretary, Washington, D.C., 15 Sept. 1953, CUL Papers, box 18, no. 1.

12. Ibid.

13. Ibid.

14. "Report of the Industrial Department, 1–31 Jan. 1949," CUL Papers, box 58, no. 7.

15. Dowdell to Mark Battle, industrial field secretary, Cleveland Urban League, 4 May 1950, CUL Papers, box 18, no. 1.

16. Untitled typewritten report, 22 Sept. 1952, CUL Papers, box 10, no. 8.

17. Untitled typewritten report, 9 Oct. 1952, CUL Papers, box 10, no. 8.

18. Untitled typewritten report, 28 Oct. 1952, CUL Papers, box 10, no. 8.

19. John A. Kieley, Coney Island Attorney to Oris E. Hamilton, director of safety, 6 Jan. 1952, Jewish Community Relation Committee Papers, box 15, no. 7, American Jewish Archives, Hebrew Union College, Cincinnati, Ohio (hereafter cited as JCRC Papers).

20. Marvin Krous, "Coney Island," *Profile* (Winter 1952): 15, JCRC Papers, box 15, no. 7.

21. Rev. Maurice McCrackin, "Statement to City Council," 7 Aug. 1952, JCRC Papers, box 15, no. 7.

22. Krous, "Coney Island," 15, JCRC Papers, box 15, no. 7.

23. Joseph A. Hall to all affiliates, 19 Nov. 1952, CUL Papers, box 36, no. 5.

24. *Cincinnati Post,* 19 May 1953, 21.

25. "Strictly Confidential," "Summary of Contacts," 18 July and 19 Nov. 1953; and 18 and 21 Jan. 1954, typewritten report, CUL Papers, box 9, no. 3. For a discussion of the Mayor's Friendly Relations Committee, see chapter 10 of this volume.

26. "Strictly Confidential," "Summary of Contacts," 18 July and 19 Nov. 1953; 18 and 21 Jan. 1954, typewritten report, CUL Papers, box 9, no. 3.

27. Ibid.

28. Ibid.

29. Ibid.

30. "Coney Island, Summary of Contacts," 21 Dec. 1954, 5 Jan. 1955, 8, 10 Mar. 1955, 13 Apr. 1955, typewritten report, CUL Papers, box 9, no. 3.

31. "Minutes of the Board of Trustees," 24 May 1955, CUL Papers, box 58, no. 7.

32. *Cincinnati Post,* 21 July 1954, 1.

33. *Cincinnati Enquirer,* 28 July 1954, 10.

34. *Cincinnati Enquirer,* 19 Aug. 1954, 16.

35. *Cincinnati Post,* 9 Sept. 1954, 3.

36. "Coney Island, Summary of Contacts," typewritten report, CUL Papers, box 9, no. 3.

37. Ibid.

38. Ibid.

39. Ibid.

40. Ibid.

41. "Coney Island, 20, 25–27 Apr. 1955, Summary of Contacts," typewritten report, CUL Papers, box 9, no. 3.

42. *Cincinnati Post,* 5 Jan. 1955, 18.

43. *Cincinnati Enquirer,* 15 Jan. 1955, 6.

44. Ibid.

45. "Summary of Contacts," 20, 25–27 Apr. 1955, typewritten report, CUL Papers, box 9, no 3.

46. Ibid.

47. Ibid.

48. "Summary of Contacts," 30 Apr. 1955, 1, 2, 7, 9, 12, 13, and 24 May 1955, 21–22 June 1955, typewritten report, CUL Papers, box 9, no. 3.

49. Ibid.

50. "Summary of Contacts, Summers: 1955, 1956, 1957, 1958, 1959, 1960," typewritten report, CUL Papers, box 9, no. 3.

51. "Summary of Contacts," 30 Apr. 1955, 1, 2, 7, 9, 12, 13, and 24 May 1955, 21–22 June 1955, typewritten report, CUL Papers, box 9, no. 3.

52. Joseph A. Hall to Thomas Augustine, acting executive director, Akron Community Service Center, 6 Jan. 1956, CUL Papers, box 36, no. 5.

53. "7–6–59, 7–8–59, 7–24–59, 11–23–59, 11–24–59," typewritten report, CUL Papers, box 9, no. 3.

54. The Cincinnati *Post-Time Star* reported riots at a rock and roll concert at Coney Island on 1 July 1950.

55. "7–6–59 . . . ,"typewritten report, CUL Papers, box 9, no. 3.

56. Ibid.

57. Ibid.

58. Ibid.

59. Ibid.

60. Ibid.

61. Joseph A. Hall to Edward L. Schott, 23 Nov. 1959, CUL Papers, box 9, no. 3.

62. "Summary of Telephone Calls," 29 Apr. 1961, 11, 15, 23 May 1961, 5, 9, 15 June 1961, CUL Papers, box 9, no. 3.

63. Ibid.

64. Wachs was not only park manager but also Schott's brother-in-law. *Cincinnati Enquirer,* 30 Jan. 1962, 1.

65. "Summary of Telephone Calls," 29 Apr. 1961, 11, 15, 23, 29 May 1961, 1, 5, 9 June 1961, CUL Papers, box 9, no. 3.

66. Ibid.

67. Ibid.

68. Ibid.

69. *Cincinnati Enquirer,* 26 May 1961, 22.

70. *Cincinnati Enquirer,* 21 May 1961, 6a.

71. Ibid.

72. Hall was out of town that day and unable to attend. *Cincinnati Enquirer,* 21 May 1961, 6a, 30 May 1961, 1; "Summary of Telephone Calls," 29 Apr. 1961, 11, 15, 23, 29 May 1961, 1, 5, 9, 15 June 1961, CUL Papers, box 9, no. 3.

73. *Cincinnati Herald,* 2 June 1961, 2.

74. Ibid.

75. There was apparently some cooperation between the Urban League and Cincinnati's civil rights groups, but the sources do not substantiate coordinated efforts. Conclusive evidence to document such an assumption can only be gained from interviews with participants. While Joseph A. Hall

agreed to an interview about his "behind-the-scenes" role, he refused to be quoted, and all references to the interview had to be deleted.

76. *Cincinnati Enquirer,* 11 Apr. 1960, 16.

77. *Cincinnati Enquirer,* 2 Aug. 1962, 4.

78. *Cincinnati Enquirer,* 15 Sept. 1963, 1.

79. *Cincinnati Enquirer, 7 July 1963, 3.*

80. Ibid.

81. *Cincinnati Enquirer,* 15 Sept. 1963, 1.

82. C.A. Harrell to city council, 3 July 1963, "Non-Violent Direct Action Demonstrations—Policy and Procedure 1963," CUL Papers, box 32, no. 7.

83. Joseph A. Hall to Stanley R. Schrotel, 20 June 1963, CUL Papers, box 32, no. 7.

84. Ibid.

85. Ibid.

86. *Cincinnati Enquirer,* 31 Dec. 1963, 32.

87. Ibid.

88. Ibid.

Contributors

NANCY BERTAUX is an associate professor of economics and human resources at Xavier University in Cincinnati, Ohio. Her research focuses on Cincinnati's nineteenth-century labor market, especially the occupational segregation of women and blacks. As a member of Cincinnati's Private Industry Council, she is also involved in job training efforts for the disadvantaged.

ROBERT A. BURNHAM is an assistant professor of history at Macon College. He is the author of "The Cincinnati Charter Revolt of 1924," in *Ethnic Diversity and Civic Identity* (1992), edited by Henry D. Shapiro and Jonathan D. Sarna.

CHARLES F. CASEY-LEININGER is currently engaged in doctoral work in the Department of History at the University of Cincinnati. His 1989 master's thesis, "Making the Second Ghetto: Avondale, 1925–1979," serves as the basis for his essay in this volume.

WILLIAM CHEEK AND AIMEE LEE CHEEK are the authors of *John Mercer Langston and the Fight for Black Freedom, 1829–65* (1989), which won the first Elliott Rudwick Award and in 1990 was named an Outstanding Book on the subject of human rights by the Gustavus Myers Center for the Study of Human Rights in the United States. William Cheek teaches American civilization and biography at San Diego State University, where he has been a member of the history faculty since 1968. He is also the author of *Black Resistance before the Civil War* (1970). Aimee Lee Cheek, a private historian in San Diego, is coauthor of "John Mercer Langston: Principles and Politics," in *Black Leaders of the Nineteenth Century* (1988), edited by Leon Litwack and August Meier. The Cheeks are collaborating on a second volume of Langston's biography, which will explore the years 1865 to his death in 1897.

VICKY DULA is the director of research at the Center for Applied Public Affairs Studies at the State University of New York at Buffalo and a Ph.D. candidate in U.S. history at Ohio State University. She is completing a project on the National Urban League, the NAACP, black workers, and the fight for a "true" Fair Labor Standards Act, based on her dissertation work in progress.

ROBERT B. FAIRBANKS is an associate professor of history at the University of Texas at Arlington. The author of *Making Better Citizens: Housing Reform and the Community Development Strategy in Cincinnati, 1890–1960* (1988) and coeditor and contributor to *Essays on Sunbelt Cities and Recent Urban America* (1990), he is currently at work on a book about business leadership in Dallas between 1930 and 1965.

STACY FLAHERTY, a historian and coordinator at the Center for Advertising History at the Smithsonian National Museum of American History, received an M.A. in American studies from George Washington University. Her essay "Boycott in Butte: Organized Labor and the Chinese Community, 1896–1987," won the Merrill C. Burlingame–K. Ross Toole Award from the Montana Historical Society.

JAMES OLIVER HORTON, professor of history and American studies at George Washington University since 1977, is also the director of the Afro-American Communities Project at the Smithsonian National Museum of American History. He coauthored *Black Bostonians: Family Life and Community Struggle in an Antebellum City* (1979) with Lois E. Horton and is the pilot series coeditor of *City of Magnificent Intentions,* a social history textbook of Washington, D.C., being used in that city's public schools. His most recent book is *Free People of Color: Essays inside the African American Community* (1993).

NINA MJAGKIJ is the director of the African American Studies Program and an assistant professor in the history department at Ball State University, Muncie, Indiana. Her most recent book is *Light in the Darkness: African Americans and the YMCA, 1852–1946* (forthcoming).

HENRY LOUIS TAYLOR, JR., is an associate professor of American studies at the State University of New York at Buffalo, founder and director of the Center for Applied Public Affairs Studies, and an adjunct professor in the Department of Planning and Design. The editor of *African Americans and the Rise of Buffalo's Post-Industrial City, 1940 to Present* (1991), he is completing a book on black surburbanization and the rise of metropolitan Cincinnati. In addition, he heads a planning and economic development organization in Buffalo and serves on a number of regional and black economic and community development committees.

ANDREA TUTTLE KORNBLUH is an associate professor of history at Raymond Walters College, University of Cincinnati, where she teaches American women's history. The author of *Lighting the Way: The Women's City Club of Cincinnati, 1915–65* and articles that examine efforts at improving race relations and building civic community in the first half of the twentieth century, she is currently working on a manuscript that chronicles the rise and fall of separate but equal social work in Cincinnati.

Name Index

Subject Index

Prejudice, 3–4, 16, 49, 52, 90, 220, 259–
60, 262, 268, 273; ethnic, 259; racial,
273; white, 158
Pressler's Cafeteria, 270
Price Hill, 263–64
Price Hill Civic Club, 263
Progressive era, 12
Proletarianization, 6
Public Health Federation, 197
Public housing, 11–12, 201–6, 235,
241, 248
Public Recreation Commission, 260
Public Works Administration (PWA),
202–3
PWA. *See* Public Works Administration

Race: barriers, 147; division of labor, 132;
hostility, 4, 84, 156; violence, 262
Race Relations Detail, 263, 265, 268
Race Relations Sunday, 210
Racism, 1–3, 5, 8–13, 16, 20, 127, 129,
145–46, 156–57, 193
Radical antislavery politics, 29
Real estate practices, 238–40
Regulation: residential land use, 6–8, 10,
175; subdivision, 8, 157, 169, 171,
175–76, 178; zoning, 15, 166
Residential land use, 7, 10; and land-rent
structure, 8; patterns of, 74, 85, 98,
100, 110, 140
Restrictive legislation, 10
Riots, 15, 19–20, 206; of 1841,
45–50, 54

Santa Maria Institute, 211
SCLC. *See* Southern Christian Leader-
ship Conference
Segregation, 1, 4, 9, 13, 32, 109–12, 115,
118, 126, 236, 282, 286, 289; occupa-
tional, 126–27; residential, 3, 10–11,
14–15, 20, 35, 157, 163–64, 235, 242,
246, 251
Shade of color, 74, 85, 88, 103,
107–9, 118
Sharecropping system, 128
Shoemaker Health and Welfare
Center, 224
Slums, 8, 10–11, 15, 170–71, 175, 177,
193–94, 198, 203, 205–6. *See also*
Ghetto-slums

SNCC. *See* Student Nonviolent Coordi-
nating Committee
Social interaction, 2, 96–98, 100, 109–10,
115–18
Social service agencies, 211, 216, 218,
221–22
Social structures, 97
Social welfare services, 210, 223, 224
Southern Christian Leadership Conference
(SCLC), 280
Spatial organization, 102–3, 108
Special Committee on Negro Housing,
197–99
Springfield Plan, 263
Springfield Republican, 263
Springmeyer School, 282
State Guard, 262
Strikebreakers, 128
Structure, 74, 92; of economic change,
126–27, 132, 144, 147
Student Nonviolent Coordinating Com-
mittee (SNCC), 280
Suburbs, 10, 14–15
Subward distribution, 100

Technical Advisory Corporation, 171
Tenements: codes, 194, 199; reform,
169–70, 194–95; regulations,
169–70, 194, 205
Territorial expansion, 161

UCPC. *See* United City Planning
Committee)
Uncle Tom's Cabin, 51
Underground Railroad, 2, 40, 43, 75, 77
Union Society of Colored Persons, 77
United City Planning Committee
(UCPC), 171
United Jewish Charities, 169–70
United Jewish Social Agencies, 211
United States Housing Authority (USHA),
204–5
Urban League, 18–19, 200, 280–84, 286–
90. *See also* Cincinnati Urban League;
National Urban League
USHA. *See* United States Housing
Authority

Vacant-land projects, 204
Victor Electric Products, 269